T0250245

Open Source
Data Warehousing
and Business
Intelligence

Open Source Data Warehousing and Business Intelligence

Lakshman Bulusu

CRC Press
Taylor & Francis Group
Boca Raton London New York

CRC Press is an imprint of the
Taylor & Francis Group, an **informa** business
AN AUERBACH BOOK

CRC Press
Taylor & Francis Group
6000 Broken Sound Parkway NW, Suite 300
Boca Raton, FL 33487-2742

© 2013 by Taylor & Francis Group, LLC
CRC Press is an imprint of Taylor & Francis Group, an Informa business

No claim to original U.S. Government works

Printed in the United States of America on acid-free paper
Version Date: 20120703

International Standard Book Number: 978-1-4398-1640-0 (Hardback)

Visit the Taylor & Francis Web site at
http://www.taylorandfrancis.com

and the CRC Press Web site at
http://www.crcpress.com

Dedication

I dedicate this book with love to my uncle, Prof. B. L. Deekshatulu, whose tender love, ever-needed care and guidance, and forgiving demeanor have shown me an illuminating path in both my professional and personal lives. I will ever remember your "first things first" that have enabled me to shine so far in my career and will pass on the message to whoever seeks them as a carrier of the same.

On the occasion of Mother's Day 2012, I also dedicate this book to my loving mother Smt. B. Sita, who has practically shown me that "East or West, Mother is the Best."

Contents

Foreword

It was nearly three decades ago when a young precocious computer geek serving the U.S. Air Force and National Security Agency (NSA) was first trained to process and analyze intelligence. Armed with what was then the latest technology and tools, I was catapulted into the world of military intelligence. I diligently pursued this field for nearly a decade and after serving under President Reagan and President Bush (the 1st one that is) and the Gulf War (again, that is, the 1st one) I was ready for something new in the "outside" world. But as Life would have it, I found myself gravitating toward what I knew best – perhaps summed up as Software, Technology, and Data—gained from all my years in military intelligence. Thus began my career of Business Intelligence (BI) which greatly involved all three components. After building more than a dozen BI solutions from the ground up and consulting to nearly fifty of the world's most prestigious and prolific organizations on the matter, I can now surely say that that young precocious computer geek has turned into an old precocious computer geek.

With the same love of the craft and a passion for intelligence and analytics, I traded the world of military intelligence for business intelligence but my end mission and goal has basically remained the same now as it was then–that is, to get the right information to the right person at the right time.

It sounds simple enough when put in these very generic points but as every experienced BI architect or developer would attest, this is absolutely easier said than done. Thus we, as BI practitioners, have all tried to deal with the current technologies and tools in hope that when properly applied, it would lead to a successful delivery of a BI solution. Open Source BI is among those that have contributed to the plethora of offerings in the current BI landscape today. With the demand for better BI and analytics, it will continue to be in the forefront of IT for years to come as different technologies, tools, and strategies are explored.

Having been a long-time practitioner with a multitude of implementations in most of the major BI software packages I tended to stay close to my expertise of the "big players". So when Mr. Bulusu approached me about the subject of Open Source BI I have to admit that I was quite surprised that he would even consider it knowing that he too had worked with the big vendors, and in fact, had authored a handful of books on using their technologies and tools. Surely, I thought, he would share an elitist view similar to the one that I harbored. It is an elitist view that in fact came to surface recently just last year when I was asked to speak on providing a small budget solution for DW and BI. For this, I admittedly shied away from even addressing at length an open source package and chose rather to address it with other alternatives.

Nevertheless, I continued this discussion with Mr. Bulusu; however, for me, his book has helped to legitimize and validate the use of Open Source BI. It just might also be the catalyst needed to help bring the subject into serious consideration for other experienced practitioners as well. As a practitioner himself, Mr. Bulusu is able to pinpoint the more critical aspects for consideration that a BI expert would truly appreciate. He does a great job of covering the subject thoroughly by first starting at a high-level covering every aspect of BI and then breaking down the components to the most granular detail applying Open Source BI's feasibility and validity as a viable solution.

As a leader of a consulting firm dedicated and focused on the BI space and touting being tool-agnostic, I now have it ready as an offering and will indeed utilize and apply Mr. Bulusu's writings when asked for an alternative. In other words, for me, Open Source BI is now a viable solution in light of the ever-changing corporate world of IT and consequently BI. As Mr. Bulusu so eloquently puts it in succinct bullets:

- No more one-size-fits-all, as there is more than one "all"
- Best-fit is the new best
- Right time is the new real-time

With Mr. Bulusu's book, I have surprisingly started on a new path of acceptance. I knew that Bulusu's thorough, meticulous approach and in-depth examination of the subject; taken from a standpoint of an experienced author, educator, and technologist has finally provided justice to this subject.

Thank you Mr. Bulusu. You have opened my eyes to Open Source BI.

Rosendo Abellera
President and CEO, BIS3

Introduction

As I begin the introduction to this book, a plethora of thoughts randomly fill my mind in regard to *open source*. From the open skies since the beginning of time to the NEW and NEXT-GEN open-source paradigm involving people–processes–pragmatics–practices NOW, *open* has become infinite—and yet it remains as finite in its ability as getting the globe in the palm of my hand while at the same time enabling me to travel back and forth, in varying degrees of function, form, and fastness. The sometimes-fast, sometimes-just-fast-enough, sometimes-too-fast, and sometimes-faster-than-I-can-think skewing and shearing dynamics of the currently trending and future-enabled open source technologies are the game-changers in information delivery—what I term as *the OPEN SOURCE PERFECT: from OPEN-NESS to OPEN-SENSE and BEYOND*, yielding a "What-I-get-is-what-I-want" solution, nothing more and nothing less, at any time and as of any point in time, thus producing, preserving, and providing currency of the desired information.

The key benefits of such a solution from a customer-centric point of view are as follows:

- Anytime, anywhere, by anyone (A-A-A) accessibility and availability, all authentic and authorized
- The right information for the right purpose to the right people at the right time (R-R-R-R)
- Uncompromising on the business basics of affordability, flexibility, reliability, stability, scalability, and efficiency
- Business assurance in terms of a single frame of reference for operational continuity, agility, and customer assurance

An open source solution is the secret sauce behind the appraisal, analyses, architecture, adoption, and adaption of such a solution, one that is at least sufficiently best-fit for meeting the demanding needs of current-day superior customer experience in the unpredictably complex web of business revolution and competitiveness. The **key differentiator** is the loosely coupled architecture that open source methodologies support, which can be easily and transparently extended to support a loosely coupled business model if needed.

Open source gains precedence when it comes to the simplicity and convenience involved in terms of being a unified and universally available, flexible, and scalable on-demand solution that is at the same time compliance-ready, implementation-ready, deployment-ready, and customer-awareness-ready. The business performance indicators from such a solution are as clearly visible from the preview of the solution implementation as the need for such indicators to drive business performance:

- *Content and context convergence* in instance, constancy, and consistence—on-premise to online to on-the-go (mobile) to out-of-premise (in the cloud)
- *Dynamic analytics* by way of metrics generation through automation
- As open source moves mainstream, *business* moves to *business-on-the-go* (or *business-on-the-fly*, to be precise). This seemingly slight shift in the business model has enormous potential to transform the business–IT–customer–social landscape of such a solution point north of the center so that:
  - The *business* accelerates in terms of improvement to involvement.
  - The *business–IT* forecast looks all CLOUD-y (irrespective of climate change!), starting from cloud bursting to crowd sourcing.
  - The *business–social* relationship gets wiser than business-as-usual, as data becomes intelligent to information-in-action.
  - The *business network* communicates and collaborates to become business competition, from inside-the-net in the real world through the Internet to the social net, resulting in competitive business processes.
  - *Business services* (including business solutions and support and operations solutions and support) evolve into *business–social*

services, thereby granting them tenure—and business assurance—through the customer lifecycle of the business.

- Businesses can leverage the so-called "gold" mines of intelligent information (as more and more data mining becomes practical) in unimaginably fast, actionable, synchronized, transparent and *social* ways, wherein users across all touchpoints can become involved interactively in a 360-degree variance to feed and feedback their (business) input. This self-serviceable input can then be auto-rewired as 'intelligent business rules" via the tenor of self-adaptability of the open source BI solution in near real time.

With all these pros come the cons, too. Business security tends to become increasingly insecure. The streams of "intelligent information" transcend the enterprise boundaries into multiple endpoints and clouds, in all their sensitivity and identity, and converge into the *social enterprise*; their security gets social too—and ensuring the *social security* of the same demands opens multiple channels for what is termed social engineering, from ethical hackers to ethical blockers and beyond—wherein the acts of hacking, phishing, VISHING, and threats become *alarmingly ethical!*

An open source solution can drastically minimize the impact of the risk while it also improves the remediation of the same through its ability to automate, accelerate, and reduce the time to recovery in easy, elastic, duplication-less, and dynamic architectural virtualization and execution capabilities. *The faster the time to insight, the faster the time to recovery—and the lesser the risk of disaster and the minimal the time spent in disaster recovery mode.*

From the combination of a people–processes–perceptions–places perspective; the evolution of business (operations) lifecycle to IT lifecycle to business–IT (solution) lifecycle to business–social lifecycle; and the customer–customization–customer experience lifecycle comes a distinctly differentiating denominator and a universally enabling factor: An open source–enabled solution is both a barometer and a benchmark-enabling bar for the end-to-end EDW/BI Oracle—from data to data-in-action, serving the business customer to the intelligent customer, and breaking through the barriers of heterogeneous data sources, time zones, platforms, technologies, methodologies, and most importantly customers with 360-degree variance in requirements-to-results!

What Does This Book Cover?

This book highlights the practical aspects of using open source data warehousing (DW) and business intelligence (BI) technologies from an end-to-end lifecycle perspective, starting from concepts to implementation and customization. It follows a lively "when-to," "why-to," and "how-to" approach to explain the key differentiators and benefits of using open source from proprietary DW and BI technologies in the database and data warehouse design, real-time ETL and data integration, and presentation services and real-time reporting phases of the end-to-end DW and BI solution. These differentiators and benefits are explained in terms of very large databases (VLDBs), scalability, high performance, stability, endurance, and ease of use that save time, effort, cost, resources, and support, and maximize return on investment (ROI), whether the solution is a totally new implementation, coexistence, codeployment, or replacement. The successful players and their products in the open source DW and BI field are taken into account while describing these details.

It concentrates on the more important pragmatic aspects involved by describing the deciding factors, key design criteria and methodologies, expert techniques, and best practices by taking into account cross-functional and multi-integration scenarios.

Who Should Read This Book?

This book is targeted toward multiple audiences. First, it is meant for the team involved in deciding, choosing, architecting, developing and implementing an open source–based DW and BI solution, whether it be the CIO looking for a maximum ROI strategy, the CTO exploring the best-fit in terms of a better-faster-simpler solution, or the business analysts/solution architects trying to figure out the optimal architecture for an *implement once/ use forever* customer-specific solution, or the design and development staff looking for a one-stop resource to uncover the under-the-hood principles, practices, and development techniques involved, or the integration experts planning an enterprise-wide *one-fits-all* integration solution to co-deploy with existing BI systems. All it assumes is a working knowledge of databases, data warehouses, and business intelligence.

Secondly, this book gives the foundational paradigms and patterns for research-in-action that can be followed by engineering and research and development (R&D) teams for innovation and invention of structurally unique business/solution/social/analytical models.

Additionally, this book is geared toward students, learners, and faculty in the academic field who are devoted to a course in open source data warehousing and business intelligence, who would find the book handy in problem–solution and best practices–techniques scenarios in terms of theory, pragmatics, and practice.

Why a Separate Book?

This book is unique in today's constantly changing and evolving market, in that it serves as a single resource for comprehensive details of an open source-based DW and BI solution that is business-centric, cross-customer-viable, cross-functional, cross-technology-based and enterprise-wide, focusing on the entire lifecycle of an open source DW and BI implementation from the concepts involved all the way through to customization.

It describes the practical aspects of using an open source approach to enterprise data warehousing (EDW) and BI by way of the technologies, tools, and methodologies involved and the better business benefit obtained thereby in terms of a business-centric, cross-functional, cross-customer, cross-technology-based solution that not only enables a better-faster-easier solution model, but also gives context-aware adaptability to changing business needs, unprecedented flexibility by way of usability and deployment—on-demand by leveraging existing resources and five-nine reliability—and is pervasive, from the legacy enterprise to the current and next-gen social enterprise.

The key standout indicator of this book is its treatment of how powerful and performing open source can be: as an enabler and benefactor of enterprise businesses without having to shake the existing business structure, and as a dynamically extensible paradigms-and-patterns expert system in form and format. As it highlights the focal points involved for such a structurally unique and dynamically intelligent business/solution/social/analytical model by way of an open source–enabled intelligence strategy as architecture-as-a-service-by-itself (AaaS) framework, as opposed to architecture-as-a-design-service, the fractal efficiencies of such an implementation grow convincingly closer to real-world customer-centric dynamics, revealed with business examples and use-case scenarios. The fine line here is that the former approach requires the AaaS as a necessary and sufficient component of the intelligence model.

The table below summarizes the primary features and their associated benefits in support of the author's preview for a separate book for open source DW and BI; this information can at least aid in boosting the potential reader's "learn-and-leverage" confidence. How well this preview can predict the same in terms of "true" benefits in practice is based on the readers' and implementers' confidence level in making a prudent decision of choice for adopting the same in desired contextual business solutions.

Feature	Corresponding Benefit
A single resource details the practical aspects of an open source DW and BI architecture from both technological and solution perspectives, while at the same time describing the "best practice" aspects for implementation of a "best-fit" solution.	This is a standout, in that <ul><li>It is the only all-in-one resource across open source DW and BI technologies.</li><li>It focuses on architecture and design as well as live implementation aspects of the best-fit solution.</li></ul>
An exclusive section devoted to best practices from an implementation perspective for customers to adopt an open source DW and BI solution (e.g., "Customization Framework" for a best-fit solution and why "best-fit" wins over the "best" solution).	1. It gives the reader practical advice from experience, which helps in improving productivity from the application project as well as professional standpoint. 2. This is also helpful for winning customer confidence and getting sponsorship for an open source DW and BI implementation. Because it explains the best-case scenario to use, it helps in quick decision making for getting a go-ahead. 3. This is indispensable for solution architecture and academic R&D projects alike, in that it provides an adoptable methodology on an "as-is" as well as on an enhancement/extensible basis.
Coverage of mission-critical and state-of-the-art trends from a user and business standpoint (e.g., "BI Beyond Reporting," "Delivering Information-On-Demand," and "Achieving Performance-On-Demand").	These are indispensable for solution architects, business analysts, executives, and academicians alike by providing an adaptable methodology on an "as-is" as well as on an enhancement/extensible basis.

Feature	Corresponding Benefit
Covers information previously unavailable or undocumented that is both technically complete and business-centric (e.g., "Accelerating Business Analytics for the Next Generation Customer—Granting A Tenure for the Customer Experience Lifecycle")	1. This makes this book an asset for any targeted audience and a standout from other titles in the market. 2. The book details the contextual specifics of approaching the "open-source solution" strategy from architecture-as-a-(business process)-service model as opposed to an architecture-as-a-design aspect, giving a preview of a new baseline trend that's both unique and innovative for a reference model for open source EDW/BI.
The last chapter ("The Prize for the Price: A Win-Win or Not?") is a real boost for success, both for the book as well as for the business-centric customer.	1. This makes this book a "great" book—a unique standout.
A book for a one-fits-all and implement-once/use-forever solution in the open source DW and BI space, written by a proven author-cum-architect-cum-educator-cum-researcher in the EDW/BI domain—open source and otherwise.	Increases the trust factor not only from the buying side, but also from business decision making and solution adoptability side, as the content is based on the author's practical experience, which match real-project needs and can be treated as "benchmark" approaches for proven and successful implementations. However, zero-trust and zero-tolerance pragmatics are emphasized for information security, thereby increasing the confidence level for information assurance.

Acknowledgements

First of all, my heartfelt thanks go to all the readers and reviewers of my previous books, starting from my first one in the year 2000. Without your feedback in some form or other, I feel my first book, as well as my successive books, would not have been a success to date.

I thank my lovely wife Anuradha and my twins Pranav and Pranati for their cooperation throughout, which served as a feedback loop of enthusiasm in me to carry on my book writing.

I thank Mr. John Wyzalek of CRC Press, as well as all of the members of the editorial and publishing team there, and Mr. Theron Shreve of Derryfield Publishing Services for their coordinated help and everlasting patience in the journey of my book from proof of concept to print.

I also thank Mr. Rosendo Abellera, CEO of BIS3, Boston, Massachusetts, for agreeing to write a forward for my book.

Finally, I thank all of the members of the open source community-especially in the areas of enterprise data warehousing and business intelligence-from sophomores to stewards to customer successes, for their efforts in contributing the same to make open source a reality.

About the Author

Lakshman Bulusu is a 20-year veteran of the IT industry with specialized expertise and academic experience in the management, supervision, mentoring, review, architectural design, and development of database, data warehousing, and business intelligence-related application development projects encompassing major industry domains such as pharmaceutical/healthcare, telecommunications, news/media, global investment and retail banking, insurance, and retail for clients across the United States, Europe, and Asia. He is well-versed in the primary Oracle technologies through Oracle11g, including SQL, PL/SQL, and SQL-embedded programming, as well as design and development of Web applications that are cross-platform and open source-based. He has expertise in data modeling and design of enterprise data warehousing/business intelligence information architectures, with multiple customer implementations to his credit. His design of application development frameworks using PL/SQL, from design to coding to testing to debugging to performance tuning to business intelligence, has been implemented in some major Fortune 500 clients in the United States. He has implemented the Common Data Quality Framework for SQL Server, based on summarization-comparison-discrepancy isolation across disparate multivendor large-scale databases. He is also an educator who has been teaching technical courses for about a decade in the areas of Oracle design, development, and optimization, and he serves on the CNS Advisory Committee of Anthem Institute (affiliated to Anthem Education Group). He has authored six books on Oracle and more than fifty educational/technical articles in journals and magazines in the United States and the United Kingdom; he has also presented at national and international conferences in the United States and the United Kingdom. He lives in New Jersey and likes to read, write, listen to, and lecture on English poetry and nonfiction when he is not working on IT projects. He can be reached at lbulusu@compunnel.com.

Chapter 1

Introduction

1.1   In This Chapter

- Data Warehousing and Business Intelligence: What, Why, How, When, When Not?
- Open Source DW and BI: Much Ado about Everything DW and BI, When Not, and Why So Much Ado?

This chapter details the foundations and frameworks of an open source–enabled EDW/BI solution from concepts to customization, the best-fit pragmatics in terms of contextual relevance and usability for implementing such a solution in the real world, and how the solution can elevate the contextual customer to an intelligent customer. From its early adoption to going mainstream, the journey of the open source Oracle has not only helped businesses as a cost-container and information-to-application integrator, but also enabled using such methodology as an innovative business model not just for delivery and deployment, but also as a singular elastic, embeddable, and executable "architecture-as-a-serviceable-process-model" that is efficient, effective, and uniquely exhaustive for anything and everything that's fit to be termed *business*. When it comes to EDW/BI, this translates to all data that's knit to such a business, from precipitation to pervasive-in-action. Leveraging open source as an AaaS, as opposed to an architecture-as-a-design aspect, enables business-to-business engagement across the dimensions of information, intellect, and intelligence at any scale whatsoever, but with a near-zero solution footprint. Thus, an open source enabled information solution by way of an open source AaaS model can be standardized as a "rules-of-engagement" blueprint as well as a "rules-of-management" blueprint—all in a unified near-zero footprint. After all, the basics of BI—business intelligence is for implementable business analytics, and business success is empirically customer success—demand the

1

same, and open source EDW/BI is as imperative as getting the implementable and empirical.

This is the key selection indicator in using open source techniques, technologies, and tools for an EDW/BI solution. It begins by opening up the high-fives of DW/BI in terms of What, Why, How, When, and When Not To—identifying the key aspects of each of these for the solution orientation spotlights three primary key performance indicators (KPIs) for an open source–enabled and –enabling EDW/BI pragmatics. It then dives into the Open Source arena of EDW/BI to explain each one of these three KPIs categorized across four major dimensions: the business landscape, the technology landscape, the programmer-to-implementer landscape, and the social landscape (which incorporates the evolving customer experience landscape, also known as the customer–user experience [C-UX] lifecycle, as an exclusive imperative in overall solution value).

1.2   Data Warehousing and Business Intelligence: What, Why, How, When, When Not?

Let's revisit this callout from the Introduction:

> From the combination of a people–processes–perceptions–places perspective; the evolution of business (operations) lifecycle to IT lifecycle to business–IT (solution) lifecycle to business–social lifecycle; and the customer–customization–customer experience lifecycle comes a distinctly differentiating denominator and a universally enabling factor: An open source–enabled solution is both a barometer and a benchmark-enabling bar for the end-to-end EDW/BI Oracle—from data to data-in-action, serving the business customer to the intelligent customer, and breaking through the barriers of heterogeneous data sources, time zones, platforms, technologies, methodologies, and most importantly customers with 360-degree variance in requirements-to-results!

To put these pragmatics into practice in the best possible manner to result in a "best-case" solution, the methodologies of data warehousing and BI optimally help draw the fine line between information centralization, consolidation, and decentralization—just that, nothing but that—from data-on-board to dashboard and everything in between. If one takes a snapshot of the current and future path of the information highway, from production to provisioning to processing to protection to prediction and security, the preview shows a "data big bang" view—one that's zoomed in and growing at lightning-fast speed. To make all of this data "work" in any and all desired fashions, it takes more than just a powerful data processing and analysis engine or tool—it requires a solution of the order of magnitude of n power-centric workhorses of data-to-information-to-knowledge-insight-full decisions enabling information, or otherwise—what can be termed an "intelligent information" churner, anytime, anywhere, and by anyone. Based on the pragmatics and practices involved in implementing such a solution, I can identify three primary business–technology–customer–social headliners that can be standardized as a necessary KPIs for the high-fives of DW and BI:

- *Taking IT Intelligence to Its Apex*: an innovative information model by design for a DBMS-based EDW/BI solution
- *Taking Business Intelligence to Its Apex*: intelligent content for insightful intent—the ability to derive intelligent decisions from the information-in-sight, i.e., information visualization for actionable business insight
- *Business* as the key driver of such a solution, as opposed to *IT*, from its inception to implementation and beyond—Self-serviceability by way of context-aware self-adaptability in terms of its relevance, importance, and significance for continuous business efficiency and effectiveness.

The first two of these serve as the necessary enablers in realizing the third. And an enterprise-wide data warehouse solution complemented by a BI solution results in a complete solution that can deliver results, to the point of a completely satisfied customer experience.

1.2.1   Taking IT Intelligence to Its Apex

Business–IT efficiency is an incessant IT evolution that resembles n-dimensional phenomena—it is constantly changing across a multitude of imperatives, most essentially across the business, technology, time, location, cost, and user experience (UX) dimensions.

- No more one-size-fits-all, as there is more than one "all"
- Best-fit is the new best
- Right time is the new real-time

- Context-specific is the new content-specific, and customer-centric can be one or a combination of any business-process touch-point
- Business context, not the prevalent technology, drives the solution architecture—hence, a "best-fit" solution is one that can mix, match, or merge any technology, methodology, or tool to get the optimal solution. The implication is that *results are the only reality—everything else is virtual reality!*

An enterprise data center can be the foundation for lightning-fast responses to market changes—but only if it can take full advantage of recent developments in servers, networking, virtualization, and cloud-computing strategies.

An enterprise solution can be an intelligent one by being context-aware, self-adaptive, and self-service-able; this can be achieved via an architectural framework that leverages the latest-and-greatest technologies, methodologies, and tools that help enable the transformation of analysis (i.e., insight from business domain, user/customer experience) into analytics, be it advanced or predictive; a framework that facilitates extreme interactivity by way of rich visualization, collaboration, and dynamic on-demand super- and sub-componentization (e.g., live on-the-fly streaming of a super- or subset of the entire end-to-end solution). The key ones in this list of technologies, methodologies, and tools are:

- Business continuity and operational efficiency end-to-end—from the desktop to the data center to the access touch point (continuous operational BI)
- Enterprise information integration (EII), enterprise application integration (EAI), e-solution-as-a-service integration on the fly—using real-time change data capture (CDC), data, and data integration services (via Web services) and service-oriented architecture (SOA)–based servicing to make it software-as-a-service (SaaS)-enabled and -enabling
- Combination of virtualization, clustering, and hybrid cloud computing for resource consolidation, compute collaboration, and business–IT SaaS

This can serve as a viable business–IT process framework for a foundational architecture for an intelligent EDW-BI solution, one that

- Delivers information intelligence using information technology: anyone/anytime/anywhere and getting the right information for the right purpose to the right people at the right time; fast, action-able, synchronized, and tested (FAST) is sharable, though distrib-uted, and serviceable (on-demand or otherwise)
- Is reusable, replicable, retainable (archival deduplication, colum-nar/hybrid-compression), refactorable, and reformable (even if it is time variant and location variant [geospatial])
- Has the ability to handle any and all types of information, from legacy to legendary (i.e., data that's insight-rich; this needn't neces-sarily be legacy data); from persistent to consistent; from just-in-time to any-point-in-time; from near-real-time to right-time; from big data to better data; from content-aware to context-aware; from single source to multisource to open source(d) (i.e., extreme flexi-bility in terms of elasticity and hot-pluggability of data sources, application sources, and other embeddable services on-the-fly)
- Is actionable from data to dashboard; from data-in-motion to dashboards-in-mobilization; from data, data everywhere to data centers everywhere

And this intelligent IT results in the UX "where's all that (huge chunks of) data gone?" for "I can only see the information that I need, and nothing else," taking IT intelligence to its apex!

1.3   Open Source DW and BI: Much Ado about Anything-to-Everything DW and BI, When Not, and Why So Much Ado?

As the design of solution architectures for Very Large Databases (VLDBs) or otherwise-sized databases continually evolves, from the primary database being a relational database management system (RDBMS) to a no-database or rather an invisible-database environment, the use of innovative technolo-gies and methodologies such as pipelining, parallelization, data grids, data-base virtualization, application grids, virtual federated views, columnar orientation at the core data model level, columnar compression, isolation, and interoperability of the "application" from the database layer thereby enable linear scalability (scaling-out), vertical scalability (scaling-in), cloud deployment, and nonlinear scalability (scaling-on-demand), data services, data integration services, etc. Also, the out-of-box database and analytic appliances and high-performance computing engines using an array of high-performing computing models like NoSQL (Not Only SQL), MapReduce (dynamically correlate and compute to reduce the algorithmic complexity), in-memory processing and/or in-memory database caching, in-database processing, and most importantly, leveraging the built-in native functionality of the RDBMS (both commercial and open source) to the optimal extent have annihilated the variance involved in the 6 degrees of separation to yield 360-degree coherence, conformance, and continuity—from proof-of-concept to performance-unto-confidence, with zero or minimal compromise otherwise. And this applies across industry verticals.

Theoretically and practically, if there is a lot of "ado" about everything DW and BI in an "open source" framework, it is in its distinctly different and uniquely universal benevolence: An open source–based DW and BI solution can yield the results of data-to-intelligent-information-in-action in a "naïve-and-natural" fashion, while subsuming and consuming any and/or all of the above solution architectures and providing better business benefits.

Keeping the above faction in view, the subsections that follow give a cue-card account of why and when an open source solution outperforms and, last but not least, when it is not a candidate for the same.

1.3.1 Taking Business Intelligence to Its Apex: Intelligent Content for Insightful Intent

In customer-sense terms, taking business intelligence to its apex simply means a fast, actionable, interactive, and rapid (FAIR) framework that is a go-ahead approach for competitive intelligence.

The so-stated competitive intelligence highway involves the following key pragmatics:

- In an universe of business (I)T, where results are the only reality, the notion of BI takes a definition that is a mix of the traditional, adaptive, and at the same time extreme—one that takes (strategic) vision as input, processes it using I-I-I (intuition, innovation, invention), and outputs a continually effective, efficient, adoptable, adaptable, evolving SaaS—or, to put it in the triangular advantage jargon, business-as-a-service (BaaS)—that is better, simpler, and faster, enables anytime/anyone/anywhere usage, and consistently, persistently, or intermittently operates on the above.

- The open source benefit comes handy in getting this set to result in the following cycle:

```
{Strategic Vision Input:I-I-I Processing:Business-
as-a-Service Output}
```

- BI that is open source–enabled and –enabling, though a 100% infrastructure-, platform-, or software-agnostic solution might not be practically feasible.
- Collective intelligence and the e-learning that spans across social and behavioral analytics, customer intelligence, real BI using information visualization as an interactive cues-enabler by way of intelligent visual analytics, and multiplex and multiflex analytics for modeling and analysis of competition.
- Sharable sourcing, storage, and access and analysis of volumes of data by way of computation-friendly and context-aware accelerators that perform in an autonomic, self-evident of the time and geolocation, socially aware, high-performing, parallel- and pipelining-capable and distributed grid generation–capable way.

The open source benefit comes handy in getting this result in the following ways:

- The bigger the data, the bigger the boon!
  - Data quality from a higher dimensional data analysis standpoint
  - Discovering knowledge in big data
  - Big data: From the visible to invisible and finally to the visible
  - Evolving (application) domains in DW and data mining
  - Multichannel analytics for modeling and analysis of competition: The comparative and competitive data becomes the evolving master data/KPI/metrics—a new dynamic imperative that happens in near real time
  - Compressing complexity, even if not compressing all data
- Selecting, implementing and supporting methodologies and processes vis-a-vis the business–technology–customer–social landscapes:
  - Quality of service (QoS)
  - Quality of conformance to business-to-social specifications

- ▪ Quality of (acceptable) performance by the business-to-social enterprise
- ▪ Web-accessible and wireless-enabled
- ■ Business–social model-driven methodology and processes, data-driven design (business–social is the driver, as opposed to business as a customer-centric driving factor)
  - ▪ From modeling to management; from rules of management to rules of engagement; from improvement to involvement—from superior C-UX to the intelligent C-UX lifecycle
  - ▪ For competitive intelligence, it has to be market-centric too
  - ▪ From properties created on the fly to aspects-as-activities relevancy-based generation, it's all data that tends to drive the implementation aspects of the solution across the extremes
- ■ Automated and dynamic test-driven development—Open source can be a core solution-and-services model for the same.
- ■ Web security and mobile (Web) security—Securing the content by breaking (the security) in intent. For example, using ethical hacking, penetration testing, static, and dynamic testing, white-listing, and the like to feed and fuel a loopback mechanism that rewires the enhancements into the security business design itself.
- ■ A next-generation framework for elastic extensibility of the business—Using derivation of (new) business analytics based on pattern recognition matching rules across the traditional to the adoptive to the extreme (power) user experience domain; from the performance of the business and perfection of the users' standpoints, it leaves a lot of room for seamlessly meeting the enterprise business needs and the resulting customer successes.
- ■ Identity management & security for higher information assurance—From data at rest to data in action to privileged user management to data protection in on-premise/online/in-the-cloud/hybrid usability environments to securing of archived data in physical and virtual environments, including secondary/tertiary/offline systems, security needs to be context-aware enabled, locally authenticated, and segregation of duties (SoD)–enabled. One of the key design indicators for this is the ability to isolate the definer(s) of the security framework from the invokers, based on the underlying business rules (i.e., to implement control as a direct and deterministic function of the business context pertaining to it) in the hands of the business managers and/or security

officers. An open source security interface enables this in an adaptable and flexible fashion by way of noninvasive and pervasive custom engines (that can reside on top of a generic domain-specific security layer). Here the term noninvasive refers to the ease of integration of the same to add/remove on demand. Pervasive refers to the ability of the specific extension to accommodate any and all functionality that such an engine services to the business in context.

- Ease of use—An intuitive and interactive user interface that necessarily consists of a business intelligence analytics interface (BIAI) that allows for n times flexibility in terms of user/context control (interactively or otherwise).
- An intelligent authentication, authorization and access interface in a single sign-on mode—Centralized control coupled with decentralized monitoring and management. This mandates a localized authentication mechanism, including claim-based authentication with delegated authorization strategy, for such an implementation to be feasible. It not only closes the security/governance, risk, compliance (GRC)/assurance loop, but also renders the EDW/BI solution more trustable by way of its quality. The complete isolation of the security landscape of the EDW/BI solution by way of an agentless enterprise security coordinator with *zero* fault-tolerance QA, *zero* loss data leakage, and *zero* visibility of personally identifiable information (PII)/sensitive information, pre-emptive, proactive, and reactive monitoring, resolution and/or remediation.
- Custom-deployable as a Web application, Web portal, thin client–based Web services and integration-enabled with existing applications (irrespective of the technologies involved) by using adapters-to-accelerators, enabling share services, and being enterprise scalable
- Health monitoring by way of diagnostic logging, health and usage data, and integration-enabled/embeddable/hot-pluggable health informatics analytics
- Granular data recovery and remote storage and backup of unstructured data in the form of binary large objects or BLOBs at a user-specified level (whose value can be dynamically set/changed)
- The key revenue drivers of an open source solution are business-as-a-direct-benefactor from the operations, processes, and support levels. As stated earlier, the trending customer dynamics of customer-centricity, the social Oracle, and doing business in the cloud (from infrastructure to interface and everything in between) have

created a new set of benchmarking metrics, like voice-of-customer (in terms of adoption, acquaint-friendliness and adaption), with near-*zero* IT involvement in return-on-customer—and these are the *new* ROI drivers for any business. Hence the corresponding business operations, processes, and UX vis-à-vis the IT-based solution-implementation are the *new* business–social–IT–UX KPIs for accurately measuring the success of an EDW/BI solution in terms of business value. The typical drivers that can benefit to the core of the methodologies involved, from an open source perspective, are as follows:

- Security, information protection, and GRC, beginning with role → risk and role → policy coupling for intelligent ID validation and verification; identity and access management–single sign on (IAM-SSO). Open source accelerates the investment versus return graph in this aspect
- Business agility via continuous operational efficiency, independent of IT decommissioning, and a consistent and superlative quality of service for the customer
- Return-on-customer (ROC) and its related derivatives, in terms of license fees, external professional services, internal services for implementation, support, and beyond; hardware costs end-to-end; and all of this in multiplex and multiflex live and deployment environments
- Immense cost savings potential, by "self-service via self-adaptability" for end-user productivity and maintenance
- Improved security and compliance, from access requests to approvals to aspects to signatures (this point is the biggest benefit of using an IAM (identity and access management) solution, and open source provides the best-of-the-breed technologies for this)
- Fill the gaps in the audit cycle: from risk identification to risk mediation to risk remediation to risk prevention, risk assurance gets an uplift. As the business processes are being audited, an expert rules engine can auto-audit the primary audit itself, from the first click to the last trickle of interactions, information flow, and implicit executed/generated data-breach stop-alerts.

- As communication happens inter- and intra- and "current" information streams are federated, an undercurrent of metadata
  streams on the information is captured and contextually tagged in
  (near) real time, and a third ultracurrent of aspect-related smart
  rules works on this undercurrent (of metadata) to subsume and
  consume in a semantic fashion, analyze and make available visual
  and decision-enabling intelligence information—intelligent
  because it can be used as business–social KPIs, and as pervasively
  as possible.
- Reality testing is a key driver that raises the value proposition to
  selecting the right solution. In this respect, the following criteria
  come into consideration:
    - Nonquantitative measures like the knowledge-and-training
      curve in terms of IT efficiency and business user productivity
    - The impact of the new/augmented solution for deployment
      and beyond
    - The GRC assurance in terms of confidence and support, and
      the corresponding certification costs, if necessary
    - A mechanism to automate "relative performance testing" using
      different snapshots of real use-case scenarios from live or near
      live (simulated) environments
- And last but not the least, the cost of securing the solution in a
  multipayload deployment platform (e.g., hybrid cloud, etc.) and
  the impact of the same on the information assurance end-to-end.

As stated in the introduction to this chapter, the focus on functionality
of an open source–based EDW/BI solution comprises a combination of the
business landscape, the solution technology landscape, the user landscape
and the social landscape. There is no single, one-size-fits-all, out-of-the-box
solution that encompasses these landscapes in terms of business, social, and
customer-user requirements and the technologies, architectures, and programming languages involved. This is because the business–social needs
(functionality and user experience lifecycle combined), the business value
(performance and lifecycle), and the technologies and methodologies used
are like snowflakes—no two are alike. However, a solution that is a *best fit* is
the ideal implementation answer that intersects all of these landscapes in
terms of convergence of information delivered; personalization by ways of
social contextualization, mobilization, and adaption; and elimination of the
amount of IT intervention.

The following list highlights the primary indicators that drive such a solution and the big picture of its end-to-end life cycle using an open source software stack—from the primary data (sources) to database(s) to the end-users' dashboard(s):

- Alignment of IT and business processes for the life cycle of the business to supplement, support, or extend the business side of the solution
- Flexibility and adaptability to new and emerging technologies (at least at the design level, in terms of solution architecture model, business, and IT process model), in case the life cycle of the technology involved in the IT solution is short compared to the life cycle of the business; this might involve extension of the existing technical architecture by adding/changing new technical modules and submodules to arrive at the same business results (scope, time, cost, and quality)
- Seamless architecture under the hood that allows for extensibility, adaptability (the ability to seamlessly incorporate business/IT changes by caching the customer experience or technology innovation), and integration—three areas critical to any architectural design from a solution life cycle perspective.
- Consistency; reusability; ease of coding, deployment, and use; effectiveness; and efficiency
- Openness in terms of usability and acceptance by the customer—native look and feel combined with seamless, rich user interface (UI) rendering
- Scalability (both for scaling out and scaling up), durability, high availability, security, portability
- Common integration platform for application development tools and applications (create/generate)
- Unified framework in terms of UI, proactive and pre-emptive testing and debugging, source code versioning, and source code configuration management

Figures 1.1, 1.2, 1.3, and 1.4 give snapshots of the solution life cycle involved from an open source perspective. It might not depict the go-ahead for a best solution, but certainly gives a strategy for a best-fit solution—a strategy that works—which is always a "win-win" compared to the "best" solution, in terms of business landscape, technology landscape, the programmer-to-implementer landscape, and the (business–)social landscape.

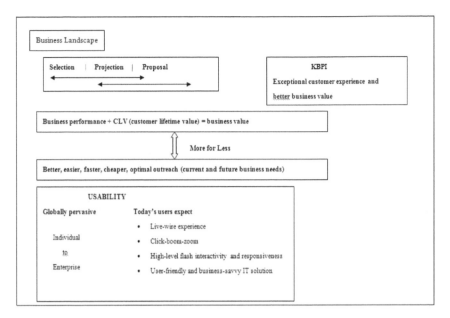

Figure 1.1   Typical solution life cycle from a business landscape.

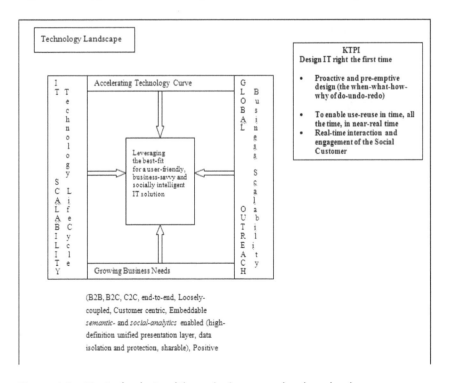

Figure 1.2   Typical solution life cycle from a technology landscape.

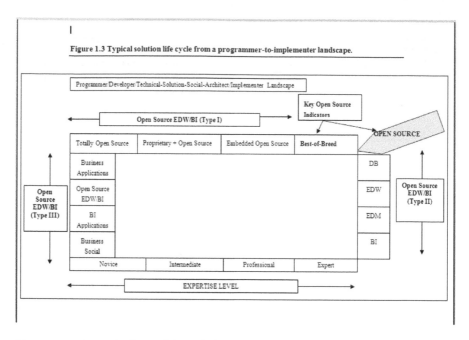

Figure 1.3   Typical solution life cycle from a programmer-to-implementer landscape.

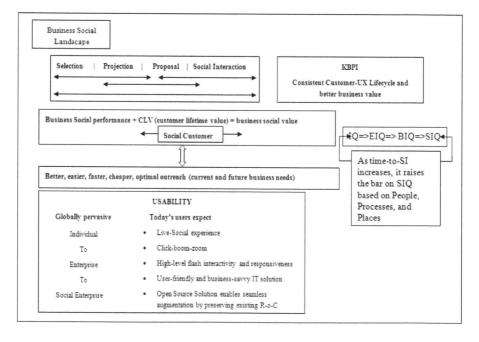

Figure 1.4   Typical solution life cycle from a business–social landscape.

SELECTION AND SUITABILITY CRITERIA FOR A PRAGMATIC AND PRUDENT SOLUTION ARCHITECTURE

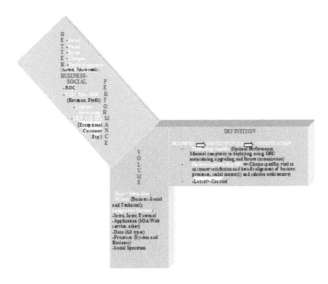

Figure 1.5   A best-fit Open Source EDW/BI solution—the big picture.

Figure 1.5 shows the big picture of primary deciding factors for a best-fit open source–enabled EDW/BI solution, not only in terms of technical accuracy and efficiency but also in terms of the ability to get what you want, from a business–social/customer–user experience lifecycle standpoint.

1.4   Summary

This chapter covered the fundamentals of an EDW/BI solution using open source technologies, tools, and techniques, starting from the data to the dashboard across the entire spectrum of the business–(social) enterprise and the social/competitive/intelligent customer. The details presented not only covered the "What's In," "When, How, Why," and "What's Not In" for these options, but also highlighted "What's Involved"—or in other words, what's needed for such a solution lifecycle. The next chapter details the foundational aspects of an open source–based EDW/BI solution in terms of architectures, technologies, and business uses.

Chapter 2

Data Warehousing and Business Intelligence: An Open Source Solution

2.1 In This Chapter

- What Is Open Source DW and BI; and How "Open" Is This Open?
- What's In, What's Not In: Available and Viable Options for Development and Deployment
- The Foundations Underneath: Architecture, Technologies, and Methodologies
- Open Source vs. Proprietary DW and BI Solutions: Key Differentiators and Integrators
- Open Source DW and BI: Uses and Abuses

This chapter details the foundations and frameworks of an open source–based enterprise data warehousing/business intelligence (EDW/BI) solution. Beginning with the notion of "open" in open source and examining the viability and availability of the architectures in context, this chapter uncovers the solution architecture in terms of design, development, and deployment, highlighting the key differentiators and integrators of adopting an open source alternative to proprietary data warehousing (DW) and business intelligence (BI) solutions. It emphasizes the *Open Source Perfect* as the trending and future direction of DW and BI by way of its business uses and abuses (to be aware of).

2.2 What Is Open Source DW and BI, and How "Open" Is This Open?

The flexibility of the architectural design enables consolidation at the infrastructure level (this can include cloud too), centralization at the administrative level, and federation at the user-control level. This gives the right balance of costs versus efficiency and involves the implementation of at least three key processes: (1) time-conscious automation, (2) context-aware and right-just-in-time recovery of the solution state, and (3) auto-reporting on the elastic provisioning, as well as the auto-auditing of the regular itself in addition to business activity monitoring, business process management, and continuous operational workflow.

How "Open" is Open Source?

- Flexibility in architecture is important for a dynamic workforce–based and multichartered services–based solution, where when a user changes roles or moves from one location to another, all of his or her access rights are updated automatically
- Rich information on user access, privileges, and provisioning activity is important to answer any GRC questions
- Enhanced security for cloud computing model is provided through extension of enterprise policies to the cloud applications
- Centralized point of control provides unified policy-based management across different systems, both on premise and in the cloud

An open source solution manages the all-inclusive environments of

```
Physical    → Virtual    → Cloud
```

by being an enabler of an

```
Intelligent    → Cloud-Ready    → Secure
```

solution, thus reducing costs and ensuring compliance.

An indispensible metric for a direly necessary business analytic, to be treated more as a business-metric than an IT-solution metric, in a very unique style! This is what is needed to raise the bar on the information assurance radar!

2.3   What's In, What's Not: Available and Viable Options for Development and Deployment

2.3.1   Semantic Analytics

Auto-generation, based on self-adaptive BI and feedback-driven business rules that mimic design, evolves the design itself. Elicit and test analytics at the source of business domain where competitive BI analytics are desired. "Competitive" comes down to "relative IQ" in terms of transforming efficiency into effectiveness for better business benefit (BBB), driven by self-service for self-adaptive functionality; time-variance; and customer-focus (the critical element to be analyzed). This approach requires timely decision making supported by confidence - continuous BI at each and every level of business domain to achieve the best privilege, with the ability to solve snags and problems in a "best-fit" manner.

2.3.2   Testing for Optimizing Quality and Automation— Accelerated!

Proactive and pre-emptive testing can guarantee an acceptable assurance level in terms of both quality of information delivered and revenue. The embeddable ability of external business components in terms of extended functionality is a near-zero impact process This can be done using open source QA accelerators for the automation and acceleration of the same across all the business (operational) lifecycle using adaptive (quantifiable) metrics.

Optimize the testing process and accelerate the quality testing by using an adaptive test automation framework that begins at the requirements analysis phase (included as part of service-level agreements, or SLAs) and is carried over all through till the customization is complete.

2.3.3   Business Rules, Real-World Perspective, Social Context

Capture business rules from a real-world perspective—customer-centric, (customer input) data-driven—and not from the implementation standpoint, and extend them to the social context domain.

Intelligent content is a direct function of the information quality delivered to the customer (with or without his/her input) and the customers' ability to derive meaningful insight from it to aid in smart decision support. The key here is that this is a cyclic process for competitive intelligence, from quantitative input to qualitative output to quantifying the same and its improvisation, and delivering output that is semantically qualitative. Self-adaptive analytics based on statistical inference and/or DM-based learning rules embedded into the solution (vis-a-vis business) workflow. *This not only involves numerical integration and optimization, but also string/text-based content aggregation and/or scholastic enumeration!*

2.3.4   Personalization Through Customizable Measures

Rein in competition by means of personalization through customizable measures, adapting for the contextualization of KPI involved:

- Introduce dynamic enumerable metrics, taking probabilistic/predictive confidence levels (based on support) calculated from competitive performance metrics (CPMs), assuming that these CPMs can scale in multiple directions and time-variant dynamics
- Use dynamic information visualization to obtain actionable business insight—federated provision for using predictive analytics for information visualization that can be then be improved for advanced prediction:
  - Apply the predictive nature of algorithms to data; predictive analytics is the next-gen level of competitive BI. The CRISP-DM 1.0 (Cross Industry Standard Practices for Data Mining) rules can be encapsulated with ease and confidence, enabling accuracy because of the platform-agnostic, cross-application, cross-tier, cross-stack integration capabilities supported by open source design
  - Use n-dimensional computing comprising graph computing, business entity relationship mining in a dynamic fashion, and high-performance computing for processing complex data structures within a "big data" domain–distributed terabyte to exabyte and beyond. All of this is done in a shared-computing (even if physically distributed) environment, in the cloud and by the cloud (using the multitenant cloud as an II-as-a-service)— it's SaaS enabled and SaaS enabling.
  - Use nested tables to enable the enumeration and processing of arbitrarily large attribute sets. Using a decision tree engine with the combination of nested tables can function as a recommendation engine for creating contextual business–social spaces. Thereby, the real value of decision making by way of giving the

control to the end-user to "craft" the desired predictive business model is realized, and the datacentric predictive analytics of the open source–based decision engine actually create the data mining model transparently with the interactive user input.

2.3.5   Leveraging the Cloud for Deployment

An open source methodology is an elevated approach to automate the deployment of a EDW/BI solution in environments with dynamically varying payloads. It gives the total control and flexibility needed to deploy and scale the solution in any desired fashion—time-variant and geolocation-variant—and on-premise, as a true hosted service, in the cloud (public, private, hybrid), or a combination of these.

2.4   The Foundations Underneath: Architecture, Technologies, and Methodologies

As stated in the beginning of the chapter, the flexibility of open source solution architecture is the key driver behind its use, apart from the cost reduction. This section details the various scenarios, from an availability and usability perspective in terms of selecting open source for an EDW/BI solution, that are viable options for the design, development, and deployment of the same. The subsections within these sections cover the use of .NET-based languages, Java/J2EE-based languages, and PHP/Ajax-based languages and highlight what's in and what's not for an Oracle11g-based embedded programming solution.

From the business–social value point, the architectures, technologies, and methodologies of an open source EDW/BI solution are enlisted below in the order of relevance, usability, and scalability:

- *An extensible model for solution implementation, integration, and operation*—from business processes to business activity to business intelligence analyses and visibility. It is a key design imperative for automation, be it on the fly or on the go. This is achieved by high-performance computing using a combination of technologies such as virtualization at the data-to-dashboard levels, real-time streaming of virtually materialized data clusters based on user-input parameters, dynamic on-demand deployment using SOA-based provisioning, software-as-a-service embedding, mobilization, information visualization and cloud computing, auto-generation, and embeddable business rules such as those related to role-based and risk-aware access control, etc.

- *Virtual business-to-business functional integration*—agile and distributed in contextual functionality, yet unified in terms of the overall business user interface (UI) via a common (centralized) repository-driven access and collaborative analysis. This is a key differentiator of open source technology, as it enables consolidation of business functions without having to create/replicate/duplicate the infrastructure underneath. And the whole concept can be elevated per business unit or per requirement in a dynamic fashion so that it scales in, scales out, and scales down with minimal downtime and impact on the live system. Real-time analytics can be pervasively correlated across the end-to-end customer space and can earn certification branding for attaining higher levels of maturity and an increased user base.

- *Intelligent information delivery*—from "data, data everywhere" to "data, data anywhere, anytime!" The often-heard problem of client-users, who complain that "All of my reports are here, but *I can't see the data I need, no matter how I do my search!*" is no misnomer—it's a fact! As alarming as it may sound, this is mostly caused by data from operational transactions being unable to get to the dashboard in near-real time. This means as the user is navigating within a single report output, the underlying data might have changed by the time he submits the request to run the same for an overlapping time-window. Open source data integration by way of virtual data federation as opposed to replication in near-real time is an intelligent solution to this very critical problem. Follow this as both the means and ends of adopting BI: Companies must be able to trace and track the silos of data that is present in various forms—from paper to prediction—across the length and breadth of the companies' resources. Then a robust BI solution can help to refine all of this data, deriving the right information that is useful to the right user at the right time. So the sooner your company gets going for the "gold data rush," the faster the *time to insight*—the time taken to analyze and arrive at "decision points" that, when implemented, can help better business/operational efficiency.

- *Simplified and user-configurable management*—automating the business process architecture through the design, deploy, test and manage phases. Be it workflow-related or business aspects that are specific in nature, automation of relative performance (quality testing or user feedback) that includes comparing two or more different business contexts of the same functional domain is a core methodology for exploratory regression analyses. And an open source approach to this is as flexible a model as it can be, in terms of dynamism and asynchrony, and also secure.

- *Analytics is the new intelligence*—from metrics to performance to social structures to advanced analytics, all deliverable on-demand and/or in near-real time. The power of Open Source EDW/BI lies in its ability to factor and refactor analytics that can be wired as part of the EDW/BI model itself, using supercomputing algorithms that are capability and capacity augmentable, multitier enabled, and at the same time optimized for time, resource consumption, effectiveness, resiliency, and most importantly hot-pluggability. This power gives the distinctly differentiating capability to embed new analytics on demand as a fledgling solution accelerator in a full-fledged running solution environment—and nothing else needs to change in terms of downtime or other mission-critical operations.

- *Dynamic information visualization for actionable business insight*— The convergence of Gigabyte-level scalability, pixel-perfect graph computing and high-performance computing of unstructured data in an efficient and transparent manner, independent of location and structure, is extreme computing in potential and the next-generation data technologies that extend beyond the relational DB sphere. And open source data and data integration services give the unprecedented levels of mishmashing required to "flatten" all of the complex data, along with its structure and across volumes of data stores. This notion can be further enhanced as *an open source framework for big data* that enables enterprisewide scalability, manipulation, partitioning, and distribution of the so called preview of intelligent information on hand and on demand. The design methodologies of virtual data federation, semantic data integration, and cloud-based information modeling are the primary collaterals that make this feasible.

- *Self-adaptable solution for self-service BI: actionable intelligence*— From contrary and complementary to complimentary and supplementary, BI has evolved to create the contextual, competitive, and self-servicing customer. Combining converged content from multiple online, on-premise, cloud, and mobile domains, the rich visualization and robust mobilization of information has realized the right-time, right-purpose, right-user, and anytime-anywhere-any-one delivery of the same. Simultaneously giving the end-user the contextual control of the same has bridged the gap between information on hand and information on demand. Real-time BI frameworks help enable bypass the enterprise data warehouse to access direct-from-OLTP data in a single-click as it is being created or updated. Predictive analytics and feedback-oriented autogenerated business rules can be auto-fed as sharable workflow at high speeds to drive the solution to become self-adaptable. They are in turn delivered as syndicated feeds that aid in insightful decision making.

An open source solution preview highlights how the Online and Mobile Controls Are Converging Conferencing, Collaboration, and Communication thereby mobile-i-zing customers in near real-time. And BI not only gives the inside truth in terms of business analytics, but also the inside scoop about how the truth was discovered, invented, and/or arrived/proved at.

- *An open source framework for information assurance*—From data-in-motion to information-in-action, relying on time-to-action as a quantitative metric is the new and heretofore scale for scoring. *Data quality and information assurance are now based on two additional BI imperatives, namely, time to insight and information visualization and viewlet materialization via (data) virtualization.* Virtualization of data enables real-time superfast streaming of information packets by dynamically generating intelligent views from the underlying metadata in sync with the query request and then tagging a semantic shell around the result-set to produce, subsume, and consume the content within the context. This capability provides a big boost for businesses dealing with huge datasets in the range of multiterabytes and beyond for the purposes of analysis and aggregation.
- And then there are alternatives to SQL-based relational data processing for highly scalable data management, data acceleration, and business continuity, such as:
  - Columnar databases (e.g., Vertica, InfoBright, etc.) in which column-orientation is a component of the core Data Model itself (as opposed to an RDBMS which is row-oriented in its very design)

- NoSQL (Not Only SQL), SQL/MapReduce (from Google's set of analytics frameworks), dynamic object caching and in-memory database caches that can function as disconnected data sources by decoupling themselves from the actual RDBMS—this accelerates query processing for extreme performance. Examples are Inter Systems Cache, eXtremeDB Cache (from McObject), PostgreSQL Plus (from EnterpriseDB) and Objectivity (for efficiency and effectiveness in object relational mapping in combination with an RDBMS or otherwise) that extend the power of in-database processing for nonrelational computing environments.
- *Information as an assured service*—This involves integration-as-a-service by way of data/information integration as a web service or cloud-based service. The key benefit of integrating data from multiple sources and in multiple formats is the single point of backup and recovery—from data loading, data syncing, data replication, data quality assessment, data loss prevention, and risk remediation, as well as other customizations where time to delivery and relevance to context are critical. Even data replication is minimized by way of de-duplication and incremental capture and store of data, metadata, and semantic tags. From data definitions, data sources, and data targets to data filters, conforming and transformative mappings, and rerouting and federated scheduling, the end-to-end data-to-information flow needs to be coherent and consistent for reliability, availability, and security (RAS), both within and beyond the enterprise
- *Interoperability and elasticity of information access and availability*—From simple to complex data processing, data virtualization, and data sharing using a single platform of computing (such as a networked or mobile virtual computing lab or a cloud-based platform-as-a-service) not only ease this process in terms of managing all of the data, but also deliver a holistic view by way of self-service. Any and all new data can be on-boarded to this sharable platform without IT intervention and rapidly mashed in the desired fashion using interactive controls to render the required results.
- *Vendor confidence in terms of popularity*—Trusted standard; certified in terms of efficiency and effectiveness; technology, customer and industry analyst research and references-based evaluation and

appraisal, augmented with customer success stories—from proof-of-concept to proven-in-customization.

- *Ideal master data management (MDM)*—An integral component of any and every data warehouse, data mart, and/or BI databoard is the master data associated with the business context of the solution. The key design indicator for MDM is the ability to link the semantic, tactical and structural gaps of the information needed. Start at the metadata level and proceed toward a shared definition of master data by putting policies into practice and ensuring data quality:
    - Data quality management on master data: quality, consistency, completeness, and synchronization
    - Data quality scorecards
    - Metadata management—Metadata starts with hard-coded data, grows, and becomes metadata once it is abstracted. Based on predictive analytics, metadata grows more and more as the EDW lifecycle progresses (as additional data sources are added, the capacity increases and hence needs to be pregrown to accommodate the same).
    - Homonyms and semantics come together when it comes to defining common ground.
    - Conformed dimensions using canonical names to converge multiple names and establishing rules that can be reused and maintained better and more easily.
    - Lock data with metadata from the business context. This approach allows easy data movement and application development, as applications are designed to be completely built on the semantic layer across all application endpoints. Here, semantic names and semantic constructs (patterns on these names) are of particular importance.
    - Data requirements analysis
    - Data quality assessment
    - Data quality inspection and control
    - Consolidation, adoption, and adaptation

2.5   Open Source versus Proprietary DW and BI Solutions: Key Differentiators and Integrators

An open source–powered solution as an accelerator in terms of its ability to extend, evolve, and elevate the EDW/BI solution in a dynamic and customer-driven fashion—without disturbing the existing infrastructure foundation—and across and beyond industry, technology, platform, and contextual boundaries. This is a key differentiating as well as an integrating factor over proprietary EDW/BI solutions in which the nativity of the information access, storage, computing, and delivery interface plays a critical role in determining the right choice of technologies, methodologies, and tools. The open source solution is, by default, a native, naïve, and natural extension, as well as providing inclusion to existing business and/or legacy solutions. Figure 2.1 depicts a high-level view of an open case for an open source solution.

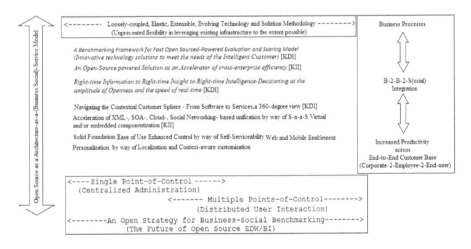

Figure 2.1   Open case for open source EDW/BI solution.

Elaborating on this, combining EDW and BI as a business domain opens the doors for potentially enormous use of an open source solution as an effective, efficient, and elastic alternative for the "Get-Set-Go" paradigm of operational efficiency and customer-driven intelligence. Here's a list of bulleted points highlighting the key differentiating indicators (KDIs) and key integrating indicators (KIIs) for the same:

- Fast cloud-powered evaluation and scoring in deploying "benchmarking" innovative technology solutions to meet the needs of the intelligent customer
- An open source–powered solution as an accelerator of cross-enterprise efficiency
- Right-time information to right-time insight to right-time intelligence, i.e., decision making at the amplitude of openness and the speed of real time!
- Building a foundation for integrating rich content and rich Internet application (RIA) on a Web 2.0 customized user interface
- Coherent and cross-platform information services, security, and management across business–social domains, using on-demand, SaaS–enabled and SaaS-enabling services. A classic example is the unification of multiple heterogeneous cloud-based services (at any of these levels—namely, SaaS, PaaS or IaaS—like OpSource Cloud, Informatica Cloud, IBM Cloud, Oracle's Exalogic Elastic Cloud, AWS EC2 Cloud, etc.) using a vendor-neutral and platform-/technology-agnostic framework, by way of virtualization of cloud services by design. This can be extended to on-premise A2A and hybrid A2A one-view collapsing, too.
- Navigating the circumstantial customer domain, from software to services—a 360° view. Examples include personalized self-service enablement, ensuring agility in dynamic scenarios (align solution strategy with solution delivery in physical/virtual/hybrid deployments)
- Acceleration of XML-, SOA-, cloud-, and social networking-based unification by way of SaaS virtual and/or embedded componentization.
- SOA security, cloud security, runtime governance, services virtualization, cross-business domain collaboration, communication, and coordination for better feedback analysis and review correlation, risk assessment, and reduction strategy leading to information, risk, and revenue assurance.

2.6 Open Source DW and BI: Uses and Abuses

The best-fit uses of open source DW and BI in terms of the pragmatics of the architectures, technologies, and methodologies involved to be put into practice can be outlined as follows:

- An open source framework for business–social integration
- An open source framework for quantifying performance of everything virtual—from data to dashboard
- An open source framework for multiplatform computing, from application to appliance: single identity, multiple densities in terms of scale, volume, throughput, multifactor security from data preparation to prediction in the cloud, quality assurance in mobile and cloud environments
- An open source information model for DW and/or BI using XML as the key component: XML has already entered the RDBMS mainstream with SQL-compliant XML queries and transactional processing going great in terms of cross-database data processing, exchange, messaging, and services. From an EDW/BI context, XML can be refactored to fit in as a model-driven component for information discovery to dissemination to delivery. This is a huge pro when dealing with unstructured and semistructured data.

The methodologies of B2B2Social integration, advanced context-aware analytics, and self-adaptable metrics can all be implemented using XML as an information hub (designed using a XML-based internal model) for breaking the complexities involved therein—resulting in a peak-point DW and BI solution from what once seemed to be a weak point in its realization.

This reminds me of the famous quote by Albert Einstein: "If the theory doesn't fit the facts, change the facts."

So if the complexity of the solution demands an out-of-normal information model, don't break the data bank; instead, fit in an XML-based model that sets the records straight.

- A open case for open source: Implementing and enforcing conforming GRC via the principles of best privileges; single point of sign-on; strong, irreversible and localized authentication complemented by delegated authorization and threat-aware controls that are fine-grained in terms of visibility, proactive and pre-emptive in enforcement ([role, risk, reign] policies), governance and audit of all processes, activity, and events including those pertaining to GRC; and security across solution deployment and execution boundaries

2.6.1   An Intelligent Query Accelerator Using an Open Cache In, Cache Out Design

Open cache in, cache out for an intelligent query accelerator is by far the most frequently needed component of any EDW/BI solution, and an intelligent open cache can be designed using behavioral analytics on the most frequently used queries and their (cached) result sets. Here are the steps involved in designing the same:

1. Using a mechanism that dynamically determines the "age" of any specific cached set, the same can be marked as "aged" or not. The key differentiator here is how the analytic function is derived and applied. A close candidate for such an algorithm is one based on the throughput in terms of query response time for each cached set, dimensioned by the size of the cache and the CBO cost of the queries. Hence, the conventional hit ratio is elevated to work on the response time by query size and cost.

For all DW and BI purposes, caching of data implicitly includes caching of the contextual metadata too.

2. Virtual federated views can be created in dynamic response to the age-refactoring results and simultaneously correlated with the statistics in database-specific dynamic performance metadata views to determine a most optimally used (or HCF-based) cache-in and a least optimally used (or LCM-based) cache-out policy.

3. Pinning the result sets for cache-in in the global shared memory or the dynamically constructed information grid enables an intelligent query accelerator in action.

In terms of abuses of open source, instead of getting into the details of the property rights of the code and the solution end to end, the following bulleted list highlights the specific business cases where open source might not be a good enabler for adoption:

■   In situations where the global and/or local dynamics of scale and serviceability (in terms of service-level agreements [SLAs] or otherwise) allow no room for an alternative approach to EDW/BI solution extension or fabrication

- Restraints in existing solutions that are either not compatible or cannot be made to comply with the functional, architectural, and technical principles and policies inherent in an open source augmentation. Examples include the "security" aspect of an open source solution being as "trustable" as a tier-1/proprietary DW and BI solution for entire spectrum of users; or supplemental context-specific regulations that are out of borders with their open source counterparts.

2.7 Summary

This chapter outlined the foundational aspects of an open source–based EDW/BI solution by opening up the viable and feasible open source solution architectures for design, development, and deployment—highlighting the key differentiators and integrators of adopting an open source alternative to proprietary DW and BI solutions. It emphasizes the *Open Source Perfect* as the trending and future direction of DW and BI by way of its business uses and abuses (to beware) and concludes by describing the design of a powerful use case implementation of an open source–based intelligent query accelerator. The next chapter explores the potential open source products and players in the current EDW/BI space and their strengths in terms of simplification, relevance, currency, and consistency in addition to the cost factor.

Chapter 3

Open Source DW & BI: Successful Players and Products

3.1 In This Chapter

- Open Source Data Warehousing and Business Intelligence Technology
- The Primary Vendors: Inventors and Presenters
- The Primary Products and Tools Set: Inclusions and Exclusions
- The Primary Users: Evaluators, Investors, Implementers and Eventual Benefiters
- The Primary Users: User, End-User, Customer and Intelligent Customer

Given that an open source strategy enables the design and implementation of an EDW/BI solution from requirements analysis to competitive intelligence analysis, its adoption has already gone mainstream, with multiple vendors and their products playing a dynamic role in the invention, evaluation, and delivery of customer-centric DW and BI solutions. From investors to implementers and end users to intelligent customers, these players have a significant role not only in gaining an edge in terms of a think-tank but also as a successful foundation for business efficiency, acceleration and value. Open source EDW/BI solutions have convincingly raised the bar on customer satisfaction by optimizing service-oriented modeling and service delivery in both physical and/or virtual environments, anytime-anywhere-anyone access, and a smarter and faster way of business operations. And open source–based advanced analytics have enabled seamless social integration of existing BI applications thus elevating "business as usual" to business–social. This chapter details the players and products of open source EDW/BI solutions that have empowered this new business model for innovation, rapid response, customer experimentation, increased utilization at the same or lower cost, and enhanced customer productivity (and hence satisfaction). Also, it has significantly reduced the dynamics of startup IT processes as well as simplified the compliance enforcement in today's multipayload deployments. Figure 3.1 depicts the end-to-end view of data warehousing technology layers. It also shows the subcomponents in each of these layers, such as data integration, data reporting, analytics, geospatial analytics, and the like.

Front End/ Reporting	Dashboards/Scorecards Visualization		Reporting Search/Discovery	
Information Delivery	Analytics Search/Discovery		Workflow Modeling	Portal GIS/Location
Data Integration Management	ETL EII	EDR EAI	ECM	
Data warehouse	Databases			
Infrastructure	Servers	Operating Systems		

Figure 3.1   End-to-end data warehousing technology overview.

Open source solutions have become viable alternatives to traditional proprietary licensed software, with more than 25 open source projects providing a wide variety of tools for data warehousing and full business intelligence software. As discussed in the earlier chapters, the open source data warehousing and business intelligence field is spread end-to-end across length and breadth of technology landscape, including:

- Infrastructure
- Data warehouse databases
- Data integration management
- Information delivery
- Front-end interfaces/reporting
- Real-time operational intelligence
- Social BI
- Context-aware, self-serviceable and interactive BI
- Competitive intelligence

The rest of this chapter takes a deep dive into the open source data warehousing industry players, their products, their customers, community, and so on.

Many references have been used in gaining access to the information provided in this chapter; these references are indicated throughout and, for ease of research, have been collected in at the end of the chapter.

3.2   Open Source Data Warehousing and Business Intelligence Technology

Enterprise caliber software is readily available for the core data warehouse and BI components. There are open source projects available for every element of the business intelligence and data warehouse stack. This includes core products such as databases as well as emerging analytic database platforms. The emergence of commercial open source accelerated development of business solutions, thereby increasing open source adoption over the last several years. Commercial open source changes the dynamics of software development by bringing these technologies to market as open source before they have a chance to go through a standard proprietary growth phase. This acceleration of the commodity process is one of the biggest effects open source has had on the enterprise software market.

The topranked open source software is provided by commercial open source vendors. Free and commercial open source software solutions are available for every possible DW/BI application, from traditional reporting and OLAP tools to advanced data mining and statistics, advanced data visualization, simulation and Webbased geographic information systems. Data integration software is a more recent entrant in the developer tools market, with ETL, data quality, and data federation options available.

Figure 3.2 summarizes the major open source products available in each of the DW/BI layers.

3.2.1   Licensing Models Followed

Software developed as open source is no different from traditional commercial software. The difference lies in a license that gives more freedom with the code than a proprietary license. Open source software (OSS) is released under a license that differs from traditional software licenses. Licensing, or how the source code is allowed to be modified and shared, can have a real impact on choosing open-source software. The license guarantees several freedoms:

Front End/ Reporting	Pentaho Jaspersoft Mondrian (Pentaho) BIRT	Jfree SpagoBI Opeal MaverIT	Palo OpenReports
Information Delivery	R Weka RapidMiner Knime	Graphviz Orange Processing Axlis	Taverna Cytoscape
Integration Management	Pentaho DI/Kettle Talend Jitterbit DataCleaner	Red Hat Apatar OSDQ Open Data Quality	Clover
Data warehouse Databases	MySQL Postgres Infobright EnterpriseDB	Ingres Firebird Palo CouchDB	SQLite MonetDB LucidDB Bizgres
Infrastructure			

Figure 3.2   Data Warehousing technology products as players of open source.

- Access to the source code
- The ability share to the code with others
- The freedom to modify and use

One misconception is that any customized changes the code must also be shared. Sharing is a requirement only the software is sold or distributed to others outside the admissible domain. If redistributed, then any changes or additions made must be provided as source code. If the open source software is not redistributed, there is no need to share the additions.

Open source software is available as a project that is maintained by a community of people who write the code and documentation, provide quality assurance, and help manage distribution. These people may be independent volunteers or contract programmers, or they may all work for a software company that maintains the software. Vendors use open source to enable a means of software production and distribution that provides lower operating costs and other benefits back to the vendor. Open source DW/BI software development and deployments, whether on premise or in the cloud, can cut licensing costs significantly.

Examples of open source licensing models are:

- *GNU General Public License (GNU GPL)*: The GNU GPL is more liberal in its views of open sourcing–derived works, in that it is in place to encourage the free sharing of code. This protects the original authors of the code by forcing new solutions based on the original project to take on the GNU GPL license as well.

- *BSD License*: The BSD license allows modifications of the code to be released into the open source world at the author's discretion. The license does not force the derived solution to also become open source; vendors can choose to open-source their code if or when it meets their business model.

3.2.2   Community versus Commercial Open Source

There are two primary models of support for open source. One is community-based open source, often called "free and open source," and the other is called commercial open source software.

In the free community model, volunteers contribute their efforts to development and maintenance. In some cases, they may be full-time employees of a nonprofit organization that owns the software, but the project does not operate like a traditional software project. There is no profit motive. The software is available free of charge to anyone who wants it.

Commercial open source was born for a different reason. Commercial open source vendors benefit by filling in the gaps in the free and open source model and thereby deriving monetary benefits. Commercial open source evolved with recognition that companies are willing to pay for support, service, and other less tangible items like indemnification or certifying interoperability, for example, of a BI tool with a given proprietary database. *A commercial open source vendor is just like a traditional software vendor, except that the source code is not obfuscated in secrecy.* This enables more and deeper interaction between customers and developers, making the open source model more community focused than the traditional model.

In contrast to the majority of free and open source projects, commercial open source vendors employ most of the project's developers and expect to make a profit while doing so. They provide the same services and support that traditional vendors do, frequently with more flexibility and lower cost. Commercial open source vendors use elements of the proprietary model, such as providing support contracts or selling non open source components that can be purchased in addition to, or in place of, the free version of the software.

> Software is truly classifiable as open source if and only if its source code is governed by an OSI certified license. Otherwise, it is not open source.

Commercial open source vendors are like proprietary vendors. The key difference is the transparency with which commercial open source vendors operate.

Third Nature conducted interviews and a survey with both consultants and IT professionals between July and August of 2009. The corresponding BeyeNETWORK Research Report titled "Open Source Solutions: Managing, Analyzing and Delivering Business Information" by Mark Madsen, http://ThirdNature.net, (www.beyeresearch.com/study/12261) includes the following paragraph, which suggests how a more committed level of transparency is lacking in proprietary vendors as opposed to their open source partners: "As one interviewee noted, 'We can see bug reports and enhancement requests made by anyone and help with prioritization by voting on their implementation. The same applies to features for upcoming releases.' This level of transparency is not often found in proprietary vendors."

3.3   The Primary Vendors: Inventors and Presenters

The communities of developers that create and contribute to open source projects make them come to life. Essentially, there are two different kinds of open source communities. First, there are pure open-source projects that are organized around independent and self-funding communities. PostgreSQL, for example, is the oldest and largest independent open source database community of this kind. The benefit of such a community is true vendor independence. The second kind of open source community can be a vendor that controls the project; that project could potentially be "purchased." MySQL is a classic example of this type. The MySQL community is autonomous but is controlled by Oracle.

3.3.1   Oracle: MySQL Vendor

In 2008, Sun Microsystems, Inc. acquired MySQL AB, an open source database company. In turn, in 2010 Oracle bought Sun Microsystems, Inc. During the Oracle and Sun acquisition transaction, the European Commission expressed concerns about the Oracle/Sun Microsystems transaction, in particular the maintenance of MySQL as a competitive force in the database market. To satisfy regulators, Oracle pledged to continue to develop and promote MySQL as an autonomous entity. Thus, MySQL became an Oracle product and has continued to flourish since then, contributing improvements where it can without compromising the essential openness of the product and process.

MySQL users should take heart from the 5.5 release and the ongoing support that Oracle has shown to this important open source relational database management system (RDBMS). It is unlikely that Oracle will try to cannibalize or otherwise compromise its open source nature or the community, and Oracle can feel comfortable with its continued involvement in MySQL. In addition to MySQL, Oracle supports conventional Oracle Database through 11gR2, Oracle TimesTen, Berkeley DB, and Oracle Exadata Database Machine in its portfolio.

MySQL is the most popular open source database; it provides high-performance, read-intensive applications. Oracle offers multiple MySQL commercial editions to meet market needs and reduces the risk, cost, and time required in developing, deploying, and managing business-critical MySQL applications. With 24×7 Oracle Premier Support, enterprises are enjoying highly reliable, secure uptime with MySQL open source environments.

Following are some of the highlights of MySQL under Oracle's stewardship:

- 70,000+ downloads a day
- MySQL named one of the Top 10 Open Source Hall of Famers by *InfoWorld*
- MySQL voted the "Best Database" by *Linux Journal* Reader's Choice Awards 2010
- More than 2,000 ISVs and OEMs entrust their products and business success to MySQL
- MySQL Workbench was named the 2009 Product of the Year, database tool category, by Developer.com

3.3.2 PostgreSQL Vendor

PostgreSQL, like many other open source programs, is not controlled by any single company; rather, a global community of developers and companies develops the system. PostgreSQL evolved from the Ingres project at the University of California at Berkeley. Michael Stonebraker started a post-Ingres project in 1985 to address the increasing issues with contemporary database systems during the early 1980s. The project was called Postgres, and its aim was to completely support types and fully describe relationships by adding only the fewest features needed, maintained entirely by the user.

In Postgres, the database "understood" relationships and could retrieve information in related tables in a natural way using rules.

The team published a number of papers describing the basis of the system in 1986; by 1988, they had a prototype version. Version 1 was released in June 1989 to a small number of users, then version 2 was released in June 1990 with a rewritten rules system. Version 3, released in 1991, rewrote the rules system once again, adding support for multiple storage managers and improving the query engine. By 1993, the number of users had increased to the point that they began to overwhelm the project with requests for support and features. The team released version 4, which was primarily a cleanup, and then ended the project.

However, because Berkeley had released Postgres under an MIT license (which enables users and developers to deal with the software without restriction), open source developers could still obtain copies and continue to develop the system. In 1994, Andrew Yu and Jolly Chen, who were graduate students at Berkeley, created Postgres95 by replacing the Ingres-based QUEL query language interpreter with one for the SQL query language, and they released the code for the new software on the Web. In July 1996, Marc Fournier at Hub.Org Networking Services provided the first non-university development server for the open source development effort. He worked with Bruce Momjian and Vadim B. Mikheev to stabilize the code inherited from Berkeley, and they released the first open source version on August 1, 1996.

That same year, the product was renamed PostgreSQL to reflect the product's support for SQL. The first PostgreSQL release formed version 6.0 in January 1997. Since then, the software has been maintained by a group of database developers and volunteers all over the world who coordinating with each other via the Internet. The PostgreSQL project continues to make major releases (approximately annually) as well as minor "bugfix" releases under the same license. The code is contributed by proprietary vendors, support companies, and open source programmers at large. (Source: http://en.wikipedia.org/wiki/PostgreSQL.)

3.3.3   Infobright

Infobright develops and markets a high performance, self-tuning analytic database specifically designed to support the growing need for analytics and business intelligence throughout the business world. This critical need for business intelligence, coupled with the dramatic growth of corporate data, has outpaced IT resources and budget within many companies. The Infobright® technology solves this problem by delivering a simple-to-manage, enterprise-class, highly scalable analytic database that offers the industry's lowest total cost of ownership (TCO). Well suited for both enterprises and as an embedded database within ISV and SaaS product offerings, Infobright's self-managing software reduces ongoing management by up to 90 percent and reduces TCO by 50 percent or more, compared to alternative approaches.

In 2008 the company released the industry's first commercial open source analytic database software, and built a strong and growing open source user community and a rapidly-growing customer base.

Infobright's software is being used by both enterprises and ISV/SaaS vendors in online marketing, advertising and gaming, telecommunications, financial services, and other industries to provide rapid access to critical business data with unmatched operational simplicity. (Source: www.graymatter.co.in/infobright-partner.html)

Per Infobright's Web site (www.infobright.com/About-Us), Infobright has been recognized for its innovative technology and the value the company provides to its customers:

- Named "Company to Watch in 2010" for Information Management by Intelligent Enterprise
- Named "Cool Vendor in Data Management and Integration 2009" by Gartner, Inc.
- Named "MySQL Partner of the Year 2009"
- "Economic Data Warehouse Choice" by Ventana Research
- Named "2008 High Performance Data Warehousing Partner of the Year" by Pentaho

3.3.4   Pentaho: Mondrian Vendor

Pentaho Corporation, headquartered in Orlando, Florida, provides a full spectrum of commercial open source BI capabilities, including reporting, analysis, dashboards, data mining, data integration, and a BI platform that have made it the world's most popular open source BI suite. Founded in 2004 by a team of business intelligence industry veterans, Pentaho is an open source business intelligence player with application software for enterprise reporting, analysis, dashboard, data mining, workflow and ETL capabilities. (Source: www.enotes.com/topic/Pentaho.)

3.3.5   Jedox: Palo Vendor

Jedox was founded by Kristian Raue in 2002 and developed by Jedox AG, a company based in Freiburg, Germany. The company currently employs approximately 60 people.

3.3.6   EnterpriseDB Vendor

EnterpriseDB is a privately held company that provides enterprise class support for PostgreSQL through its product Postgres Plus Standard Server, which is PostgreSQL with extra bundled modules. The company also offers Postgres Plus Advanced Server, which adds compatibility software to simplify application migration from other databases.

The company was founded in March 2004 by Denis Lussier and Andy Astor. Though Denis Lussier moved on to found OpenSCG in mid-2009 and Andy Astor joined Asurion in early 2009, EnterpriseDB is presently headquartered in Massachusetts and has offices in New Jersey, Europe, and Asia. Ed Boyajian is the current President and CEO. (Source: www.enotes.com/topic/EnterpriseDB)

3.3.7   Dynamo BI and Eigenbase: LucidDB Vendor

LucidDB was started as a collaboration between LucidEra, Inc. and The Eigenbase Project (a nonprofit organization). Much of the technology was adapted from an earlier venture (Broadbase Software, which produced the industry's first turn-key data mart product).

LucidEra acquired the rights to this codebase, integrated it into the pluggable DBMS framework provided by Eigenbase, and contributed the result (LucidDB) back to Eigenbase as open source software under the terms of the GPL.

The Dynamo BI Web site gives the history for LucidDB: "Much of the original algorithms and technology for the LucidDB column store was developed at Broadbase software, which was acquired by Kana in 2001. LucidEra acquired the IP to the database, and rewrote the core pieces to run in Eigenbase frameworks. Eigenbase frameworks and LucidDB have been a multi-year joint development effort between multiple data management startups." (Source: www.dynamobi.com/c/community/history-and-statistics.)

The Eigenbase Project provides an extensible open source platform for building specialized data management systems in a wide variety of application spaces. LucidEra went out of business in June 2009, but Eigenbase continues to sponsor the community effort, providing project hosting resources such as source control and release management. Eigenbase also oversees coordination with related projects. Most recently, a new company called Dynamo BI has picked up the baton and is commercializing the technology under the name DynamoDB. (Source: www.luciddb.org/html/projectfaq.html.)

3.3.8   GreenPlum Vendor

On July 6, 2010, EMC Corporation acquired Greenplum and continues to develop the technology marketed under the Greenplum name. Greenplum used to be a privately held database software company located in San Mateo, California, specializing in enterprise data cloud solutions for large-scale data warehousing and analytics. Greenplum was formed in 2003 by the merger of Metapa and Didera to develop data warehousing solution built on open source software. Greenplum was led by pioneers in open source, database systems, data warehousing, supercomputing, and Internet performance acceleration with technical staff from companies such as Oracle, Sybase, Informix, Teradata, Netezza, Tandem, and Sun.

The Greenplum Database is built from modified PostgreSQL in a massively parallel processing (MPP) database.

3.3.9   Hadoop Project

The Apache Hadoop project develops open source software for reliable, scalable, distributed computing. According to the Apache wiki (http://wiki.apache.org/incubator/BigtopProposal), Hadoop includes these sub-projects:

- *Hadoop Common*: The common utilities that support the other Hadoop subprojects
- *HDFS*: A distributed file system that provides high throughput access to application data

- *MapReduce*: A software framework for distributed processing of large data sets on compute clusters

Other Hadoop-related projects at Apache are outlined on the Hadoop Web site (http://hadoop.apache.org) and include:

- *Avro*: A data serialization system
- *Chukwa*: A data collection system for managing large distributed systems
- *HBase*: A scalable, distributed database that supports structured data storage for large tables
- *Hive*: A data warehouse infrastructure that provides data summarization and ad hoc querying
- *Mahout*: A scalable machine learning and data mining library
- *Pig*: A high-level data-flow language and execution framework for parallel computation
- *ZooKeeper*: A high-performance coordination service for distributed applications

3.3.10   HadoopDB

According to the Connecticut Technology Council's "Tech Companies to Watch" blog, digital information is increasing tenfold every five years, and current database management systems are already struggling to keep up. HadoopDB is an open source parallel database capable of performing high speed analytics on this new generation of "Big Data" to address the data management problem. Using a hybrid architecture, HadoopDB combines the scalability of Hadoop with the high performance of relational databases on structured data. The result is a database that scales linearly, using inexpensive commodity hardware, and that can return query results nearly 10 times faster than IBM's DB2 and nearly 50 times faster than Hadoop—increasing performance while reducing cost per terabyte and TCO. (Source: http://ct.typepad.com/c2w/2010/12/hadoopdb.html.)

3.3.11   Talend

Talend describes itself as one of the largest pure-play vendors of open source software. The company offers an array of middleware solutions that address both data management and application integration needs. Talend has become a major player in open source data management, a position reinforced by its acquisition in 2010 of Sopera, a player in open source application integration, resulting in Talend becoming a global player in open source middleware. Talend makes enterprise grade data management and application integration solutions available to organizations of all sizes. The company offers open and innovative software solutions with the flexibility to meet the data management and application integration needs of all types of organizations. (Source: www.talend.com/open-source-provider/overview.php.)

Talend is the first provider of open source data integration software. After three years of intense research and development, and with solid financial backing from leading investment firms, Talend revolutionized the world of data integration when it released the first version of Talend Open Studio in 2006. Talend's solutions are used primarily for migration and integration between operational systems, as well as for ETL (Extract, Transform, Load) for BI and data warehousing. Unlike proprietary, closed solutions, which are only affordable for the largest organizations, Talend makes enterprise-class data integration solutions affordable to organizations of all sizes. (Source: www.infobright.com/Customers_Partners/talend.)

3.4   The Primary Products and Tools Set: Inclusions and Exclusions

3.4.1   Open Source Databases

Open source databases have been in existence for many years. Most of the engineering effort for OSS databases is focused on transaction processing. In general, open source databases are smaller in size than their proprietary counterparts.

Database sizes have increased significantly across all industries during the past few years. Most open source analytic databases are aimed at databases less than 5 terabytes in size. Lack of data warehouse–specific scaling and performance features, query performance, and performance related to data size and scalability or to user concurrency are some of the issues with open source databases.

Following is the list of open source databases in the industry:

- MySQL
- Postgres
- Infobright
- Mondrian

- Palo
- EnterpriseDB
- LucidDB
- Greenplum
- Talend and Talend Unified Platform
- Ingres
- Firebird
- CouchDB
- SQLite
- MonetDB
- Bizgres

MySQL

An article by Jim Mlodgenski in *eWeek* comparing PostgreSQL and MySQL outlines this history of MySQL's development. The MySQL community's beginnings are in the commercial world. MySQL was started in Sweden in 1994, out of a need to have a high-speed database behind Web sites. It was released to the open source world a few years later under the control of MySQL AB. This commercial control helped MySQL become one of the most widely used databases in the world (a factor that led to Sun's 2008 acquisition of MySQL AB). The popularity of MySQL also became a major factor in the European Union's acceptance of the Oracle acquisition of Sun, which was finalized in 2010. (Source: Jim Mlodgenski, "PostgreSQL vs. MySQL: How to Select the Right Open-Source Database," *eWeek*, October 21, 2010. Available at http://mobile.eweek.com/c/a/Linux-and-Open-Source/PostgreSQL-vs-MySQL-How-to-Select-the-Right-OpenSource-Database.)

MySQL's easy administration, excellent read performance, and transparent support for large text and binary objects make it the top choice for many Web sites.

As the most popular open source database, MySQL has a deserved reputation resulting from its legacy of performance and simplicity. MySQL was designed to be a fast indexed sequential access method (ISAM) data store for Web sites. This type of work load—which is characterized as a read-mostly load, with many small queries—has led to features such as a query cache that improves MySQL's performance even further. This concentration on performance has inspired features such as MySQL Cluster, which allows the database to scale beyond a single physical server.

One of MySQL's greatest strengths is its pluggable storage engines. MyISAM, MySQL's default storage engine, provides the performance for read-mostly environments, and the InnoDB storage engine provides the transaction robustness necessary for write-intensive applications.

There are a number of third-party storage engines, such as Brighthouse and DB2, that add even more capabilities to MySQL. This flexibility allows administrators to tune a MySQL instance based on the needs of the individual tables. MySQL, the traditionally strong database for Web applications, is also used by applications requiring transactional support. The key is that either option has the flexibility to handle a large range of uses, but one may be a better technical or business choice based on individual circumstances.

Oracle outlines the key benefits of MySQL as (source: www.oracle.com/us/products/mysql/index.html):

- *Ease of use*—Go from download to complete installation in less than 15 minutes
- *Low TCO*—Deploy MySQL for mission-critical applications with significant cost savings compared to Microsoft SQL Server
- *Scalability and performance*—Meet the scalability and performance requirements of the most trafficked Web sites and the most demanding applications
- *Production support*—Oracle Premier Support helps lower the total cost and risk of owning MySQL solutions

Oracle offers MySQL in the following six editions:

1. *MySQL Community Edition*—A freely downloadable version that is a fully integrated, transaction-safe, ACID-compliant database with full commit, rollback, crash recovery, and row-level locking capabilities. (Source: www.oracle.com/us/products/mysql/mysql-communityserver/index.html)

2. *MySQL Classic Edition*—The ideal embedded database for ISVs, OEMs, and VARs developing read-intensive applications using the MyISAM storage engine.(Source: www.oracle.com/us/products/mysql/mysqlclassic/index.html)

3. *MySQL as an Embedded Database (OEM/ISV)*—A full-featured, zero-administration database for ISVs, OEMs, and VARs; it can be embedded into their products to gain a competitive edge, faster time to market, and significant cost reduction.

4. *MySQL Standard Edition Subscription*—Includes InnoDB, making it a fully integrated transaction-safe, ACID-compliant database.

5. *MySQL Enterprise Edition Subscription*—Includes a comprehensive set of MySQL production, backup, monitoring, modeling, development, and administration tools.

6. *MySQL Cluster Carrier Grade Edition Subscription (MySQL Cluster CGE)*—Delivers predictable, millisecond response times that enable it to service tens of thousands of transactions per second. It also provides linear database scalability by providing support for in-memory and disk-based data, automatic data partitioning with load balancing, and the ability to add nodes to a running cluster with zero downtime. (Sources: www.mysql.com/products/cluster and www.oracle.com/us/products/mysql/mysqlcluster/index.html.)

PostgreSQL

PostgreSQL excels in terms of robustness and power for handling transactional enterprise applications, but it is also used to support many Web applications.

In September 2010, the PostgreSQL Global Development Group released the most anticipated PostgreSQL 9.0 object-relational database system. PostgreSQL 9.0 includes built-in, binary replication, and over a dozen other major features that will appeal to everyone from Web developers to database hackers.

PostgreSQL is an open source object-relational database system, with more than 15 years of active development and a proven architecture that has earned it a strong reputation for reliability, data integrity, and correctness. It runs on all major operating systems, including Linux, UNIX, and Microsoft Windows.

An enterprise class database, PostgreSQL has features such as Multi-Version Concurrency Control (MVCC), point-in-time recovery, tablespaces, asynchronous replication, nested transactions (savepoints), online/hot backups, a sophisticated query planner/optimizer, and write ahead logging for fault tolerance.

An article by Jim Mlodgenski in *eWeek* comparing PostgreSQL and MySQL describes the core architecture of PostgreSQL as enabling other community groups to build more advanced features into PostgreSQL through add-on modules. A perfect example of this is PostgreSQL's geospatial support, a functionality from a module called PostGIS, which is a simple extension to PostgreSQL that arguably makes it the strongest spatial, open source or commercial database.

Mlodgenski also describes a further extension to PostgreSQL: the ability to have many different types of stored procedure languages, enabling developers to build server-side code using the best language for their needs. For example, a trigger that needs to perform complex text processing can be written in Perl in order to utilize its strong regular expression functionality. (Source: Jim Mlodgenski, "PostgreSQL vs. MySQL: How to Select the Right Open-Source Database," *eWeek*, October 21, 2010. Available at http://mobile.eweek.com/c/a/Linux-and-Open-Source/PostgreSQL-vs-MySQL-How-to-Select-the-Right-OpenSource-Database.)

PostgreSQL's Web site (www.postgresql.org/about) states that PostgreSQL runs stored procedures in more than a dozen programming languages, including Java, Perl, Python, Ruby, Tcl, C/C++, and its own PL/pgSQL, which is similar to Oracle's PL/SQL. Included with its standard function library are hundreds of built-in functions that range from basic math and string operations to cryptography and Oracle compatibility. Triggers and stored procedures can be written in C and loaded into the database as a library, allowing great flexibility in extending its capabilities. Similarly, PostgreSQL includes a framework that allows developers to define and create their own custom data types along with supporting functions and operators that define their behavior.

There are also many library interfaces as well, allowing various languages both compiled and interpreted to interface with PostgreSQL. There are interfaces for Java (JDBC), ODBC, Perl, Python, Ruby, C, C++, PHP, Lisp, Scheme, and Qt just to name a few.

Infobright

Infobright's company fact sheet (www.infobright.com/?ACT=62&resource_id=34) describes Infobright as "the high performance database for analytic applications and data marts, used by both enterprises and ISV/SaaS companies who need fast query response with unmatched administrative simplicity: no indexes, no data partitioning, and no manual tuning."

Infobright uses intelligence, not hardware, to drive query performance:

- Creates information about the data upon load, automatically
- Uses this to eliminate or reduce the need to access data to respond to a query

■ The less data that needs to be accessed, the faster the response

This is a huge performance benefit to the customer, in that:

■ There is no need to preplan queries, create indexes, or tune for performance
■ Ad hoc queries are as fast as anticipated queries, so users have total flexibility
■ Data compression of 10:1 to 40:1, meaning a lot less storage is needed
■ Queries that may take hours with other databases run in minutes; queries that take minutes with other databases run in seconds

Infobright offers an open source and a commercial edition of its software, which are designed to handle data volumes up to 50 TB.

Infobright describes its products as follows: "Infobright Enterprise Edition (IEE) is the commercial version of our software, and Infobright Community Edition (ICE) is our freely-available, open source product you can download by clicking on the Download Community Edition button on the right. IEE includes enhanced features often needed for production and operational support, technical support and services, product warranty and other benefits of a commercial license." (Source: www.infobright.com/Products.)

Mondrian

Pentaho Analysis Services Community Edition, known as Mondrian, is an online analytical processing (OLAP) server written in Java that enables business users to analyze large quantities of data in real time. Users explore business data by drilling into and cross-tabulating information with speed-of-thought response times to complex analytical queries. It supports the MDX (multidimensional expressions) query language and the XML for Analysis and olap4j interface specifications. Mondrian reads from SQL and other data sources and aggregates data in a memory cache.

Mondrian is used for:

■ High performance, interactive analysis of large or small volumes of information
■ Dimensional exploration of data (for example analyzing sales by product line, by region, by time period)

- Parsing of the MDX language into SQL to retrieve answers to dimensional queries
- High-speed queries through the use of aggregate tables in the RDBMS
- Advanced calculations using the calculation expressions of the MDX language

(Sources: http://mondrian.pentaho.com and http://en.wikipedia.org/wiki/Mondrian_OLAP_server.)

Palo

Wikipedia (http://en.wikipedia.org/wiki/Palo_(OLAP_database)) describes Palo as a memory resident multidimensional (OLAP or MOLAP) database server that is typically used as a BI tool for controlling and budgeting purposes, with spreadsheet software acting as the user interface. Beyond the multidimensional data concept, Palo enables multiple users to share a single centralized data storage.

This type of database helps in handling complex data models for business management and statistics. Apart from multidimensional queries, data can also be written back and consolidated in real time. To give rapid access to all data, Palo stores it in the memory during runtime. The server is available as open source and closed source.

Palo for Excel is a open source add-in for Microsoft Excel. There is also an open source add-in for OpenOffice.org named PalOOCa, with Java and Web client also available from the JPalo project. Palo can also be integrated into other systems via its Java, PHP, C/C++, and .NET client libraries. It is fairly easy to communicate with Palo OLAP Server, since it uses REST.

Beginning in October 2008, Palo has supported XML for Analysis and MDX APIs for connectivity, as well as OLE DB for OLAP interface, which allows standard Excel Pivot Tables to serve as a client tool.

Palo Suite is a tightly integrated framework consisting of:

- Palo MOLAP Server
- Palo ETL Server
- Palo Web (Palo Spreadsheet: Connection, User, ETL, File and Report Manager)
- Palo for Excel
- Palo Supervision Server
- Palo Client Libraries

The data in Palo database is stored as a cube in the Palo MOLAP server. The Palo Excel Add-In component is used as a service to communicate between the Excel and the Palo MOLAP Server.

Palo for Excel

Palo for Excel is an open source business intelligence solution for planning, analysis, reporting and consolidation. Palo provides relevant dimensions of corporate information to be viewed and analyzed at the same time. Palo for Excel includes the OLAP Server Database, plus the Microsoft Excel add-in (alternatively Open Office add-in) which allows the customer to build a complete business intelligence solution.

Following are the main features of Palo for Excel and Palo OLAP Server:

- Write-back
- User rights
- Cell-based
- Multidimensional
- Hierarchical
- Memory-based and real-time computation–capable
- Server-based
- Subsets
- Rules
- Palo Suite

Palo Suite is available as a community and a premium edition, with the premium version offering extended software assurance and support functionalities. Palo Suite combines all four of Jedox's core applications—OLAP Server, Palo Web, Palo ETL Server, and Palo for Excel—into a single comprehensive and customizable BI platform. The platform is completely based on open source products representing a high-end BI solution that is available entirely free of any license fees. The primary focus points of the Palo Suite are:

Palo OLAP Server, the key module of the Palo Suite, offers increased stability and performance, as well as new logical algorithms. It is a multiuser, high-performance data server application that allows workers throughout an enterprise to access, change, and collaborate on BI data instantaneously. Furthermore, it offers a real-time aggregation through the multidimensional data model.

Palo Web combines all Palo components in a Web interface. Here all actions can be carried out, given the user rights that are claimed, allow Palo Web access. Designers can administrate and create Web-based reports, model the OLAP database, or monitor ETL processes. Business users are able to view planning and analysis reporting in Palo Web.

The *Palo Suite* allows users direct access via Microsoft Excel and Open Office Calc by including Palo for Excel. By doing so, existing applications (mostly Excel based) can easily be migrated and find further use. Entry into the Palo Suite via Palo for Excel is simple and can be achieved without previous Palo experience.

Palo ETL Server is a Web-based data acquisition tool that extracts, transforms, and loads data from transactional systems, data warehouses, and other external sources. The application accepts data from relational database management systems, SAP, Web services, and much more.

(Source: www.palo.net.)

Palo SAP Connectivity

The Palo SAP Connectivity is an additional component of Palo ETL, which offers additional types of connections and extractions to access SAP Systems directly. Palo can now be integrated optimally into SAP environments.

SAP data can be extracted at the table level or from views of the SAP Data Dictionary. Similarly, a flexible access to SAP Remote Function Calls (RFC) and to the SAP Business Application Programming Interface (BAPI) is possible. The ETL process is fully modeled using a graphic Web frontend, without the need for programming.

The extraction of data from SAP Business Warehouse (BW/BI) is put into practice easily: BW info objects can be loaded directly as dimension into Palo OLAP, including all the original attributes, texts, and hierarchies. Transaction data is transferred with high performance from BW Data Store Objects (DSOs). While accessing SAP R/3 and ERP Systems, hierarchies for cost centers and profit centers with a specific extraction type can be carried over directly.

SAP R/3 and ERP system users who do not require full BW functionality can now use the Palo Suite and Palo SAP Connectivity as an easy and very flexible alternative to a BI platform which can be installed quickly and is ideal for use by professionals. SAP BW system users might access consolidated data from the SAP BW Data Warehouse Layer for OLAP analyses.

(Sources: www.abraneo.com/products/ and www.jedox.com/en/products/jedox-etl/etl-fuer-sap.html)

Palo OLAP Accelerator (GPU)

Palo GPU was developed in cooperation with researchers from the University of Freiburg and the University of Western Australia, co-funded by the German Research Foundation (DFG) and Jedox. It is a technology that uses Nvidia GPU hardware to speed up large data processing jobs.

In addition to the CPU of the server, Palo GPU uses the tremendous computing capacity of Nvidia graphics cards (GPUs) to speed up large OLAP aggregations. Modern GPUs come with hundreds of so-called streaming processors and with several gigabytes of graphics memory that enable the direct storage of cube data on the GPU.

Palo GPU relies heavily on this kind of parallel computation, thus speeding up aggregations (e.g., the calculation of consolidated Palo cube cells).

(Source: www.jedox.com/en/products/jedox-olap-accelerator.)

EnterpriseDB

Wikipedia states that EnterpriseDB offers two distributions based on PostgreSQL with additional features and commercial support. These distributions are available for free download and are supported on several different platforms, including Linux, Microsoft Windows, and Oracle Solaris. The distributions include connectors for the most common programming languages and environments, including: JDBC, ODBC, .NET, ESQL / C++, Perl, Python, and PHP.

- *PostgreSQL*—The parts developed by the Postgres community
- *Postgres Plus Standard Server*—All the features of PostgreSQL, plus additional QA testing, integrated components, tuning, and one-click install
- *Postgres Plus Advanced Server*—All the features of Postgres Standard Server plus Oracle compatibility, scalability features, and DBA and developer tools; it can run Oracle applications written for Oracle databases by revising the core of PostgreSQL to recognize Oracle's PL/SQL as well as handle data replication to and from Oracle.

EnterpriseDB also offers services and support options for Postgres, including remote DBA services, tuning, developer support and training.

(Source: http://en.wikipedia.org/wiki/EnterpriseDB.)

EnterpriseDB builds Postgres Plus Products
In addition to contributing to the community version of PostgreSQL, EnterpriseDB also builds and markets Postgres Plus Standard Server and Postgres Plus Advanced Server. Enterprise DB describes Standard Server as "a professionally packaged version of the community open source project plus other complimentary open source projects all wrapped inside a friendly one click installer." (Source: www.enterprisedb.com/products-services-training/products/postgresql-overview.)

Postgres Plus Advanced Server adds numerous enterprise class features to Postgres Plus, allowing organizations of all sizes to replace or compliment their existing commercial databases with incredibly low Total Cost of Ownership without sacrificing performance or critical features.

- *Postgres Plus Standard Server*—The data sheet for the Postgres Plus Standard Server (available at www.scribd.com/doc/41350066/Data-Sheet-PP-Standard-Server-20100726) describes the product as being made for developers and smaller organizations in need of a robust relational database that is quick and easy to install, ready to handle a variety of transaction and reporting work profiles, and able to scale for large user and data loads. Based on PostgreSQL, Standard Server is packed with pre-bundled enterprise modules for spatial data handling, job scheduling, connection pooling, replication, caching and more. And Standard Server provides graphical tools like pgAdmin and the HQ Monitoring consoles for DBAs and developers.
- Note: Per the EnterpriseDB site (www.enterprisedb.com/products-services-training/products-overview/postgres-plus-standard-server/product-lifecycle-postgre), "Postgres Plus Standard Server was retired from new sales on November 4, 2011. Current subscribers will still be covered for maintenance and support . . . ."
- *Postgres Plus Advanced Server*—The data sheet for the Postgres Plus Advanced Server (available at http://get.enterprisedb.com/datasheets/Data_Sheet_PP_Advanced_Server_20100927.pdf) describes the product as delivering the stability, innovation, and low cost of open source software with the high power features of leading commercial databases. If you want Oracle-like features and wish to preserve your current PL/SQL-driven applications (or code new systems in PL/SQL without the Oracle price tag), then look no further than Postgres Plus Advanced Server. Winner of multiple awards and used in all industries its easy to see why IBM, Netezza,

NTT and others look to Advanced Server for open source power and economy.

LucidDB Product

LucidDB is an open source relational database management system that was purpose-built entirely for data warehousing, OLAP services, and BI. It is based on key architectural considerations such as column-store, bitmap indexing, hash join/aggregation, and page-level multiversioning.

LucidDB is purpose-built for flexible, high-performance analytics, including integrated ETL and OLAP capabilities, with very little administration required. LucidDB performs faster than traditional row store databases, without any additional tuning.

Most database systems (both proprietary and open-source) start life with a focus on transaction processing capabilities; analytical capabilities are bolted on as an afterthought. By contrast, every component of LucidDB was designed with the requirements of flexible, high-performance data integration and sophisticated query processing in mind. Moreover, comprehensiveness within the focused scope of its architecture means simplicity for the user: no database administrator required.

LucidDB's unique architecture allows you to achieve great performance using only a single off-the-shelf Linux or Windows server.

(Sources: www.luciddb.org/html/main.html, www.luciddb.org/html/projectfaq.html.)

Greenplum

In 2005, Greenplum released an enterprise-level massively parallel processing (MPP) version of PostgreSQL called Greenplum Database. The Data Warehouse Solution Web site (www.datawarehousesolution.net/greenplum-open-source-data-warehouse/Data_Warehouse_for_Beginners)   describes Greenplum Database as "the industry's first massively parallel processing (MPP) database server based on open-source technology. It is explicitly designed to support business intelligence (BI) applications and large, multiterabyte data warehouses."

Greenplum Database, based on PostgreSQL, is the first open source–powered database server that can scale to support multiterabyte data warehousing demands.

The Greenplum Data Computing Appliance (DCA) is a purpose-built, highly scalable, parallel data warehousing appliance that architecturally integrates database, compute, storage and network into a single, easy-to-manage enterprise-class system. Designed for rapid analysis of data volumes scaling into petabytes, the Greenplum DCA is a powerful platform for unifying business intelligence and advanced analytics enterprise-wide. The Greenplum DCA is proven to provide the industry's fastest data loading capabilities and in turn, to rapidly deliver real business value to customers reducing investments of money, time and effort. (Source: EMC Greenplum Data Computing Appliance fact sheet, www.greenplum.com/sites/default/files/h7419.5-greenplum-dca-ds.pdf.)

- *Greenplum Data Computing Appliance*—The Greenplum DCA provides data analysts, IT, and business executives with value out-of-the-box.
  - Appliance Simplicity – Easy to install and manage; dramatically simplifies your data warehousing (DW) and analytics infrastructure
  - Rapid deployment - Fast time to value for important BI and analytic initiatives that impact your bottom line
  - Extreme performance and scalability – MPP architecture; supports thousands of users and very complex mixed-workloads, grows to meet the demands of the business
  - Enterprise-class reliability and availability – Greater than 99.99% uptime
- *Greenplum Database*—Greenplum Database 4.0 is a major release of Greenplum's industry-leading massively parallel processing (MPP) database product.
- *Greenplum Chorus*—Greenplum Chorus is software that empowers people within an enterprise to more easily collaborate and derive insight from their data. As the first commercial Enterprise Data Cloud platform, it provides the key services necessary for organizations wrestling with all data-big and small, structured and unstructured-to realize the benefits of private cloud computing techniques and social collaboration for enterprise data warehousing and analytics. Chorus serves the needs of data analysts, IT, and business executives with three core pillars of functionality:
  - Self-service provisioning of data marts and secure, controlled sandboxes relieve IT of the management overhead and operational complexity usually associated with data mart deployment

- Data services allow analysts to effortlessly discover, combine, and share useful datasets within and across data marts
- Data collaboration provides rich social networking capabilities that link data and data analysts, accelerating collaboration and insight

  (Source: www.greenplum.com/sites/default/files/
  EMC_Greenplum_Chorus_DS_0.pdf)

- *Greenplum Analytics Lab*—Greenplum Analytics Lab, is a package of services, technology and training delivered by Greenplum's team of leading Data Scientists. Customers and prospects interested in learning about best practices for analytics on the Greenplum platform can apply for participation in the Greenplum Analytics Lab, in which their analysts and database administrators work in partnership with Greenplum's team of statisticians and modelers to quickly solve real business problems.
  (Source: www.greenplum.com/sites/default/files/
  EMC_Greenplum_Analytics_Lab_DS_1.pdf.)

- *Greenplum Database: Single-Node Edition*—Free version of Greenplum Database gives data analysts access to Greenplum's high-performance database for large-scale analytical projects outside the enterprise data warehouse (EDW). The Single-Node Edition is a state-of-the-art parallel analytic database, and can participate as a distributed node of Greenplum's Enterprise Data Cloud -- allowing centralized management, data discovery and data sharing across databases. Other features of Greenplum Database - Single-Node Edition include:
  - Unlimited production usage on a single commodity x86 server using up to 2 CPU sockets (and unlimited CPU cores), or in a single virtual machine using up to 8 virtual CPU cores
  - Fully parallel SQL and MapReduce processing leverages multi-core parallel-processing engine for every query
  - No storage capacity cap – from GBs to 10s of TBs
  - Hybrid row and column-oriented processing
  - Free community support as well as a low-cost, paid support option
  - Ability to expand beyond Single-Node Edition to a multi-node massively-parallel Greenplum Database deployment

(Source: www.prweb.com/releases/2009/10/prweb3071834.htm)

- *Greenplum Performance Monitor*—Greenplum Database 3.3 includes a highly interactive Web-based performance monitoring tool—the Greenplum Performance Monitor. This tool connects to the Greenplum Database's low-level performance tracking infrastructure to provide a powerful graphical view into the system and the queries running within it. It provides both real-time and historic information about:
  - System resource utilization, including CPU, memory, network, disk I/O, swap, and more
  - Queries in the system, including full query text, and a wide range of relevant information (user, database, resource consumption, etc.)
  - Internals of any query, including the query plan and real-time information about individual scans, joins and more
  - This information is available via a secure Web login, and allows database administrators (DBAs) to see all queries in the system while restricting end-users to seeing just the queries that they initiated. With these capabilities, DBAs can proactively:
    - Comprehend how the system is being used — both in real-time and trending over time
    - Identify and diagnose problem queries, while they are running — detect skew, runaway queries, etc.
    - Review and balance the query load on the system by better optimizing and scheduling the query load

Talend and Talend Unified Platform

Talend describes its Talend Unified Platform (www.talend.com/products-data-integration/talend-products.php) as the foundation of all Talend Solutions. The Unified Platform is an open platform to consolidate disparate projects and reinvent how data management is implemented across teams and the entire organization. A single development studio (based on Eclipse) provides consistency across integration, quality and master data projects so resources can be shared and reutilized, while remaining open, intuitive and economical. Talend's data management solutions cover three key domains:

- Data Integration
- Data Quality

- Master Data Management

Data Integration Solutions

Talend's data integration solutions provide organizations with powerful and extensible data integration within and beyond the enterprise.

- *Talend Open Studio for Data Integration*—This comes with an open source GPL license and includes the essential components of data integration, such as ETL/ELT support, Business Modeler, Job Designer, Context Management, and Versioning.
- *Talend Enterprise Data Integration*—This is a comprehensive suite designed for pervasive data integration and comprises team, professional, cluster and big data editions. It comes with an open source subscription license and includes enhanced features such as dynamic schemas, data lineage, shared repository, impact analysis, change data capture, reference projects, and business rules (with the exception of the team edition which doesn't support business rules). The big data edition also supports FileScale and Hadoop computing.

Data Quality Solutions

Talend's data quality solutions provide organizations with accurate and detailed insight and monitoring of any business data and deliver a comprehensive set of features to improve the quality and effectiveness of critical data assets.

- *Talend Open Profiler*—The first open source data profiling solution, Talend Open Profiler, allows business users or data analysts to perform a quality assessment, detect anomalies and highlight issues in their corporate data assets. It provides detailed reports with visual indicators that enable analysts to quickly and accurately gain insight into the quality of their data.
- *Talend Data Quality*—High quality data improves business analytics to increase revenues and can provide massive operation efficiencies to decrease costs. Talend Data Quality cleanses inaccurate and inconsistent data, identifies and resolves duplicate records and provides the capability to augment and enhance your data. It extends profiling with real time dashboards for insight into quality and also provides the conduit to not only identify issues but to automatically create processes to resolve and clean data.

Master Data Management (MDM) Solutions

Talend MDM allows organizations to master any data, in any domain without constraint. This unique approach unites data integration, data quality, master data, and business process management in a single comprehensive solution to meet any master data challenges.

- *Talend MDM—Community Edition* is the only open source MDM solution. It implements a data model that allows the modeling and maintenance of any master data. It includes all the features to integrate profiles and master your data, and extends those features with capabilities to orchestrate automated processes and interactions with systems to synchronize master data across any organization.
- *Talend MDM—Enterprise Edition* enables teams to establish and enforce data governance process and collaborate on master data. It also includes capabilities to implement business rules to survive master data records as well as manual stewardship tools. This proactive approach to data quality improves data analysis and streamlines operations.

  More information is available at www.talend.com.

Ingres

Ingres's company product sheet (http://downloads.actian.com/online/collaterals/ps/IngresDatabase-PS.pdf) describes Ingres as follows: "Ingres database is the leading enterprise open source database. It supports very large database systems in demanding operational environments. A commercially supported, open source database management system (DBMS) that reduces IT costs and time to value, Ingres Database provides exceptional performance, availability, scalability, security, and extensive manageability features."

The uniqueness of the Ingres database is its ability to provide "true" enterprise open source capabilities that meet business objectives by fulfilling the following basic requirements that span the enter IT infrastructure of the enterprise (software, middleware and hardware):

- High availability for your mission-critical needs by supporting failover clustering, online backup with point-in-time restore, online index and table reorganization, seamless upgrade process, replication, dual log support, journaling by table, and parallel reorganization and optimization with the DBMS

- High performance by way of support for mixed workloads, SMP and multicore processor hardware, large data sets, large user sets and multithreaded architecture
- Providing a secure environment for data and applications by way of pluggable authentication modules (PAMs) for user authentication and support for roles, role separation, Kerberos, and auditing
- Keeping IT costs low by way of an open source subscription model that provides transparency, choice, control, and value to the customers; integrated appliance offerings such as Ingres Icebreaker BI Appliance; backward compatibility; rapid problem resolution; and support for industry-recognized database management tools such as TOAD, Nagios, Squirrel, and Ingres Visual DBA
- Increasing flexibility to manage volatile markets thereby Reducing developer costs and risks by way of standards compliance to SQL92 and SQL03 (90%); API support for C, C++, Perl, Python, PHP, and .NET; rapid application development with Ingres Open-ROAD; legacy support for COBOL and FORTRAN; backward compatibility and the ability to leverage the same database for development and production needs
- Providing enterprise-capable support and services when you need them by way of Follow-the-Sun support mode, 15-year lifecycle support, enterprise-caliber support and service staff, and a rich experience of providing robust, professional support to enterprise clients.

(Source: Deb Woods, "What is Enterprise Open Source? Ensuring your IT infrastructure can support your business," 2008, Ingres Corporation. Available at www.actian.com/products/ingres)

Firebird

Firebird is a true universal open source database (www.firebirdsql.org) distributed under the IDPL or Initial Developer's Public License model. It is an RDBMS that supports cross-platform and cross-operating-system database development compliant with many ANSI SQL standard functionality. The "About Firebird" section of Firebird's Web site (www.firebirdsql.org/en/about-firebird) states that "It has been used in production systems, under a variety of names, since 1981." Firebird is truly open source and universal in that:

- It is free for commercial and academic usage, with zero license fees and no restricted or double licensing (e.g., for installation, activation, etc.).
- It supports an open choice of development and reporting tools, operating system and architecture, hardware and no vendor lock-in.
- It supports all major platforms and OS including Windows, Linux (both 32-bit and 64-bit) Mac, FreeBSD, HP-UX, etc.
- It is based on multigenerational architecture that enables development and deployment of hybrid OLTP and OLAP ecosystems. As described in the "Features" section on Firefox's Web site (www.firebirdsql.org/en/features), "This makes Firebird database capable of serving simultaneously as both an analytical and operational data store, because readers do not block writers and when accessing the same data under most conditions."
- It includes a rich feature-set and developer-friendly SQL language by way of its comprehensive ANSI SQL92 compliance, support for common table expressions (CTE), flexible transaction management, stored procedures (SP) including selectable SP, cross-database queries, user-defined functions, and active tables (concept and events).
- It provides inherent logging and monitoring features by way of trace API and rich set of monitoring tables (MON$) that enable real-time monitoring, SQL debugging, and auditing functionality such as events, partial or fill-time logging, and remote logging.
- It provides a robust security framework by way of Windows Trusted Authentication, user- and role-based authentication and management, exclusive rights to access UDFs and external tables, and grants.
- It supports comprehensive text search by way of its integration with Sphinx, full-text search engine.
- It supports a host of deployment options ranging from an embedded version (in dll), Native Windows Installer, as a service or application, as an RPM or tar gz build, or a custom "100% silent" installer to read-only deployments, such as on CD, DVD, Blu-ray, etc., and a lightweight installation (up to 4MB).
  (Source: www.firebirdsql.org/en/features)

CouchDB

CouchDB is a document-oriented database for querying and indexing of documents using JavaScript as the query language in a fashion similar to MapReduce (http://couchdb.apache.org). It is a project of Apache Software Foundation and is distributed under the Apache License for collaborative open source software development.

As described in the introduction section of its Web site (available at http://couchdb.apache.org/docs/intro.html), "CouchDB is a peer based distributed database system. Any number of CouchDB hosts (servers and offline-clients) can have independent 'replica copies' of the same database, where applications have full database interactivity (query, add, edit, delete). When back online or on a schedule, database changes are replicated bi-directionally."

CouchDB:

- Is a document database server that exposes a RESTful JSON API which can be accessed from any HTTP-enabled SDK
- Is programmed using Erlang, a functional programming language that provides scalability and extensibility in a simple-to-use manner
- Is schema-less in that it supports structured views on semistructured document data and management of disparate documents

SQLite

SQLite's Web site (www.sqlite.org) states that "SQLite is a software library that implements a self-contained, serverless, zero-configuration, transactional SQL database engine. SQLite is the most widely deployed SQL database engine in the world. The source code for SQLite is in the public domain."

Customers who use SQLite can benefit in the following ways:

- No maintenance hassle
- Suited for PoC implementations with the feature-set of a fully functional transactional RDBMS
- Easy access to data across multiple platforms with almost no portability concerns
  (Source: www.sqlite.org/features.html)

MonetDB

MonetDB is as a pioneer by way of being a "proper" disk-based column-store database and as outlined on its home page (www.monetdb.org/Home): ". . . since 2011 column store technology as pioneered in MonetDB has found its way into the product offerings of all major commercial database vendors." It is distributed under the liberal open-source license.

As described in the column-store features section of its Web site (www.monetdb.org/Home/Features), "Its three-level software stack, comprised of SQL front-end, tactical-optimizers, and columnar abstract-machine kernel, provide[s] a flexible environment to customize it many different ways. A rich collection of linked-in libraries provide functionality for temporal data types, math routine, strings, and URLs."

MonetDB uses

- Vectorized primitives—simple hard-coded operators—to improve computational efficiency
- Pipelined query evaluation and result materialization for increased scalability of both data and user sets

This dramatically saves disk I/O when scan-intensive queries need a few columns, and at the same time it eliminates the need for an expression interpreter while evaluating column expression there by accelerating query response time.

Bizgres

Bizgres is an optimized and scalable BI and data warehousing version of PostgreSQL. It is distributed under the open BSD license. As described in an article by Burleson Consulting (www.dba-oracle.com/t_edb_bizgres.htm), "Bizgres is the premiere, open source BI and Data Warehousing solution. Bizgres is a fork of PostgreSQL that adds needed Very Large Database (VLDB) support to PostgreSQL. All code added or changed for Bizgres is offered back to the PostgreSQL team for incorporation to the base product. Bizgres does not currently support MS-Windows."

3.4.2   Open Source Data Integration

Open source integration software is used in performing the following tasks:

- Batch ETL for a data warehouse or mart

- Operational integration
- Data migration efforts
- Data quality efforts
- Master data management efforts
- Low-latency ETL for a data warehouse or mart
- Semantic data integration

The following outlines the open source data integration tool providers in the emerging and next-gen data integration solutions:

- Pentaho DI/Kettle
- Talend
- Jitterbit
- DataCleaner
- Red Hat
- Informatica
- Ingres Vectorwise (a unique player in terms of productizing a vector-enabled, context-aware, self-adaptable, intelligent DW and DI solution)
- Expressor (for semantic data integration)
- OpCloud (for cloud data integration)
- Pentaho Data Integration/Kettle

Pentaho Data Integration/Kettle

Pentaho Data Integration (PDI, also called Kettle) is the component of Pentaho responsible for extract, transform and load (ETL) processes. Though ETL tools are most frequently used in data warehouses environments, PDI can also be used for other purposes:

- Migrating data between applications or databases
- Exporting data from databases to flat files
- Loading data massively into databases
- Data cleansing
- Integrating applications

Kettle is easy to use, where every process is created with a graphical tool where you specify what to do without writing code to indicate how to do it. Kettle can be used as a standalone application, or it can be used as part of the larger Pentaho Suite. As an ETL tool, it is the most popular open source tool available. Kettle supports a vast array of input and output formats, including text files, data sheets, and commercial and free database engines. Moreover, the transformation capabilities of Kettle allow you to manipulate data with very few limitations.

(Source: http://wiki.pentaho.com/display/EAI/Pentaho+Data+Integration+(Kettle)+Tutorial.)

Talend: Data Integration Solutions

Talend's data integration solutions provide a powerful set of tools to meet any integration requirement, from basic transformations to the most complex operational integration issues, data migration and capture, as well as data replication, synchronization and application upgrades.

- *Talend Open Studio* is Talend's innovative and powerful flagship product. Available as an open source download, Talend Open Studio is a packaged and ready-to-install data integration solution that delivers more than 400 components to meet the integration requirements of any organization, regardless of size or level of expertise.
- *Talend Enterprise Data Integration* is an open source enterprise data integration solution that satisfies the most challenging and complex process requirements of enterprise development and scales to manage massive volumes of data.

Talend Integration Suite is a subscription service that extends the award-winning Talend Open Studio with advanced features to facilitate collaboration among large teams and provide professional-grade technical support and capabilities to ease enterprise-scale deployments. Talend Integration Suite is offered in various editions: Team Edition, Professional Edition and Enterprise Edition. Further, Talend Integration Suite MPx enables massively parallel processing and Talend Integration Suite RTx provides real-time capabilities.

(Source: www.talend.com/products-data-integration/talend-products.php.)

Jitterbit

Jitterbit data integration software can be used for the following tasks:

- *Application Integration* for tying together distributed and incompatible applications and systems

- *Cloud/SaaS Integration* by securely and reliably connecting data beyond your firewall with your on-premise infrastructure
- *ETL and Data Integration* to retrieve and process data for analysis and reporting quickly, reliably, and accurately
- *Business Process Integration* by automating business processes both within an organization and across customers, partners, and supply chains.

Jitterbit is the Integration Solution of choice for more than 5,000 organizations, with customers including Continental Airlines, NASA, and Balfour Beatty Construction.

DataCleaner

DataCleaner is an Open Source application for profiling, validating and comparing data to administer and monitor data quality in order to ensure that data is useful and applicable to the business needs. DataCleaner is the free alternative to software for master data management (MDM) methodologies, data warehousing (DW) projects, statistical research, preparation for extract-transform-load (ETL) activities and more. (Source: www.sqlis.com/sqlis/post/Data-Profiling-without-SSIS.aspx)

DataCleaner has the following components (as outlined in the Wikipedia article on DataCleaner, http://en.wikipedia.org/wiki/DataCleaner):

- *DataCleaner Profiler*: The Profiler in DataCleaner enables the user to gain insight in to the content of the data store. The profiler can calculate and present a lot of interesting metrics that will help the user become aware and understand data quality issues. Examples of such metrics are distribution of values, max/min/average values, patterns used in values etc.
- *DataCleaner Validator*: The Validator assumes a higher degree of data insight since it enables the user to create business rules for the data to honor. Rules for data can be defined in a variety of ways such Java scripts, lookup dictionaries, regular expressions and more.
- *DataCleaner Comparator*: The Comparator enables a user to compare two separate datastores and look for values from one data store within another data store and vice versa.

DataCleaner is the flagship application of the eobjects.org open source community. The project was founded in late 2007 by Danish student Kasper Sørensen.

Red Hat

According to Red Hat's investor Web site (http://investors.redhat.com/ releasedetail.cfm?releaseid=376330), Red Hat acquired MetaMatrix in April 2007. The data services technology of MetaMatrix is Teiid. Teiid is an open source community project with the goal of delivering EII (enterprise information integration) with both relational and XML data virtualization. Teiid focuses on data virtualization, which enables real-time access to data across heterogeneous data sources without copying or moving the data from the systems of record. Its JDBC (Java Database Connectivity) and Web Services interfaces are designed to provide straightforward integration with both custom and commercial off-the-shelf applications.

Informatica

Informatica Corporation provides data integration software and services that empower your organization to access, integrate, and trust all its information assets, giving your organization a competitive advantage in today's global information economy. As the independent data integration leader, Informatica has a proven track record of success helping the world's leading companies leverage all their information assets to grow revenues, improve profitability, and increase customer loyalty. That is why Informatica is known as the data integration company. (Source: www.technologyexecutivesclub.com/sponsorpages/informatica.php.)

Per Informatica's press release of March 1, 2011 (www.informatica.com/us/company/news-and-events-calendar/press-releases/03012011-netsuite.aspx), "Informatica is the world's tier-1 independent provider of data integration software. Organizations around the world gain a competitive advantage in today's global information economy with timely, relevant and trustworthy data for their top business imperatives. More than 4,100 enterprises worldwide rely on Informatica to access, integrate and trust their information assets held in the traditional enterprise, off premise and in the Cloud."

The Informatica Platform (outlined at www.informatica.co.za/products.asp) is the first comprehensive, unified, and open software platform specifically designed for data integration. The company's open, platform-neutral software accesses data of virtually all types, making it accessible, meaningful, and usable to the people and processes that need it. With products that encourage collaboration across the enterprise, Informatica reduces costs, speeds time to results, and scales to handle data integration projects of any size or complexity.

This platform includes the following modules:

- Enterprise Data Integration
- Informatica PowerCenter
- Informatica PowerExchange
- Informatica Data Explorer
- Informatica Data Quality
- Informatica Identity Resolution
- B2B Data Exchange
- Informatica B2B Data Transformation
- Informatica B2B Data Exchange
- Application Information Lifecycle Management
- Informatica Data Archive
- Informatica Data Masking
- Informatica Data Subset
- Cloud Data Integration
- Informatica Cloud
- Complex Event Processing
- RulePoint
- Master Data Management
- Ultra Messaging

3.4.3   Open Source Business Intelligence

Aashish Debral, whose blog "Know Business Intelligence & Data Warehousing" reports on BI issues and opportunities, reported that ". . . the year 2005 saw the start of 10 new open source projects related to data analytics, specifically business intelligence and data warehousing." Of these, five were BI suites, providing either several unified components or comprehensive solutions for BI. The year 2000 had opened the doors for research into open source projects for data warehouse solutions: Jetstream was invented for extract, transform, load (ETL) operations, Mondrian as an OLAP engine, and jPivot as a front end to Mondrian. In 2007, there were more than 45 projects related to data analytics, covering databases, ETL/ EAI (Enterprise Application Integration), reporting, OLAP, portals, dashboards, data mining, GIS and visualization. Since then, all of these have evolved by leaps and bounds to accommodate the next generation trends of real-time BI, competitive BI, agile BI methodologies, virtualization at all levels of DW and BI solution stack, and more. (Source: Aashish Debral, "OSBI 2—Introduction to Open Source BI," blog entry posted September 21, 2010; available at http://knowbi.blogspot.com/2010/09/osbi-2-intro-duction-to-open-source-bi.html)

The only open source projects that qualify as comprehensive BI suites are BEE, Jaspersoft, Pentaho, and SpagoBI.

The following lists key business intelligence tasks where open source software is used as an indispensable asset:

- Static reports
- Dashboards
- Interactive reports
- Application database reports
- Embedded application reports
- OLAP
- Advanced analytics, which includes predictive analytics, dynamic information visualization and content mashing, and the integration of BI, BPM, EPM, and social networking

Below is a list of BI tool providers:

- Pentaho
- Jaspersoft
- Mondrian (a Pentaho project)
- BIRT
- Jfree
- SpagoBI
- OpenI
- MarverIT
- Palo
- OpenReports
- VitalSigns
- BEE
- Bizgres
- BPM Conseil
- MicroStrategy
- LyzaSoft

The primary and predominantly adopted players are briefly described below.

Jaspersoft

Jaspersoft provides the business intelligence suite enabling business decision making through interactive, web-based reports, dashboards and analysis. Jaspersoft leverages commercial open source business model and provides end-to-end BI capabilities. The BI suite includes enterprise reporting, ad hoc query, dashboards, OLAP and in-memory analysis, and data integration. Jaspersoft enables companies to adapt to the new, virtualized world by providing a complete spectrum of on-premise, multitenant SaaS and cloud-based deployment options for both embedded and standalone business intelligence.

Jaspersoft's open source business intelligence software products are built to solve specific decision-making challenges. JasperSoft BI software includes the following functionalities (from www.jaspersoft.com/products):

- *Reporting*: Design interactive pixel perfect and/or ad hoc based reports for the web, the printer or mobile device.
- *Dashboards*: Build multireport dashboards with internal or external data for executives and knowledge workers.
- *Analysis*: Explore data with powerful relational OLAP or in-memory analysis against any data source.
- *Data Integration*: Build data marts or warehouses from several disparate relational or non-relational data sources.
- *BI Platform*: Centrally store, secure, and distribute reports, dashboards, and analysis views across your organization or the web.

Jaspersoft describes its solutions (www.jaspersoft.com/solutions) by stating that Jaspersoft's modular, scalable, standards-based architecture provides the flexibility needed to easily deploy in any environment, with the following flavors:

- Embedded BI
- Standalone BI
- Cloud BI
- SaaS BI (both SaaS-enabling and SaasS-enabled)

Jaspersoft offers both commercial editions as well as community projects to help tailor the right solution to the right problem. One such project is Jasperforge, detailed at www.jasperforge.org.

BIRT: Actuate/Eclipse BIRT

Actuate's Rich Information Application-ready, open source–based BI tools can be deployed in any pre-existing or new development project to create a progressive, collaborative reporting environment that allows developers, report writers and end users to create and/or use applications rich in interactivity, depth, span and complexity. With the Business Intelligence and Reporting Tools (BIRT) Project at its core, the Actuate suite of BIRT-based products creates an environment that is virtually boundless; an infrastructure in which to build and deploy Rich Information Applications without Limits. (Source: www.infobright.com/Customers_Partners/actuate.)

In describing the Business Intelligence and Reporting Tools (BIRT) Project, Wikipedia states that it "is an open source software project that provides reporting and business intelligence capabilities for rich client and Web applications, especially those based on Java and Java EE."

BIRT's two main components are a visual report designer within the Eclipse IDE for creating BIRT Reports and a runtime component for generating reports that can be deployed to any Java environment. The BIRT project also includes a charting engine that is fully integrated into the report designer but also can be used on its own to integrate charts into an application.

BIRT Report designs are persisted as XML and can access a number of different data sources including SQL databases, JDO Data Stores, JFire Scripting Objects, POJOs, XML and Web Services. (Source: http://en.wikipedia.org/wiki/BIRT_Project)

BIRT, which runs on the Eclipse IDE, provides a set of reporting and data visualization tools and technologies used by developers to build rich information applications. It includes the basic tools required for reporting: the ability to design reports and to display report data. Actuate's product Web site (www.actuate.com/products/eclipse-birt/summary) states that open source BIRT includes the following functions and features:

- Multiple development and design tools
- Extensible data access
- Data customization
- Programmability

- Flexible data presentation
- Component reuse/libraries
- Easy integration
- Internationalization

ActuateOne, a commercial product suite built on BIRT, provides value-added products that speed up BIRT implementation, automate and secure reporting, and provide the tools required for interactive report creation and customization. (Source: www.actuate.com/products/eclipse-birt/summary.)

BIRT is a top-level software project within the Eclipse Foundation, an independent not-for-profit consortium of software industry vendors, and an open source community. The project is supported by an active community of users (at BIRT Exchange) and developers (at the Eclipse.org BIRT Project page). (Source: http://en.wikipedia.org/wiki/BIRT_Project.)

In 2004, Actuate Corporation founded the Eclipse BIRT Project with the cooperation of the Eclipse Foundation(www.actuate.com/products/eclipse-birt/summary). Actuate continues to co-lead what has become the most successful open source BI toolset in existence today. More than 750,000 developers use BIRT, proving that BIRT is easily adopted and is, for many, the development environment of choice.

Additional information is available at the following URLs:

- www.eclipse.org/birt
- www.birt-exchange.com

JFree

As described in the Web site (www.JFree.org), "JFree.org is home to a number of free software projects targeting the Java platform." The most prominent among them that deserve a BI analysis perspective are JFreeChart, Orson Chart Beans, Eastwood Charts, JCommon, and JWorkbook. Of these Eastwood Charts (www.jfree.org/eastwood) is an independent and open source implementation of the Google Chart API. The rendering of the actual charts is done by JFreeChart.

The remainder of them are all free or open source API in multiple variations of the Java open source specifications.

- JFreeChart is tailored towards J2EE applications, applets, servlets, and JSP. (Source: www.jfree.org/jfreechart)

- Orson Chart Beans is based on JavaBeans specification. (Source: www.jfree.org/orson)
- JCommon is an embeddable Java class library that is used by JFree-Chart and Pentaho Reporting. It is distributed under the GNU Lesser General Public Licence (LGPL). (Source: www.jfree.org/jcommon)
- JWorkbook is a similar library for generating spreadsheet files from Java. It has an Excel plug-in with limited support for the same and is distributed under the GNU Lesser General Public Licence (LGPL). (Source: www.jfree.org/jworkbook)

SpagoBI

(Section adapted from the SpagoWorld Web site: www.spagoworld.org/xwiki/bin/view/SpagoBI/BIComponents.)
SpagoBI, an open source BI suite with all analytical areas of BI projects and engines, offers a range of entirely open source analytical tools:

- *Reporting*—SpagoBI enables the realization of structured reports using structured information views (e.g., lists, tables, crosstabs, graphs) and can export them using several formats. SpagoBI integrates the reporting engines BIRT, JasperReport, and BusinessObjects 6.5.
- *OLAP*—SpagoBI allows multidimensional analysis through OLAP engines. The users can monitor the data on different detail levels and from different perspectives, through drill-down, drill-across, slice-and-dice, drill-through processes. SpagoBI integrates the OLAP engines JPivot/Mondrian, JPalo/Mondrian, and JPivot/XMLA Server.
- *Chart*—SpagoBI offers a graphics engine based on JFreeChart that enables development of single ready-to-use graphical and interactive widgets.
- *Dashboard*—SpagoBI offers a graph visualization engine in SWF format, enabling the display of KPIs for real-time graphical performance views.
- *KPI*—SpagoBI offers tools to create, manage, view, and browse KPI hierarchical models, through different methods, calculation rules, thresholds, and alarm rules.

- *Cockpits*—SpagoBI offers an engine for the realization of complex cockpits which allows aggregation of several documents into a single view, connecting them with one another
- *GEO/GIS*—SpagoBI offers some geographical engines capable of advanced analytics for setting real-time connections between the geographical data and the business data of the Data Warehouse. SpagoBI offers two engines in this domain:
  - The GEO engine uses a static catalogue in order to display data, allowing users to dynamically reaggregate the information according to geographical hierarchies (e.g., nation, country, city).
  - The GIS engine interacts with real spatial systems according to the WFS/WMS scheme.
- *Data Mining*—SpagoBI allows advanced data analysis thanks to data mining processes that target the discovery of hidden information patterns among a great amount of data. SpagoBI integrates Weka as an open source data mining tool.
- *Query by Example*—SpagoBI offers a Query by Example engine, which is suitable for those cases in which the free inquiry of data and the extraction of data are more important than their graphical structure and structural layout
- *Smart Filter*—SpagoBI offers an engine to create simple enquiry forms.
- *Accessible Reporting*—SpagoBI offers an engine to generate tabular reports.
- *RT Console*—SpagoBI offers an engine that enables the production real-time monitoring consoles to be used in business, applicative or BAM processes.
- *Dossier*—SpagoBI offers an engine that enables the automatic creation of organized report dossiers, enriched with the attending notes and information, posted by users to comment data.
- *ETL*—SpagoBI allows loading data according to the common ETL logic or data warehouse vitalization logic, which, for example, qualifies users to manage simultaneous data directly on the data warehouse. SpagoBI's ETL engine integrates the open source product TOS (Talend Open Studio).
- *Office*—SpagoBI offers a specific engine for the publication of personal documents in BI environments, realized through commonly used Office tools.

OpenI

OpenI is an open source BI application for on-demand or SaaS deployments. Based on J2EE, OpenI is an out-of-the-box solution that can easily visualize data from OLAP and relational databases, where users can build and publish interactive reports, analyses, and dashboards. (Source: http://wiki.openi.org/openi-2-0/openi-20-RC2-release-notes.)

Sandeep Giri, one of OpenI's developers, stated on the SourceForge forums that OpenI can be used right out of the box, as opposed to an SDK (software development kit) on top of which a BI developer will build a BI application. "Hence," he says, "a lot of our work has gone towards making the installation increasingly easier, being able to just point to an OLAP data source and start publishing analyses/dashboards without having to write code, supporting Microsoft Analysis services, etc." (Source: http://sourceforge.net/projects/openi/forums/forum/478298/topic/3489996, second comment.)

OpenI's Web site states that OpenI adds key features for a complete BI application (http://openi.org/2009/how-is-openi-different-from-jpivot):

- Security—Either via its own user management or by integrating to existing OLAP or custom authentication, OpenI enables restrictions to analyses based on user permissions
- Dashboard—OpenI has complete dashboard creation and management
- Create/Save Reports—OpenI provides a well-defined XML structure (.analysis files) that works as a report definition language (RDL) to save and manage reports; it also supports the notion of public versus private reports
- Navigation—OpenI provides a full file explorer–like UI to navigate through multiple analyses and manage them in folders
- Report customization by dragging/dropping attributes to columns, rows, and filters
- Tabbed view of tables and charts
- Provides results of an OLAP drill through as a text file dump or publish result set to a custom Web API
- Explore data feature that lets you "eyeball" data in a cube without having to create individual reports—which is very handy for exploratory analysis
- Concept of "projects" to enable multitenant reporting (i.e., the same application can serve multiple clients). An on-demand can

leverage this to serve multiple client accounts separately from a single Web application instance

- Administration UI to manage accounts, application, data sources, and many other tasks that you'd otherwise have to do by hand-editing a configuration file

OpenI was founded in 2005.

MarvelIT

MarvelIT builds complete open source Business Information solutions for the small to medium business enterprise market. MarvelIT DASH is a dashboard solution based on the Apache Jetspeed 2 Enterprise Portal and MarverIT Dashboard Portlets. MarverIT DASH enables the process of creating and maintaining a web based business intelligence dashboard for all users. This has established MarvelIT as a prominent player in the open source BI space with customer successes, including the projects outlines on the company's Clients Web page (www.marvelit.com/clients.html):

- BIGresearch collects data on consumer behavior and future buying patterns. A hosted dashboard solution provides a rich experience for their clients to analyze monthly metrics.
- Aladdin Bail Bonds has 44 offices California that enter daily metrics and obtain operational insights via a hosted dashboard solution.
- Delta Health Technologies uses DASH to display key operational metrics for their management team.
- Physicians Computer Company is using DASH to build executive management dashboards.
- Guidance Software is using DASH to monitor key operational metrics and simplify executive reporting and analysis.
- Insight Health Corp. implemented DASH to deliver operational DASHBOARDS at a fraction of the cost of implementing Business Objects Dashboard Manager.

OpenReports

OpenReports is a Web reporting solution that provides browser-based, parameter-driven, dynamic report generation and flexible report scheduling capabilities.

As described on the company's Web site, http://www.oreports.com, OpenReports supports a variety of open source reporting engines, including

JasperReports, JFreeReport, JXLS, and Eclipse BIRT, to support a wide range of reporting requirements and capabilities. OpenReports also includes QueryReports and ChartReports, easy-to-create SQL-based reports that do not require a predefined report definition. In addition, OpenReports now supports OLAP, via Mondrian and JPivot.

OpenReports provides a Web-based report generation and administration interface with the following features:

- Support for a wide variety of export formats
- Web based administration
- Flexible scheduling
- Comprehensive report parameter support
- Fine-grained security controls access functionality
- Report auditing
- Support for multiple JNDI or Connection Pool DataSources
- Support for drill-down reports and external application integration

OpenReports Professional is the commercial version of OpenReports. OpenReports was developed by Open Source Software Solutions, LLC, a Hartford, Connecticut based provider of open source business intelligence tools and services.

VitalSigns

Per the Linux Softpedia site (http://linux.softpedia.com/get/Programming/Quality-Assurance-and-Testing/VitalSigns-15463.shtml), VitalSigns provides an easy to use application for logging report data over time and reporting that data in an easy-to-digest format. It is written so that it is extensible, enabling the user to retrieve report data from anywhere and report it in any desired fashion.

BEE

Gilbert Griño of the BloxChronicles blog describes the BEE Project as "an open source suite of Business Intelligence tools which combines ETL engine and a ROLAP server for mid-size businesses" (http://bloxchronicles.blogspot.com/2006/03/open-source-bi-review-bee-project.html).   He also states (http://bloxchronicles.blogspot.com/2006/02/business-intelligence-links.html) that the BI Suite of tools is ideal for midsize companies that have 50GB or less of data. BEE has ETL, uses ROLAP, and is under the GPL license.

Bizgres

Bizgres is the an open source, production ready database server focused exclusively on supporting Business Intelligence applications. Bizgres targets entry-level and departmental workloads such as data marts and reporting applications in the 10–300 Gigabyte range. (Source: www.opensource-it.com/open_source_business_intelligence_software)

BPM Conseil

BPM Conseil is the French leader of Open Source BI, and the developer of Vanilla, the first True Open Source Business Process and Business Intelligence Platform. By aggregating leading development and administration studios such as FreeAnalysis (Olap), FreeMetrics (BSC), FreeDashboard, FreeWebReport and BIPortal, along with advanced Web 2.0 interfaces, Vanilla enables companies to bring a new level of information intelligence to their business operations. (Source: www.infobright.com/ Customers_Partners/bpm_conseil)

MicroStrategy

Infobright's Customers and Partners Web page on MicroStrategy (www.infobright.com/Customers_Partners/microstrategy) describes the company as "a global leader in business intelligence and performance management technology" that is providing reporting, analysis, and monitoring software to enable leading organizations to make better business decisions every day. MicroStrategy empowers business users to make informed decisions by providing timely, relevant, and accurate answers to their business questions.

MicroStrategy provides enterprise-wide BI standardization that is designed to support the most demanding BI applications, with advanced technical capabilities, sophisticated analytics, and superior data and user scalability. Leading companies and government organizations worldwide have chosen MicroStrategy as their enterprise business intelligence standard.

MicroStrategy is built from a single integrated and efficient architectural foundation with an intuitive Web interface that enables business users to seamlessly access enterprise data for enhanced decision making. MicroStrategy engineers its software for reliability, scalability, security, and ease of administration.

MicroStrategy offers Dynamic Enterprise Dashboards™, which combine advanced data visualization and animation with MicroStrategy's industrial-strength BI platform to deliver highly intuitive digital dashboards that yield greater business insight than traditional graphs and grids. Business users can intuitively flip through many perspectives of corporate performance, allowing them to quickly and easily identify problems and diagnose root causes.

LyzaSoft

Infobright's Customers and Partners Web page on LyzaSoft (www.infobright.com/Customers_Partners/lyzasoft) says that the company's products blend the best of BI and social media to deliver a collaborative intelligence experience for the enterprise:

- Lyza Studio is a downloaded workstation application where Power Users can explore enterprise databases, create custom data integrations across multiple sources, and design charts and dashboards which can then be published to Lyza Commons for other people to use. It runs on your desktop or laptop.
- Lyza Commons is a web-based collaboration hub where everyone in your workgroup can participate in the intelligence process – search, comment, blog, rate, forward, bookmark, etc. It runs on either an internal web server, a dedicated cloud, or a public cloud.
- Lyza Foundry is a automation and scheduling application to which popular or important processes are promoted by the community moderator. It runs on a server inside your company's firewall.

3.4.4   Open Source Business Analytics

The following is a list of open source analytics tools in the industry:

- R
- Weka
- RapidMiner
- Knime
- Graphviz
- Orange
- Processing
- Axiis
- Taverna
- Cytoscape

R

R is a GNU project, an open source language and software environment for statistical computing and graphics that is similar to the S language and environment developed at Bell Laboratories by John Chambers and colleagues. This section is based on GNU's Web page on R (www.gnu.org/software/r).

R provides a wide variety of statistical (linear and nonlinear modeling, classical statistical tests, time-series analysis, classification, clustering) and graphical techniques, and is highly extensible. The S language is often the vehicle of choice for research in statistical methodology, and R provides an open source route to participation in that activity.

R is an integrated suite of software facilities for data manipulation, calculation and graphical display, including:

- An effective data handling and storage facility
- A suite of operators for calculations on arrays, in particular matrices
- Collection of intermediate tools for data analysis
- Graphical facilities for data analysis and display either on-screen or on hardcopy
- Programming language which includes conditionals, loops, user-defined recursive functions and input and output facilities

Weka

Wikepedia (http://en.wikipedia.org/wiki/Weka_(machine_learning)) describes Weka (the Waikato Environment for Knowledge Analysis) as a machine learning software written in Java, developed at the University of Waikato, New Zealand.

The Weka workbench contains a collection of visualization tools and algorithms for data analysis and predictive modeling, together with graphical user interfaces. Its advantages include:

- Portability, as it is fully implemented in the Java programming language and thus runs on almost any modern computing platform
- A comprehensive collection of data preprocessing and modeling techniques
- Ease-of-use by a novice, due to the graphical user interfaces it contains

Weka supports standard data mining tasks such as data preprocessing, clustering, classification, regression, visualization, and feature selection.

All of Weka's techniques are predicated on the assumption that the data is available as a single flat file or relation, where each data point is described by a fixed number of attributes (normally, numeric or nominal attributes, but some other attribute types are also supported). Weka provides access to SQL databases using Java Database Connectivity and can process the result returned by a database query.

Weka's user interface is the Explorer, but essentially the same functionality can be accessed through the component-based Knowledge Flow interface and from the command line. The Explorer interface has several panels that give access to the main components of the workbench:

- The Preprocess panel has facilities for importing data from a database, a CSV file, and the like, and for preprocessing this data using a so-called filtering algorithm. These filters can be used to transform the data (e.g., turning numeric attributes into discrete ones) and make it possible to delete instances and attributes according to specific criteria
- The Classify panel enables the user to apply classification and regression algorithms (indiscriminately called classifiers in Weka) to the resulting dataset, to estimate the accuracy of the resulting predictive model, and to visualize erroneous predictions, ROC curves, etc., or the model itself (if the model is amenable to visualization like, e.g., a decision tree)
- The Associate panel provides access to association rule learners that attempt to identify all important interrelationships between attributes in the data
- The Cluster panel gives access to the clustering techniques in Weka (e.g., the simple k-means algorithm). There is also an implementation of the expectation maximization algorithm for learning a mixture of normal distributions
- The Select attributes panel provides algorithms for identifying the most predictive attributes in a dataset
- The Visualize panel shows a scatter plot matrix, where individual scatter plots can be selected and enlarged, and analyzed further using various selection operators

Weka is open source software available under the GNU General Public License. Pentaho is a major sponsor of Weka development. Additional information can be found at www.cs.waikato.ac.nz/ml/weka.

RapidMiner

RapidMiner (formerly YALE, Yet Another Learning Environment) is an open source environment for machine learning and data mining experiments. RapidMiner is used for data mining tasks. The Community Edition of RapidMiner (formerly "Yale") is an open source toolkit for data mining. It is available as a stand-alone application for data analysis and as a data mining engine for the integration into own products.

RapidMiner provides:

- Data integration, analytical ETL, data analysis, and reporting in a single suite
- Graphical user interface for the design of analysis processes
- Repositories for process, data and metadata handling
- Metadata transformation solution
- Support for on-the-fly error recognition and quick fixes

RapidMiner provides a GUI to design an analytical pipeline, called the "operator tree." The GUI generates an XML (eXtensible Markup Language) file that defines the analytical processes the user wishes to apply to the data. This file is then read by RapidMiner to run the analyses automatically. The initial version was developed by the Artificial Intelligence Unit of University of Dortmund since 2001. It is distributed under the AGPL license, and has been hosted by SourceForge since 2004.

RapidMiner provides more than 500 operators for the primary machine learning procedures, including input and output, data preprocessing, and visualization. It is written in the Java programming language and therefore can work on all popular operating systems. It also integrates learning schemes and attributes-based evaluators of the Weka learning environment.

(Source: www.enotes.com/topic/RapidMiner)

KNIME

KNIME, the Konstanz Information Miner, is an open source data analytics, reporting and integration platform. KNIME integrates components for machine learning and data mining. The graphical user interface allows the quick and easy assembly of nodes for data preprocessing (ETL: Extraction, Transformation, Loading), for modeling and data analysis and visualization.

KNIME allows integration of different data loading, processing, transformation, analysis and visual exploration modules without the focus on any particular application area.

KNIME allows users to visually create data flows (or pipelines), selectively execute some or all analysis steps, and later inspect the results, models, and interactive views. KNIME is written in Java and based on Eclipse and makes use of its extension mechanism to add plugins providing additional functionality. The core version already includes hundreds of modules for data integration (file I/O, database nodes supporting all common database management systems), data transformation (filter, converter, combiner) as well as the commonly used methods for data analysis and visualization. With the free Report Designer extension, KNIME workflows can be used as data sets to create report templates that can be exported to document formats like doc, ppt, xls, pdf and others. Additional capabilities of KNIME include:

- KNIMEs core-architecture allows processing of large data volumes that are only limited by the available hard disk space. E.g. KNIME allows analysis of 300 million customer addresses, 20 million cell images and 10 million molecular structures.
- Additional plug-ins allows the integration of methods for Text Mining, Image Mining, as well as time series analysis.
- KNIME has the capability to integrate with various other Open-Source-projects, e.g. machine learning algorithms from Weka, the statistics package R, as well as LibSVM, JFreeChart, ImageJ, and the chemistry development kit CDK.

KNIME though implemented in Java, allows for wrappers calling other 3GL code in addition to providing nodes that can run Java, Python, Perl and other script fragments.

KNIME is released under GPLv3. KNIME (since 2006) is being used in pharmaceutical research, also in other verticals like CRM customer data analysis, business intelligence and financial data analysis.

The Development of KNIME was started January 2004 by a team of software engineers at Konstanz University as a proprietary product. The original developer team headed by Michael Berthold came from a company in the Silicon Valley providing software for the pharmaceutical industry. The Development of KNIME was started January 2004 by a team of software engineers at Konstanz University as a proprietary product.

(Source: www.enotes.com/topic/KNIME)

Graphviz

Graphviz (short for Graph Visualization Software) is a package of open source tools initiated by AT&T Research Labs for drawing graphs specified in DOT language scripts. It also provides libraries for software applications to use the tools. Graphviz is Free Software licensed under the Common Public License. (Source: www.enotes.com/topic/Graphviz.)

Graphviz consists of a graph description language named the DOT language and a set of tools that can generate and/or process DOT files (http://graphviz.softpedia.com). Graphviz is open source graph visualization software. It has several main graph layout programs.

The Graphviz layout programs take descriptions of graphs in a simple text language, and make diagrams in several useful formats such as images and SVG for web pages, Postscript for inclusion in PDF or other documents; or display in an interactive graph browser. *Graphviz also supports GXL, an XML dialect.* Additional information can be obtained from the Web sites: www.graphviz.org and www.research.att.com/software_tools

Orange

Orange is a component-based machine learning library for Python developed at Laboratory of Artificial Intelligence, Faculty of Computer and Information Science, University of Ljubljana, Slovenia.

From the leaflet "Orange: Data Mining: Fruitful and Fun," (www.ailab.si/orange/wp/orange-leaflet.pdf), Orange is a library of C++ core objects and routines that includes a large variety of standard and not-so-standard machine learning and data mining algorithms, plus routines for data input and manipulation. Orange is also a scriptable environment for fast prototyping of new algorithms and testing schemes. It is a collection of Python-based modules that sit over the core library and implement some functionality for which execution time is not crucial and which is easier done in Python than in C++. This includes a variety of tasks such as pretty-print of decision trees, attribute subset, bagging and boosting, and alike.

Orange also includes a set of graphical widgets that use methods from core library and range modules. Through visual programming, widgets can be assembled together into an application by a visual programming tool called Orange Canvas. All these together make an Orange, a comprehensive, component-based framework for machine learning and data mining, intended for both experienced users and researchers in machine learning who want to develop and test their own algorithms while reusing as much of the code as possible, and for those just entering who can enjoy in powerful while easy-to-use visual programming environment.

Orange features include (from http://orange.biolab.si/features.html):

- Visual programming—Design your data analysis process through visual programming. Orange remembers your choices, suggests most frequently used combinations, and intelligently chooses which communication channels to use.
- Visualization—Orange is packed with different visualizations, from scatterplots, bar charts, trees, to dendrograms, networks and heatmaps.
- Interaction and data analytics—Actions seamlessly propagate through data analysis schema. Selection of data subset in one widget can automatically trigger change of display in the other one. By combining various widgets you can design data analytics framework of choice.
- Large toolbox—Over 100 widgets and growing. Coverage of most of standard data analysis tasks.
- Scripting interface—With Python interface, programming new algorithms and developing data analysis procedures is pure joy.

Processing (An Open Source Programming Language)

Processing is an open source programming language and environment to create images, animations, and interactions. The Processing software runs on the Mac, Windows, and GNU/Linux platforms. Processing software exports applets for the Web or standalone applications for Mac, Windows, and GNU/Linux. Graphics from Processing programs may also be exported as PDF, DXF, or TIFF files and many other file formats.

Processing was founded by Ben Fry and Casey Reas in 2001 while both were John Maeda's students at the MIT Media Lab. Further development has taken place at the Interaction Design Institute Ivrea, Carnegie Mellon University, and the UCLA.

Initially developed to serve as a software sketchbook and to teach fundamentals of computer programming within a visual context, Processing also has evolved into a tool for generating finished professional work. Today, there are tens of thousands of students, artists, designers, researchers, and hobbyists who use Processing for learning, prototyping, and production. Additional details can be found at http://processing.org.

Axiis

Axiis's Web site (www.axiis.org) describes Axiis as "an open source data visualization framework designed for beginner and expert developers alike. Axiis provides both pre-built visualization components as well as abstract layout patterns and rendering classes that allows to create unique visualizations."

Axiis is built upon the Degrafa graphics framework and Adobe Flex 3.

The "About" page (www.axiis.org/about.html) states that Axiis gives developers the ability to define their data visualizations through concise and intuitive markup. Axiis provides granular framework, allowing developers to mix and match components and build complex output by compositing together basic building blocks. We have specifically avoided long OO inheritance chains to keep our class structures flat and interchangeable.

Axiis is an open source project, under an MIT license. Additional details are available at www.axiis.org.

Taverna

Taverna (www.taverna.org.uk) is an open source and domain independent Workflow Management System—a suite of tools used to design and execute scientific workflows and aid *in silico* experimentation. The applications of Taverna in various domains have been implemented or deployed using various platforms and technologies:

- Standalone Workbench (used by the majority of projects)
- As a server
- On a grid or using services on a grid
- On a cloud
- Behind a portal
- Bundled with other products

The Taverna suite is written in Java and includes the Taverna Engine (used for enacting workflows) that powers both the Taverna Workbench (the desktop client application) and the Taverna Server (which allows remote execution of workflows).

The development of Taverna started as a combined effort of the University of Manchester and EBI. Taverna has been created by the myGrid team and funded through the OMII-UK. Some 350+ organizations around the world, both academic and commercial, are known to use Taverna.

Cytoscape

Cytoscape is an open source software platform for visualizing complex networks and integrating these with any type of attribute data. Cytoscape provides plug-ins for various kinds of problem domains, including bioinformatics, social network analysis, and semantic Web.

Cytoscape is a bioinformatics software platform for visualizing molecular interaction networks and integrating with gene expression profiles and other state data. Additional features are available as plugins.

Cytoscape was originally created at the Institute of Systems Biology in Seattle in 2002. Now, it is developed by an international consortium of open source developers. Additional details can be obtained at www.cytoscape.org.

3.5   The Primary Users: User, End-User, Customer and Intelligent Customer

Open source projects are, by definition, all about the community. Open source DW and BI software provides access to a large number of users worldwide that corporations like Oracle might not reach any other way. Open source DW and BI software community represents a worldwide laboratory of development, support, and QA engineers who contribute the fruits of their labors freely in return for the free use of the software. Open source DW and BI software enables enterprises to build upon its user community from the grassroots, and to discover variant technology and usage models at a fraction of the cost of conventional research and development.

3.5.1   MySQL

There are more than 767 enterprises from 24 industry segments, including large corporations to small businesses around the world, using MySQL open source database. Out of these767 enterprises, 19 of them use MySQL as a data warehousing application. Table 3.1 lists the primary industry functional domains adopting MySQL to evolve in the DW and BI solution space.

3.5.2   PostgreSQL

The postgresql.com Web site lists more than 83 enterprises from 13 industry segments, including large corporations to small businesses around the world, using PostgresSQL open source database.

MySQL Data Warehouse Customers	
Industry	Company
Business Intelligence Analytics	Infobright
	MIT Lincoln Lab
Education	University of Kent
Financial Services	Nomura Research Institute
Government	Pottawattamie County
Government/Aerospace, Defense	Los Alamos National Laboratory
	BlueLithium
Media & Entertainment	LiveRail
Mining & Natural Resources	Fortum
Technology: Hardware	Xerox
	Cox Communications
	Flexilis Inc.
	Polystar OSIX
Telecom	Tellme Networks
	Evite
	MyPoints
Web: Ecommerce	ZipRealty
Web: Social Networks	Mindspark
	True North Corporation

Figure 3.3   Subset of MySQL DW customer base.

The PostgreSQL community is one of the oldest, largest and fastest-growing communities of its kind, and has flourished to the point where, today, there are more than 1,000 contributors and more than 30,000 members.

The key advantage to the large community is the interaction between users and developers, which allows users to become directly involved in the design of new features. This diverse community is the model that many other open source communities strive for.

PostgresSQL's prominent customers include:

- Yahoo!, for Web user behavioral analysis and storage of two petabytes; it is claimed to be the largest data warehouse, using a heavily modified version of PostgreSQL with an entirely different column-based storage engine and different query processing layer. While for performance, storage, and query purposes the database bears little resemblance to PostgreSQL, the front-end maintains compatibility so that Yahoo! can use many off-the-shelf tools already written to interact with PostgreSQL.
- MySpace, a popular social networking Web site, is using Aster nCluster Database for data warehousing, which is built on unmodified PostgreSQL.

- OpenStreetMap, a collaborative project to create a free editable map of the world.
- Afilias, domain registries for .org, .info and others.
- Sony Online multiplayer online games.
- BASF, shopping platform for their agribusiness portal.
- hi5.com, social networking portal
- reddit.com social news Web site.
- Skype VoIP application, central business databases.
- Sun xVM, Sun's virtualization and datacenter automation suite.
- Evergreen, an open source integrated library system providing an online public access catalog along with cataloging, management, and other functions for hundreds of libraries in the United States, Canada, and elsewhere.
  MusicBrainz, an open online music encyclopedia.
  The International Space Station, for collecting telemetry data in orbit and replicating to the ground.
  MyYearbook, a social networking site.

3.5.3   Mondrian Customers

Several organizations around the world depend on Pentaho to make faster and better business decisions that positively impact their bottom lines.

3.5.4   Palo Customers

Palo's customer reference list consists of 31 major enterprises from the United States and Europe.

3.5.5   EnterpriseDB Customers

There are over 270 enterprises from 16 industry segments including large corporations to small businesses around the world using EnterpriseDB products. Customers around the world depend on EnterpriseDB for products, services and expertise.

3.5.6   LucidDB Customers

LucidDB has more than 100+ trial/customer deployments

3.5.7 Greenplum Customers

"Greenplum has more than 100 customers in verticals ranging from financial services and telco to Internet, retail, transportation, and pharmaceuticals. Greenplum customers include Fox, NASDAQ, Zions Bancorporation, Reliance Communications, NYSE Euronext, Bakrie Telecom, T-Mobile, Sears, Sony, and Skype" (from the Wikipedia entry on Greenplum: en.wikipedia.org/wiki/Greenplum). One of their largest and most prominent customers is eBay, which is running a multipetabyte system.

3.5.8 Talend Customers

Talend is the recognized market leader in open source data integration and data quality solutions. Talend's users and customers span all industries, geographies, and company sizes.

Many large organizations around the globe use Talend's products and services to optimize the costs of data integration, data quality, Master Data Management (MDM) and application integration. With an ever growing number of product downloads and paying customers, Talend offers the most widely used and deployed data management solutions in the world.

There are more than 85 enterprises from 12 industry segments, from large corporations to small businesses around the world, using Talend's open source solutions.

3.6 Summary

This chapter explored the potential open source products and players in the current EDW/BI space and their strengths in terms of simplification, relevance, currency, and consistency in addition to the cost factor. It provided a compare-and-contrast approach to the major open source products and their functionality. It is to be noted that the similarities among them are generally limited to their being open source. Each one of them has its own distinctive best-fit use cases, with only a small amount of overlap with other products in its category. In either case, they are high-quality open source software systems that should be given a considerable analysis of thought over the more expensive proprietary systems—especially in light of today's tough economy as well, given the unparalleled gains in business–social efficiency and customer-centric experience lifecycle.

The next chapter delves into the details of analyses, evaluation and selection criteria for an open source EDW/BI solution—one that fits as a best case solution for information-centricity.

3.7   References

The following references have been used in gaining access to the information provided in this chapter:

- General Open Source Information
    - Aashish Debral, "OSBI 2—Introduction to Open Source BI," blog entry posted September 21, 2010. (Available at http://knowbi.blogspot.com/2010/09/osbi-2-introduction-to-open-source-bi.html)
    - Doug Dineley and High Mobley, "Slideshow: Top 10 Open Source Hall of Famers," *InfoWorld*, August 16, 2009. (Available at www.infoworld.com/d/open-source/top-10-open-source-hall-famers-848)
    - Mark Madsen, "Open Source Solutions: Managing, Analyzing and Delivering Business Information", BeyeNETWORK research study published December 8, 2009. (Available at http://www.beyeresearch.com/study/12261)
    - Mark Madsden, "Size of Data Warehouses: Peek at Open Source Survey Results," blog entry posted April 29, 2009. (Available at www.b-eye-network.com/blogs/madsen/archives/2009/04/size_of_data_wa.php)
    - Open source software to build private and public clouds:
        - The Open Stack Web site, www.openstack.org
        - Claudia Imhoff, "Open Sesame: Why Open Source BI and Data WarehousingSolutions are Gaining in Acceptance," paper published October 2008. (Available at www.scribd.com/doc/11647223/Claudia-Imhoff-PhD-Examines-Why-Open-Source-BI-and-Data-Warehousing-Solutions-Are-Gaining-in-Acceptance)
        - Claudia Imhoff, "Is open source BI for you?" blog entry posted April 22, 2005. (Available at www.b-eye-network.com/blogs/imhoff/archives/2005/04/is_open_source.php)

- Actuate/Eclipse BIRT
  - www.actuate.com/products/eclipse-birt/summary
  - http://en.wikipedia.org/wiki/BIRT_Project
  - www.infobright.com/Customers_Partners/actuate
  - www.eclipse.org/birt
  - www.birt-exchange.com
- BEE
  - Gilbert Griño, "Open Source BI Review: BEE Project," blog post to BloxChronicles, March 15, 2006. (Available at http://bloxchronicles.blogspot.com/2006/03/open-source-bi-review-bee-project.html.)
  - Gilbert Griño, "Business Intelligence Links," blog post to BloxChronicles, February 22, 2006. (Available at http://blox-chronicles.blogspot.com/2006/02/business-intelligence-links.html.)
- Bizgres
  - www.opensource-it.com/open_source_business_intelligence_software
- BPM Conseil
  - www.infobright.com/Customers_Partners/bpm_conseil
- Cytoscape
  - www.cytoscape.org
- DataCleaner
  - eobjects.org
  - http://en.wikipedia.org/wiki/DataCleaner
  - www.sqlis.com/sqlis/post/Data-Profiling-without-SSIS.aspx
- EnterpriseDB
  - www.enterprisedb.com
  - www.enotes.com/topic/EnterpriseDB
  - http://en.wikipedia.org/wiki/EnterpriseDB
  - www.enterprisedb.com/products-services-training/products/postgresql-overview
  - http://get.enterprisedb.com/datasheets/Data_Sheet_PP_Advanced_Server_20100927.pdf
  - Enterprise/Postgres: www.scribd.com/doc/41350066/Data-Sheet-PP-Standard-Server-20100726
- Graphviz
  - www.graphviz.org

- www.enotes.com/topic/Graphviz
- http://graphviz.softpedia.com
- www.research.att.com/software_tools
- Greenplum
  - www.greenplum.com
  - www.greenplum.com/sites/default/files/EMC_Greenplum_Chorus_DS_0.pdf
  - www.greenplum.com/sites/default/files/EMC_Greenplum_Analytics_Lab_DS_1.pdf
  - www.prweb.com/releases/2009/10/prweb3071834.htm
  - www.datawarehousesolution.net/greenplum-open-source-data-warehouse/Data_Warehouse_for_Beginners
  - en.wikipedia.org/wiki/Greenplum
- Hadoop
  - http://hadoop.apache.org
  - http://wiki.apache.org/incubator/BigtopProposal
  - http://ct.typepad.com/c2w/2010/12/hadoopdb.html
- Infobright
  - www.infobright.com/About-Us
  - www.graymatter.co.in/infobright-partner.html
- Informatica
  - www.technologyexecutivesclub.com/sponsorpages/informatica.php
  - www.informatica.com/us/company/news-and-events-calendar/press-releases/03012011-netsuite.aspx
  - www.informatica.co.za/products.asp
- Jaspersoft
  - www.jaspersoft.com/products
  - www.jaspersoft.com/solutions
  - www.jasperforge.org
- KNIME
  - www.enotes.com/topic/KNIME
- LucidDB
  - www.luciddb.org/html/projectfaq.html
  - www.dynamobi.com/c/community/history-and-statistics
  - www.eigenbase.org
- LyzaSoft
  - www.infobright.com/Customers_Partners/lyzasoft

- ∑MarvelIT
  - www.marvelit.com/clients.html
- MicroStrategy
  - www.infobright.com/Customers_Partners/microstrategy
- MySQL
  - www.oracle.com/us/products/mysql/index.html
  - www.mysql.com/why-mysql/awards
  - www.oracle.com/us/products/mysql/mysqlcommunityserver/index.html
  - www.oracle.com/us/products/mysql/mysqlclassic/index.html
  - www.mysql.com/products/cluster
  - www.oracle.com/us/products/mysql/mysqlcluster/index.html
  - www.mysql.com/customers/operatingsystem
  - Jim Mlodgenski, "PostgreSQL vs. MySQL: How to Select the Right Open-Source Database," *eWeek*, October 21, 2010. Available at http://mobile.eweek.com/c/a/Linux-and-Open-Source/PostgreSQL-vs-MySQL-How-to-Select-the-Right-OpenSource-Database
- OpenI
  - http://wiki.openi.org/openi-2-0/openi-20-RC2-release-notes
  - http://openi.org/2009/how-is-openi-different-from-jpivot
  - http://sourceforge.net/projects/openi/forums/forum/478298/topic/3489996
- Open Reports
  - http://oreports.com
- Palo/Jedox
  - www.palo.net
  - http://en.wikipedia.org/wiki/Palo_(OLAP_database)
  - www.jedox.com/en/products/jedox-etl/etl-fuer-sap.html
  - www.jedox.com/en/products/jedox-olap-accelerator
  - www.jedox.com/en/about-jedox/success-stories.html
  - www.abraneo.com/products
- Pentaho
  - http://mondrian.pentaho.com
  - www.enotes.com/topic/Pentaho
  - http://en.wikipedia.org/wiki/Mondrian_OLAP_server
  - http://wiki.pentaho.com/display/EAI/Pentaho+Data+Integration+(Kettle)+Tutorial

- PostgreSQL
  - www.postgresql.org/about
  - http://en.wikipedia.org/wiki/PostgreSQL
  - The Postgres Plus Advanced Server data sheet: http://get.enterprisedb.com/datasheets/Data_Sheet_PP_Advanced_Server_20100927.pdf
  - The Postgres Plus Standard Server data sheet: www.scribd.com/doc/41350066/Data-Sheet-PP-Standard-Server-20100726
  - www.enterprisedb.com/products-services-training/products-overview/postgres-plus-standard-server/product-lifecycle-postgre
  - Jim Mlodgenski, "PostgreSQL vs. MySQL: How to Select the Right Open-Source Database," *eWeek*, October 21, 2010. Available at http://mobile.eweek.com/c/a/Linux-and-Open-Source/PostgreSQL-vs-MySQL-How-to-Select-the-Right-OpenSource-Database
- R
  - www.gnu.org/software/r
- RapidMiner
  - www.enotes.com/topic/RapidMiner
- Red Hat
  - http://investors.redhat.com/releasedetail.cfm?releaseid=376330
- SpagoBI
  - www.spagoworld.org/xwiki/bin/view/SpagoBI/BIComponents
- Talend
  - www.talend.com/open-source-provider/overview.php
  - www.talend.com/products-data-integration/talend-products.php
  - www.infobright.com/Customers_Partners/talend
- Taverna
  - www.taverna.org.uk
- VitalSigns
  - http://linux.softpedia.com/get/Programming/Quality-Assurance-and-Testing/VitalSigns-15463.shtml
- Weka
  - www.cs.waikato.ac.nz/ml/weka
  - http://en.wikipedia.org/wiki/Weka_(machine_learning)

Chapter 4

Analysis, Evaluation and Selection

4.1 In This Chapter

- Essential Criteria for Requirements Analysis of an Open Source DW and BI Solution
- Key and Critical Deciding Factors in Selecting a Solution
- Evaluation Criteria for Choosing a Vendor-Specific Platform and Solution
- The Final Pick: An Information-Driven and Customer-Centric Solution, and a Best-of-Breed Product/Platform and Solution Convergence Key Indicator Checklist

This chapter delves into the details of analysis, evaluation, and selection criteria for an open source EDW/BI solution—one that fits as a best case solution for information centricity; intelligent information integration by way of availability, security, integrity, and information assurance; and solution efficiency in terms of scalable performance and stability. Enumerating the essential criteria for building a business case by way of determining the need for an open source DW and BI solution, the chapter goes on to build the deciding matrix for such a solution based on the key business indicators mapped across to the IT, customer-/user, and business–social landscapes—with usability, self-serviceability, adoption, and adaptation as the core selection criteria. In the following section, it outlines the key selection indicators (KSIs), which are an analog of the same deciding matrix from a vendor-specific platform and solution perspective. The final section closes this loop by confirming a key indicator checklist for the same—one that serves as a best fit for an information-driven and customer-centric solution in line with the business–social context—a solution that is *Open Source Perfect* and stands out as the trending and future directional roadmap of DW and BI by way of its business uses.

Reference(s) have been used in gaining access to the information provided in this chapter; these references are indicated throughout and, for ease of research, have been collected in at the end of the chapter.

4.2   Essential Criteria for Requirements Analysis of an Open Source DW and BI solution

The requirements analysis of an open source DW and BI solution can very well begin with the *business–social* solution landscape as the scope of the targeted solution. Whether the applications are legacy or brand new, it seems as inevitable as it is evident that the technology, business models, customers, and customer needs and behaviors will evolve, and the big bang of data/content in any and all possible dimensions (transcending the confines of time, space, and location) will be constantly and dynamically changing. As a result, existing as well as new solutions/applications mandate a best-of-breed approach to elevation, escalation, and efficiency with zero-tolerance and minimal impact on their operational and business capabilities.

As this trend continues, the requirements tend to become somewhat elastic to accommodate business growth, which also trends to grow elastically. Enlisted below are the essential criteria to be included as part of the requirements analysis phase for an open source DW and BI solution that would help in identifying best-of-breed selection KPIs. Getting the requirements analysis right the first time achieves the right design the first time, which in turn helps in getting the right software architecture the first time, which ultimately results in getting the right solution the first time.

- The convergence of product, platform, and place (intelligent information integration; anyone/anytime/anywhere access; right data/ right user/right job/right time delivery)
- The convergence of architecture, alignment, and automation (e.g., technologies, design methodologies, frameworks, standards)
- The convergence of people, processes, and perfection (usability, business-savvy, customer/end user–centric and self-serviceable, consistent, context-aware, flexible, and social-friendly—leveraging social content by way of dynamic social contact & feedback, enterprise performance management)
- The convergence of embeddable, existential, and evolving
- The convergence of the customer-user experience, feedback, and efficiency—the business domain meeting the social content domain for competitive intelligence (for deriving KPI from crowd-sourcing

and cloud-bursting to isolate potential value from customers' behavior, activity monitoring, and action-response analyses)

The key selection indicators (KSIs) must be objectively evaluated against the typical DW & BI functionality as executed by real-world customers/end users and the frequency of their respective usage. This gives a more accurate "value" specification in terms of both the qualitative and quantitative effects and affects of such a selection on the real-world implementation.

Intelligent information integration by way of availability, security, integrity, and information assurance is and must be the central requirement for any EDW solution, and an open source solution aids in achieving a simpler, better, faster, cheaper implementation of deployment of the same for faster time to delivery and faster time to insight, as well as better insight and sometimes getting beyond BI. The corresponding criteria boil down to the following enlisted set:

- Streamline and semantically align structured/unstructured data using data services, data integration services, and/or real-time embeddability (for data-in-store, data-in-motion, and data as it is being created)—from the point of ingestion to the point of interpretation (insight)
- Virtualization of data, data-views, databases, dashboards, and mash-boards—cross-(business)-dimensions and cross-(user)-contexts, irrespective of time, space, or location
- Virtual data federation in place of in-memory data replication for real-time, right-time data syndication; materialization and distributed data replication to service high-volume based high-performance queries
- Dynamic streaming of any or all of the above, from data sourcing to storage (in-memory or persistent) to synchronization to syndication to semantic-visualization (anytime, anywhere, anyone)
- Collaborative and noncollaborative shareability of data with internal (existing, on-premise, within-the-enterprise scope) and external (beyond-the-enterprise scope, yet needed/added on-demand; cloud-based; other extranet–based) applications
- Improvisation of KPI-based analytics for consistency, currency and continuity in terms of business-operational efficiency and

customer–user experience (C-UX)—the key indicator here to note is that integration and improvisation of new/variant data impacts the associated business processes in context and, more often, in a deterministic manner. Hence, agility, mobility, and visibility are the key imperatives to be taken into account. This is especially critical when the analysis involves complex datasets with interrelated data elements—identifying the hidden relationships and establishing a symbolic linkage that can translate optimally to business semantics.

- Automation and acceleration by way of hybrid methodologies, blending TDD with model-driven design and solution/code-accelerators; unit testing blended with simulation and emulation (elevation, escalation) of core as well as surrounding functionality

- If evolution by way of EFM and back-looping of the same by way of additional/optimized business rules/metrics is one side of getting beyond BI, measuring performance in a quantifiable fashion—in a constantly dynamic data/information life-cycle, from production to perfection, involving multiplexed, multiflex, and context-aware semantics—and exponentially exploding in volume-is the other inevitable side of getting beyond BI, also referred as continuous operational intelligence on live, streamed data or competitive intelligence

4.3   Key and Critical Deciding Factors in Selecting a Solution

An open source EDW/BI solution must facilitate a seamless, transparent, secure and highly visible architecture for the pervasive business user, from the corporate executive to the technofunctional executive to the business analyst to the data steward to the knowledge specialist—no matter what these users' interaction touchpoint is. The architectural design must have the flexibility to enable consolidation at the infrastructure level (this can include cloud too), centralization at the administrative level, and federation at the user-control level. This gives the right balance of costs versus efficiency and involves putting at least three key processes in place: time-conscious automation, context-aware and right-just-in-time recovery of the solution state, and auto-reporting on the elastic provisioning, as well as the auto-auditing of the regular itself in addition to business activity monitoring, business process management, and continuous operational workflow.

4.3.1   The Selection-Action Preview

To this effect, the following list outlines four key deciding factors in selecting such a solution, keeping in perspective the current and next-gen business–IT–customer–social 360° view:

1. Leverage the potential of the cloud to create an "umbrella view" to monitor, mine, and maintain data across application and business tiers securely and reliably, while improving customer experience—thus gaining customer confidence and information assurance—yet with the flexibility of a stricter, stronger, more continuous and more customer/end user–driven interactive dynamic provisioning—a *customer-centric cloud*. This in turn aids in robust competitive BI.

2. Achieve "more (functionality) with less (time, cost, complexity, results)" by creating, consuming, and subsuming Web services based on XML technologies. This enables the on-demand creation of a *common compute cloud* that acts as a container for core business–specific functionality. Add-ons can be seamlessly integrated using Web services or SaaS-based embeddable services for customization. The key indicator here is to ensure that the business users and knowledge specialists can handle this well, without having to code or know SQL.

3. Combine the customer-centric cloud and the common compute cloud via cloud-to-cloud elastic integration. Using the same mechanisms of XML, Web services or embeddable services can result in a unique and distinct *collaborative (customer-centric) compute cloud*.

4. Use open source EDW/BI models to create a *custom test bed* that enables seamless testing for solution performance and information access and accuracy—one that works efficiently in both on-premise and virtualized environments.

The key indicator here is that
  Relevancy AND Accuracy → Constant
  (tend to be always)

The business drivers that are key to deciding on a solution that envisions the selection–action preview are as follows:

- An open venue for businesses to consider the open source option—from corporate to business analyst to IT analyst to social analyst to the (social) customer/end user
- The extent to which the solution functionality desired aligns with the corresponding industry-specific growing and future trends:
  - How easy it is to retain the existing infrastructure and to extend, enhance, and augment the same with additional functionality
  - Whether it goes beyond the trending baselines and benchmarks to introduce extra-rich functionality to gain that extra mile in the competition-to-be
  - Mash the above two criteria, using a best-of-context approach to decide upon the best-fit solution that is current- and future-proof and delivers value in terms of the end-to-end customer experience lifecycle

The key indicator here is not to miss out on the desired functionality—a necessary and sufficient condition to classify the solution implementation as a customer success.

The Open Source Perfect: From Legacy-Scope to Leading-Scope

This approach demands an increase in design-to-delivery costs, a substantial learning curve for the business user, and on-demand customization by way of context-specific and customer-centric personalization. An open source design model that is multiflex, multiplexed, and leverages existing systems is a trustable, customer success–based best fit to implement the same.

- Anywhere, anyone, anytime access to the solution, whether the customer/end user is in-network or out-of-network. This requires solution availability across multiple payloads, multiple endpoints such as on-premise, on-line, on-mobile, or on a shared basis, and accessed via cloud-based platforms, other endpoint-compliant devices, and the like. The key drivers here are cross-anywhere interoperability that does not compromise the reliability, availability, and security of the end-to-end information

---

The Open Source Perfect: From Proof-of-Model to Pervasive-Model

Open source EDW/BI solutions have gained mainstream adoption with proven business use cases and customer success stories. In certain cases, they have been benchmarked to surpass existing/proprietary solutions in usability and efficiency, with standout features such as business-user configurable and hot-pluggable business2business and legacy2next-gen solution integration. They accomplish this by enabling

---

- A data-centric model
- Unprecedented flexibility in terms of a self-adaptive solution for self-serviceable BI
- Enterprise-wide scalability for processing large data sets involving relational and nonrelational data at subsecond response times, the expanding user-base, and most exceptionally, analysis and mining of operational data in near-real time
- Simple and single-click deployment on-demand
- Built-in feedback-driven autorewired evolution for competitive intelligence

---

Open Source technologies and frameworks have enabled better, easier, faster, and cheaper implementation of this functionality, using sophisticated technologies such as open connectivity frameworks, dynamic virtualization, collaboration methodologies that integrate the all–social platform (from social media to social mining). provide user-configurable interactive action–response interfaces that can be used in sync with existing/alternate desktop tools, and enable real-time application and on-demand streaming, automation of BPM, business process automation (BPO), and acceleration of the same.

- Legacy interface to user-driven interactive intelligent interface
- Business and operations impact—Impact of efficiency versus the effectiveness of the resulting solution across current trending competition, as well as time-variant and geolocation-variant dimensions

- Situational impact; the above impact was measured against "economic" indicators
- Transformation involves business process management (BPM): business rules improvisation, business process optimization, and business process automation to align and sync with current and enhanced BI functionality, from dynamic workflow management to BPA to BI-A (BI Automation)

The Open Source Perfect: From Core to Cloud

An open source EDW/BI model as a data-driven model by way of dynamic information interoperability is an indispensable imperative for deciding the architecture and orchestration of the target solution. This is the key driver for any and all types of integration, including consolidation—from core enterprise to cloud.

- Compliance w/existing and new open source technologies injected into the derived solution
- Customer/user confidence—adoption, awareness, and adaptation—from seamless to superior
- (Dynamic) digital dictionary of change management end-to-end, before and after the solution deployment and going forward—one that acts a ledger for EDW/BI compliance. This is by far the most challenging yet demandingly necessary business functionality when it comes to a new/optimized/augmented solution implementation across the enterprise scope. An open source strategy in implementing it is, at the least, the best-fit viable, operational-specific, secure and risk-aware methodology that at the same time delivers a customer experience that's on par with (or superior to) current business efficiency

The Open Source Perfect: From Customer-Centric to Compliance-Centric

The open source standards are by definition GRC-compliant; hence any EDW/BI solution that adopts these standards-based technologies, techniques, and tools is to a certain extent already compliance-centric. The key variable is the change management processes in each and every customized/derived/architected Open Source EDW/BI solution—from existing to extending and beyond. The power of open source, in terms of its usability, delivery, and adaptive accommodation, comes in handy to implement of GRC controls that can be put in the hands of appropriate business users—from enterprise business policies to beyond-the-enterprise industry-specific regulatory compliance, including internal and external auditing—thus allowing those users to execute custom or additional related processes. The key indicator here is that the business user can execute the same, just as any other normal business function, irrespective of what the changes are, in an on-demand and policy-variant fashion and without any impedance mismatch between the previous and the newer software versions.

- Re-usable solution layers:
  - Isolate database (DB) layer from solution access layer
  - Isolate BPM and BPO (business process outsourcing) layers from data access; and the data integration layer from the application/application-component integration layer from the SOA-based provisioning/presentation/delivery layer; maintain all of them in synchrony for currency, consistency, and completeness via XML Messaging services or ESB

The following subsection describes five best practices any company can adopt that can raise their business intelligence quotient (BIQ).

4.3.2   Raising your BIQ: Five Things Your Company Can Do Now

This subsection briefly introduces the notion of BIQ, or business intelligence quotient, and how it can be used as a metric for accelerating time to insight and keeping the customer/end user in perspective. It lists the five best practices companies can follow right now to graduate from a *good company* to a *great company* and finally to an *intelligent company*. The content of this sub-section is adapted from a Focus.com research brief by the author titled "Raising your BIQ (Business Intelligence Quotient): 5 Things Your Company Can Do NOW" (available at www.focus.com/briefs/raising-your-biq-business-intelligence-quotient-five-things).

Strategies

With a multitude of IQs being used in trying to measure success (IQ, emotional IQ, social IQ, and, most mystic of all, spiritual IQ), it seems to make sense to do the same for business or companies to quantify their performance 360°, not just from a ROI perspective but from a customer/end user experience perspective. As trivial as it may seem, this is by no means an easy task. Viewing a company as a conglomerate of people performing in various roles and driven by a set of business processes, the accuracy of such an IQ extends beyond numbers. The words "win-win" create *business value* only when the business benefits of easier, faster, simpler, sharper decision-making capabilities by all users—from the corporate to the front desk—are realized when they are needed most. To this effect, here is a list of high-fives that enable companies of any size and industry vertical to raise the bar on BIQ:

1. *State and restate the fact that BI is everybody's business*: This is a key driver in BI adoption and empowerment by all users of a BI solution, from the corporate staff to the customer/end user. Hence, teaching that better BI means better decision making that leads to efficient actionable analyses across the company spectrum (i.e., the *why* and *what* of a BI solution) is a KPI because it brings everyone to the same vision. A unified view of the contextual customer is the KPI for a higher BIQ.

2. *Data, data everywhere—but I can't see it, no matter how I do my search*: This is both the means and ends of adopting BI: Companies must be able to trace and track the silos of data present in various forms—from paper to prediction—across the length and breadth of the companies' resources. Only then can a robust BI Solution help "refine" this data to derive the right information, useful to the right user at the right time. So, the sooner your company joins the "gold data rush," the faster the time to insight (the time taken to analyze and arrive at "decision points" that, when implemented, can help in a better business/operational efficiency).

3. *Enumerate the potential of BI as an innovative invention of a superior customer experience*: BI grants autonomy to the customer/end user by providing self-service functionality combined with interactive and responsive controls that place the power to drive the business solution in those users' hands. Companies should focus on differentiating between customer and end user in terms of power users and contextual business roles. This is the new dynamics of being customer-centric. Proper enlisting of users versus roles versus business needs, and maintaining the "independence and isolation of data/metadata access and presentation" is vital to a higher BIQ. This is where managed metadata comes

into play by allowing some of the business context to be custom defined by the end users! By correlating customer/end user centric aspects with their BI solutions already in place, companies can efficiently manage their metadata and streamline their business processes.

4. *Right-time information is the new BI imperative, and it prevents the data burst*: From real time to right time, time and data truly don't wait for any user today! This can be both real-time and point-in-time or just-in-time; the relevance and authenticity of information enables efficient use of the same and is essential to a better BIQ. And the ability to integrate/interoperate with multiple existing solutions and data sources provides a value beyond revenue. Nothing is more critical to a business than the consistency, currency, and protection of all of its data *cum* information in a way that is secure, reliable, and available anytime, from anywhere, and by anyone authorized. To this effect, companies must lay out security and GRC policies per requirements, from the earliest stages in their operational lifecycle (a typical plan starts from concepts and continues through to customization). This approach ensures that the data/information lifecycle goes in sync with the business process lifecycle. Enforcing multifactor authentication, distributed data replication, and/or data federation/syndication; rich search analytics, and industry standards-based architecture go a long way in getting the right data at the right time in the hands of the right user.

5. *Consider BI as a strategic solution for your business*: BI is more than just a decision-making tool. For any company, it is an evolving solution that reinvents itself based on customer/end user experience to adapt to the customers'/users' changing needs from time to time. Thereby, it extends beyond intelligence to become a strategic decision-making enabler. Companies must keep this focus when deciding on a BI solution—they need one that can adapt to current and future business requirements. By choosing a solution that includes this adaptability, the return-on-customer will be higher, which is an intelligent metric for quantifying success—both in terms of business value and customer/end user experience. This requires a self-adaptable BI solution that enables a greater degree of self-service BI. A "best-fit" IT solution based on gap-fit analysis, in terms of access optimization, embedded analytics, SaaS-enablement, and

operational BI capabilities, accelerates the operational efficiency. This again raises the BIQ: Better insights yield better results!

Results

The next generation of BI is driven by a new dynamics of customer-centric imperatives, including faster time to insight, right-time information availability and accessibility, enhanced self-service by way of self-adaptability, business process–driven and business services–oriented, multitenancy enabled, and reliance on active and passive security and compliance. Not having merely the ability to analyze "big data" but the ability to enable "big decisions" that add strategic value, derived from any and every data source, however big or small, across the enterprise, BIQ is the new business–IT KPI for a BI solution. A fine-grained analysis of business-centric requirements, followed by a robust plan for putting the above outlined principles into practice can help companies in raising the BIQ—and ensuring an *intelligent* company, one that is tailored toward and geared by the customer/end user.

4.4   Evaluation Criteria for Choosing a Vendor-Specific Platform and Solution

When it comes to open source software evaluation, the gridlock of being presented with more than one best choice is a trending confrontation. The precise and decisive selection of the best-of-the-best is a function of the following key evaluation indicators as differentiating criteria:

- A thorough profiling of the vendor's product/platform/solution to establish the gap-fit analysis report between the product's functionality (in terms of alignment with the "as-is" market trends) business-wise and technology-wise; conformance with industry-specific standards (as well as any additional domain-specific rules of the game, like those that are "restriction-based"); elevation and/or escalation of feature set/policy frameworks, if necessary; and whether the vendor is recognized by any national/international evaluator/research-group reviews, such as those performed by *Information Week*, Technology Evaluation Center, Gartner Magic Quadrant, or Forrester Research Group, to name a few.

The key here is to evaluate the vendor's product/platform from a customer-centric standpoint and let the technology follow after this first (necessary and sufficient) pass.

- Whether the product/platform/solution includes business-operations-centric feature set, toolkits, and user-configurable controls, as opposed to being IT-centric, immaterial of how rich, robust, and next generational the technology might be. *This is a must-have metric that goes a long way toward ensuring that solution selected will be asset to the business, both tactically and strategically.*
- Whether the implementation of the product/platform/solution can creatively and effectively raise the bar on customer-user experience by being a simpler and superior solution that stands out as competitively business-centric, rather than just elevating the ROI/lowering the TCO (total cost of ownership). This means the vision of the customer/end user as measured/measurable by the associated feedback must be able to bring in a better return on customer (ROC) and a greater customer experience lifecycle. Though in certain cases this might not seem totally feasible due the lack of prior deployments/restricted domain usage, most of the open source EDW/BI vendor-solution specifics can be evaluated by using one or more of proofs of concept, peer reviews based on technology versus business–social functionality matrix and customer success stories.

As an evolving paradigm, leveraging the use of open source methodologies to build a pervasive pseudo-deployment environment—one in which both business and IT uses can drive the solution in context to their every possible functional use and their fair share of feedback—that is monitored, measured, and quantified, resulting in a dense ranking of the candidate solution's context-specific relevancy as a finalist. The open source technologies and architectures available today make the build and deployment of such evaluation test-beds rapid, effective, and easily navigable, as well as elastic, by being able to accept dynamic datasets and other business process–driven inputs to quickly spin context-specific instances for the business/organization.

- Whether the vendor-specific solution offers dynamic scope creep for future enhancements/extensibility/regulatory improvisations and/or de-commissioning (if need be) that is acceptable by indus-try-level standards. *This includes loosely-coupled solution components interoperability, Web-based access and use anytime, anywhere, by any-one, near zero-trust, zero-loss security, and near zero-IT intervention.*

Drilling down further into these three key aspects, the evaluation crite-ria refactor into the following:

- How much of dynamic functionality can the specific platform or solution support in terms of development to deployment—risk-driven processes such as those that can work in times of crisis? *The key indicator here is the flexibility and efficiency of build and deploy-ment automation.*
- How easily and quickly can the business-specific processes be ingested or taken in by the platform in question so that they can be made "operational" to align with the IT processes, thereby enabling them to be execution-ready? This method of agile incor-poration must have an associated agile ingestion process in place that can be executed, managed, and customized as needed with the least IT intervention possible. The key here is the ability of the selected software solution to be as intelligent as possible in terms of being business context–aware by way of the variant attributes, so that it can autodetect and autorank what needs to be changed, along with suggesting how to do it.

This can be implemented by using dynamic data-driven search and metadata gathering based on the changing operational context and ana-lyzing the same using a self-learning software algorithm that applies advanced analytics and/or prediction-based coding to output multiple alternatives and score them in relevancy-based order. The results can then be pipelined into a second such algorithm that renders the sugges-tive alternatives as near real–time visualizations for business users—marking them as optimally actionable.

- What is the extent to which the vendor product/solution can sup-port integration, from business, social, and IT perspectives? This includes a combination of collaboration, communication, and cooperation from text to context and everything in between.

- How do we leap from faster time to insight to faster time to quality of service (QOS)? The level and severity of protection and compliance supported by the product when it comes to critical and sensitive information, from raw data sourcing to data warehousing to information integration, access, and availability to overall solution quality and efficiency. Data integrity is vital to information assurance, and builds the trust factor into the vendor–customer relationship. This in turn ensures that the specific solution lands into the so-called "zero-tolerance" zone. This kicks in two major tasks—testing in parallel and testing across multiple combinations of heterogeneous and homogeneous platforms. Hence, the vendor-specific testing product must be platform-agnostic; load balance–enabled to thrive in business environments running on a massive scale of users, resources, and data; and at the same hot-pluggable for a test, untest, retest scenario.

  This can be done by verifying the product using database hardening, ethical hacking, penetration testing, advanced point-of-delivery security (e.g., Web browser, mobile device, remote access–enabled systems, etc.), criticalities involved in risk mitigation, privileged-user access, and manual elevation/escalation of these privileges.

The key indicators here are:

- To employ an industry-compliant third-party test-bed that uses a snapshot of context-specific "live" datasets that are deidentified in all ways required—and perform this evaluation in a "moving the clock-hand in any random direction" fashion while still maintaining the end-to-end business operational workflow, including simulating mobile and agile (e.g., virtual) test-bed platforms if necessary.
- To understand that there is a difference between testing for functionality and testing for quality. The former involves testing that is more business-driven in terms of supporting functional business processes and must accommodate the full spectrum of business and operational processes in terms of functionality and their performance. The latter is more dynamic and business-process extensible; it involves additional criteria to prove how the vendor product is capable of:

- Quantifying quality and QOS in terms of deep-dive testing to detect the unknowns, the inherent flexibility for variance, and the skewing required to gain fine-grained visibility into application behavior as it is responding to change.
- Prediction-based analysis
- Self-serviceability
- The testing can even extend beyond the above to allow for the nonfunctional people-related, interaction-driven social aspect–oriented testing.
- Can even extend beyond the above to allow for the nonfunctional people-related, interaction-driven social aspect–oriented testing.

The vendor solution must qualify in all these testing categories and thus support seamless SOA-based integration with the third-party test bed and follow a process-oriented testing methodology.

- When it comes to open source software testing, there are at least a dozen tier-1 tools and techniques that have the capability for extreme functionality and performance testing in unique and innovative ways, like the trending Black Duck Software's Black Duck Suite and Black Duck KnowledgeBase (an evolutionary solution that accelerates testing and management of using and integrating Open Source Software in legacy, existing, and new business–IT–social environments); Phoronix Test Suite, based on the OpenBenchmarking.org's Open Source Testing Framework; Zend Technologies's Drupal-based Open Source Social Publishing Platform for Benchmarking; the Testing as a Service (TaaS) testing platform from Wipro and IBM's Rational Performance Testing (RPT) Services (Next-Generation O-demand Testing platforms); Parasoft Concerto; Smartesoft Testing Solutions (particularly SmarteScript and SmarteStudio);TechExcel's DevTest Suite; and MicorFocus's SilkCentral Test Manger, SilkTest, and SilkPerformer. A distinct class of browser-based BI software is also available from Tableau Software.

4.5   The Final Pick: An Information-Driven, Customer-Centric Solution, and a Best-of-Breed Product/Platform and Solution Convergence Key Indicator Checklist

The final pick can be as innovative and dominating by way of uniqueness and universality as being the foundational framework for an open-context EDW/BI solution that can embrace not only open source technologies, frameworks, methodologies, tools, and metrics, but also business–social context specifics and situational, location-variant, time-variant, collaborative, and continuous BI that is flexible, scalable, and elastic enough to self-adapt, self-manage, self-service, and self-evolve (by way of automeasurement and autoloopback based on input feedback). This can serve as a business–social operations model in itself for open source–based EDW/BI build-deploy-extend customer successes, as well as going beyond BI via its inherent self-evolution as a sort of autobenchmarking.

To this effect, herewith listed are the key indicators for such a best-of-breed and convergent EDW/BI solution. These indicators are lattice-based, as opposed to ladder-based, in terms of relevance and significance:

- Can open source meet cloud source? This is the ability of the open source EDW/BI solution to be capable of being designed, developed, tested, tuned, and/or deployed in a cloud-based environment or a shared cloud environment. And how business-friendly is the customer experience going to be? This is a key criterion to strategic business interests, as businesses big and small tend to leverage advanced and customized business analytics as easily and quickly as possible to respond to dynamic changes in business requirements.

Can open source meet cloud source? Enterprise evolution is a best-fit combination of experience, efficiency, and expertise, with the ability to get as close as possible to 360° of integration (agile and mobile at the same time).

- Eased architectural complexity of the solution with the evolution of technology
- Efficiency in processing more complex data/content structures
- Secure and single-click solution deployment that is end user–/business user–configurable

- Elastic scaling on demand, resulting in faster time to deploy without inhibiting production environments
- Embeddable business analytics that are both statically and dynamically augmented by benchmarking of the same, automated and accelerated
- Delivering a unified customer view of the business–social contextual content and/or the SaaS-enabling, SaaS-enabled integration of the same. Technically speaking, this translates into high-performance computing by leveraging virtual data federation and syndication of all forms of data, from structured and relational to semistructured, unstructured, hierarchical, or URL-based content and social content from the majority of social networking sites.
- The ability to divide and conquer by way of context-aware and risk-resilient componentization of business processes and the associated functionality that can be delivered by using a services-enabled software architecture. The key here is reusability of both the business-specific and customer-centric components as well as the corresponding services.

Figure 4.1 illustrates the correlation between open source and cloud source by way of virtualization and other key indicators that factor into the selection process of an EDW/BI solution. These criteria count as the Primary selection indicators to make any open source–based EDW/BI solution both compliance-proof and future-proof, end-to-end. Figures 4.2 and 4.3 show sketches depicting high-level views of the key selection performance indicators (KSPIs) of an *Open Source Perfect* EDW/BI solution that can be considered for the final pick.

4.6   Summary

This chapter dealt with the foundational basics in deciding upon an open source–based EDW/BI solution. It highlighted the key selection criteria emphasizing on the requirements analysis phase and the critical deciding factors in solution selection from techniques, technologies, and tools available; and then presented a preview of the selection–action process results. Finally, it outlined a cross-correlation between open source and cloud source in terms of the primary selection criteria for achieving what the author calls the *Open Source Perfect* EDW/BI solution. The next chapter dives deeply into the design and architectural pragmatics of current and next-generation open source technologies and methodologies, along with the use of the same in an optimal manner.

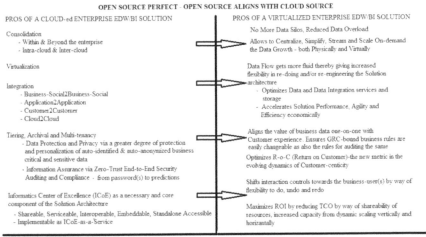

Figure 4.1   Correlation between open source and cloud source by way of virtualization and other key indicators as the primary selection indicators for a compliance-proof and future-proof EDW/BI solution, end-to-end.

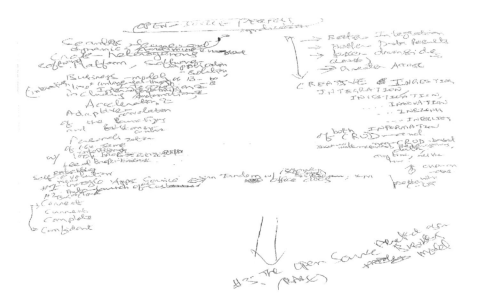

Figure 4.2   A sketch depicting a high-level view of the key selection performance indicators (KSPIs) of an Open Source Perfect EDW/BI solution.

Figure 4.3   A sketch depicting another high-level view of the key selection performance indicators (KSPI) of an Open Source Perfect EDW/
BI solution.

4.7   References

The following references have been used in gaining access to the information provided in this chapter:

- General BI Information
    - Lakshman Bulusu, "Raising your BIQ (Business Intelligence
    Quotient): 5 Things Your Company Can Do NOW."
    Focus.com Research Brief, published August 30, 2010 (avail-
    able at www.focus.com/briefs/raising-your-biq-business-intelli-
    gence-quotient-five-things).
    - Lakshman Bulusu, "Raising your BIQ (Business Intelligence
    Quotient): 5 Things Your Company Can Do NOW." Business
    Intelligence   Overview,   October   2010   (available   at
    www.scribd.com/doc/72571012/2010-10-Business-Intelli-
    gence-Overview).

Chapter 5

Design and Architecture: Technologies and Methodologies by Dissection

5.1 In This Chapter

- The Primary Aspects of DW and BI from a Usability Perspective: Strategic BI, Pervasive BI, Operational BI, and BI On-Demand
- Design and Architecture Considerations for the Primary BI Perspectives
- Information-Centric, Business-Centric, and Customer-Centric Architecture: A Three-in-One Convergence, for Better or Worse
- Open Source DW and BI Architecture
- Why and How an Open Source Architecture Delivers a Better Enterprisewide Solution
- Open Source Data Architecture: Under the Hood
- Open Source Data Warehouse Architecture: Under the Hood
- Open Source BI Architecture: Under the Hood
- The Vendor/Platform Product(s)/Tools(s) That Fit into the Open DW and BI Architecture
- Best Practices: Use and Reuse

This chapter delves into the details of Open Source DW and BI design methodologies. The opening section gives a brief insight into the classification of DW and BI aspects based on scope of business and purpose of use in the context of business operations and business users. The subsequent sections elaborate on the key design considerations therein, highlighting the benefit of unified EDW/BI convergence via information-centricity, business-centricity and customer-centricity as well as the architecture of the essential open source EDW/BI solution components, such as the data and information management layer, the EDW layer, and the BI layer. The chapter concludes by outlining the best practices to put in place for a best-fit and successful implementation.

5.2   The Primary Aspects of DW and BI from a Usability Perspective: Strategic BI, Pervasive BI, Operational BI, and BI On-Demand

Starting from principles to pragmatics to practice, DW and BI involves at least the following aspects that directly impact the information usability and the design architecture of such a solution:

- Scope of BI use (lifecycle of BI adoption): pervasive, competitive, strategic, tactical
- Purpose of BI use (business operations context): traditional/analytical, operational, predictive
- Purpose of BI use (business user context): information-centric, business-centric, customer-centric (consumer, customer, competitor)

Pervasive DW and BI refers to the adoption of such a solution across all functional business touchpoints, from the help desk, front office, and support to the departmental units, lines of business, and corporate units, to across-the-enterprise and business-to-business consolidation, and into the cloud.

Strategic BI refers to using the implemented solution and the underlying business analytics for deriving a strategic value from it—the implication being that such a solution is future-proof and can easily, effectively, and efficiently adapt to the strategic KPI of the business by supporting the road ahead in addition to being the go ahead. Generally, *strategic* refers to the enterprise as a whole, but can also be inclusive to a particular line of business, for example.

Tactical BI is just the opposite, in that it is intended to meet the current (just-in-time, real-time, right-time) demands of the business enterprise. It can be pervasive or restrictive to a specific business functional unit.

Operational BI is typical in that it facilitates information access, analysis, and delivery directly from operational (OLTP) systems in near-real time as the data is being created. This is extremely useful for tactical purposes and real-time data analysis on an as-is basis. It is also helpful in sourcing information for prediction-based reasoning and decision support.

The implementation of continuous operational BI processes as part of the overall enterprise BI strategy is recommended.

BI on demand is more *right*-time BI enablement than *real*-time BI, which is continuous. This suits the anytime-anyone-anywhere BI consumer, in that it combines pervasive BI, tactical BI, analytical BI, and operational BI on an as-needed basis.

5.3   Design and Architecture Considerations for the Primary BI Perspectives

The case for architecture as a precedence factor can be argued about in any perspective, from design to design patterns to methodologies to mechanisms in action. But the business value of architecture as a key benefactor for any software solution in general, and any EDW/BI in particular, is tangibly seen when a EDW/BI solution is built from scratch or an existing one is augmented, customized, or personalized, keeping in mind the fundamental facts about design and architecture that follow as the key quintessential indicators for the pragmatics of such a solution realization.

Architecture and Its Associated Design as the Key Quintessential Indicators for the Pragmatics of any EDW/BI Solution Realization

Architecture is the mechanism for action that drives a particular EDW/BI solution. This simply says that for a solution to be actionable (i.e., up and running),the underlying mechanism matters first and foremost—not the technologies or tools or algorithms involved. An optimal mechanism-for-action yields an optimal mechanism-in-action solution.

There is an inherent difference between architecture and design. And this applies to solution architecture and solution design in the same way that it does to information/usability architecture and information design. Architecture is the combination of one or multiple designs to arrive at a best-fit mechanism by which the target solution can be "constructed" to be up and running. Design, on the other hand, is a set of one or more computational, mathematical, or accelerating algorithms and the associated patterns that help build the individual components, which are then blended together by the mechanism called architecture.

Though architecture is unique for any given solution, it is generic in that a given solution architecture can be template-enabled as a reference model, provided its contextual domain includes a common ground in terms of the design and mechanism involved and targets a specific business domain—for example, EDW/BI for communications—or a usability imperative—for example, EDW/BI for business efficiency—that in turn share the same necessary requirements. This difference is tangibly critical when it comes to architecting a customer-centric EDW/BI solution in which the above core generic architecture is layered, but not in silos, by another piece of mechanism for action that is only specific to the particular business customer or end user in perspective. The uniqueness of architecture versus design also becomes cognizant in EDW/BI solutions targeted toward competitive intelligence and situation-aware collaborative intelligence.

5.3.1   The Case for Architecture as a Precedence Factor

An innovative open source–based EDW/BI solution requires an innovative software architecture model as a foundation for driving such a solution from principles to pragmatics. At times, this necessitates going beyond the BI dashboard and the cloud to get to what the data-to-dashboard journey does not reveal. This in turn requires that the end-to-end architecture and the underlying software design components support the traceability of the functional misfits in first-time and repeated use of such a solution. Remember that this needs to be part of the requirements analysis which is performed before the logical design and solution architecture begins. With the skyrocketing data growth—in volume and structure—and the increasing speed and reliability demands of the solution with the growth of the customer-/end user–crowd, the role of architecture is not only critical but in fact indispensible to operational efficiency. The customer experience, in terms of "live use" feedback and/or industry-based successes, is a vital source of feeds that can provide the so-called ground-rules for such a design framework. Having the flexibility and ease to extend or reengineer the same based on dynamic business needs—thus delivering a solution that is can fit-in on-demand into the business-social landscape—is an effective and efficient way for the solution to be fully functional and at the same time sustainable throughout the customer lifecycle. This raises the bar on the customer confidence level from the usability and reliability perspective and at the same time proves to be a solution with a key constant imperative—that of being best-fit on-demand—leveraging the benefits of collective and contextual intelligence. Thus, there is no such theory as the total (final solution) equals the sum of its parts (i.e., each and every component of the solution); rather, at any point, a (contextual) part of the solution can itself become the total solution for another customer-centric context. Getting the requirements analysis right the first time gets the design right the first time, which in turn gets the solution architecture right the first time, ultimately resulting in delivery of the right (and loosely-coupled) solution the first time.

The question "Why performance matters?" is essentially evolved to "Why performance factors?" It is this key performance indicator of performance factoring into prediction-enabled insights (by way of Predictive Analytics) across state, time, and spatial variances that becomes the necessary driver behind an "architecture-as-the-precedence"factor. Conforming to and standardizing this as a software architecture best practice for a best-fit solution can lead to its adoption as a key prediction indicator for a solution that can deliver actionable BI.

An innovative software architecture commands the code behind the EDW/BI solution to be executed in a way that delivers results in an elastically flexible and manner, while at the same time ensuring that continuity, concurrency, and consistency are preserved throughout the lifecycle if the business domain that uses it.

5.4   Information-Centric, Business-Centric, and Customer-Centric Architecture: A Three-in-One Convergence, for Better or Worse

As stated in the beginning of the chapter, a EDW/BI solution can be specialized according to the purpose of use from the context of the business user. These pertain to such a solution being information-centric, business-centric, and customer-centric, or a combination of any or all of these. In this section, the pros and cons (if any) of a three-in-one convergence of these three imperatives are highlighted.

Information-centricity refers to the EDW/BI solution being geared towards productizing the solution, the primary purpose of which is to deliver an out-of-the-box EDW/BI solution that can be POC (or proof-of-concept) tested and deployed in a single pass. Customization and extensibility are treated as add-ons to this out-of-the-box solution. An information-centric solution can be more restrictive in nature by being inclusive of specific industry domains such as networking and communications, global investment banking, or the like; or it can be made available as a less restrictive EDW/BI model that can be improvised and extended to a full-fledged BI system by leveraging existing infrastructure, or embedded as a EDW/BI add-on to existing non-BI applications. This is useful for both analytical reporting and operational BI. Hence, the architectural design patterns are primarily based on data-driven EDW/BI KPI in line with the business industry domain.

Business-centricity refers to the EDW/BI being geared to meet business operations and operational (OLTP) needs in sync with the business functional processes and support. Hence there is no productizing concept, even though the EDW/BI solution is still information-centric by way of supporting the business domain–specific functionality. This kind of a solution is more specific business process–driven as opposed to being 100 percent data-centric. Another difference is that it might include specific governance policies internal to the business segment/company, implemented as business rules, and some or all of a greater set of generic industry domain–compliant GRC policies. This can also be a packaged solution architected primarily as a cluster of custom EDW/BI modules to result in a *corporate intelligence center*.

Customer-centricity refers to a fine-grained level of implementation of the business-centric EDW/BI solution. The key drivers for such a breakdown can be by consumer, by customer (a domain of consumers specific to the particular business), or by competitor (that is generally a superset of customer-centricity, but supporting competitive BI to dissect, analyze, and derive a decisive business analytics model that boots the customer to a competitor level through cross-correlation, collaboration, and continuous operational intelligence—and in real time. Such a BI solution needs to be risk-aware of the constantly market competition and dynamically adapt itself to aid in actionable intelligence.

When it comes to pros and cons, there is no hard and fast rule as to which type of EDW/BI solution is best suited in terms of business need. By carefully planning and defining the business requirements in collaboration with the business teams like business analysts, data stewards, and the like, cross-correlating them with key business drives (such as leveraging existing infrastructure, integration-only purposed solutions that can seamlessly co-exist with non-BI or existing BI systems), and assessing the risk versus assurance ratio and TCO versus ROC (return on customer) business value and the suitability from a customer adoption/experience perspective, any or all of these types of EDW/BI can be a best-fit for implementation in the real world.

A unified EDW/BI convergence by way of information-centricity, business-centricity and customer-centricity is always a best-of-breed benefit in that it enables, eases, and accelerates the EDW/BI operations to run in pace with the other business operations—thereby enhancing the information sharing and actionable decision support processes in the following ways:

1. Unification of on-premise, online, on-device, and in-the-cloud deployments for EDW/BI anytime, anywhere, by anyone.

2. Enabling businesses to obtain a BI solution that conforms to the paradigm "my business is primary driver of my solution." This approach not only minimizes risk, but also builds trust in terms of business value, assurance, and customer confidence.

3. Enables the business operations to stay ahead of the competition for both current and strategic needs. For example, as the social intelligence context evolves to a greater/newer level, it becomes simpler for the EDW/BI solution to incorporate new social metrics and adapt to the changing social context.

4. Enables business operations and users to use the EDW/BI solution with zero or minimal IT dependence, thereby reducing time, cost, effort, and increasing intrabusiness (and sometimes interbusiness) collaboration.

5.5 Open Source DW and BI Architecture

An open source DW and BI architecture is and should be a solution that is business–social friendly and an enabler of creative insight-phyla for the enterprise BI user. The following describes one typical framework that can be followed to start with, in the architecture of a typical open source DW and BI solution by design:

- Get to the intent-context-content aspects of the desired solution.
- Get to the rules-of-the-thumb that must be implemented to realize the desired solution. This requires the zoom-in clarity of the surrounding (business) context and, based on the same, deciding the right content to include in the architecture: the design patterns and the corresponding algorithms for loosely-coupled flexibility and the optimization patterns for elevating the design to conform to risk-awareness, context-awareness (including MDM policies), and governance, risk, and compliance.

- Get to the details of usability in terms of intelligent information integration, time to deliver, time to insight, and the new imperative of time to adapt. In addition, get to a customer-user experience across every point of interaction by way of *Quality of Service (QOS)* and *Quality of Assurance (QOA)*.

The following subsections outline the design pragmatics, patterns and components involved in a solution that is both unique and universal from concepts to customization. The architectural backbone is based on using the *Open Source Perfect* framework for a Web-based interactive business model integration, which can be a blueprint for an open source EDW/BI anytime-anyone-anywhere solution architecture.

A business use case for such an implementation can be:

Automating and accelerating the compliance-centric standardization of a context-aware EDW/BI solution and in-cloud deployments of the same to gain subsecond response times and intelligent infolets in traditional and cloud business operations

---

5.5.1   Pragmatics and Design Patterns

Pragmatics and design patterns comprise the methodologies by which each component of the solution can be designed so that it is self-sufficient in terms of being embeddable or stand-alone hot-pluggable as well as the mechanism(s) for putting all of the pieces together. Here's an overview of a typical implementation of the same from a SDLC perspective:

- Extreme model-driven development framework
- Collaborative modeling and design
    - Analyze, design and build business rules of exceptional QOS and QOA (quality and efficiency by way of performance, price, and precision; and trustworthiness by way of reliability, high availability, security, risk-tolerant assurance and come-back customer-user experience)
    - Embeddable UML-based (analytics) engines and standards-based extension plug-ins
    - End-to-end traceability

- Integrated coding, debugging, and visualization rule sets and toolsets
- Integrated business modeling vis-a-vis solution architecture (design) modeling
- Flexibility and comfort zone–like ease in overcoming the limitations of security and pricing, while guaranteeing optimal uptime and the multitenant model of a "my-solution-my-way" usability experience

---

Design using one methodology and deploy using an entirely different one.

- Development of an extensible and customizable application programming interface (API) for the end-to-end EDW/BI to be generated from within an open database (DB) such as Ingres or Ingres Vectorwise, and/or a closed-source DB such as Oracle11g, Sybase, MS-SQL Server or similar, by only using this API and the variant parameters involved (this includes extensible data visualization too)

5.5.2   Components

An open source framework can enable implementation of a complete abstraction layer—from infrastructure (or hardware) to Web application server to DB server to personalized UI to VMware (in virtual environments)—exposable via an API or visualization–based platform layer. The key components for putting the pieces together to enable such a flexible and elastic architecture include:

- Easy-to-deliver interactive and consistent solution for inter- and intraplatform integration
- A high-performance predictive analytics engine; approximation is better than computation for accuracy in a predictive analytics domain
- A codeless user experience from technical users to business users and beyond
- Reusable data visualization services for transforming Flash/Flex-based user interface (UI)-lets to analogous video graphics modes by way of HTML5 enablement, using a combination of CSS, HTML, and SVG
- Swift performance analysis

- Extensible and extensive support for leveraging native database functionality (including multiple disparate databases)
- The new *Open Source Perfect* BI imperative, *time to adapt,* which implies a self-adaptive solution for self-serviceable BI. This stands out by introducing line-of-business user interaction–driven UI controls
- Using data, database, data integration, and dashboard-level virtualization for dynamic contextual solution delivery, immaterial of the target deployment platform; virtualization does not necessarily have to be true infrastructure server–based VMware-driven virtualization, but an inherent self-constructive mechanism of creating information sets on the fly based on the context and content variance(s)

5.6   Why and How an Open Source Architecture Delivers a Better Enterprisewide Solution

An open source architecture eases the EDW/BI solution implementation from design to deployment and beyond, by way of a dynamic plug-and-play mechanism that bypasses the so-called "nativity" specific to a particular technology or vendor solution—one that enables an unified convergence of build-your-own and buy-and-extend in a scalable, flexible, and transparent and efficient manner—by letting the business (customer/user) be the primary decision maker in terms of the choice that optimizes the business value. This is due to the fact that an open source–enabled architecture is by definition a reference model for enabling such a leveled abstraction on-demand, on top of or around existing implementations or as a totally new one.

Immaterial of the source and target requirements, contexts, workloads, and users involved, an open source EDW/BI architecture is functionally more *natural or naïve* than *native*—thus ensuring that the resulting solution is foolproof and future-proof at the same time. The following table elaborates on these aspects by building a blueprint for an open source intelligent information integration architecture (referred to as $OSI^{3}A$ for the purposes of this book).

Table 5.1   OSI^{3}A: An Open Source Intelligent Information Integration Architecture.

OSI^{3}A—Open Source Intelligent Information Integration Architecture	
Mechanism for Action	**Mechanism in Action**
Scope: context or content or both? Does the order matter?	An insightful overview from the business, IT, C-UX, and social perspectives
Architecture	Principles, practices, pragmatics and performance
Next-generation dynamics	**Time to perform** ■ (access, assurance, availability, authorization, authentication, anytime-any-one-anywhere access, precedence of right data over near real–time data, fast/actionable/synchronized/tested [FAST], and the innovative time to virtualized [Data to Dashboard]) **Time to insight** **Time to adapt** ■ (a self-adaptable BI solution for self-serviceable BI) **QOS and QOA** ■ (response time, resolution time, customer satisfaction levels) **Business intelligence quotient (BIQ), competitive intelligence quotient (CIQ), social intelligence quotient (SIQ)** ■ (Social media is also a platform for advanced analytics to track, correlate, and analyze customer behavior for competitive intelligence)
Tools, suites, platforms and patterns in trend	The road-ahead evolves as the go-ahead

Table 5.1   OSI³A: An Open Source Intelligent Information Integration Architecture.

OSI³A—Open Source Intelligent Information Integration Architecture	
Mechanism for Action	**Mechanism in Action**
Architecture reference model	Integration tips, traps, techniques, technologies, trends, and trendsetters: ■ Information integration is both an enabler and accelerator of business and IT interaction. ■ An enhanced view of information demands an enhanced/new performance metrics that in turn open up a use case for an enhanced, extended, or new business analytics platform. This new analytics platform is best implemented and driven by an open source–based architecture that can serve as a reference model for subsequent implementations/customizations in terms of effectiveness, efficiency, and adaptability.
The ISAP (integrate, share, act, and perform) paradigm	Information sharing to information streaming and everything in between, from: ■ Cross-user collaboration to cross-border interoperability (within and beyond the business2social enterprise and [end] client to cloud), to context-aware customer-centricity, to ■ On-demand personalized solution versioning (information-centric vs. business-centric vs. customer-centric), to ■ Cloud bursting to crowd sourcing across the social spectrum (social Web, social "live" interaction, social non-Web media) People, processes, precedent priorities, and pragmatics working together—from the end client user to the intelligent customer. Collaboration should not lead to disablement of existing interoperability.

- Information Services
- Information Integration Services

These information services must enable, automate, and accelerate the following functionality:

- Continuous, contextual, collaborative and competitive (adaptive) information processing regardless of the source, destination, transformation, structure, volume, or presentation of the data/content involved.
- Avoidance of redundancy, silos, and unnecessary replication of data, regardless of the number of data/information systems being integrated. This includes autointeroperability of relational and object/nonrelational data, in transit and in storage.
- Ability to leverage the multithreading, thread scheduling, resource sharing and synchronous or asynchronous execution and control of the underlying database and/or in-memory cache or disconnected data source.
- Ability to leverage and adapt cloud-based data processing and delivery architectures that are embeddable into the EDW/BI solution and vice versa
- Right time is the new real time, and the data architecture must emulate a design that guarantees time-criticality and location independence in addition to fast performance and agentless delivery of the information in context.

5.8   Open Source Data Warehouse Architecture: Under the Hood

The key to an EDW implementation lies in its ability to provide anytime, anywhere, anyone one-on-one with right time/right data/right user/right purpose information availability and accessibility of all data, big or small for historical and current analyses purposes, as well as near real–time availability of transactional data directly from OLTP systems processed in a information-centric, user-specific fashion. Hence the underlying architecture of the EDW provides the above functionality by using a combination of information usability designs, such as:

- *Dynamic data warehousing*: The underlying EDW model is designed in a way that is synchronous, aligned, adaptable in terms of functionality, and fast-actionable-dimensional in terms of implementation. An open source data model typically conforms to the dimensional normal form and follows a hybrid column *cum* row orientation, with the actual data being stored in a columnar fashion and the associated abstraction view being presented in rows. This approach enables the best fit, as it can be embedded into any row-based or column-based databases that power existing data warehouses or data marts. Pipelined paralleled streaming can be used for source data consolidation as well as information delivery with virtualized services. Compute-intensive analysis is enabled by using big data architectures such as Hadoop/MapReduce, high-performance clustering based on contextual datasets, NoSQL-enabled algorithms, and unstructured to structured data conversion to fit into relational online analytical processing (ROLAP) implementations. The key here is there is no need for indexing, replication, or dimensional cube processing, as all data is flattened into either columnar or grid-based structures with the underlying data modeled in a ROLAP fashion.

This enables dynamic updates of changed data and, thereby, the underlying business processes as they occur by way of delivering timely and accurate information to the EDW and the BI user interface.

- *Dynamic and elastic integration of EDW information with advanced analytics*: These analytics are predefined or autogenerated on the fly, using a information grid that is constructed as the source data is processed, based on the type, content, and relationship(s) between the various data elements, as well as the metadata around them. The advanced analytics are implemented as stored metrics that contain the original information (cast or as is) plus the KPI-specific content as one actionable data element. Data quality engineering and data mining models enable deep-dive exploration of the data to discover inherent but hidden relationships and semantics between data, as well as extraction of derived metadata, in addition to data enhancements through profiling, segmentation, masking, encryption, and Extract-Transform-Load/Extract-Load-Transform (ETL/EL-T) processes.

The key here is that both structured and unstructured data is unified into a single context-aware infolet that serves as an abstraction layer between the underlying data design and the UI. This is reusable and can be made persistent and embeddable on demand into any other information system that needs it. Also, a lateral view of the same across business-centric dimensions can be dynamically constructed and exposed on demand. Self-service capability and adaptability of the infolet to changing needs and times is made possible by autogeneration of optimized and/or new business rules based on C-UX that are rewired into the data architecture workflow by event-driven action-response mechanisms.

- *Data compression based on row-orientation, column-orientation or a combination of both*: Depending on the context of the content involved, some type of data compression is used to maximize storage of the same and minimize resource-consumption
- *Data subsuming, consuming, and delivery*: Optimized by high-performance ETL/EL-T and augmented by dynamic data virtualization and federation, as opposed to syndication, prioritization of dimensional hierarchies based on synchrony that is dynamically inherited from super- and sub-infolets.
- *Information services and information integration services*: These services are exposed via SQL-enabled or services-based APIs that are native-compliant with the target database being used to result in an optimized data access layer.
- *Addressing data analytics*: An intelligent analytics model is designed that automatically decides the right choice of computation mechanism for processing and generating metrics by way of SQL, NoSQL, or a combination of both. This proves efficient in complex objects to relational computing, thereby rendering the target information in any specific format desired. This process consists of the following essential steps:

    1. Quality-proof and transform the data in accordance with the target EDW design strategy in terms of conformance, governance, and usability

    2. Design functionally specific data-driven mechanisms, either physical or virtualization enabled, that meet the demands of

information-centricity, consumer-centricity, and business-centricity (domain-specific)

3. Design an efficient information management mechanism to orchestrate the data flow in sync with the work flows and dynamic constraints involved.

5.9 Open Source BI Architecture: Under the Hood

The key to BI implementation lies in its ability to provide real-life information visualization by way of multiseries charts, graphs depicting analyzed results of multistructured data sets across multiple business domains, and time series–based and trend-based reports for statistical forecasting, as well as prediction-based analytics. Customizable smartboards by way of dynamically generated marts of enterprise BI dashboard(s), and just-in-time delivery of the same (or on-demand), take BI to the next level in terms of an intelligent, innovative, and informational business–IT interface.

The underlying architecture is based on three key patterns: *event-driven design*, *SOA-based delivery*, and *customer-centric contextualization*. Getting into the details gives the following step-by-step procedure:

1. The open source BI architecture includes the core components of BI: traditional reporting, operational BI, ad hoc querying, and dashboarding. These functions can be statically or dynamically (on-demand) leveraged or in an embeddable fashion and are deployable in on-premise, mobile, online, and/or hybrid cloud environments.

2. The open source BI architecture must allow single sign-on (SSO), immaterial of the platform, time and location from where the user accesses the solution. Using open source as a model for designing a SSO component results in a stronger authentication and authorization implementation for a "login-once-for-all-that-I-am-privileged-to-do" functionality that is also capable of unifying the process to make it laterally agnostic to the target access platform.

3. The open source BI architecture must enable easy and dynamic componentization of the business intelligence platform, business analytics platform, and end-to-end performance and customer experience platform, in a hot-pluggable and embeddable fashion—without losing the synchronicity and consistency of both

operational and analytical information. Though solutions based on proprietary software in the likes of Oracle11g Application Integration Architecture and so on can be used to implement this, an open source–based engine is a best-fit for both intra-application and external solution integration, especially when varying in customizations.

4. Using on-the-fly integrated data (in whatever form it might be) that has been "flattened" into a seamless reusable infolet (visual, nonvisual, or a mix and merge of both) to render to the end-client RIA dashboard. The *techniques of dynamic warehousing* discussed in the previous section aid and accelerate this implementation. Binding the customer-specific variant attributes at runtime to this infolet that has the core domain-specific functionality already embedded into it makes this process realizable as well as situational, competitive, and adaptable. The 3-tuplet consisting of

```
(geo-location, time, trending-business functions)
```

   are the necessary input variants to this infolet. These inputs can be user-interaction driven or auto-derived by using self-learning intelligence based on previous inputs. In either case, these trigger an event-based autostart that turns on the elastic execution involved.

5. Once the customer-centric personalized infolet is built, it is easily to deliver it using an SOA-based model that internally churns multiple deliverylets using virtualization, dynamic streaming, hot-pluggable Web services (exposed as WS-executables or as API), virtual application(s) services, and the like.

6. The query capabilities must support SQL-based access and multidimensional query analysis (using the popular MDX query language, XQuery, or the more generic DMX). True entity framework–based analytics can be enabled using a database-independent query language by way of encapsulation and abstraction based on open source API like those supported by Groovy, Ruby, NoSQL, Hadoop/MapReduce, PHP, Python, and the like.

7. The most important part of this architecture is the *contextualization process* that bridges the existing/newly generated initial info-

let with the customer-centric 3-tuplet described above via an autoenabled link process (AKA a dynamic business process), an intelligent analytics-driven object, and the like, which it then integrates into the solution workflow to autorun in line with the rest of the process tasks. A similar approach can be followed for decoupling this personalized customer component if need be.

8. The mechanism of right-time data virtualization using virtual federated views enables the delivery of on-demand dashboards with consumer-centric information. This approach, supplemented by dynamic dashboarding using live application streaming, offers a scalable solution that can be as pervasively available as desired, from the currently located BI center to the cloud BI center—changing the pragmatics of information delivery from *right here, right now* to *anywhere, anytime*.

9. A self-sufficient BI platform will always be a front-runner for BI solution adoption. This in turn implies that the BI solution be self-contained and complete in its functionality and platform environment without having to augment the BI solution with missing components like data integration (DI), data quality (DQ), complementary reporting modules, and the like. And this applies to embeddable or SaaS-enabled scenarios in a industry domain–agnostic manner. Most of the enterprise open source BI editions are compatible to meet this requirement. However, community editions of the same are more componentized in availability to support custom orientation of existing BI environments. Sometimes a blended approach of the two might give the benefit of a best-fit solution.

10. The greater the elasticity of a BI platform, the greater its usability, thereby enabling a pervasive BI adoption and user experience. Such a solution can be architected by using self-sufficient BI solutions that support end-to-end BI functionality from source data integration through information management through EDW, BI, and extensibility. The alternative approach is to use tightly or loosely coupled integration and hot-pluggable componentization

based on the specific requirements in place. An example of a typical design pattern for the latter is shown in Table 5.2:

Table 5.2   Typical open source business intelligence solution architecture that is loosely-coupled, hot-pluggable, componentized, and cloud-enabled.

BI Solution Function	BI Vendor Product/Suite
BI layer	Jaspersoft Business Intelligence
Enterprise data warehouse layer	Vertica Analytic Database
Data integration and information management layer	Talend DI, Talend ESB and Web Services–based Information and Information Integration Services
Cloud deployment layer	AWS EC2 Cloud
End-to-end orchestration and cloud management	Opscode Chef Integration or RightScale Cloud orchestration

11.   A self-serviceable BI solution brings self-adaptable business intelligence, thereby improving and evolving the effectiveness for the consumer-centricity, customer-centricity, and competitor-centricity of open source BI, tactically and strategically.

An open source model enables this implementation in an efficient, effective, elastic, and embeddable fashion by registering this as a dynamically created-and-executable business process (one for the coupling and another for the decoupling), based on a set of configuration parameters. It is prudent to aim for a solution that can provide tighter cross-product integration across lines-of-business and thereby future-proof the same for strategic business purposes.

Figure 5.1 illustrates an architectural design view of an open source EDW/BI-as-a-service solution as an enabler and accelerator of competitive business.

5.10   The Vendor/Platform Product(s)/Tools(s) That Fit into the Open DW and BI Architecture

Taking into account the seamless strata of an EDW/BI solution as explained to this point, the vendor/platform specific product(s)/tool(s) that are a best

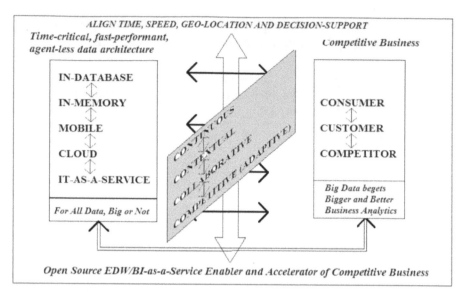

Figure 5.1   An architectural design view of an open source EDW/BI-as-a-service
solution as an enabler and accelerator of competitive business.

fit into the open source EDW/BI solution landscape can be broadly categorized as follows:

- Information integration, usability, and management (across data
  sources, applications and business domains)
- EDW: models to management
- BI: models to interaction to management to strategic business
  decision support (via analytics and visualization)

All of these have business-centric rules and policies as well as governance rules—all clear and efficient—to enable complete 24×7 visibility
into the business processes, zero trust security, zero fault tolerance, scalable performance and a confidence of assurance enabling customer
experience that is persistent across the tactical, operational, and line of
business consumer/customer/competitor user domain(s).

The subsections that follow discuss the key industry players based on
the above categorization.

5.10.1   Information Integration, Usability and Management (Across Data Sources, Applications and Business Domains)

This includes data integration at the data source level, data services level, and data delivery level; includes data quality to ensure accuracy and right-time (and real-time) data availability; and extends beyond data to dynamically accelerate the information integration and management related to the business operations and operational processes in context. The major vendors/products in this arena are discussed in the subsections that follow.

Talend Data Integration Suite

Talend is a revolutionary industry leader in open source data integration, management and application integration. The Talend difference is in its ability to offer its solution portfolio available to organizations of all sizes and for multi-purpose integration needs.

Talend is recognized and positioned by Gartner, Inc. in the "Visionaries" quadrant of the "Magic Quadrant for Data Integration Tools" and by Lead411 as "one of the largest pure play vendors of open source software, offering a breadth of middleware solutions that address both data management and application integration needs," Bloor Research's Research Director says, "In any market, open source represents a potentially disruptive approach. However, relatively few vendors are effectively organized [sic] to take advantage of such disruption. Talend is an exception." Other major industry leaders agree: Talend Data Management Suite is a comprehensive solution for information integration (operational data integration and analytical ETL for EDW/BI), optimizing data quality, data synchronization, MDM (including operational BI–enabling transactional MDM), and its IOA-centric Agile Information Integration Architecture. Its primary and unique products and tools include Talend Open Studio and Talend Integration Suite for DI, Talend Open Profiler and Talend Data Quality for DQ, Talend MDM for MDM, Talend Services Factory, Talend Integration Factory (both available as Community Editions), Talend ESB Standard Edition, Talend ASF Enterprise Edition for Application Integration and Information Lifecycle Management, Talend Integration Express as an enhanced version of Talend Open Studio that enables collaborative development and deployment and execution monitoring, Talend Open Source ETL Solution for BI for analytical and operational data integration. Talend also supports the functionality to leverage Hadoop/MapReduce in its Data Integration framework.

Talend leverages start-of-the-industry and next-generation technologies like SOA-enabled and IOA-centric information (integration) architecture as well as real-time and right-time data delivery by using data virtualization and semantic data integration capabilities. Talend's Web site is www.talend.com.

expressor 3.0 Community Edition

This is an open source next-generation data integration suite consisting of expressor Studio—a complete and user-friendly data integration module with built-in reusable ETL mappings. Distinctly differentiating in its ability to provide effective and efficient semantic data integration by way of its Semantic Types, expressor 3.0 enables dynamic point-to-point data mappings, faster processing via its embedded engine and an expert peer community for collaboration and support. Further information is available at www.expressor-software.com/products-overview.htm and www.expressor-Studio.com.

Astera's Centerprise Data Integration Platform

This is another next-generation DI platform that provides a user-friendly visual, drag-and-drop platform that enables and accelerates the development, testing, and deployment of the complex integration flows with the flexibility and efficiency of customizable integration intervals, high-performance big-data processing, built-in data validation and profiling—all at an optimal TCO/ROC ratio. Additional information can be found at www.astera.com.

Pervasive Software's Integration Suite

This is Pervasive Software's unique and innovative integration solution for connecting cloud-based systems and applications to on-premise ones in a universally interoperable fashion. And this includes data integration to information management across any existing or cloud-enabled solution, end to end. The collateral products Pervasive DataSolutions and Pervasive Business Xchange enable the same level of connectivity, with the former tailored toward popular business and consumer applications such as SAP, EPM, and ERP, and the latter suited for B2B information interchange. One typical use of both of these (or the latter alone) was in architecting recently trending information exchanges like the HIE (Health Information Exchange) that extend information sharing beyond the data sharing functionality. The Web site www.pervasive.com has the relevant in-depth details about these products and the technologies underneath and use cases of each.

5.10.2   EDW: Models to Management

The top-ranked EDW vendors in the industry are InfoBright (an analytic database vendor), Vertica (a virtualized analytic database), MySQL (the most popular open source RDBMS) and Ingres VectorWise (the breakthrough industry-recognized open source DB and analytics engine that enables extreme parallelization and vectorization to enhance and accelerate CPU-aware computation, independent of the DB/EDW involved. This is a powerful tool for high-performance analytics that involve CPU-intensive data processing).

When it comes to advanced analytics, Interop Cache, Hadoop/MapReduce (from Google), Objectivity, McObjects precision management, EnterpriseDB, AsterData (and Aster nCluster), and Noetix Analytics are the primary candidates.

The top-ranked Hadoop Projects for advanced analytics and big data–centered BI include:

- Cascading (a JVM-based library and API for creating and consolidating complex data-intensive processes into a single deployable JAR file callable from the CLI or via a shell)
- Mahout (an efficient AI-based library for generating intelligent analytics on a Hadoop cluster of datasets)
- Hive (a way to query a Hadoop cluster by using a SQL-compliant language called QL; very useful for needles in haystacks of big data in the range of petabytes)
- AVRO (a data serialization engine for Hadoop, useful for "vanilla flattening" complex unstructured datasets)
- STORM (a real-time Hadoop-free engine for a fast and efficient stack-based load balancer for optimized resource utilization)

For cloud-based EDW, advanced analytics, and predictive analytics, OpCloud, Electric Cloud, and RightScale enable the effective and efficient development, implementation, deployment, information sharing, pervasive storage, and extensibility of data to information, to applications, to multi-tenancy-enabled solutions, and to efficient orchestration and management of cloud-centric hosting, integration, and hybrid implementations.

5.10.3   BI: Models to Interaction to Management to Strategic Business Decision Support (via Analytics and Visualization)

As open source adoption is increasingly going mainstream, the power and potential of open source BI as a viable alternative for existing and new BI deployments is becoming recognized, from the front office to the cross-corporate business domain. The following paragraphs describe some BI vendor products/tools that are among the top five trending and next generation solutions—from community to commercial editions that enable a rich, robust, and trustable implementation, including collaboration, architecture, functionality, scalability, and next-gen technology compliance, such as enabling HADOOP integration, SaaS-enabling and SaaS-enabled, and the like.

Actuate BIRT BI Platform

Actuate BIRT is the leading "pure play" traditional BI platform that enables rich and robust reporting, including OLAP-centric analytical and production reporting with operational BI and mobile BI, scaling to the multiterabyte level and enabling load balancing. Actuate BIRT components include its reputed iServer and eReports, BIRT Data Objects for in-database/in-memory analysis, and the BIRT iPhone application and BIRT Mobile Virtual Appliance for BI on the go (a combination of BIRT onDemand and BIRT Mobile Viewer). Actuate BIRT also provides the ability to integrate with any open source OEM for data integration, EDW, or business analytics. Additionally, Actuate BIRT provides a BIRT onDemand Smart SaaS Solution for BI and Reporting (that is implemented as a platform-as-a-service, or PaaS) for true hosting, or cloud-enabling the same. It also enables rich (geo-)data visualization by way of its Flash Maps and Map It (Google Maps) components. Actuate BIRT is a part of the Eclipse project and supports the Eclipse IDE. Additional information is available at www.birtexchange.org and www.BIRTonDemand.com.

JasperSoft Enterprise

Jaspersoft Enterprise is by far the most pervasive open source BI solution in terms of its BI domain inclusion, full-fledged functionality, and scalability. Its product suite includes JasperReports and iReports for core reporting; JasperServer for repository, security, dash boarding, ad hoc querying, and in-memory analysis; JasperAnalysis for OLAP, and also uses industry-standard open source components such as Talend for DI, InfoBright (an analytical database),Vertica (a virtualized analytical database) and Ingres VectorWise for EDW, integrates System R for advanced analytics, and RightScale (a cloud management platform) as its end-to-end orchestration bus to run BI natively in a cloud environment. The key JasperSoft differentiators are its ability to be both a "free and open source solution" (or FOSS) and a "commercial open source solution" (or COSS) at the same time, unprecedented support for multitenancy, mash-up dashboarding (dynamically), SaaS-enabling and SaaS-enabled BI capabilities, and Hadoop integration, which makes it one of the most competitive BI solutions in terms of scalability of open source BI. Further information is available at www.jaspersoft.com.

Pentaho Enterprise BI Suite

Pentaho Enterprise offers a comprehensive and integrated open source BI suite with almost full ownership of components. The Pentaho BI Suite comprises Pentaho Reporting, its enterprise reporting module; Kettle for ETL Integration; Mondrian-based OLAP with a graphical user interface (GUI) based on JPivot and an interactive dashboard interface from Lucidera; and advanced analytics based on Weka. Pentaho's uniqueness lies in its capability for Hadoop Integration and the tight integration of components across its BI stack, thereby providing the extra benefit of simpler and better impact and data lineage analysis as well as solution-centric troubleshooting. Additional details are available at www.pentaho.com.

KNIME (Konstanz Information Miner)

This product offers a user-friendly and comprehensive open source data integration, computation, interactive analysis, and exploration platform that delivers scalable and efficient predictive analytics for EDW/BI by way of big data discovery, mining, and analysis that is visualization-enabled and powered by artificial intelligence–driven design patterns. This is a key driver for deriving inherent yet invisible data relationships in unstructured data, including those involving semantics. Details about the KNIME platform and its included enterprise products can be found at www.KNIME.com.

Pervasive DataRush

This is a great product for architecting highly scalable and parallel-computation-centric data mining and predictive analytics frameworks, especially those involving graph-based rich data, semantic Web–based data, and similar other very large database (VLDB)–related BI, including operational BI. This is also a product of Pervasive Software.

Pervasive DataCloud2

This is in line with other Pervasive Software products; it is highly efficient and productive PaaS that lets businesses of any size, any data volume(s) and any data-based requirements to design, develop, and deploy a EDW/BI cloud-based solution in a "My Cloud, My Way" flexible manner and at a fraction of the cost of enterprise/proprietary solutions. Currently enabled for AWS, Microsoft Azure, and Force.com, this product eases the cost, size and complexity of anytime, anywhere, anyone EDW/BI solution availability and personalization. Further details can be found at http://cloud.pervasive.com.

5.11 Best Practices: Use and Reuse

An open source–based solution model is a richer and actionable solution model that is as live in its functionality as much as it is open:

- Agile, aligned (synchronous), and adaptable (in terms of flexibility for personalization and extendibility); and context-centric, risk-aware
- Continuous, consumer-centric, collaborative, and competition-enabled
- Simplified, secure, and scalable (highly)

Taking these factors into account and the architectures underneath as explained in the earlier sections, here's a list of best practices that can be followed to help achieve a next level EDW/BI implementation:

- *Dynamic data warehousing*, providing the capability to derive, subsume, or consume a consumer-centric EDW on demand from a centralized DW or data mart targeted toward a specific consumer, as opposed to a specific business-context or delivery platform or functionality—from its core to all of its corners. This is, in other words, placing the controls in the hands of the consumer to input specifications on demand that are used by the underlying DW or data mart architecture to construct a personalized "my data warehouse, my way" instance of the EDW.
- *Dynamic and elastic integration of EDW with advanced analytics*, using data virtualization as a enabler and accelerator, and realizing business analytics as formalized metrics containing common core content augmented by domain-specific KPI.

- *Dynamic and elastic integration of BI and business analytics* to result in intelligent business informatics.
- *Unifying user interface and user experience*, based on the usability experience measured as a numeric indicator of confidence and strategic value.
- *SQL-enabled API exposure*, for any and all involving EDW/BI platforms-as-a-service.
- *On-demand transformation of EDW/BI model* to an open source consortium-compliant format that is externally URL-accessible or downloadable, and vice-versa.
- *Open source as open cloud*, providing cloud enablement in terms of state-full and secure backup and restoration, online processing, physical-to-virtual dynamic provisioning, automatic deployment and decommissioning, and interoperability with the semantic Web, Web 2.0, and social networking platforms.
- *Self-serviceable BI for a self-adaptable BI solution*, because the adaptability of a solution is its ability in dynamically and consistently respond to feedback or failures to the point of success as the surrounding content and/or context change. This quintessential for an EDW/BI solution that is self-serviceable.

5.12   Summary

This chapter concentrated on the open source DW and BI design methodologies. Starting with a brief discussion on the classification of DW and BI aspects based on scope of business and purpose of use in the context of business operations and business users, it goes on to emphasize the key design considerations therein, the architecture of the essential open source EDW/BI solution components (such as the data and information management layer, the EDW layer, and the BI layer) and concludes by outlining the best practices to follow for a best-fit pragmatics implementation. The next chapter delves into similar aspects of BI from the operational BI perspective and discusses why operational BI is critical in today's business dynamics.

Chapter 6

Operational BI and Open Source

6.1 In This Chapter

- Why a Separate Chapter on Operational BI and Open Source?
- Operational BI by Dissection
- Design and Architecture Considerations for Operational BI
- Why, When and How Operational BI Plays a Significant Role
- Operational BI Data Architecture: Under the Hood
- A Reusable Information Integration Model: From Real Time to Right Time
- Operational BI Architecture: Under the Hood
- Fitting Open Source Vendor/Platform Product(s)/Tools(s) into the Operational BI Architecture
- Best Practices: Use and Reuse

To delve into the architecture of a open source DW and BI solution for operational BI, it is critical to note that the design considerations underneath *do not* necessarily translate one-on-one with the analogous algorithms, techniques and best practices. This chapter outlines the details of the same from an operational BI perspective. The opening section gives a brief description of what operational BI has that's missing from the rest of BI, and why that missing functionality is so necessary for BI implementation. Though the key business indicators of open source DW and BI remain the same from the customer-centricity, usability, and value points of view, there are certain key technofunctional and business–social standpoints that require quite a different design for optimal scalability, services, and value. The essential components requiring change are the *access–adopt–automate–adapt* mechanisms and the *real time–to–right time information analysis–to–delivery* being treated as isolated yet possibly mutually exclusive design paradigms, with operational BI as a byproduct of the rest of BI but the vice-versa being possible. This means that an operational BI solution can co-exist without an EDW across the pervasive BI landscape. The sections that follow elaborate on these specific aspects, highlighting the need for the same and for the architecture of the inherent solution components involved—focusing on the data and information management and the BI layers (and seemingly ignoring the EDW layer). It concludes by outlining the best practices to put in place for a best fit and successful implementation.

6.2   Why a Separate Chapter on Operational BI and Open Source?

Operational BI provides the capability to stream dynamic updates to constantly changing data in transactional information systems directly to the BI user interface (UI), bypassing the EDW on an as-is (near real–time) basis, continuously and consistently, so that the BI analyses, reporting, visualizations, and predictive analytics that require this information get it in a timely and accurate manner. This functionality is of primary importance to actionable decision making at the speed of business (operations). Hence an exclusive chapter on operational BI is necessary for the following reasons:

1.   Time-critical data is needed for many BI solutions to derive analytics based on the same as the data is being created or changed—sometimes in subsecond intervals. This means the currency of the data is so material that it is to be delivered in sync one-on-one, with state of its creation aligning with the state of its delivery to a near 360° level of accuracy. Add a geospatial attribute to this and it means the BI solution needs to access and process the operational data as if all of it were residing local to the BI—independent of the time and location where it is being sourced. Examples are BI solutions are required to be situation aware, such as those analyzing microblogged data, networking traffic, and surveillance information generated in real time as the associated events are occurring. The typical BI use cases for the same provide fine-grained visibility into real-life events and capture the relevant information for just-in-time reporting, as well as autogeneration of metadata based on the raw data in real time. Examples of this are high-volume big-data traffic in networking and communications, as well as health information exchanges that include patient monitoring systems to monitor the "live" status of subjects in lifesaving situations or detect any "live-wire" anomalies arising from the same.

2. BI solutions can enable and accelerate continuous and competitive intelligence by extracting business value from data market trending in real time and applying high-performance analytics to the same to derive productive metrics that can aid in constant and comparative decision support, enabling the business to stay ahead of the competition. A typical use case for this is *prediction-based BI using real-time data visualization*.

3. Intelligent feedback recognition and response are necessary to enable and enhance self-serviceability for self-adaptability of the BI solution, based on real-time capture of the end-to-end user experience one-on-one with the business operations lifecycle. This functionality will create and/or evolve a context-aware, risk-aware, consumer-centric, and data-driven intelligent feedback recognition and response system. A typical use case for this is autoevolving the BI solution for better business competency, sustainable competition, and come-back customer experience lifecycle.

6.3   Operational BI by Dissection

Operational BI is emerging as a new dimension of mainstream BI, specifically when autogenerated data growth is increasing at an alarming rate. This is addition to the OLTP transactional data being created all the time. The primary difference between autogenerated (otherwise called machine-generated) data and the OLTP data is the former is created as the latter is being created—in the form of click-streams, Web-generated data such as social content or online content that is syndicated in real-time, log-based data resulting from fine-grained monitoring such as network logs and activity logs, telecommunications-based CDRs, and sensory content that are created faster than business operations, as well as markets-based trading systems. This data carries a lot of meaningful content in terms of the underlying patterns and variations that directly translate to customer behaviors, usage trends, collaborative content as it happens in real life, and so on; it is a top-tier candidate for analysis and study for further improvisation and intelligence. However, given the huge volume of the same and the fast rate at which it is generated, a high-bandwidth, high-throughput analytic engine is needed for the mining, analysis, visualization, and reporting of the same. This has introduced a next level of analysis to traditional BI processing (which can include big data too, but is primarily persistent in nature, is populated on a frequency basis, and is preanalyzed for aggregation, summarization, and optimization).

The pragmatics of Operational BI as a next-level BI spectrum include:

- *Intelligent information integration*: Anyone–anytime–anywhere access, combined with right-data, right-user, right-job, right-time delivery directly from an information system that is transactional in nature. This means there is no scope for partial transaction isolation when it comes to data delivery. In other words, information needs to be pulled from the OLTP system as it is being committed there, with near-zero latency and converted, processed, analyzed, and delivered to the BI system synchronously. This process demands compute-intensive and data-intensive operations, as the traditional EDW processes like extract-transform-load (ETL), aggregation, and analytics need to converge into one single-pass process that is extremely dynamic and time-sensitive. The key necessary ingredient is data quality assurance of the operational data. The pragmatics demand a convergence of architecture, alignment, and automation of the EDW/BI processes to work in coherence and continuous collaboration by optimizing the time-to-analysis, thereby performing ultra-fast analysis of the operational data without worrying about the EDW and the associated mechanisms for faster query execution.

  - Extract the transactional data live from heterogeneous sources in multiple formats, which can include external file systems, nonrelational data, unstructured data, and data with deep-dive hierarchical relationships embedded in them. This has some overhead in terms of performance when traditional ETL processes are used to handle the data extraction, profiling, cleansing, and federation involved.
  - Conform to the custom BI solution in place with respect to Web scalability, computational complexity, and 24×7 availability. This in turn cascades to the unstructured-to-structured data processing and rendering, which can involve on-disk-like object data to relational data mappings and the contextual semantics. Of greater value is such data with embedded semantic relationships.
  - Keep operational BI metrics effective and continuous to obtain improved business value from them and improve the visibility of operational landscape, providing better decision support and evolution beyond BI.

- *The combination of virtual data federation, data virtualization, and elastic caching* with an SOA-centric data-in-transit transmission and delivery mechanism enables information analytics in an "as-is" state. This is used to perfect the master data management strategy of the overall BI solution by simultaneously identifying, deidentifying, and generating business-critical metadata on the same and syncing it with the EDW master data management (MDM) repository or otherwise as an independent MDM module.

This eminence of operational BI does not in any way make the world of BI any smaller than it was before, and the rest of BI is equally important as operational BI for any enterprise needing converged analysis of transactional and historical data. To this day, almost every business needs the historical data in place, immaterial of the period of retention of such data for purposes like trend-based reporting and forecasting, such as the legendary projections and proposals for capital-expense needs and/or strategic-directional roadmaps. The compare-and-contrast between the two is explained in Table 6.1.

Table 6.1 Comparison and contrast between operational BI and the rest of BI.

Operational BI	Rest of BI
Enables just-in-time analysis and insight, as is required in situations like generating performance ranking score-cards as the scores are being generated in a real-life contest, and auto-dense-ranking the cards, determining the standard deviation relative to current situational attributes, and determining the best among the best.	Typically enables point-in-time analyses on persistent data—historical or once transactional in nature—that has been conformed to current EDW requirements; usually the data is aggregated, summarized, and optimized for faster querying purposes.
Typically does not include large number of dimensional attributes (i.e., columns) for analysis	May or may not include large column-based analyses
Primarily uses data virtualization (dynamic construction of virtual viewlets of information) and elastic caching to accelerate and automate the information consumption, customization and delivery—live in-memory processing	Primarily uses storage-based data access, a combination of disk-based, in-database, and in-memory processing including data virtualization, clustering, and a predefined and dimensional data model optimized for storage and query efficiency

Table 6.1　Comparison and contrast between operational BI and the rest of BI.

Operational BI	Rest of BI
Has no special query optimization needs for subsecond response like indexing, partitioning or fine-grained tuning on a regular basis. Typically column-oriented in nature, with operational data involving multiple record-like columns being flattened into a single columnar storage format topped by intelligent knowledge grids that enable on-the-fly fast analysis by way of being query-aware.	Generally row-oriented in nature, in case of traditional DW by way of a dimensional ROLAP/OLAP model and augmented by column-based dynamic grids that store/analyze information on an aggregated basis. This requires special indexing, partitioning, and projections of data-subsets, with cube-based preprocessing for faster querying and storage.
When it comes to data visualization involving large number of column dimensions, a columnar data model delivers a highly scalable and efficient performance.	Though analytical and high-performing in nature, traditional BI systems that rely on noncolumnar orientation are suited for historical analysis involving a lesser degree of columnar dimensionality, even when the data volumes are high.
Does not alter the state of the existing EDW unless the operational data involved is stored in the EDW. Sometimes it is two-way buffering of the same data, with the transactional simultaneously federated to the BI system and to the EDW without losing currency and consistency.	Typically alters the state of the existing EDW, as it uses the same as the primary information source for BI analysis.
An open source architectural approach delivers the best-fit solution in an easier, better, faster, and cheaper manner to both these types of BI, by intelligently enabling and accelerating the dynamic combination of both approaches depending on the data itself at the point of analysis. This means it has the ability to leverage the context of the data values and learn from them in cross-correlation with subjective and objective patterns of the data element(s) in question— and derive the optimal approach to query the same, using a combination of supervised, unsupervised, and statistical algorithms, enhanced compute-efficient techniques like Hadoop/MapReduce and NoSQL, and seamlessly coupled object-relational and in-memory processing.	

Hence, it is worthy enough to state that operational BI is not a replacement for the rest of BI, but an extension to the rest of BI for efficient analysis and reporting of OLTP data and new data that is generated in real-time. Therefore, operational augments the capabilities of the rest of BI solutions in today's information ecosystem by way of being adaptive one-on-one with the changes taking place therein.

Intelligent information integration by way of availability, security, integrity, and information assurance is and must be the central requirement for any EDW solution, and an open source solution aids in an simpler-better-faster-cheaper implementation of deployment of the same for faster time to delivery and faster time to insight, as well as better insight and sometimes getting beyond BI. And the corresponding criteria boil down to the following enlisted set:

- Streamline and semantically align structured/unstructured data using data services, data integration services, and/or real-time embeddability (for data in store, data in motion, and data as it is being created)—from the point of ingestion to the point of interpretation (insight)
- Virtualization of data, data-views, databases, dashboards, and mashboards—cross-(business)-dimensions and cross-(user)-contexts, and irrespective of time, space, or location
- Virtual data federation in place of in-memory data replication for real-time, right-time data syndication; materialization and distributed data replication to service high volume–based high-performance queries
- Dynamic streaming of any or all of the above, from data sourcing to storage (in-memory or persistent) to synchronization to syndication to semantic-visualization (anytime, anywhere, anyone)
- Collaborative and noncollaborative shareability of data with internal (existing, on premise, within the enterprise scope) and external applications (beyond the enterprise scope, yet needed/added on-demand; cloud-based; or other extranet based)
- Improvisation of KPI-based analytics for consistency, currency, and continuity in terms of business-operational efficiency and customer-user experience—the key indicator here to note is that integration and improvisation of new/variant data impacts the associated business processes in context, and more often in a deterministic manner. Hence, agility, mobility, and visibility are the key imperatives to be taken into account. This is especially critical when the analysis involves complex datasets with interrelated data elements—identifying the hidden relationships and establishing a symbolic linkage that can translate optimally to business semantics.

- Automation and acceleration by way of hybrid methodologies—blending test-driven development (TDD) with model-driven design and solution/code accelerators; unit testing blended with simulation and emulation (elevation, escalation) of core, as well as surrounding functionality

If evolution by way of enterprise feedback management (EFM) and back-looping of the same by way of additional and/or optimized business rules/metrics is one side of moving beyond BI, measuring performance in a quantifiable fashion—in a constantly dynamic data/information lifecycle—from production to perfection. Involving multiplexed, multiflex, and context-aware semantics—and exponentially exploding in volume—is the other inevitable side of getting beyond BI, also referred as continuous operational intelligence on live, streamed data, or competitive intelligence.

6.4   Design and Architecture Considerations for Operational BI

The case for architecture as a precedence factor can be argued from any perspective—from design to design patterns to methodologies to mechanisms in action. But the business value of architecture as a key benefactor for any software solution in general and any EDW/BI in particular is tangibly seen when *operational BI is built as an inherent component of such a solution by way of a building a streamlined BI in flow to BI on the go solution, taking the following stated imperatives about design and architecture as key quintessential indicators for the pragmatics of such a solution realization*:

- Big data poses greater challenges when it comes to realizing actionable insight and true business value from this data, especially when such data is in its raw form—and this might not necessarily be compatible with the target BI format.
- Leveraging cloud is a big benefit for solving this problem, from design to delivery and cloud integration of the same; functioning in isolation from the rest the EDW/BI components is as challenging as it is demanding.
- Creating an effective measurable performance strategy, from design to delivery:
  - From data sourcing to semantic transformation to dynamic metadata creation and processing to advanced analytics creation, the rules of the game deviate variably from the standard

case of through-the-EDW BI—*operational BI demands a design that is persistent and variable at the same time.*

■ From applications to applicationlets to application-intelligent bots, the formal design, design patterns, architecture, and orchestration of the same differ in significant contrast.

- Applying dynamic data federation, streaming, and end-point computing (in-memory database [IMDB], embeddable analytics engine, high-performing SQL-enabled API and XML-serviced (remote) method invocation) for mobility, visibility, and agility—from architecture to access ability to availability to standards-enabled optimization to audit-enabled governance, as well as automation of the same.

- No compromising on relevancy of the information presented; because operational BI gets to the data as it is being changed, any latency that is sufficient enough to change the state of the data when it was created and the state of the same data when it reaches the BI platform is critical to the relevancy of the same—all along the way in its journey to the dashboard. For example, though the changed (in this case new) data is federated to the operational BI engine, still it might be necessary to mash it up with existing data in the EDW to get the "relevant" result set (e.g., to report the number of prospective customers for a CRM-based BI application). Data from a transactional CRM system like Salesforce.com or eSalestrack.com, which is dynamically sourced to the BI engine via virtual data federation, must be combined in near real–time with those already existing in the EDW for the same primary business dimensions.

6.5   Operational BI Data Architecture: Under the Hood

Real-time data interoperability is the key driver for implementing operational BI and is needed for right-time information management, from reporting to real-world business analytics in action. The architecture must also enable merging of this real-time data with machine-generated data in a coherent and consistent fashion (and sometimes support the on-demand grid-elasticity of adding/removing OLTP data sources on the fly). Hence, the design components for such architecture typically involve the following:

- Identification and validation of operational data sources needed
- Data quality, portability, and assurance

- Scalability
- User authentication mechanisms
- Data transmission mechanisms
- Data security checkpoints
- Operational data attributes: form, format, size, whether future-proof in its variability or static after an incremental period; whether multitenant in serviceability; location dependent or not, in addition to time dependency; how self-manageable it will be post-BI
- Structured storage with or without co-location
- Business rules centralization with semantic personalization—This levels out the entire enterprise usability experience on the common grounds of being naïve and native in delivering the same user-friendly experience immaterial of the technology, architecture and delivery platforms.
- SaaS-enabled/-enabling open source (cloud) platforms.
- Adherence to industry-relevant, international, and regulatory standards without compromising on the core open source specifications. These include the information-oriented architecture (IOA) devised by The Bloor Group, which levels out the dynamic interoperability between the BI world and the non-BI world (those who need the information from an operational BI system from an operations standpoint)—but existing as two disparate systems and communicating with each other using data services and data integration services
- Painless migration, dynamic capacity planning and multiworkload balancing, and continuous workflow orchestration.
- Impact of operational data movement pre- and post-BI, including those of governance and lifecycle management

Putting the above principles into practice involves the following implementation mechanisms for an operational BI data architecture (OBIDA):

1. A comprehensive *data virtualization* engine that enables the mix/mash/merge of *operational data* and *enterprise data*. Either of these can be big data or mission-critical data. This is also comprised of application-aware adapters that emulate the "native" capabilities of the consuming application.

2.   An *in-memory analytics* engine that enables high-performing data-intensive computations for subsecond query responses that incorporate virtual data federation (as opposed to replication) and distributed caching. In other words, it seeks to maintain an "always-available" active cluster of postcomputation consolidated datasets in memory that can serve as disconnected infolets.

3.   A *dynamic data contextualization* engine that is modular and data context–aware, generating data services and data integration services on the fly to intelligently decide the data and the relevant processing and delivery algorithms needed, based solely on the input data itself and its linked relationships—to construct a context around the resulting data that satisfies the user request in a best-fit manner. This in a way adapts to the data changes in relevance and responds with an optimized execution mechanism thereby providing the business–social enterprise with information on a wider range of amplitudes, as well as introducing self-serviceability.

4.   An *advanced predictive analytics engine* that uses data mining–driven prediction-based rules with those from descriptive analysis to dynamically graph the linkage among the past, present, and (probably tangible) future trends. This can be stored as a *predictive business informatics model* for reusability in the BI layer.

5.   A *cloud-enabled data delivery and cloud-enabling data integration* engine that enables:

   a.   Push-pull data consolidation in the cloud and in a collaborative manner across functional domains securely and instantly—a critical requirement for operational BI—thereby allowing real-time decision making that's better purposed for taking actions. By using a private or hybrid cloud, such as CloudOne, OpCloud, or Salesforce.com Chatter, operational BI can be implemented in one single platform—without worrying about the IT hardening required in traditional environments.

   b.   Open source–based model generation of the same to result in an IOA-centric *pervasive cloud-based integration (PCI) model.*

6.6　A Reusable Information Integration Model: From Real- Time to Right Time

This subsection outlines the design patterns for business case for using the above stated PCI Model. Here are the details:

1. The key differentiator between real-time and right time, when it comes to information integration, is that the former focuses more on instant data availability as the data is created or changed, whereas the latter primarily involves timely sharing of information, immaterial of its source. Together, these two translate to the composite imperative of *anytime, anywhere, anyone* and right time/right data/right user information availability, accessibility, and interoperability, with zero (or minimal) latency, yet uncompromising in quality by way of consistency, coherency, and computability.

2. For a design that supports this composite imperative, it is necessary to leverage data virtualization and advanced analytical mechanisms to accurately access and share the data in a lossless and efficient manner. The key design patterns for implementing the same are by using changed data capture (CDC), distributed data replication, and data federation. The last two of these can be implemented by introducing virtual data federation supplemented by in-memory replication of the same in an intelligently context-aware and distributed fashion. And data virtualization is going to be the primary technique used to build this design.

3. The changed data capture (CDC) is quintessential for capturing only the deltas in real-time from operational systems, auto-syncing the changes with the rest of the data (already processed and ready-to-operate) thereby streamlining the underlying process into the information management workflow. The output from this step is redirected to the BI layer, which uses just-in-time virtual data federation and streaming replication to distribute or syndicate the final insight-enabled information to the BI engine. Sometimes the BI engine can handle the later step to achieve more consumer-centric information collaboration. Also, advanced analytical algorithms can be applied in this step to derive a higher level of intelligence by using visualization and descriptive and prediction-based analysis.

4. Having all of these steps performed in a single PCI platform accel-
    erates the time to delivery and time to insight of the necessary
    information, in a one-click install, implement, deploy fashion for
    continuous and collaborative data sharing and processing.

5. For already existing applications, a service-oriented architecture
    (SOA) data bus can be used to service this PCI component for
    enabling point-to-point data flows in a seamless and transparent
    fashion.

The business advantages from such an implementation—operational
efficiency, business continuity, and continuous BI, which sit at the core of
any operational BI solution—will drive adaptive and competitive BI.

6.7   Operational BI Architecture: Under the Hood

Operational BI is one of the primary business drivers for competitive intelligence, as it enables on-the-spot analysis of dynamic business trends as they
are happening (minus the near-zero network latency involved) without having to significantly impact any existing transactional systems or other co-
existing applications. This is a huge advantage in terms of value entitlement
for both the business and its customers, as it provides

- Instant interactivity without compromising performance
- Squares the distribution of simple to complex information, allowing flexibility at the same time

---

The new business analytics imperative is a collaborative customer experience for Intelligent Customization. This necessitates a dynamic data
warehouse supplemented by dynamic BI. The right business analytics
deliver the right time BI.

And if the techniques of data virtualization, distributed data syndication and computation, virtual data federation, real-time to right time
streaming, and asynchronous CDC are extrapolated to the application
integration level, these imperatives translate as key design indicators for an
operational BI architecture under the hood. Implementing the same is
feasible using information services and information management services—exposed via direct SQL–enabled API or as Web services in their
own relevant context. The case for using an open SQL–enabled API is

strong from the standpoint of commonality, uniformity by being database independent, native-compliant, and natural language semantics–agnostic, and the ability to be embedded or SaaS enabled.

The design pragmatics for such architecture can include:

1. Information services and information management services that encompass MDM services as similar submodule. The essential component needed here is the metadata content versus context capture, computation, and consolidation, as well as a managed metadata service that can be delivered as an open source model for managed metadata. The implementation of the same can leverage the dynamic data contextualization engine (described in the previous section) at its core, powered by bridge services that can handle the synchrony versus cumulative performance.

2. Application-to-application services that enable cross-domain information interoperability by way of continuous operational BI and elastic functionality. These services can also be componentized as process services tailored toward pervasive business analytics by transforming them into open source business process analytic models that can be further supplemented by visualizations, mash-ups, and on-demand onboarding of external content elements. A lead component of these services can be a *data mash-up engine* that functions as a dynamic data warehouse (in-memory or as an embedded engine) churning data into meaningful information—synchronizing the global content with the local context for customer-centric informatics.

3. Decisive and dedicated measures in terms of a *unified BI analytics platform*—On-premise, cloud, hybrid, computation-processing shareability; embeddable, SaaS enabling and SaaS enabled. This can be implemented by designing a model that emulates the functionality of semantic business services, intelligent autogeneration of decision rules (these can be different from the more generic business rules in context), and live dashboarding.

4. Semantic business services—On-the-fly intelligent search and contextual tagging that echo business-friendly semantics. This is necessary for *pervasive BI analytics* in terms of an engaging customer experience as it suits all types of business analysts, not just the tech-savvy. Hence, the dynamic localized tagging of the information, made accessible in a way that every business user

understands, truly does aid in simple, quick, and insightful analysis. This in turn increases the customer experience lifecycle. The implementation of the same involves data-driven extraction, segmentation, and qualification of semantic metadata using dynamic parallel processing and taxonomy construction via Web 2.0 and Web 3.0 based methodologies and text mining and structuring algorithms. This is where multiple information designs collage to form an information architecture that is both receptive and adaptive to user-interaction based input.

5. Intelligent decision rules generation based on content-context behavior of the operational data elements, whether individual or set based. This accelerates the pervasive BI process effectiveness and efficiency while still enabling dedicated business analytics at individual business unit level.

6. Business analytics frameworks that leverage the predictive informatics model with analytical insight from the BI engine—to support on-demand creation and business–process enablement of the same. This brings agility and decisive potential to the end-to-end collaborative customer landscape.

7. Application-aware intelligent selectivity based on auto-derived intelligence, leveraging the symbolic, semantic, and lineage relationships between the various data values: data virtualization versus data clustering versus hybrid approach. The resulting value proposition is customized analytics needed for location-specific operational data, to cite a typical business use case.

8. Correlated analysis of operational data from multiple interoperating systems—A KPI-driven cumulative performance scorecarding (i.e., results-centric quantification and ranking) across functional domains, business units, divisions, and departments, measured against the end-to-end customer experience in terms of satisfaction and confidence, gives a close-to-accurate picture of whether the operational BI solution lifecycle is one-on-one with the business operations lifecycle valued over the key ranking indicators (of customer-user experience). This requires fine-grained monitoring, event-based segmentation, and process-aware recognition by a deterministic results-oriented algorithm applied to heuristic behavioral patterns as input—using BI and

enterprise performance response as an open-ended metric for the point of inflection.

6.8   Fitting Open Source Vendor/Platform Product(s)/ Tools(s) into the Operational BI Architecture

This section describes some BI vendor products/tools that are among the top five trending and next generation solutions from community to commercial editions that enable rich, robust, and trustable implementation of operational BI—by way of dynamic ETL, dynamic warehousing, and on-demand BI compliance—without compromising on collaboration, architecture, functionality, scalability, and next-gen technology.

6.8.1   Talend Data Integration

Talend Open Studio enables collaborative development and deployment, as well as execution monitoring. Talend Open Source ETL Adapters (both SOA based and business process compliant) enable analytical and operational data integration on demand into the BI system(s). Talend's Open Source Adapters support dynamic ETL and data warehousing in accordance with the target BI platform's specific nativity and efficiency, making Talend uniquely poised to become the open source vendor of choice, for providing the most flexible and comprehensive information integration and intelligence platform – for any BI domain and competition. Almost any EDW/BI Solution that is open standards–compliant from data to dashboard can leverage Talend ETL and DI engines that can be easily and efficiently integrated into new or online environments. This seems to be a huge plus for customer-friendly solution adoption.

6.8.2   expressor 3.0 Community Edition

This is an open source next-generation data integration suite consisting of *expressor Studio*, a complete and user-friendly data integration module with built-in reusable ETL mappings. It retains the same level of its distinct differentiation when it comes to operational BI, in its ability to provide effective and efficient semantic data integration. *expressor* DI stands out as a pervasive open source vendor for operational BI, where semantic integration of any/all types of information can be plain-transformed in a business rules of context–compliant manner—yielding the same or higher value in terms of business scope and customer experience. Additional details are available at www.expressor-software.com/products-overview.htm and www.expressorStudio.com.

6.8.3 Advanced Analytics Engines for Operational BI

Interop Cache, Hadoop/MapReduce (from Google), Objectivity, McObjects precision management, EnterpriseDB, AsterData (and Aster nCluster)—all of these products support on-demand and XML-enabled real-time analytics. And the cloud-based dynamic EDW/advanced analytics/predictive analytics providers, such as OpCloud, Electric Cloud, or RightScale, enable the effective and efficient development, implementation, deployment, information sharing, pervasive storage, and extensibility of data to information, to applications, to multitenancy-enabled solutions, and on to efficient orchestration and management of cloud-centric hosting, integration, and hybrid implementations.

6.8.4 Astera's Centerprise Data Integration Platform

This is another next-generation DI platform that provides a user-friendly, visual, drag-and-drop platform that enables and accelerates the development, testing, and deployment of the complex integration flows with the flexibility and efficiency of customizable integration intervals, high-performance big-data processing, and built-in data validation and profiling—all at an optimal TCO/ROC ratio. Additional information can be found at www.astera.com.

6.8.5 Actuate BIRT BI Platform

Actuate BIRT is the leading "pure play" BI platform, enabling rich and robust reporting for operational BI and mobile BI—scaling to the multiterabyte level and enabling load balancing. Actuate BIRT components include its reputed iServer and eReports, BIRT Data Objects for in-database/in-memory analysis, and the BIRT iPhone application and BIRT Mobile Virtual Appliance for BI-on-the-go (a combination of BIRT onDemand and BIRT Mobile Viewer). Actuate BIRT also provides the ability to integrate with any open source OEM (original equipment manufacturer) for data integration, EDW, or business analytics. Additionally, Actuate BIRT provides a BIRT onDemand Smart SaaS Solution for BI and reporting (implemented as PaaS) for true hosting or cloud-enabling the same. It also enables rich (geo-)data visualization via its Flash Maps and Map It (Google Maps) components. Actuate BIRT is a part of the Eclipse project and supports the Eclipse IDE. Additional information is available at www.birt-exchange.org and www.BIRTonDemand.com.

6.8.6   JasperSoft Enterprise

Jaspersoft Enterprise is by far the most pervasive open source BI solution in terms of its BI domain inclusion, full-fledged functionality, and scalability. Its product suite includes JasperReports and iReports for core reporting; JasperServer for repository, security, dashboarding, ad hoc querying, and in-memory analysis; and JasperAnalysis for OLAP; it also uses the industry-standard open source components such as Talend for DI, InfoBright (an analytical database),Vertica (a virtualized analytical database) and Ingres VectorWise for EDW. Additionally, it integrates System R for advanced analytics and uses RightScale (a cloud management platform) as its end-to-end orchestration bus to run BI natively in a cloud environment. The key JasperSoft differentiators are its ability to be both a "free and open source source solution" (FOSS) and a "commercial open source solution" (COSS) at the same time, its unprecedented support for multitenancy, its mash-up dashboarding (dynamic), its SaaS-enabling and SaaS-enabled BI capabilities, and its Hadoop integration, all of which combine to make it one of the most competitive BI solutions in terms of scalability of open source BI. Further information is available at www.jaspersoft.com.

6.8.7   Pentaho Enterprise BI Suite

Pentaho Enterprise offers a comprehensive and integrated open source BI suite with almost full ownership of components. Pentaho BI Suite comprises Pentaho Reporting, its enterprise reporting module; Kettle for ETL integration; Mondrian-based OLAP with a GUI based on JPivot and an interactive dashboard interface from Lucidera; and advanced analytics based on Weka. Pentaho's uniqueness lies in its capability for Hadoop integration and the tight integration of components across its BI stack, thereby providing the extra benefit of simpler and better impact and data lineage analysis as well as solution-centric troubleshooting. Additional details are available at www.pentaho.com.

6.8.8   KNIME (Konstanz Information Miner)

This product offers a user-friendly and comprehensive open source data integration, computation, interactive analysis and exploration platform that delivers scalable and efficient predictive analytics for Operational BI by way of big data discovery, mining and analysis that is visualization-enabled and powered by artificial intelligence driven design patterns. This is a key driver for deriving inherent yet invisible data relationships in unstructured data including those involving semantics. Details about the KNIME platform and its included enterprise products can be found at www.KNIME.com.

6.8.9   Pervasive DataRush

This is a great product for architecting highly scalable and parallel-computation-centric data mining and predictive analytics frameworks, especially those involving graph-based rich data, semantic Web–based data and similar other very large database (VLDB)–related operational BI.

6.8.10   Pervasive DataCloud2

This is in line with other Pervasive Software products; it is highly efficient and productive PaaS that lets businesses of any size, any data volume(s), and any data-based requirements to design, develop, and deploy a operational BI cloud-based solution in a "My Cloud, My Way" flexible manner and at a fraction of the cost of enterprise/proprietary solutions. Currently enabled for AWS, Microsoft Azure, and Force.com, it eases the cost, size, and complexity of anytime–anywhere–anyone BI solution availability and personalization. Further details can be found at cloud.pervasive.com.

6.9   Best Practices: Use and Reuse

The operational BI component of an open source EDW/BI solution enables agile business operations by allowing the consumer–customer–competitor to use the inherent business functionality that the solution was intended to support in an efficient, effective, and extensible manner for the lifecycle of the business in context. By being able to implement the business processes that accelerate continuous operational integration and business continuity (including on-demand needs), operational BI seems to keep the business (processes) in motion, syncing the near real–time and right time information access, analytics, and availability—for the duration of the enterprise information lifecycle, as well as for the lifecycle of the business operations—independent of the lifecycle of the technologies and tools involved. And the use of open source architecture(s) for implementing such a solution makes this methodology more systemic, holistic, next-generational, and tangible. This directly produces the following use cases that can be standardized as best practices in terms of intelligent use and reuse:

1.   An architectural design that meets both tactile and strategic business informatics by way of real-time and right time analytics, predictive and decisive, and one that scores high in terms of proactive metrics, measurement, and management of actionable business decisions, as well as from the trustable assurance point of view. This paves the path for deriving an intelligent operational BI delivery model from the implemented architecture that can be used as a universal *open source software operational BI delivery model* across functional boundaries, deployment boundaries, and programming language boundaries, including those that are 4GL, AI-based, API-based, and declarative.

2.   A strong use case of using such a methodology can be to extract and deliver operational BI metrics of high function-ranking value as a reusable model that can be integrated with existing/other enterprise applications, including legacy, at a fraction of the cost and multiple times the quality—all using a lightweight footprint.

3.   Another much-needed business case for using such a model can be the pervasive integration and implementation of an EPM-centric performance tracking, profiling, measurement, analysis, reporting, and optimization.

Such an EPM-centric model can serve as the foundational framework for any EDW/BI tailored solution by way of an intelligent performance analytics model that is facts-based and authentic in terms of quality of metrics; communicative and collaborative for cross-touch-point integration and informatics; and available in open source–based and extensible access management (XAM) formats such as UML models, XML models, or other IOA-compliant formats. This makes the solution both evolutionary and revolutionary. An exemplary implementation of this can be to effectively, efficiently and adaptively integrate proprietary EDW/BI solutions with existing EPM systems, using a common metrics model for performance management.

6.10 Summary

This chapter described the open source DW and BI design methodologies for operational BI solutions and support. Starting with a brief discussion on the scope of operational BI and its purpose of use in the context of business operations and business users, the chapter goes on to emphasize the reasons that operational BI deserves special architectures for information integration and describe the key business contexts and content one on one. It concludes by outlining the best practices to follow for a best-fit pragmatics implementation. The next chapter delves into solution aspects of EDW/BI, but with the primary focus on the development and deployment of such a solution using open source methodologies.

Chapter 7

Development and Deployment

7.1 In this Chapter

- Development Options, Dissected
- Deployment Options, Dissected
- Integration Options, Dissected
  - Multisource, Multidimension
- DW and BI Usability and Deployment: Best Solution versus Best-Fit Solution
- Leveraging the Best-Fit Solution: Primary Considerations
  - Better, Easier, Faster as the Hitchhiker's Rule
  - Dynamism and Flash—Real Output in Real Time in Real World
  - Interactivity
  - Better Responsiveness, User Adoptability, and Transparency (of Underlying Analytics)
- Fitting the Vendor/Platform Product(s)/tTools(s): A Development and Deployment Standpoint
- Best Practices: Use and Reuse

7.2 Introduction

When it comes to using open source methodologies for implementing the *Open Source Perfect* solution for enterprise data warehouse/business intelligence (EDW/BI), the development options come in independent choices that are compliant with the primary selection criteria of architectural design; ease complexity; are proven in terms of performance; are flexible, including the ability to undo changes with minimal overhead; and are customer-certified. Still, the selected options can be state of the art as long as they are based on open source. After all, this is the unique potential of open source methodologies—they come standard and grant almost 360° of freedom to the SDLC (software development life cycle) and the customer-user experience lifecycle.

7.3 Development Options, Dissected

An EDW development and deployment methodology is based on the way the EDW design has been architected, which in turn is built on the ways the requirements analysis, planning and preparation strategies have been laid out. Thus, the development options go hand-in-hand with the design options (also known as the business processes), and the deployment options go hand-in-hand with the business operations (AKA the execution of the business processes)—in other words, the execution of the design-based developed solution. Thus a good design leads to a good software solution, which in turn needs good development pragmatics. Therefore, a good deployment depends on the good design and development practices for a best-fit solution operations lifecycle. A best-fit EDW/BI option must include the following technical propositions in its design and development checklists:

- Leveraging CPU power for high-performance computing as a first priority, followed by memory-based computing, is definitely a gain from the various analytical perspectives. Combining both requires a balanced approach that optimizes speed versus the volume of data to be processed, the volume of data to be returned, the complexity of computation, the resource utilization, and the scaling factor, in addition to the {time, geolocation, access-point} variants. Although deriving a linear equation out of this is nearly impossible (to the best of the author's knowledge of EDW/BI solution performance benchmarking to date), certain trade-offs in terms of data inputs, processing schedules, and constraints on outputs can provide a solution that can exceed efficiency expectations.
- Bringing the data as close as possible to where the processing takes place, which can involve co-locating CPU and RAM, using multiple-core CPUs in a single processor, and scaling the CPU and memory on-demand.
- Optimizing the data model itself, using column orientation, row orientation, object orientation, and hybrid orientation as an inherent "hardwired" feature of the data model itself. This aspect is unique to open source databases, and makes them very efficient for business analysis, BI, and business analytics processing.

- Clustering the data at the database (DB) level involves merging multiple instances of the DB either physically or virtually to unify the data at the end-to-end enterprise level.
- Clustering the data at the customer/consumer/competitor level involves merging data from multiple sources into a single (business) view of the same that can be contained as a single presentable component, independent of the data sources and processing involved as long as the inputs, computation, and outputs conform to the same business-contextual dimensions, rules, and results. In turn, clustering the data at the DB level (described in the previous point) might be used as an underlying design criterion
- Optimizing the data at the organization level involves logical and/ or physical reorganization of the data for effective and efficient processing. Typical strategies include partitioning of data based on business-centric queries; slicing and dicing the data at the storage level by means of compression (columnar or otherwise); autoenabling the logging of all data being queried to ease audit-trails and historical data lineage; storing the data on low input/output (I/O)– intensive physical media, such as solid state disk (SSD) and Flash caches in addition to disk-based storage; bringing the data storage unit concept as close as possible to the processing unit concept—or in other words, unifying the storage at the network level, as in NAS (network attached storage), SAN (storage area network), storage clusters, and the like.
- Optimizing processing power at the computation level involves using parallelization and pipelining of data computations and query processing, thus giving the ability to speed up computation at exponential levels. Column orientation (as stated earlier) is one such optimization where data is stored as a single column vertical as opposed to traditional row-oriented databases where data is stored in a row-by-column table format. Speed of computation can also be optimized by enabling shared-resource computing, as in shared memory, shared CPU, shared storage and shared platform configurations. Cloud computing is one such computing architecture that enables share-all in terms of computing resources *and* share-nothing in terms of independent physical infrastructures, along with elastic flexibility for dynamic on-demand provisioning, as well as data, database, dataset, data-view, and semantic virtualization of disparate/linear data and content.

■ Optimizing processing power at the client computation level involves the caching of dynamic result sets and in-memory database, as well as disconnected data-sourcing, which the EDW functions as an offline data warehouse without losing its "live" functionality.

Any or all of these options used in combination yield ultra-fast query performance for data transformations, dynamic extract, transform, and load (ETL) operations, dynamic data warehousing, aggregation and summarization of data based on n dimensions, context-aware computation, and analysis based on a dynamic set of dimensions, data visualization for real-time interactivity, data mining and heuristics-based search, data exploration, data simulation/emulation, prediction-based analysis, and dynamic content integration such as on-the-fly mash-ups, dynamic dashboarding and mashboarding, and the like.

Given the large scope of using open source methodologies for EDW/BI solutions, dissecting the corresponding development options boils down to one or more of the following development pragmatics, which are at least sufficient (if not necessary) for a customer implementation that can score a success:

1. Pervasive BI combined with real-time BI (including situation-aware, risk-aware), continuous operational BI and right-time BI (right time/right data/right user/right purpose, plus anyone, anytime, anywhere) enables competitive BI.

2. Dynamic EDW, ETL, and BI enable context-aware business analytics that in turn accelerate continuous BI—be it operational or EDW-based BI.

3. Semantic analytics model–driven development is to be treated as part and parcel of the solution implementation—a recommended imperative, though not a required one (in certain cases). It can be developed using business-centric, customer/consumer/competitor–specific business rules that are directly embeddable into existing or new EDW/BI environments and become part of the end-to-end business process workflow.

This enables business domain–compliant consistency across multiple business units, systems, and users, thereby delivering the same user experience on the front-end and common ontology–based unification of disparate dimensions, attributes, key identifiers, and business rules at the logical design, physical design, computation, and presentation levels of information.

The typical implementation algorithm for the codex of a semantic analytics model includes:

- Transforming foreign function interfaces (FFIs) into application programming interfaces (APIs) using purpose-built designs that can pertain to context-tailored functionality from localized highest common factors to globalized least common denominators.
- Implementing context-driven designs using domain-specific languages that are a mix/match/merge of independent or embedded programming languages such as Python or derived from language-based frameworks such as Ruby on Rails, Groovy on Grails, Semantic Markup Languages, ontology-based frameworks, and the like.
- The underlying code patterns are driven by high-level embedding-enabled design. Expressor3.0 Semantic Analytics Engine is a strong customer success–proven example of this type of implementation, in which additional design criteria such as context-aware and performance-centric parallelization are induced into the semantic metrics to optimize relevance, efficiency, and scalability.

The key imperative is that a context-driven design can be made more generic by way of using it to validate itself. A good example of this is to validate the interoperability of development and testing of the inherent model on a target solution such as master data management (MDM) or customer relationship management (CRM) with the variant being the domain-specific context.

4. Cloud-sourced development platforms include the cloud-based platform-as-a-service or a combination of platform-as-a-service and (software-as-a-service; infrastructure-as-a-service) implemented as solution-as-a-service as the predominant development methodology to go. Cloud technologies can also be used for business-to-business, application to application, and customer/con-

sumer/competitor to customer/consumer/competitor integration, as well as (geolocation, time, end-point) agnostic solution deployment and accessibility—in a matter of minutes to hours to a few days. This goes in line with the design paradigm of using open source to cloud source.

5. Virtualization-powered coding and/or componentization, integrated with semantic analytics, gives the flexibility and elasticity needed without affecting the time to delivery and time to perform. With right-time BI having precedence over real-time BI as the key design-to-delivery indicator, data-to-dashboard virtualization is the key technology imperative in realizing this implementation.

6. An open testing model means that you *test as you develop* for *pay-as-you-go*. Open source–based solutions still need the robustness and resilience of fault tolerance and extreme performance, especially when it comes to security, compliance, functionality, and user friendliness. As the business saying goes, "the customer is always right." It is critical that the EDW/BI solution always functions to the level of customer acceptability. Hence, the imperative of testing as you develop for pay-as-you-go must be made a governing requirement of the development strategy. This also contributes to the key performance points that determine the overall solution efficiency, as required by EPM.

7. An open security model isolates solution security and information privacy through a hybrid approach that separates user identity from solution context in terms of geolocation and interaction touchpoint. This is a key design and development imperative to implementing a balanced approach that enables proactive security with trusted identity. Tying the customer/consumer/competitor–specific GRC policies into this design results in an open security model that is *Pervasive* (from the perimeter to the persistent store), *Public*, and *Private* (or the *Open PPP Security Model for short*) at the same time.

Pragmatics of the Open PPP Security Model, by way of algorithmic rules driving such a model:

- Multiply the authentication and authorization with a context-anonymous identifier, or PPP key, that cannot be made persistent and is tied to the actual data-content ID key. A combination of PKI and access control list (ACL) policy–based obfuscation can be used to generate the above PPP key.
- The above key is applied to every interaction level of the solution, both implicit and explicit—from the perimeter to the server levels to the endpoint(s), including applying to data in transit bidirectionally
- Use stateless modularization to implement the associated coding routines as API
- Use state-full execution with the context specifics as the dynamic argument that creates a new state for each API call
- Enable componentization of the same by SOA-enabled encapsulation and Web service–based runtime invocation, independent of the target deployment infrastructure

8. Use a solution efficiency scorecard to focus on key performance points.

Solution efficiency extends beyond measuring overall performance in terms of request/response times and the ability to handle large volumes of data in significantly lower amounts of time. It involves a number of imperatives, the measurement of which contributes to solution efficiency and the business value. Figure 7.1 gives a high-level view of the key imperatives, otherwise called indicators, to be taken into account one-on-one with the KPI (that are directly proportional to business value).

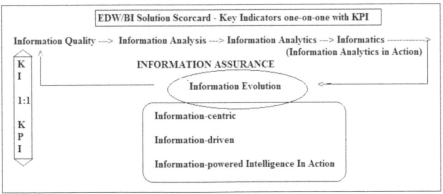

Figure 7.1   EDW/BI solution scorecard: Key indicators one-on-one with KPI

As is evident from the diagrammatic representation, solution efficiency is based on:

- Measuring the continuity of the optimal performance and its deviation with respect to the baseline, benchmarked by the domain-context variables, as the solution lifecycle progresses from strategy to strategic (experimental errors and exceptions excluded in a marginally acceptable range)

- Quantifying the standard deviation of the possibly various deviations resulting from the above step by using scholastic and stochastic algorithms to determine the relevancy of the desired results in correlation with the context involved. This key imperative is as dynamic and central to the business as the solution parameters that determine the results. As an example, use statistical models to measure the rate of deviation by time period; pipeline the same by qualifiers such as predictive metrics, and upscale factors so as to determine the future probabilistic return on customer (ROC). This supportively makes the measurement dynamic in its value that scores the *business value or the assured rate of ROC* beyond the currently realized solution boundaries.

- Advanced analytics can be derived based on machine-generated data coupled with throughput and scalability by way of usage analysis one-on-one with {time, geolocation, globalization, localization, anytime/anywhere/anyone, right information for the right purpose to the right people at the right time}. This formula can be implemented for short-term responses, long-term outcomes, outlier scenarios, distributed payloads, and time-agnostic cum place-agnostic emulations. Although this entire set of analytics might not be feasible to implement for measurement, subsets of the same can be implemented using key database and data warehouse road blockers such as:

-
    - Using information-centricity based on large data sets that return very low analyzed sets
    - Using information-driven processes to determine the inter-component resource contention, trade-off between memory usage, and data loss prevention
    - Using information-powered analytics to prioritize relevance over prevalence

7.4   Deployment Options, Dissected

Akin to development, the "start small, grow big" approach applies to deployment strategies as well. The pioneers of enterprise data warehousing and BI have dished out the best practices of EDW/BI architectures, which include the coupling of core functional components with add-on components. A scenario that illustrates this well is integrating a centralized BI dashboard on top of EDW components across the enterprise. An open source–based divide-and-conquer approach to solution deployment can follow the following pragmatics for a viable best-fit option:

- A non-silos approach to pipeline the various EDW components and channelize the same to the BI dashboard to sustain consistency and continuity of information flow balanced against the on-demand and prime-time scalability of the same.
- Though unbounded in terms of enterprise scale and service, an EDW can be deployed using a push-through mechanism by way of a service-orientation policy that dynamically creates a sort of virtual deployment environment (VDE). This can be implemented in a simulated deployment platform to which components (that in essence can be individual solutions by themselves) are added based on context-specific variables; the resulting VDE goes through the iterations of standardize, test, operate, optimize, and freeze.
- This allows for composite imperatives to be implemented as required by the underlying business processes, resulting in a set of best-of-breed KPIs for overall solution deployment. As an example, deploying beyond the solution perimeter boundaries requires an extensible security model that is capable of hardening the controls and policies necessary to consume and subsume cloud services across each additional layer beyond the perimeter. The anytime, anywhere, anyone implementation is a valid deployment use case that demands such strengthened security.
- All of the above steps can be implemented as a reusable and agile VDE SOA module. Here are a few guidelines on how this can be done:
    - The key deployment indicator to be noted here is that the architectural framework of the VDE SOA module does not change. It is the inputs to this engine that vary based on the business context and content. And this works across all

deployment environments from the early stages of conceptualization to commoditization.

■ This mechanism can be further fine-grained to adapt to hybrid business domains like streamlining a CRM system with continuous operational BI and the like.

The primary deployment strategies for EDW/BI solution can be classified as shown below in Table 7.1:

Table 7.1   Primary deployment strategies for an open source EDW/BI solution.

Usability from the Customer/Consumer/ Competitor Perspective	Key Architectural Imperative	Key Delivery Infrastructure
As a stand-alone solution	Deploy once, use multiple	Standalone S/W appliance
As a share-enabled solution	Deploy once, use multiple, with sharing enabled over the network as multiple thin client installations	S/W appliance over a network with multiple thin client installations
As a hosted solution	Software service hosted on a single server with shared access via collaborative (application-server powered) UI	Digital dashboards, online Web spaces, on-demand "live" apps
As a service-enabled (SOA-enabled) solution	Embedded and embeddable solution components, in line with the host (target) solution	S/W analytic engines, hot-pluggable modules, solution-in-a-box, integration services
As a platform-enabled solution (cloud-based)	SaaS, PaaS, IaaS (The degree of control that can be placed in the hands of the end user in terms of interaction, extensibility, and elastic flexibility)	Web-services, solution-cloud-in-a-box, VDI-enabled cloud PCs (AKA VDI-enabled solution-in-a-cloud)

Table 7.1   Primary deployment strategies for an open source EDW/BI solution.

Usability from the Customer/Consumer/Competitor Perspective	Key Architectural Imperative	Key Delivery Infrastructure
As an on-device solution	Localized solution with delegated end-user privileges and centralized administration	Self-service kiosks, on-boarded mobile apps, content-aware VDIs/Cloud PCs (PC-over-IP enabled; PC-over-IP)
As an on-demand solution	Real-time, right-time, anyone/anywhere/anytime accessible solution with built-in multi-tenancy; virtual machine (VM) solution by isolating the underlying hardware hosted on a server-virtualized VM	Personalized S/W appliances, solution-on-demand thin/zero clients, VDI (or H/W isolated) solution-as-a-PC, virtual-machine solution
As an online solution	As a Web-enabled solution using a unified cross-browser agnostic and/or compatible portal, Web application, virtualized solution streamed on-demand, SOA-enabled Web service	Rich Internet applications (RIA), customer/consumer/ competitor-aware solution-lets, solution-as-a-Web service

Urban{code} has pioneered the automation and acceleration of the build-test-deploy-release processes with its Enterprise DevOps Solution. Additional details can be obtained from www.urbancode.com. This innovative open source–based deployment platform is a best-fit choice for iterative solution deployment, be it migration to cloud-based environments, custom deployments using selective software components, or automation of deployment infrastructures already in place.

Riverbed's Cloud Management Solution helps custom-orchestrate the EDW/BI solution stack to enable business-friendly deployments onto and from the cloud, including on-demand and real-time deployments.

Fiberlink's MaaS360 Platform is a true SaaS platform that uses mobility-as-a-service to deliver software solutions on a higher level of deployment by converging Mobile deployments onto their Enterprise App

Stores—optimizing delivery to anyone, anytime, anywhere as well as achieving the right information for the right purpose to the right people at the right time. *This model can be extended using open source–based integration and virtualization methodologies to custom-build an integrated unified deployment platform for mobility that is application-aware and device-agnostic at the same time.*

Eucalyptus's (PaaS based) Private Cloud enables quick build-and-deploy solutions for custom EDW/BI implementations.

7.5   Integration Options, Dissected

Integration options involve inter- and intracomponent coupling/decoupling at any level of the solution tiers, *without disturbing* the existing solution as such, both operationally and functionally. The phrase *without disturbing* emphasizes the following:

1. Zero or minimal impact on live user environments

2. Scaling the application solution to extend the business needs in terms of resources, data volumes, and user-requested functionality add-ons

3. Load-balancing the solution environment as additional resources are added/removed

4. Transparent fail-over mechanisms during server outages (planned or unplanned)

5. Stand-by solutions to support live business operations during system/database crashes including during disaster recovery

6. Any or all of the above without having to redesign the core and critical component architecture(s) of the solution

This list seems to be too much hype to be practical, but these are very likely situations in almost every EDW/BI environments—more so when dealing with high data volumes and high traffic volumes, where even a downtime of less than a minute is mission critical.

Keeping these factors in mind, the open source integration options available can at best reduce to near zero lossless transition from pre- to postintegration scenarios. Given the elasticity of selection, implementation, and extension of open source methodologies, the primary integration options are as follows:

- *Data/content/information integration and functional integration across the dimensions of security, controllability, compliance, and performance.* This is done by breaking the data silos by transforming ambiguous content into actionable and/or anonymous information. The anonymous ID protects PII and other business-specific sensitive data by using identity masking that surpasses native database-level unmasking. This can be implemented as a business rule for GRC-adherence and embedded into the solution KPI using segregation of duties (SoD) and security information event management (SIEM) mechanisms. *This can be the gold standard for data and functional integration across the security, compliance, and controllability dimensions in terms of preventing and preempting unauthorized privileges escalation, privileges elevation, and unwarranted privileged user access.*

Open source enablement is a game-changer when it comes to adding this additional tier of fine grained anyone-anywhere-anytime access control (FGA^{3}AC) not only to the DB level but also to every other level of solution architecture. Isolating the different layers of the EDW/BI solution—DB tier, middleware tier, BI tier, and presentation tier—and applying the FGA^{3}AC to each, as well to each of the intercomponent integration layers delivers an intelligent integration implementation framework that is coordinated, consistent and continuous and therefore aligns with the Open Source Perfect.

- *Integration by emulating virtual data generation.* This involves dynamic clustering of data from multiple sources in real time/at the right time to service user queries without having to relocate or move the associated data elements pertaining to the query request–response workflow. In some cases, it can be precalculated and stored persistently (and refreshed on-demand) or intermittently (using caching mechanisms) to boost the query performance.
- *Integration by emulating an offline EDW.* This is done by a persistent in-memory database cache that is autorefreshed whenever the underlying source data changes also called a disconnected data source. This allows the actual EDW to be offline while the disconnected DW is functioning online (or transparently seems

to be)—and any and all data changes are autopushed to this disconnected engine.

- *Integration by using services orientation that allows stateless and state-preserved integration options in a hot-pluggable way.* The frequently used options in this category are:
  - Embedding of add-on modules using loosely coupled threads. This refers to integrating the add-on engine in line with the solution process workflow so that it executes in sync as part of the overall end-to-end execution. Decoupling is handled in a similar manner. This is also considered as a SaaS-enabled strategy.
  - SaaS enabling strategy for embedding of add-on modules. This is primarily focused on the ability to integrate into the driving module (i.e., the add-on in most cases) so that it can be part of another SaaS-enabled system or a standalone module. This is a key integration differentiator, as it allows bidirectional embedding—a very essential requirement for Integration services. Integration services are by themselves software engines that are used in the intercomponent integration of a solution. The subtle difference here is that this module contains the transport or messaging or servicing mechanism by which the actual solution ingredients are made to interoperate.
  - Customer success–backed examples include Talend Integration Suite for comprehensive data services and data-integration services, including SOA-enabled Enterprise Integration Bus. Jaspersoft's BI engine is both SaaS enabled and SaaS enabling; Actuate/BIRT's Reporting Solutions are too. Key open source–based next-gen databases like Vertica, InfoBright, EmbeddedDB, and Ingres Vectorwise all use this type of integration at the data/data services levels. And the same holds good for the BI layer on top of the EDW/analytic DB layer.
  - This methodology also works on proprietary DBs like Oracle, DB2, Sybase, MS SQL Server, and the like, as the required add-ons can be integrated in a similar fashion using native-compliant connectors or adapters.
- *Integration by way of analytics.* This refers to the automachine generation of business rules and aligning the same as part of the dynamic solution workflow based on on-the-fly add-on functionality. Typical examples are on-demand streaming of advanced

analytics, as well as federation/virtual syndication of the same to target systems.

- *Integration by way of virtualization.* This is an extension of on-demand integration and works for both data integration and data integration services. This is accomplished by virtual data federation (AKA on-demand replication/servicing based on multivariant changing inputs), cloud-enabled integration, wireless mobility–based coupling and decoupling, and the like.

- *Integration using cloud enablement.* This is listed as separate category in that it goes beyond the above stated integration methods to enable business-to-business integration across pervasive solutions environments, endpoint/access point–based integration that is highly dynamic in nature and mandates extreme elasticity. Cloud-enabled integration necessarily uses virtualization, not merely at the data and database levels, but also at the solution tier–based application levels and external-to-internal systems levels. It is by far the most innovative and cost-effective method of integration to enable on-demand BI, anytime/anywhere/anyone BI, and the like—and it does preserve the reliability, security, and availability of the overall solution by using hybrid (private/public cloud merging) clouds, SOA-based gateways at each integration point of the solution (including Web perimeters), beyond-the-firewall access points, and the like.

7.6   Multiple Sources, Multiple Dimensions

Referring to the FGA^{3}AC security model described in the first point of the previous bullet list as part of data/content/information integration and functional integration across the dimensions of security and compliance, consider integrating the security model in place with the necessary policies and controls for the custom cloud services using multifactored information, identity and intervention management rules that meet governance, risk, and compliance (GRC) requirements in terms of internal and external authentication and authorization protocols. Here the multiple sources refer to the security model in place, the internal-to-external authentication and authorization, as well as the extensible add-ons to be designed with respect to the multiple dimensions of information, identity, and intervention protection, preemption, and prevention. This paradigm applies to any integration model across multiple sources and multiple dimensions, where sources can be treated to be more source-of-data/content/information/application-centric and dimensions can vary across multiple business variables on which the business analysis, BI, and business analytics are based.

7.7   DW and BI Usability and Deployment: Best Solution versus Best-Fit Solution

Open source makes it feasible and flexible to architect the information design that can essentially emulate a *best-fit* orchestration with respect to changing solution ecosystem. And it enables this in a way that:

- Is intelligent enough to dynamically balance deterministic versus nondeterministic business process efficiency across information flow sets and hybrid payloads that include the big data sets.
- Is adaptive in its ability to dynamically isolate, but not separate, the "unique" from the "universal" solution behaviors. These behaviors refer to throughput performance, scaling factors, and the various business dimensions. Once the behaviors are isolated, it becomes relatively easier to enumerate a workflow that can execute universally (across a wide range of deployments) but is still unique in behavior when grouped by the constantly changing variants. Customer-trusted examples include those of the likes of
    - Talend's Enterprise Service Bus is for open source–based integration of any/all permutations of data/data integration services
    - Voxel's VoxSTRUCTURE, described as "The Fabric for a Flexible Internet Infrastructure" (www.voxel.net), is a brilliant architectural design that is open source and technology-agnostic; more importantly, it is one that explores beyond today's cloud computing domain and and derives yet another "Infrastructure That Always Fits" (www.voxel.net).
    - Cloudera's Cloudera Enterprise 3.5 leverages the Hadoop and MapReduce frameworks to deliver a unique, yet universally (adoptable and adaptable) platform for very large data sets analytics (www.cloudera.com).
    - Electric Cloud's automation, acceleration, and quality improvement platform is particularly tailored for private clouds (www.electric-cloud.com).

This type of hybrid computation empowers the EDW/BI solution to perform in a three-in-one parallelized–pipelined–partitioned execution flow that sets the bar on adaptability to a converging high-value point, regardless of the spectrum of inputs, filters, and process variations.

A very good use case for this can be implementing a custom-integral module that coalesces the spectrum of KPI for the mobility, Flash (live video), VoIP, and Video-over-IP domains into a relational database management system (RDBMS)–compliant transformable information model. This model can be used as data source, data model, data template, or a combination of these to extend and deliver an agile services interface (ASI).

- The one-of-a-kind property of an RDBMS-based EDW/BI solution—whether it is row-oriented, column-oriented, hybrid row/column–oriented or multidimensionally oriented—in its very data model design is its capability to process and present the inherent data and its interrelationships synchronized across any and/or all solution boundaries. Yet as computation intensity scales in the order of 10^{12} plus and workload increases in n-factor multiples, the interaction and interrelationships between data flows and the associated data values become more and more complex. *These result in nonlinear proportionalities between information processing and information value thereby obtained.* An open source–enabled "information machine" (AKA, analytics engines, informatics-powered appliances, specialized information models and data-flow constructs, etc.) breaks this complexity by way of cross-technology-based architecture(s) that enable flexible and efficient coordination-cum-correlation of the interaction-flows vs. inter-relationships change dynamics. The key open source–based architecture drivers that can be used are:
  - Lossless redundancy (by way of data/database/data flow virtualization)
  - State-full decoupling between the interaction and interrelationship components (by way of representational state transfer [REST] architecture–/service-oriented architecture [SOA]–based service models); this not only preserves the state of the components but also cache-enables the contextual/situational state of the end-to-end user experience

- Consistency in the interrelationships chain to prevent any inadvertent results due to *extreme versus non-extreme* variances (manual or machine-initiated) in (data–values, data–relationships) pairs
- Autogeneration of a self-adaptable EDW/BI engine for self-serviceable BI (by using the above rules as the underlying design pragmatics)

This delivers a solution that is loosely coupled in terms of elastic componentization, as well as tightly integrated in terms of state-preserved interaction and interdependence.

A practical use case of using this implementation is outlined in the next section under the subsection "Better Responsiveness and User Adoptability."

7.8   Leveraging the Best-Fit Solution: Primary Considerations

Taking into consideration the solution life cycle involved from an open source perspective, it is evident that leveraging a best-fit approach for such solution implementation is always a prudent strategy in terms of techno-functional accuracy and winning customer confidence. The preview of the best-fit solution proof-of-concept (PoC) speaks volumes when it comes to customer satisfaction by way of a solution preview. This section explains the key practices for DW and BI solution usability in terms of best-fit development, deployment, integration, interaction, and implementation considerations. Consider the primary drivers of the better, faster, easier paradigm as the baseline or an analogue of hitchhiker's rule 42 (to leverage a best-fit solution); the extent to which dynamism and Flash-based interactivity play a role in enabling real output in real time in real world business implementations; and the role of mobility as another significant aspect that is gaining momentum among next-gen business strategies and easing the usability by way of wireless interaction—from corporate to customer. Finally, it emphasizes the notion of better-results–oriented customer success by way of better responsiveness, user adoptability, and transparency as the value-driver of the overall best-fit solution. To reiterate this fact, we revisit Figure 1.5 of Chapter 1, which gives a high-level view of a best-fit open source EDW/BI solution. This figure is reproduced here in Figure 7.2.

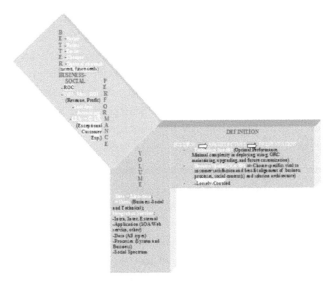

Figure 7.2   A best-fit open source EDW/BI solution—the big picture.

7.9   Better, Faster, Easier as the Hitchhiker's Rule

Using business process-centric analytics in combination with implementation, improvisation, and intelligence-driven KPI is the first hitchhiker's rule for a B-B-B EDW/BI solution. This gets the business closer to the competition than to the industry-domain at large.

Implement the *Open Source Perfect* solution by augmenting better, faster, easier with the competitive trends in customer-centric dynamics that personalize the customer experience into consumer-centricity, customer-centricity, and competitor-centricity, rather than the more traditional business-centricity as a primary driver. This requires factoring the *Optimal Outreach* attribute into the solution value, thereby extending the solution usability to the business/IT/customer-user experience/social landscape. The architecture pragmatics for the same involve:

Analyze → Visualize → Virtualize → Mobilize → Appliance

processes to be streamlined, synchronized, and executed in line with the end-to-end solution development, deployment, adoption, customization, adaptation and evolution.

7.9.1   Dynamism and Flash—Real Output in Real Time in the Real World

The key considerations for achieving real output in real time in the real world are directly in line with how well the hitchhiker's rule of better, easier, and faster (in terms of solution architecture and business results) can be synchronized with the key *value* drivers of context awareness; business roles–compliant administration, accessibility, availability and analytics; and customer experience. And the critical backbone that runs through these two frames of reference is the dynamism involved in the solution implementation, usage, and reliability over time, access point, and location variance.

In the real world, time and location play a critical role when it comes to customer experience that is in line with the colloquial saying "in a flash." That's the kind of dynamism that users demand in the current world of exponentially growing data volumes, user bases, and access devices. It wouldn't be an extrapolation to state that business lifecycles are tending to be as dynamic as the cycle of real life—and this requires the solution and solution-usage lifecycles to catch up in sync.

Figure 7.3 is a diagrammatic representation of the correlation between key technology indicators versus key business–social indicators for cross-domain dynamism.

The primary levers for a best-fit implementation are:

1.   Virtual data federation (for data and data store(s) replication)

2.   Real-time and on-demand syndication (for access, availability, and on-demand solution deployment)

3.   Component-agnostic mediation platform, using (private) cloud both as an initiator and generator for cross-component and inter-solution process mediation

7.9.2   Interactivity

Use cloud-enabled wireless integration to deliver wireless interapplication interactivity by way of:

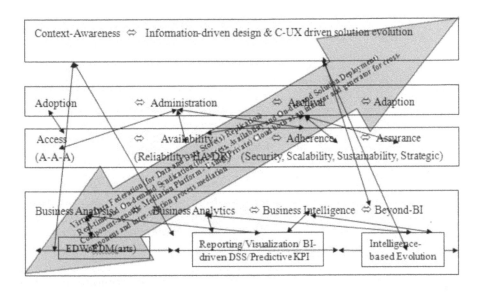

Figure 7.3   Visual depicting the correlation between key technology indicators versus key business–social indicators for cross-domain dynamism.

- Push and pop services implementation for on-demand interaction (transparently wired into the solution workflow or by cascading of the same) to push through and chain the interdependencies
- Drag-and-drop services implementation to enable shared cross-GUI interaction
- Online interaction across heterogeneous content and document management platforms like Microsoft SharePoint (a proprietary collaboration platform) or Alfresco Content and Document System - an open source enterprise content management (ECM) system and document management platform.

Figure 7.4 is a diagrammatic illustration of the concept of leveraging wireless cloud-enabled development and deployment platforms for cross-solution, cross-business-contextual-domains interaction and collaboration.

7.10   Better Responsiveness, User Adoptability, and Transparency

The framework stated above for implementing wireless interactivity using cloud-enabled wireless integration can be extended to the next level to deliver a self-serviceable wireless interactivity engine by architecting the

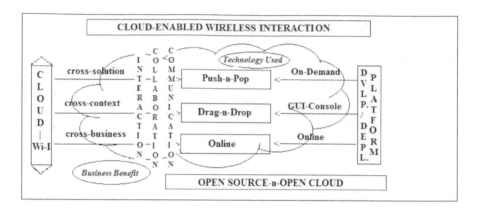

Figure 7.4   Using open source and open cloud to deliver wireless cloud-enabled interactivity

extensibility pragmatics in line with the framework of combining loosely coupled elastic componentization with tightly integrated interaction (as described in the previous section titled ***DW and BI usability and deployment: best solution vs. best-fit solution***) to *transparently integrate the customer experience lifecycle* into it. The customer-user experience engine can be a prebuilt system (like EPM and EFM solutions) or one that can be designed using feedback-based patterns. Such an engine can reduce the ROC and increase the interactivity/responsiveness usability experience of the end user. A typical design methodology for the same can involve:

- Transforming raw data into semantics-based information by using data virtualization to extract metadata, dynamically parse it, and surround it with proper context so that it complies with the customer-centric master data
- Transforming this information into user-accessible, shareable, and far more unifying knowledge imperatives that are reusable on a common ground (domain, customer/consumer/competitor, business rules–driven, policy-managed, Web/wireless-agnostic, and the like.)
- Transforming knowledge through user-analyzed insights that drive the autogeneration of situational metrics for adaptive intelligence that are pragmatically actionable
- Transforming this actionable intelligence by putting it into business practice to realize real-world business value

- Transcending beyond intelligence to autoevolve this act-intelligence by iterative use of this engine to arrive at a best-fit self-adaptable BI solution through self-serviceable BI—competitive BI that delivers situational, risk-aware competency across the business–social user spectrum

---

Real-world business use implementations of such solutions can include:

- Health informatics centers of excellence and health information exchanges
- Bidirectional patient2doctor and patient2patient communication, collaboration, and interoperability

When it comes to transparency of the inline metrics, the proposed best-fit solution works with user-satisfied efficiency that is visible enough (AKA transparent) in terms of expected return on results, with the analytics-behind-the-processes autoexecuting invisibly (AKA transparently).

Using Beyond-BI KPI to Raise the Bar on Quantifying Quality

Using beyond-BI KPI to raise the bar on quantifying quality gives the best-fit solution a competitive edge over the best-built solution. Here's an implementation strategy for raising the bar on quantifying quality using open source–based methodologies:

1. Take *relay* situations into account in addition to *delay* scenarios. Efficiency is not limited to latency and subsecond response times alone, and in all likelihood be sensitive to *out-of-way* behaviors as well. The replay mechanism can help "replay" the particular problem scenario in real-world-centric simulated environments—which are hard to reproduce in production environments—by feeding the EDW/BI solution with scaled-up/scaled-back inputs. The corresponding design rules can be framed by applying predictive-analytic algorithms that combine uplift modeling with periodicity/priority/preventability behavior semantics.

2. Apply the "knowledge is *(quality)* power" principle to find the sweet spots, hot spots, and blind spots, and run analyze/apply/approve/visualize progression to zero in on key intelligence indicators such as "*There is nothing like completeness or non-completeness*

when it comes to accuracy of prediction-enabled metrics." Typical industry implementations of the same using open source trendsetters are customer experience management solutions like Vovici's Customer Call Center and Contact Center Software, which uses context-based tags as key qualifiers to measure intangibles.

The key decision-making imperative here is to know the differences between "hardwiring" and "brainwiring" and the subsequent selection and application of the same (right information for the right purpose to the right people at the right time). Statistical inferences are no more than a baseline for deriving probabilistic preferences when it comes to forecasting behaviors as opposed to forecasting trends, as the outliers tend to be the only viable decision drivers. The former involves higher levels of nonlinear complexities than the latter. Examples are qualifiers like "It works best for me" and "It's been rated the best by a highly competent solution evaluator" are only as relative in significance as they are in terms of their inherent functionalities. "It works best for me" and that is all my business wants, so "rated best" comes lower in order of preference-cum-precedence in this situation. BI-based advanced analytics for situational awareness are critical for a successful implementation of the same, and open source gives all the necessary handles to interplay the customer behavior dynamics in any/all needed perspectives.

---

3.   Consider the set of *all data points* a highly reliable input for benchmarking predictive analytics KPIs; dynamically sliding the bar on this baseline as this input set changes over time and other related variants is a necessary and sufficient condition for an *acceptable accuracy value.* An outlier point is not necessarily an inflexion point or deflection point and sometimes can be a point-of-measure by way of hidden metadata tagged to it that might be the actual scoring point to determine the acceptable accuracy. A converging data mining–based KPI that extends the "confidence and support" imperatives to correlate and cross-relate the "as-of," "as-is," and "what if" metrics to autogenerate a next-gen KPI: *prediction accuracy value.*

7.11   Fitting the Vendor/Platform Product(s)/tTools(s): A Development and Deployment Standpoint

Given the depth and breadth of open source–based EDW/BI solution development and deployment methodologies, listing a comprehensive set of vendor/platform product(s)/tool(s) takes an effort more exhaustive than the pervasive scope of the open source EDW/BI domain itself. Table 7.2 narrows this list into set of vendors/platforms and the key functionality specific to each of them one-on-one with respect to development, deployment, and integration aspects involved. This can be used a viable starting checklist while evaluating potential vendors/platforms for business use.

Table 7.2   A starting checklist of potential vendors/platforms for EDW/BI solution implementation.

Key Imperative from a Development/ Deployment/ Integration Standpoint	Vendor/Platform for Best-Fit Leverage	Vendor/Platform-Specific Functionality for a Best-Fit Value
Development/ Deployment	**Urban{code}** Enterprise DevOps Solution www.urbancode.com	Pioneering solution for the automation and acceleration of build–test–deploy–release processes. As an open source–based deployment platform, it is a best-fit choice for iterative solution deployments such as:

- Migration to cloud-based environments
- Custom deployments using selective software components
- Automation of existing deployment infrastructures in place

Table 7.2 A starting checklist of potential vendors/platforms for EDW/BI solution implementation. (continued)

Development/ Deployment	Vovici's Customer Call Center and Contact Center Software Solutions	Enterprise performance management and customer experience management that focus on the voice of the customer.
Development/ Deployment	Cloudera's Cloudera Enterprise 3.5 www.cloudera.com	An intelligent platform based on the Hadoop and MapReduce frameworks to deliver a unique, yet universally (adoptable and adaptable) solution for very large data set–centric analytics.
Development/ Deployment	Electric Cloud www.electric-cloud.com	Automation, acceleration, and quality improvement platform particularly tailored for private cloud implementations
Development/ Integration	Recommind.com's suite of products based on its Context Optimized Relevancy Engine (CORE) technology	Text analytics–driven advanced analytics engine that has proven business use cases in enterprise feedback management in combination with business analytics to unleash potential traits in customer satisfaction— from business to social landscapes

Table 7.2   A starting checklist of potential vendors/platforms for EDW/BI solution implementation. (continued)

Development/ Deployment	Amazon Elastic Compute Cloud (EC2) Amazon Simple Storage Service (S3) Amazon SimpleDB Amazon Relational Database Service (RDS) Amazon Simple Queue Service (SQS) Amazon Elastic MapReduce Amazon VPC (Virtual Private Cloud) Amazon Machine Image (AMI) http://aws.amazon.com/ec2 http://aws.amazon.com	Amazon EC2 is a cloud-enabled Web Service that supports better-easier-faster Web-scale computing. Amazon S3, SimpleDB, RDS, and SQS are other Amazon Web services to augment EC2 functionality for a best-fit solution delivery. S3 is a Web service for Web-based data/content/big-data storage and retrieval by way of any-time/anywhere/anyone access and on-boarding. SimpleDB and RDS are cloud-enabled Web services for high-performance query execution and RDBMS set-up to scale-up in EC2 instances. SQS is a Web service that enables development and deployment of advanced analytics on VLDB sources for efficiency and scalability. This is useful for embedding of high-performance analytic engines in businesses requiring BI centers of excellence.

Table 7.2   A starting checklist of potential vendors/platforms for EDW/BI solution implementation. (continued)

		Using a combination of Amazon VPC instances and Elastic MapReduce, customers can leverage a massive cloud computing platform that is customer/consumer/ competitor–centric. AMI is a prepackaged EC2 platform for automated and accelerated EC2 instance deployment.
Integration	Talend's Integration Suite Talend Enterprise Service Bus Talend Master Data Management (MDM)	Open source–based integration of any/all permutations of data/ data integration services, including solution component-to-component integration, workflow integration, and MDM functionality. MDM is essential for customer-specific business dimensional data integration and is critical for any EDW/BI solution implementation.
Development/ Deployment	OpSource Cloud www.opsource.net/Services/Cloud-Hosting OpSource On-Demand www.opsource.net	A comprehensive suite for cloud enablement, from analysis to adoption by way of public/ private cloud interaction, integration, delivery, and extension that provides a virtual private cloud within the public cloud without compromising on reliability, availability, and security and governance, risk, and compliance.

Table 7.2   A starting checklist of potential vendors/platforms for EDW/BI solution implementation. (continued)

Development/ Deployment	NextLabs's Information Risk Management Solution(s) www.nextlabs.com	A comprehensive data loss prevention (DLP)–based solution for enterprise rights management, which the vendor calls information risk management. The solution is unique in that it strictly adheres to the OASIS (oasis-open.org) standard for eXtended Access Control Markup Language (XACML)-driven security. The solution delivers transparent rights management with built-in content-aware rights/policies enforcement given the context for that content.
Deployment/ Integration (primarily cloud-enabled)	Rightscale's Cloud Management Solution	Innovative in its design to custom-orchestrate the EDW/BI solution stack and enable business-friendly deployments onto and from the cloud, including on-demand and real-time deployments.

Table 7.2   A starting checklist of potential vendors/platforms for EDW/BI solution implementation. (continued)

Development/ Deployment/ Integration	Vertica, InfoBright, EmbeddedDB, Ingres Vectorwise, MySQL	Open source–based next-gen analytic/EDW centric databases
	Jaspersoft's BI Solution(s)	SaaS-enabled and -enabling BI platform
	Actuate/BIRT's Reporting Solutions - (Business Intelligence Reporting Tools)	SaaS-enabled and -enabling BI Suite
	Talend Integration Suite for comprehensive data services and data-integration services including SOA-enabled Enterprise Integration Bus.	For all of the listed open source DBs specialized for EDW, solution architects can use this type of integration at the data/data services levels. The same holds true for the listed BI tools for integration at the BI layer on top of the EDW/analytic DB layer.
Development/ Deployment	Voxel's VoxSTRUCTURE (The Fabric for a Flexible Internet Infrastructure) (Source: www.voxel.net/voxel-technology)	An architectural design and development framework that is open source, technology agnostic, and most importantly, explores beyond today's cloud computing domain, deriving yet another infrastructure that always fits.

Table 7.2   A starting checklist of potential vendors/platforms for EDW/BI solution implementation. (continued)

Development/ Deployment	Fiberlink's MaaS360 Platform	A pure SaaS platform that uses mobility as a service to deliver software solutions on a higher level of deployment by converging mobile deployments onto their enterprise app stores, for anytime/ anywhere/anyone access and getting the right information for the right purpose to the right people at the right time.
Development/ Deployment	CloudShare's Cloud-Based Demo Center Surgient CloudExpress (cloud automation software)	A cloud-based SaaS platform that can be used for instant proofs-of-concept (POCs) by performing in-seconds replication of custom solution environments distributed across multiple demo-sites with a centralized management and monitoring console.
	Surgient CloudExpress (cloud automation software)"	This use can be extended to create BI centers of excellence as a service and BI centers of excellence in a box by leveraging IaaS and PaaS via open source–centric soft-coupling with cloud automation engines that bridge enterprise-level BI centers and the cloud-enabled BI centers of excellence as a service

Table 7.2   A starting checklist of potential vendors/platforms for EDW/BI solution implementation. (continued)

Development/ Deployment	Eucalyptus's (PaaS based) Private Cloud	Enables quick build-and-deploy solutions for custom EDW/BI implementations

7.12   Best Practices: Use and Reuse

Here's a list of best practices for leveraging the development and deployment methodologies outlined in the this chapter that can be put into real world use to attain, sustain, and retain solution adoptability, usability and adaptability for the term of the customer lifecycle:

- *Instant and Intelligent POC on Demand*: Leveraging existing proprietary infrastructure and using an open source–based EDW/BI solution to demonstrate the proof of concept behind the prototype to show how best the solution fits into target implementation domain gets done in a simple and self-serviceable manner as the design and architecture of the EDW/BI solution supports it. This enables the business users to take control of the POC instance and drive it by interactive input/output to get to the bottom of the "what the POC delivers is exactly what the business needs" imperative—from the high-level conceptual view to the end user–customer experience view.

- *Built-to-Test Collateral Business Models*: An open source EDW/BI solution by way of its open choice of development and deployment options allows any business customer/consumer/competitor to build collateral technofunctional models for EDW/BI that can be tested using scaled-up and scaled-out variations of the mission-critical business dimensions for tactical use or as part of a strategic initiative. By doing this, the customer/consumer/competitor gains some competitive advantage beforehand in the cross-vertical business operations that is running "as is." As an example, the collateral POCs can help boost corporate budgetary approvals for the company's subsidiaries that require some kind of variations from the original POC-based operations model. These can then be implemented with significantly less TCO (total cost of ownership) for live production environments, enabling companies to seamlessly expand their business from built-to-test to built-to-last.

- *Vendor-Agnostic Implementations*: By using the development and deployment options explained in this chapter, companies can eliminate vendor lock-ins by basing their selection of choice on the requirements-centricity at a more fine-grained level. Since the design allows for isolation of EDW and BI layers as well as the integration level, a best-fit choice at each required level can enable cross-functional components in place—without losing the backbone strength of their integration—across the changing business needs.

- *Better Operational BI Begets Better Business Operations*: This is in a way a "necessity come true" for many businesses, especially for small to medium-sized businesses in which BI is primarily used for determining progressive business growth by way of facts-based reporting, forecasting of revenue based on current and changing market trends, and the like as the business is operating. This requires real-time contextual information fed and analyzed for feedback to get to its efficiency score at the speed of the business operations. The development and deployment options highlighted in this chapter are by far proven to be customer friendly and yield accurate results on a real-world time-to-time and location-to-location basis. Sometimes this model can help in upscaling the business ahead of time—*a KPI for planning and preparation for the road ahead that delivers continuous operational BI for competitive intelligence.*

- *Creating a Social Intelligence and Analysis Engine*: An ideal use of open source EDW/BI methodologies is merging text analytics with BI and business analytics to autogenerate KPI for fine-grained exploration of feedback-based content from social networking sites and/or live conversations to quantify the customer satisfaction quotient at several levels of utilization. This can be integrated into the BI/advanced analytics/predictive analytics layer of any target online analytical processing (OLAP)– or online transaction processing (OLTP)–based scoring system for information assurance, risk assurance, productivity measurement, and the like.

7.13   Summary

This chapter dealt with the essential details of the development, deployment, and integration options available that can be leveraged for a best-fit open source EDW/BI solution implementation. Beginning with the key development options that emphasized the ins and outs of using each of them, the following section dove deeply into the essential deployment options, followed by an analogous coverage of the various integration options factoring into the solution implementation. Special sections focusing on DW and BI usability and deployment by way of comparison between best and best-fit solutions, and the primary considerations in leveraging a best-fit solution implementation as a win-win strategy laid down the necessary content befitting such a solution adoption. Finally, it outlined a correlation between open source vendor(s)/platform(s) and development/deployment/integration aspects by enlisting a checklist of the same. The chapter concluded with some best practices for use and reuse in terms of the development and deployment options discussed. The next chapter discusses the best practices for data management in granular detail from data sources to data delivery and the cross-dynamism and analytics involved across each interaction point of the end-to-end EDW/BI solution spectrum.

Chapter 8

Best Practices for Data Management

8.1   In This Chapter

- Best Fit of Open Source in EDW Implementation
- Best Practices for Using Open Source as a BI-Only Methodology for Data/Information Delivery
- Best Practices for the Data Lifecycle in a Typical EDW Lifecycle
- Best Practices for the Information Lifecycle as It Moves into the BI Lifecycle
- Best Practices for Auditing Data Access, as It Makes Its Way via the EDW and Directly (Bypassing the EDW) to the BI Dashboard
- Best Practices for using XML in the Open Source EDW/BI Space
- Best Practices for a Unified Information Integrity and Security Framework
- Object to Relational Mapping: A Necessity or Just a Convenience?
- Summary

8.2   Introduction

This chapter focuses on the best practices for data management in granular detail from data sources to data delivery, as well as the cross-dynamism and analytics involved across each interaction point of the end-to-end enterprise data warehouse/business intelligence (EDW/BI) solution spectrum. When it comes to data management, there are some essential indicators in terms of categorizing the landscape, keeping in mind that the customer/consumer/competitor (AKA the users producing, consuming, and subsuming the data) are the driving factor. And data management by design is a matrix-management scenario in the real world. Add to this the *big data* rapidly changing dimension and the complexity of management becomes analogous to managing a maze of n dimensions. The good news, though, is that as data evolved in structure, function, and volume, so did the technologies, architectures, and methodologies in place for creating, accessing, assessing, delivering, distributing, and dimensionally conforming that data in a correlated fashion. Using open source methodologies to implement the *Open Source Perfect* data management platform for EDW/BI is perhaps the best-fit practice option in today's data-centric, wireless, information-seeking world. Managing and analyzing data and its associated master data and metadata is critical to any business's operational and strategic success.

8.3   Best Fit of Open Source in EDW Implementation

Open source–based methodologies have befitting usability when it comes to EDW implementations, new or existing. The openness of standards—not only in terms of breadth or coverage of the target domain diversity but also in terms of depth when it comes to individual business solution tiers across the domain—provides *a unified set of adoptable standards and their subsequent implementation as business rules for horizontal and vertical business solution growth/optimization—from concepts to components to compliance and beyond.* Given the variety in choice of development options that are compliant with the primary selection criteria of architectural design, that ease complexity, and that are proven in terms of performance and flexibility, including the ability to undo changes with minimal overhead and customer-certification, here's a list of four best-practice use cases for leveraging open source as a development methodology in the EDW solution lifecycle:

1.   Given the *n*-dimensional complexity of data management having a matrix-oriented scope in terms of credibility, confidentiality, and functionality, using open source components as standalone or service-oriented add-ons can deliver a grid-controlled design to the data management platform. Using each of these components for stateless and state-enabled persistence across inter- and intradata tiers, the request-to-response and data-to-information flows are independently implementable across contextual domains, capacity, and scaling and efficiency factors—from articulation to administration. This is done by dynamically transforming the underlying process-to-model (data to information) conversion, followed by automation/scheduled execution with respect to the set of attributes/observations fit into the request-to-response context view. This in turns ripples into the return on customer (ROC) of the EDW solution by allowing segregation of duties, central-to-control and access to

the right information for the right purpose to the right people at the right time, as well as anytime, anywhere, anyone delivery of information to intelligence.

2. Open source is a best fit when it comes to the integration of existing EDW implementations with new and/or other solutions across solution boundaries. The integration options described in Chapter 7 in the section entitled "Integration Options: Dissected" can be used in developing a specialized-to-generalized *dynamic integration service* that can cross-connect across all required geolocated solution(s) to establish a converged EDW center with global presence and local scope. This technique can be used to establish custom EDW in a box that can encompass multiple distributed context-centric data marts/operational data stores (or ODS).

3. For lossless composition and decomposition of data and information, open source–based data and data integration models facilitate the design and development of redistributable, reconfigurable workflows for data consolidation, coalescing, and co-location by business function, orientation (i.e., emulating the business-model), and scoping (this includes levels of scalability, both tactical and strategic). This approach addresses the key business requirement of a having a common customer context in view for all data, all the time. The realizable business value from this benefit runs into unprecedented levels of customer satisfaction, not to mention the billions of dollars in cost savings—and all of this through an architecture that is flexible enough to adapt to changing data growth and easy to implement using a "build-once-deploy-many" strategy.

4. Last but not least, an open source EDW model enables reliable and sustainable adaptability to constant change, immaterial of the immensity or intensity of that change, by bringing the change-deltas as close as possible to the crux of data, with zero or minimal data movement, via its elasticity-powered, virtualization-enabled support to identify, understand, and quantify patterns of change using relative measurement metrics. This comes with a lot of dynamism surrounding the business solution, such as context-aware, application-aware, and risk-aware capabilities that can considered *360°-change-aware*. These capabilities are vital to any EDW solution deployment, as they automate the key

imperatives of information security and assurance that in turn drive business risk assurance.

8.4   Best Practices for Using Open Source as a BI-Only Methodology for Data/Information Delivery

Using open source as a BI-only methodology for 360°-change-aware information delivery begins with a conceptual view, depicted in Figure 8.1, that illustrates how open source methodologies can be used for data/information delivery in the context of BI-only deployments.

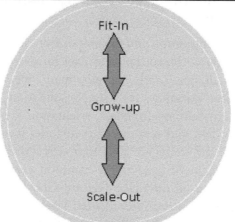

Analysis, Analytics, Decision-making ⇔ Self-Service BI, Self-Adaptable BI, Self-Manageable BI solution

Fit-In

Grow-up

Scale-Out

Common-Customer-Context (in View) Grid ⇔ My Data, My Way, Anywhere, Anytime, All the time

Figure 8.1   Using open source as a BI-only methodology for 360°-change-aware information delivery: a conceptual view.

Mobile BI and pervasive BI also play a pivotal role in this aspect.

8.4.1   Mobile BI and Pervasive BI

High-performance virtualization is a transforming design paradigm that can enable and enhance the information architecture so that mobility is integrated into the solution workflow visibly and with near-zero impact, from end point (cross-device) to enterprise point (cross-enterprise). Since each mobile device is independent in terms of its native functionality, an open source design based on this approach enables development of device-aware native services (at the service-oriented architecture or SOA tier), each of which is generated from the high-performance virtual services platform and then services the requesting endpoint device, using real-time federation of the common virtual engine by autoadapting to the native functionality in context. It does this by tagging the native context to the SOA-enabled/-enabling service cached on the end device and passed on as part of the request URL or stored on the sourcing end itself by preregistering the device-specific metadata. Note that the metadata that stores the per-device context is derived from a unified MDM model (XML-enabled or otherwise) using primary KIs based on mobile communication protocols and generic-to-native driver compatibility standards.

The key technology indicator driving this strategy is cloud computing that offers an easy and secure platform for building, testing, deploying, and optimizing the solution before freezing the proof of Concept (POC) for real-world usage.

The key imperatives involved are:

- BI pertaining to the business user role played by each domain data practitioner, from data scope analyst to data scientist to business analyst.
- BI pertaining to the functional domain, including administration, planning, customer engagement, data-centric connectivity, access, shareability and distributed processing with and without data replication and/or deduplication, and EDW vaulting versus co-locating.
- BI-aware data analytics, which comprise examining the uses to which data can be put for BI as a targeted domain as opposed to doing the same from a general data management perspective:
    - Using disconnected analytics as connection bases for BI-enablement by way of data integration→information integration→intelligent information integration. By using a grid-based distributed topology of these individual connection bases, a supertopology of analytics anchors can be articulated that is both load balanced and elastic in computation. Such dynamic information architectures are illustrative of those used in building knowledge grids for high-performance querying, as

in Vertica, InfoBright, MySQL-based, and other intertier cache-clusters for coherency, and they are best suited for unstructured data processing across relational-to-object-to-multidimensional solution boundaries. To shed some light on the commercial database (DB) side, Oracle's grid computing architecture and the larger Oracle Enterprise Grid are based on a similar design methodology.

- Using computation-in-depth enabled architectures for data analysis and storage without having to relocate or replicate the data.
- Scale-out enabled storage (persistent flash cache, SSD, or a hybrid leverage of the same) to balance memory input/output (I/O) versus disk I/O.
- High-performance data analysis and metrics generation by way of in-memory virtual replication, distributed data processing, partial transaction isolation by way of functionality partitioning and cross-DB distribution of data by {domain-context, content, custom-context} grouping, inter- and intrapipelining for real-time data sharing, and the like. This delivers real-time analysis to the reporting and analytic components, optimizing and scaling query performance for operational BI, which is an ideal use case for a BI-only scenario—especially for high-performing queries in which a single query involves processing of data volumes in the range of million records per second.

8.5　Best Practices for the Data Lifecycle in a Typical EDW Lifecycle

- Data Quality, Data Profiling, and Data Loss Prevention Components
- Data Integration Component
  - Data Integration: ETL–ELT versus EII versus EAI vs. I-I-I
  - Master Data Management (Including Metadata Management)
  - Using Data Integration as a Service

There are a set of best practices that can be followed for managing the data lifecycle in a typical EDW operations cycle. Depending on the functional specs and data/information usage, an open source–enabled information architecture can be used as assessor, enabler, enhancer, augmenter, accelerator, or a combination of these to address business needs in a load-balanced way in terms of time, scale, geography, and personalization variants. Here cost is assumed as a prerequisite factor for the same. Here's a list of some of the most widely used strategies today and next-generation trends:

1. A proprietary RDBMS for the enterprise foundation data warehouse on standard hardware as hardware layered over software, customized for EDW needs *and* using open source as the primary data access component for interapplication collaboration (e.g., Oracle, IBM DB2, MS SQL Server, etc.), complemented by open source–based high-performance caches for streaming/federating data to and from the source-to-target across each integration point, like Talend's extract, transform, load (ETL)-engines, Greenplum's Data Computing Appliance, or Hadoop/MapReduce–based SQL-engines for extreme query performance, and the like.

2. An out-of-the-box data warehouse appliance that gives direct install–configure–use capability optimized specifically for OLAP performance, with built-in flexibility for scaling and availability. Examples include Oracle's recently announced (at OOW 2011: October 2–5, 2011) Exalytics In-Memory Analytics Appliance, Oracle's Exadata and Exalogic (all three proprietary to Oracle), IBM's Netezza Twinfin Appliance, EMC Greenplum's DW Appliance, Noetix Analytics Platform, and the like.

3. A special purpose DBMS engineered for EDW and advanced analytical processing that includes a combination of next-generation information architectures from parallel computing to performance computing by way of columnar data model design, hybrid columnar compression using application-aware and hardware-enabled computation algorithms, and dynamic information grid generation based on the actual data and/or metadata involved. Open source examples include Vertica, InfoBright, Paraccel, SybaseIQ, Ingres Vectorwise, EnterpriseDB (based on postgreSQL), MySQL Analytics Engines, and the like.

4. In-memory databases and distributed file systems functioning as extended data warehouses that can be online in memory but offline when it comes to the actual underlying database management system or relational database management system (DBMS/RDBMS)—disconnected from it. This gives the power of data/

information access anytime, anywhere, to anyone. Examples are the Google's HDFS and HBase, InterSystems Caché, Oracle Exalytics In-Memory Analytics Database (the software component of the Oracle Exalytics Appliance), and the like.

8.5.1   Data Quality, Data Profiling, and Data Loss Prevention Components

Data quality, today and beyond, shares the dimensions of data profiling, data discovery, data clustering, data masking, data securing (by way of encryption and other ways), data loss prevention (by way of bidirectional tracing, tracking, and logging of data transport in prime time), and the trending imperatives of data virtualization, data co-location, and data-to-knowledge grids and the underlying workflows in action across (static data, slowly changing dimensions (SCDs), rapidly changing dimensions (RCDs), data-in-transit, data-in-the-clouds) asynchronously and synchronously.

Open source–based data quality methodologies, from open standards to open source services, have enabled the integration, elevation, and classification of data in the following ways for the *persistent, pervasive, and prevalent (relevance and relative customer use) treatment of the same for quality of such data*:

- Structured with the unstructured
- SQL-enabled with the Non-SQL enabled, including XML, NoSQL, and intelligent integrated queries
- Asynchronous with the synchronous
- Static, slowly changing, rapidly changing, and elastically varying dimensions
- At-rest with In-motion
- Silos with seamless with layered
- Experimental, historical, analytical, experiential, social, transactional, canonical, qualifying, anonymously identifiable, self-serviceable, autogenerated, machine-generated, hierarchical, and a combination of these types of data
- Homogeneous with heterogeneous, by way of services and processes in addition to structure and content
- Data integration with data migration with data upgrade, data enhancement, and multifactor data matrix formulation
- Relational with nonrelational with spatial with multidimensional with unknown dimensional

- Data-intensive with compute-intensive
- Share-all enabled with share-nothing enabled

The key technical processes for data quality are:

1. *Exploration-based data discovery*: What the data means function-ally, the source of that data and its identity, how the data can be used in a best-fit manner, and why it is a best fit. This requires figuring out the data-to-data linkages, both contextually and by studying the actual data values.

2. *Extraction-based data profiling and segmentation*: This involves metadata or context around the data. This is a necessary input to the MDM module to enhance the data further by unifying the same in structure, type compliance, semantics, and patterns-based metadata processing.

3. *Data cleansing*: This comprises refreshing and refining the data for target domain compatibility.

4. *Data quality (pre-, post-) certification*: This consists of a precertifi-cation that uses the data to be quality tested as a sample training set for deriving the qualifiers, followed by using the derived met-rics to measure the quality of the actual data as a postprocess for baselining and improvisation.

Some of the best practices from the methodology standpoint can involve:

- *Exclusive audit-based logging at the data access layer*: This is highly essential for designing a *common native interface* that accesses data and presents it by adapting it to the receiving domain's native for-mat. The advantage of this native-enablement is to bring the data being adapted as close to the storage and processing pragmatics of the receiver DB. This eliminates the overheads of additional appli-cation programming interface (API) calls and reduces the number of copy-by-value passes and dynamic memory management. Also, when such data is hierarchical in nature, it enables autoinheritance of the target DB's compilation and execution capabilities. And an open source–based adaptive native analyzer can be designed using the pragmatics outlined in the Chapter 7 section entitled "Devel-opment Options: Dissected."

This engine can be used on the user-facing side as embedded analytics while presenting information on demand. At this stage, it is a recommended best practice to avoid the use of SQL unless such usage is prevalent by compliance at the presentation layer. The trending push-to mechanism can be used to implement the same. The next sections will outline how easy and beneficial this is, where it reiterates the best practice of isolating the EDW, enterprise data access, and enterprise BI layers of any EDW/BI solution. *This is a best-fit topology for usage flexibility by enabling the elasticity of demand and supply (AKA, elasticity by scalability and availability).*

- *Web-enablement by way of adaptive data quality metrics*: Web 2.0 with Web 3.0, semantic with nonsemantic, and unification of the same using *contextual semantic expressions* tags that denormalize terminology-based expressions (user friendly) with semantic expressions (business friendly) using composite transformations constructed using regular expressions, ontology rules, and tokenized parsing based on (autogenerated) common ground of metadata and master data definitions.

- *KPI-focused metrics, measures, measurements, and models*; These include multitier test cases and multitier test beds as a standalone run, as a service, in line with integration workflow, in the database as a API call, online as part of business operations cycle, and so on

The key here is to profile data via fine-grained differentiators that reveal the inhibitors, exhibitors, and prohibitory and required data items, along with their context. This aids in the critical phase of data profiling by allowing all data to be qualified by context, from raw to rich to robust.

- *Role-centric, rules-based, responsibilities-driven, and results-oriented analysis and analytics*: Here, *role* is a multifactor rule, itself comprising {role-by-authority, role-by-function, role-by-context, role-by-information-identity}. *Though there is some overlap between these four types of roles, the fine-line divider is the way the information is supposed to be consumed by way of usage.* This difference becomes conspicuous when the corresponding metrics are autogenerated rather than predefined for registration, unregistration, and {severity-level, data-domain content hierarchy}–based dynamic allocation.

A real-world use case is qualifying pre-aggregated or summarized data to derive metrics that can drive other aggregated or nonaggregated data in an analogous fashion. When the only data available is at least one level above raw data or base-level data, the de-aggregation or synthesis of the same to derive meaningful metrics for data quality is a necessary condition to be met. Data mining techniques based on exploratory analysis can be used to uncover the common ground hidden in such data. Here the key quality metric is visibility of the hidden patterns {content, context} to the finest possible atomic level.

- *SOA-enabled, SaaS-enabled and -enabling, embeddable, hot-pluggable, out-of-the-box, and high performance–enabled SQL/hybrid data quality engines*: These engines include hardwired and algorithms-driven analytics and analysis platforms delivered as cache-resident computing platforms or software appliances.
- *Cloud computing–enabled quality engines with configurable endpoint controls and technofunctionality tailored data-quality process models*: A typical model can be based on the following process key performance initiatives:
  - Determining the primary data element to be used as the outlier or in-the-neighborhood by using fuzzy logic–based learning algorithms that leverage real-time constraints-induced intelligence. This guarantees that the quality of the measuring ruler is as close to the behavior of the outcome as it is supposed to be.
  - An implementation of the same needs some homework to be done at the requirements planning and preview stages of the solution test cycle(s), as data quality needs prequalification of the data to be used as potential test-bed and the rules-set surrounding it. This approach could be thought of as data driving data to reach the optimal quality level possible. It is like taking the fingerprints of the measures needed from the data itself, which is "native" to the data these measures will use to qualify (verify, validate, and certify). Code design can be done

following the patterns of self-similarity testing algorithms and the like.

- Trace the activity logs for all data from database to the data flow to the end user and store the results in a common format (e.g., XML- or SQL-enabled). This information can be used to analyze the data-driving-data patterns (as stated in the previous bullet point) using metadata extractors and feeding the output of the same into data quality analyzers.

- Customer feedback and on-demand ratification of the qualifiers involved based on the same in an iterative fashion are key to accelerating the metrics for quality of data, and must be included as part of the data quality analytics set. This constitutes metrics that can be applied as qualifiers as well as quantifiers, as the authenticity of such metrics is established because they are derived from and tested on these dual datasets, from lineage to anchorage. MDM models can help accelerate this process by bridging between the data in analysis and the data analytics to ensure coherency and consistency across the solution scope.

- Once completed, these rules can be encapsulated into a generic or specific data quality certification engine primarily based on delivering the optimal time to quality with security; governance, risk, and compliance; and other necessary add-ons being enabled by way of extension qualifiers.

It is recommended that all of the quality control measures use a common set of end-to-end compliant tools, techniques, methodologies, and elastic platforms for modeling, development, deployment, testing, and real world–simulated analyses.

Data Loss Prevention (DLP)

This can be qualified in at least two different ways: first, the "unnoticeable" data leakage as it moves from its source to target usage, and second, the data lost during the process of applying transformations on the same. The difference is that the former can refer to data being left behind after leaving the source but before getting to the transformation engine; the latter can involve the data losing its identity (functional value) as its value is etched by applying data transformations such as masking, deidentification, encryption, and data hardening by enclosing a domain-level rules set, and the like.

The first of these problems can be solved by implementing data virtualization as a data quality measure. This can be done in the following ways:

- *Constrain the movement of data to the minimal extent possible*: This means views based on multiple data sources powered by context-specific logic can be used to dynamically answer query requests without having to physically move the data (location-wise) using data replication, duplication, and the like. This limits the actual data-in-motion by ensuring that *data is moved only as needed*. Co-location of multiple data sets (homogeneous or heterogeneous) using clustering techniques, performance-optimized multijoin views, and dynamic virtual data federation are some of the best-fit techniques for implementing the same. Sometimes, even virtual caching (AKA caching by user-session, by memory-scope, or inter-session caching) or domain-level segmented cache clusters can accelerate this process.
- *Take data virtualization to a higher level by enabling it at the interdatabase, interdimension, and interapplication levels*: This is realizable by architecting persistent distributed caching that can be accessed in real time or on demand, and can operate in a offline fashion. The key here is to preserve the state of this cache by using data-busing services, also called data-integration services, that keep the offline cache in sync with the online data store(s).
- *Use key-value pairs as pointers to the actual data rows*: These store a hash-mapped ID and a relevant context combination determined by meta-data one-on-one with master data and fact-based data. Then using any of the above two techniques the data quality KPI can be implemented as analytics that can then be applied in real-world scenarios to result in qualified-informatics.
- *Automate and SOA-enable the above workflow by using it as a DLP-service corresponding to the business DLP process*: This is a pre-emptive practice that prevents relapses in data loss by ensuring continuous execution of the DLP-process as part of the subsuming business process-flow.

The second of the two problems, i.e. data getting misrepresented during the processing phase via masking etc. can be prevented in the following ways:

- *Perform bi-directional scanning of the data to the atomic level (as far as possible)*: This process dissects the data based on reengineering and reverse-engineering, as it is used from source-to-target. A selected criteria set, such as {priority-level, usage-context, domain-context} in this order and partitioning vertically across this combination but using a composite-hashed key containing these three as the key members, gives a collateral result that puts the business rules-to-data rules to be used into segmented vertical buckets that define when to stripe the data and when not to; as well as when to strip/crop the data and when not to. Such rules can be extended to multitier levels to implement complex metrics for multitenant partitioning of the analysis involved.

- *Preserve the identity for cross-tier interoperation of the data*: This is vital when data moves from one tier level to another, meaning from the DB to the application or middleware level(s) and vice versa. Here, deidentification and anonymous representation for commonality are used as best practices to preserve and protect the unnecessary context of the data being exposed by way of its content. The solution again lies in using a common functional representation based on the context-domain with the exceptions (of data involved) being saved to be treated differently. A host of masking and encryption algorithms are available based on the {content, context} combination, but the primary driver of the underlying algorithm is the 3-tuple {priority-level, usage-context, domain-context} that uniquely identifies both the amplitude and recursion-depth of the identity operation involved. Examples are {1, sensitive-data, ALL_DOMAINS}, {0, securing-data, ALL_DOMAINS}, and so on. Here, the second 3-tuple emphasizes on a higher priority than the first by establishing it as a baseline—as the default measure to be enforced.

  An access-control list based on the 3-tuple elements can also be used to white-list the desired combinations. The order does matter here.

  When it comes to local versus global, the default baseline still applies to the local, and *the local overrides the global*.

A hybrid approach combining both of the previous approaches gives a best-of-breed approach by structuring the data loss prevention rules-set into a layered dimension of data quality that can be standardized as a new imperative quality-of-(data-content)-identity. This concept can be generalized to extend into the BI space so that it evolves into quality-of-content-identity-intelligence analytics.

8.5.2   The Data Integration Component

As the EDW life-cycle progresses from data sourcing to data movement and beyond, data integration (or DI for short) becomes a key component in orchestrating overall data processing, distribution, advanced analysis, and most importantly data quality in terms of ensuring consistency and relevancy of the same. As new data sources are added and new content needs to be autogenerated across point-to-point and solution boundaries, data integration needs a collaborative and adaptive mechanism in place by which it can produce, consume, and service multiple cross-dimensional request-to-response and cross-component information access, availability, and authenticity. This requires a common framework for architecting the DI services end-to-end, the essential design criteria of which are laid out in the *Common Frame of Architecture for DI (CFA-for-DI)*.

Common Frame of Architecture for DI

- Commonality in agility
- Commonality in computation: using open source embeddable in-database analytics (a platform that supports development, testing, and deployment of such analytic metrics on an on-demand, customizable basis)
- Commonality in storage
- Commonality in transformation
- Commonality in presentation
- Commonality in optimization
- Commonality in access
- Commonality in conformance (to static, slowly changing, and rapidly changing dimensions)
- Commonality in relevance to user preference(s)
- Commonality in persistence (across shared and cross-solution boundaries)
- Commonality in identification and deidentification by *role* (usability: what it does and in what *n* ways), *rule* (implementation of the usability role), *linkage and lineage*, and *change management*

(subjectively by collapsing into a unified view and objectively by contextualizing as usage dictates)

By introducing the technology–methodology stack vertically through the CFA-for-DI set of criteria, the best practice pragmatics boil down to the following list:

- *A unified computing platform for interaction and interoperation*: This gives the power to harness scalability without hurting performance by way of share-enabled computing leveraging share-enabled resources. Here, resources include not only the solution platform ecosystem in terms of hardware, OS, software, and middleware but also sharing primary, secondary, and tertiary memory, as well as the CPU utilization at every possible tier of the solution infrastructure. This approach involves using principles of collaborative comput-ing—integrating intra- and interapplications as well as external (off-enterprise-scope) applications like social software systems on an on-demand (on-the-fly) basis.
- *On-demand scalability with always-on availability*: Security and assurance are critical factors in this case. Augmenting on-demand solutions with customer configurable lock-in security controls, sys-tem-level encryption controls and remote-access-aware analytics is one way to securitize EDW/BI solutions in- and outside of the enterprise usage scope. Open source DI metrics automated by dynamic content-fits-context workflows and/or SOA-enabled inte-gration services eliminate the need for third-party systems with analogous functionality in at least two ways. First, they allow industry standards and company-specific policies for the same to be incorporated into a single analytics base that is extensible and reusable cross-customer, cross-platform, cross-temporal, and cross-geo. Second, DI services can be used to bridge the gap between what's in and what's needed when the customer scope leverages externalized engines/tools for the same. This way, an open source DI service/engine can function as a collaborative development, deployment, and delivery mechanism that can be standardized into an open source collaborative DI framework for pervasive adoption. In regards to availability assurance, an open source–based (data) integration service can be implemented as follows:

- Automate the above stated DI workflows into a preintegrated and streamlined process flow. The only required input to this subsuming process will be the context handle dynamics.
- Pass the dynamic context as a stateless or persistent object instance, XML-instance, Context Model instance (via pre-configured Context Domains).
- In addition use a runtime generated version of one or more combination(s) of the above (via virtualization using dynamic parameter binding) to handle variable arguments as needed.

- *Query reuse and optimization, as well as query result-set reuse and cache-enabled storage.*
- The four Ds (Discover-Derive-Decision-Demonstrate) of data exploration and extraction of patterns from it to put to use, reuse, and improved use.
- *Avoiding pre-defined aggregation and summarization by way of application-aware context caching (tagged to the appropriate content by using {request, response} paired identifiers)*: This can include caching the related workflow that is responsible for servicing the request. At runtime, the appropriate content is processed on the input context using a hybrid-computation mechanism—one that does SQL processing, including implicit recursive SQL, and a second that uses non-SQL processing (AKA Hadoop/MapReduce–based metrics, NoSQL (Not only SQL), and the like) in parallel—akin to a dynamic virtual analytics engine.
- *Using streams-based processing for fast unstructured content searching*: This can be done by leveraging data vaults that are configurable on demand and are Flash-cached to enable interactive disconnected analysis for all offline requests as well as those originating online, be it from Web, mobile, social, or combinations of these deployment platforms.

The Dimensions of Data Integration: ETL–ELT versus EII versus EAI versus I-I-I

On a broader scale, data integration can be considered the backbone for EDW in terms of the end-to-end data lifecycle as it moves from data assimilation to data dissemination. The primary dimensions of DI revolve around the following four aspects:

- *Information Architecture*: Involves three primary dimensions, namely, *Data Modeling, Data Quality,* and *Data (Services) Virtualization*. From instant information access to intelligent information access instantly, data integration methodologies directly influence the information architecture by way of data as a service, information as a service, DI as a service, and dynamic query services— employing techniques such as data virtualization and clustering at the logical level to stream one-to-many and many-to-one query result-sets by processing them in-memory, in-database, and/or with resident caching.
- *Data Management*: Includes administration of all data, all the time, as well as data messaging, massaging, and transmission.
- *Extreme Data Convergence*: This includes knowing what the data can do relative to a particular dynamic context and what else can complement this data for comprehensive metadata extraction/generation and subsequent integration of the same, to better aid in business analysis, analytics, and intelligence-oriented decision metrics. Master data management is key to metadata management using customer data and other related data.
- *Extreme Data Continuity*: This pertains to the commonality in agility principle and enforces continuity of business (solution) operations by way of being able to autoadapt continuous changes in DI, from requirements specifications to BI and beyond. SOA enablement of continuous data integration and dynamic query services can be used to implement this.

The critical factor here is in figuring out the best-fit methodology to differentiate between management and use of such data from the customer/consumer/competitor standpoint. The essential qualifiers for this methodology are agility, data quality, data profiling, data virtualization, and secure data assurance at the very least.

The key business drivers for data integration are:

- Data quality—qualifiers and quantifiers as quality control measures
- Data services for EDW and BI by way of extract, transform, load and extract, load, transform (ETL–ELT) and data and database virtualization (especially distributed data delivery on-demand)

- Data services for operational BI (where there is no EDW needed) via data virtualization at the data sourcing end as well as the data servicing end, supplemented by in-memory, in-database, and in-application processing
- Data-cycle extensibility by way of dynamic data distribution on demand (AKA dynamic data grid), centralization and/or decentralization, synchronization, migration, and dynamic data commissioning and decommissioning
- Isolating DI processes from data access to application processes, which facilitates solution platform-agnostic interoperability; open source methodology is a perfect way to realize this goal. Here isolation refers to the DI servicing mechanisms as opposed to Data Services themselves.

The ETL–ELT (Extract, Transform, Load—Extract, Load, Transform) dimension of DI is a necessary component for the data assimilation phase of DI. It involves sourcing data from multiple sources, immaterial of the structure and storage characteristics of such data. The *discover, derive* imperatives of the four Ds paradigm (i.e.. *discover, derive, decide, demonstrate)* can aid in the ETL–ELT dimension of DI by implementing a methodology as outlined below:

- *Apply the principles of commonality in relevance and conformance* when selecting data sources for a solution scope. This can be done by enlisting all *necessary and sufficient* customer data sources (master data, legacy data, historical data, archived data, offline data, electronic system of records, real-time data) along with the real-world use-case context of every such data set in the list. The phrase *use-case context* includes the business process, lineage, and spread of such data across the business and social (internal and external) scope of use, as well as the technology used for the same, to the extent allowable for the traceability of the same. This is the first step to start with for DI to be productive.
- Apply the principle of commonality in transformation to categorize the data extracted by the business-centric qualifiers of data quality, compliance, governance, target usage context, and most importantly the degree of change involved in such data over the EDW lifecycle. *The one simple cue card to follow to derive a common qualifier across all of these is to apply the single source of scope as outlined in the solution SLA(s).*

- Then apply the technology drivers by way of CFA-for-DI to flatten out the data from the point of source through the points of complexity to arrive at a common database of structured and unstructured content that is the first layer of output from the DI process. This in turn is used for the subsequent Transform-Load—Load-Transform phases of ETL–ELT.

Enumerating the dimension of EII, or enterprise information integration, involves more than just ETL–ELT. Though the latter is a necessary component for EII, it involves a more fine-grained scoping in that it includes the information architecture, data management, and extreme data convergence to be taken into account for implementation. The design qualifiers for EII include but are not limited to the following:

- Applying the principles of commonality in computation, storage, persistence, presentation, access, and optimization across every point of interaction, interoperation, request–response servicing, bidirectional data flow, and conversion variations for multitenancy.
- Applying the principle of commonality in optimization to isolate the architectural tiers by business context as opposed to architectural convenience—for example, a typical modular EDW architecture can involve a common data source base for the ETL–ELT tier; a common data computation tier; and a common information presentation tier; all flexibly coupled by way of light footprint DI services and/or SOA-enabled/-embedded DI engines.
- Applying the CFA-for-DI using replication techniques, especially techniques of virtual replication for efficient data distribution and query results set delivery. Here replication can even apply to the individual DI workflows, multiple ETL–ELT modules, and multiple information architectures, predesigned and ready to be reused. The design and development techniques of real-time information streaming, coalescing point-to-point and peer-to-peer (AKA system-to-system) datasets for processing and overriding traditional ACID properties and data integration methods of physical replication and so forth of RDBMS to leverage dynamic objects, stateless caching of information for anytime availability, and transparent auto-update of the same for consistency are the major implementation rules for the same.
- Applying a combination of the above to achieve commonality in agility is quintessential to today's growth in all-data, both

incrementally and exponentially in correlation with the growth in change requirements. The primary focus is on *how to improve the business solution and operations processes as the needs of the business constantly change to ensure business continuity.*

The key imperative in agility is continuity—business continuity. From continuous requirements specifications to continuous integration to continuous delivery to continuity in deployment to continuous (business AKA solution lifecycle) operations, managing continuity of change in order (or, in other words, managing continuous change) demands at least two things to be constant in implementation, namely, continuous [operational] integration of data and continuous [operational] intelligence. Of special emphasis is the phrase "continuity in order." This does not necessarily mean order in terms of sequence of occurrence, but is more indicative of the ability to align the change as it happens with the business (AKA solution) operations in a transparent and effective manner—without disturbing the operational aspects of the live running solution.

- Implementing the above process as a closed-loop DI workflow to ensure that data changes are pervasively reflected from the ETL–ELT tier to the EDW tier, the BI tier, and the point-of-access tier; to prevent loss and consistency of information, continuous event-based logging of business activity, EDW activity, and customer/user experience activity (treated as an event separate from business activity)—using technologies such as global log vaults, log vaulting by business context, user context, application solution context, solution component context, bidirectional data flow context and DI workflow context greatly improves the security, regulatory compliance, information management, and customer experience dynamics that make up the overall value of the solution.

Master Data Management (Including Metadata Management)

Master data management (MDM) is the business value driver for any EDW/BI solution by way of taking into account all the enclosing and enclosable business dimensions or attributes necessary for the actual facts-based analysis, advanced analytics, and/or BI. These business dimensions are referred to as master data or the necessary business-critical and business solution–specific attributes that define the (key, value) pairs for data and information contexts on which all business analysis, analytics, and intelligence are based.

Master data management refers to the functional lifecycle management of these business dimensions with respect to business analysis, business processes, and business user-centricity.

Metadata management refers to the software design, derivation, development, configuration, transformation, and optimal leverage of the functional master data domain in terms of data quality, security, quality assurance, processing and testing for triage-lineage-linkage, to create an analogous technical metadata (or data about the master data) management platform that exhibits the following characteristics:

- Coherency and consistency with the MDM from start to finish
- Adaptability to growth in data and change management of related master data, any time and all the time
- The business value or return on customer (ROC) of master data management comes from the ever-challenging and user-experience-centric task of delivering a *single collaborative customer view* that presents the landscape of all business-related information across users, context domains, scoping, and master data dimensions. This is different from a single source of truth in that there can be multiple master data marts involved in a single EDW solution, and there can be multiple collaborative customer views, each pertaining to a single business enterprise scope. However, all of these can be integrated to facilitate mix/merge of one or more these to meet on-demand user requirements.
- A quality MDM design begins at the point of planning and progresses through the EDW lifecycle, with DI as the mechanism for conforming the changing master data across scale, uniformity in content, and dynamism to service multiple consumers—across the EDW and BI tiers as well as for externalization.

Master data management is taking prerequisite data in diversity to a higher level of information in uniformity so that multiple disparate data elements can "talk" to each other using a common metalanguage. This in a way extends the concept of language-independent querying to the domain of master data.

The key business drivers for MDM are:

- Master data modeling that outlines a conceptual view of all master reference data—highly imperative for the 'Unified Customer View' pragmatics in all EDW/BI solutions. MDM models can aid in accelerating this process by bridging 'data-in-analysis' with the 'data-analytics' to ensure coherency and consistency across the solution scope.
- MDM models allow for dynamic context switching between disparate domains, which in turn accelerates the delivery of dynamic data services necessary in dynamic data warehousing implementations and the like.
- Customer reference data, standardized by business scope, industry-segment, usability roles, functionality domains, and cross-referencing.
- Dedicated and integrated deployment of MDM as a service for any/all target IT environments with minimal change management and near-zero IT administration.
- The technical implementation details from MDM to metadata management can consist of the following best practices:
- Like data quality, master data management must begin at the data sourcing phase of DI to ultimately result in a robust MDM model that can be reused, or even unused, for best fit, multiple times. The MDM model must be elegant enough to present a conceptual view of what the collaborative customer view is going to be.
- The design patterns of metadata must mimic those of the underlying master data, though not necessarily one-to-one. This is because one or more master data entities can be mapped to one metadata dimension by way of dimensional normalization. And this is done for the purposes of query performance as well as storage simplification. Dimensional normalization and denormalization are two overlapping design patterns, yet they differ in terms of MDM-specific rules. The difference lies not just in denormalizing cascading dimensions of the super-type→sub-type category, but in developing data flow maps that can be convoluted into data mapping models (which are often more logical than physical) for MDM-specific purposes, such as:
  - Physical implementation of the master data hierarchies via specialization and generalization of logical models.

- On-the-fly synchronization of master data to enable dynamic integration of the same, to reflect in the collaborative customer view.
- API-enabled invocation of the MDM model(s) as independent calls that operate on metasets of grouped master data information. This is useful in implementing collaborative master data integration services via SOA or pure Web services.
- Semantic virtualization across heterogeneous master data domains to generate business rules that can operate on such inputs to output common identifiers that work across the contextual business-user domain. This can be implemented by storing the metadata of each master data domain, using data mapping models to coalesce multiple related taxonomies into one user-acceptable descriptor that expresses commonality in meaning, and then tagging this descriptor to any number of workflows that pertain to master data integration.
- Apply governance, risk, and compliance (GRC) and security policies by way of segregation of duties, same origin policy vulnerabilities, Security Information and Event Management (SIEM), Infrastructure-network inherent topology-centric policies.
- Last but not least, make the above design persistent by way of a data dictionary, a unified MDM model, or a repository-driven catalog.

Using Data Integration as a Service

A service-oriented architecture (SOA)–based methodology is recommended as a best practice for implementing data integration (DI) in terms of operations and orchestration. DI as a service takes DI to the next level by structuring the DI into modular and distributed entities, each of which can independently work on a specific function for which it is implemented, and then having all of the individual components coordinate for connectivity, consumption, and integration to deliver the final results. The best practice methodology drivers for implementing this are using data virtualization as an enabler and accelerator of DI as a service to BI as a service and extending it to solution as a service enabler, as well as other development strategies as described in Chapter 7 As an example, a typical SOA-centric DI service can involve:

- Complex Data Synthesis Component—for handling unstructured data
- Distributed Workload Component—for handling data functionality-wise, efficiency-wise, or homogeneity/heterogeneity/hybrid payloads–wise
- Orchestration Component—for coordinating the intercomponent process, resource, and messaging via dynamic workflows generation for Reliability-Availability-Security (or R-A-S)
- Change Management Component—for handling real-time, on-demand, batch-oriented or
- Dynamic Allocation Component—for handling the right data service to the right DI service component

---

DI as a service can be easily extended and elevated to information integration as a service to cover the end-to-end DI in a single pass with interconnected (loosely coupled, lightweight) DI as a service components. This can be used to develop A reference architecture for a unified Intelligent-Information-Integration (or I-I-I) framework.

The key here lies in the ability to use DI in a flexible, elastically scalable fashion by just configuring the details, while the SOA transport and orchestration mechanisms autohandle the dynamism involved.

- An SOA approach allows for unordered to ordered transformation from silos to structures that can be reused or represented in an adoptive manner in relatively change-enabled ecosystems.
- SOA-enabled DI services can be delivered as SaaS based or true-hosted embeddable DI engines, immaterial of the source outgoing and incoming IT infrastructure.
- SOA-centric DI services are cloud computing–compliant and can be deployed in cloud environments for a variety of reasons, starting from DI beyond the enterprise to the enterprise cloud and the like.

A business case for using DI as a service can be one that assesses the risk impact and assurance of a data loss prevention (DLP) model. Using a live dataset and a set of DLP rules driving the DLP model, DI as a service can be designed to:

- Detect leakages in data

- Classify them into distinctly different categories:
  - Ignorable data drops, with zero-or minimal impact on data quality
  - High-impact data drops that affect the data quality control metrics, thereby potentially narrowing the quality assurance window
  - Intelligent data drops that function as process-centric input to test-case generators for identifying event-triggered error spots during {pre-process, process, post-process} execution tasks, such as scheduler boundary conditions, threshold baseliners, morphed transformations for unstructured data processing, Web-site traffic dependent 'data sops' that are countable as valid for data trickling scenarios, and the like
- Integrate both the above pieces by using a third DI piece. It is to be noted that each of the above pieces can be implemented as data as a service, though, when it comes to the logic to be applied to enabling such functionality. The DI as a service plays a pivotal role in interpiece orchestration, input/output (I/O), and component-state consistency end-to-end.

8.6   Best Practices for the Information Lifecycle as It Moves into the BI Lifecycle

As data analysis crosses the chasms of online, mobile, predictive, and prime time analytics, it is standardized as a *business analysis process*, thereby inventing the need for business analytics or, in other words, the generation of business rules that when implemented as self-contained metriclets (Business Rule → Associated Business KPI) deliver decision support capabilities to end user.

8.6.1   The Data Analysis Component: The Dimensions of Data Analysis in Terms of Online Analytics vs. Predictive Analytics vs. Real-Time Analytics vs. Advanced Analytics

Analytics are derived/discovered/autogenerated metrics that aid in data-driven, usage-based decision making. By using analytics, the value of a *business process* can be qualified and made to perform at the most optimal level by way of uncovering the best-fit process (and methodology) behind that *business process* in terms of when and how, as opposed to accelerating the what, why, and where components. Some of the best-practice recommendations in this regard are as follows:

- Increasing effectiveness, efficiency, and extensibility of data-to-information improvement, insight, and intelligence. This is because they provide commonality in measurement across multiple domains, channels, and platforms and thus are of greater value in terms of enrichment, quality, and faster time to insight. In this respect, analytics can be predefined, stored for reuse, created on the fly (as in case of operational BI), and/or advanced to a higher level by deploying them as a context-centric foundational platform of metrics-based intelligence. As an example, the same set of analytics can be used for mobile BI, reports-driven BI, or for that matter anywhere, as long as the BI usage context is the same.
- Analytics can help in self service–based report generation or interactive/collaborative shared analysis. Examples are dynamic dashboarding, cross-dimensional integrity, always-on persistence, relevance-in-depth context tagging, and the like.

If collaboration can be perceived as being user oriented, coordination can be viewed as being process oriented, and communication is conceivable as spanning the entire amplitude between these two boundaries. In this perspective, analytics are both the producers and consumers for intertier, intratier, and extratier solution communication of information in a flexible, adaptive, and responsive fashion. Solutions-multiple, common analytics, normalized intelligence—this is the Next Generation BI Model.™

- *Analytics can be used to streamline BI deployments*, using advanced analytics that publish business rules as dynamic drivers for automation and orchestration of cross-platform deployments by integrating the business operations landscape with next-gen deployment landscape via stateless decoupling by way of SaaS, SOA-embeddable metrics, and the most pervasively used user platforms like social media. This means this set of preintegrated analytics can be adopted as a dynamic deployment and delivery model that consists for model to model–, rules to rules–, and standards to standards–based common set of deployment rulesets and measures that work across the solution scope. This means going beyond tech-savvy to gain an edge over on-demand, faster time to service productivity. The classic example of today's IT convergence via a unified infrastructure that blends mobility, agility, and visibility in an elastic fashion is one of the use cases where this type of dynamic deployment and delivery model can be put into practice. *In this case, the instant delivery on demand of BI solution by mobile-enabling it on the fly is the key value imperative of using such a methodology.*

■ The *quality-of-content-identity-intelligence* metric (described earlier in the subsection on data loss prevention, or DLP) can be taken to the next level to be implemented as an advanced analytic for data mining that combines the qualitative and quantitative measures from the respective training datasets to provide a more accurate prediction that is greater in confidence and support.

A business use case of using such an analytics-based factor can be to power an advanced predictive analytics model for businesses requiring real-time intelligent information visualization solutions.

The high five of data analysis from an EDW/BI perspective can be enlisted as:

1. Cross-process componentization for the same context domain and extension/contraction of the same

2. Autohandling of growth and change dynamics especially identification and handling ambiguity in changes

3. Self-manageable metrics via autooptimization in extreme load and stress conditions like dynamic load-balancing, and auto-rollback capability during outlier and out-of-context "missed" states

4. Self-recoverability via persistent state caching, immaterial of the underlying frameworks such as BASE over ACID, SEAM, RESTful, and the like, without losing integrity of information

5. Self-adaptable metrics by way of context awareness and realistic and relative correlation

Business intelligence can be a slowly changing dimension from the business domain's effective, efficient, and evolving context, given that it meets the solution usability lifecycle over a consistent time period, but competitive BI is a rapidly changing dimension, and the *Open Source Perfect* needs to handle this by way of the following:

- The Next-Gen Business–Social Operational Model: *Open Source Perfect*. Leverage it to implement competitive BI, thereby transforming the business operations model, one analytic at a time
- The Next-Gen Customer-Centricity: Do-it-yourself (DIY) "concept"-centric, context-enabled business pie
- The Next-Gen Customer: The intelligent customer, from corporate to end user; on-premise to cloud to crowd
- The Next-Gen Desktop: Virtual Desktop Infrastructure (VDI), anywhere, anytime, for anyone
- The Next-Gen Internet: IPv6 enablement
- The Next-Gen Business–Social: BI for Information and technology convergence:
  - Mobile, Web, virtual environments
  - Voice, video, and data
  - Shared, collaborative, social cooperative, interoperable, hot-pluggable, distributed
  - Dedicated, competitive, context-aware, risk-aware
  - Adaptive BI for adaptive self-service
  - Information-sourcing, -producing, -subsuming, -consuming, -assuring

---

Advanced metrics for integrated reasoning or collective intelligence:

- Accelerating competitive intelligence across the dimensions of time, space, referential domains, and customer/consumer/competitor experiences by eliminating point-to-point, access-point, and inter-process boundaries
- Adopting a process modeling approach to align the underlying business process models with decision support models at every stage of the intelligent information realization: inception, implementation, visualization, customization, personalization, and the information continuum

---

Some of the trending and next-gen best practices for a best-fit DIY BI solution can be enumerated as follows:

- *Enable on-demand decision support.* This gives trusted IT-free business solution adoption by reducing the reliance on IT significantly. Note that this does not enable an IT-less business ecosystem, which is practically unthinkable.
- *Reiterate the best practice of isolating the enterprise data warehouse, enterprise data access, and enterprise BI layers of any EDW/BI solution.* This is a best-fit topology for usage flexibility by way of elasticity of demand and supply (AKA elasticity by scalability and availability).
- Use advanced business analytics as a supplement to EDW and not as a (total, semitotal) replacement of the same.
- Use *disconnected analytics* as *connection bases for BI enablement,* by using DI, information integration, and intelligent information integration in the dynamics of messaging to massaging data as it progresses from tier-to-tier. This engine can be used as embedded analytics while presenting information on demand and in real time. At this stage, it is a recommended best practice to process data using the "data-shift" paradigm,which autodelegates the processing by allocating the right data to be processed at the right place(the most optimal SQL-enabled and/or hybrid engine). This helps accelerate the process by bridging the data in analysis with the data analytics to ensure coherency and consistency across the solution scope.
- *Use the disconnected analytics methodology on MDM models to aid in closing the semantic spread,* by integrating master data and creating new metadata during the process, as well as unifying annotation complexity by way of a common language of terminology that works across the latitude of users' demands for business friendliness.
- *Realize multidimensional data to be delivered on demand* by constructing virtual cubes that use relational aggregation on any/all data in context to group, cross-reference, and summarize at various levels (rollup, dense multiscore, etc.). The virtual cubes can be created and delivered by a data virtualization API that in turn leverages predefined materialized views kept in sync with fact-based data, including all the dependent dimensional data. A recommended approach is to follow a blended strategy that enables:

- Using a ROLAP model to structure and store data for greater SQL-enabled processing and storage efficiency, as close to the DBMS engine as possible.
- Using a columnar data model to accelerate access performance; this can be part of a dynamic data grid.
- Using a semantics-enabled data mapping model to synthesize and analyze both structured and unstructured data in a bidirectional fashion. This can be enabled by using the various development techniques as described earlier in this chapter and in Chapter 7 ("Development Options: Dissected" and "Deployment Options: Dissected").
- Using a semantics-enabled integrated information presentation model to construct a unified view that delivers consistent results with respect to the request, immaterial of how the underlying data is stored, structured, processed, aggregated, or analyzed, and most importantly independent of how such data behaves by way of transit, transmission, and automanipulation.
- Last but not least, making each of the above layers independent to enable stand-alone implementation and execution of the same in multiple solution spaces—by being to deploy on existing infrastructure while at the same time ensuring a consistent transition and operations.

Open source enabling of the same can benefit the business from its ability to:

- Construct a connected solution implementation that provides global access to all information, anytime, anywhere, by anyone—yet preserves the GRC and SOP compliance.
- Internally personalize by using on-demand services and extending them to connect to the external solution domains with minimal downtime.
- Proactively scale and dynamically load-balance based on both solution resource utilization and customer-centric demand.
- Customize the production and consumption of data/content as well as the sharing and coordination of services as desired (e.g., publish–subscribe, Web services, portal-enabled, cloud-based, smart devices–based, etc.) This approach allows users to reuse the

information in multiple ways, such as application-aware, by-user, hot-pluggable, and one-click visual solution components.

■ Create and leverage dynamic user experiences by increasing interactive customer engagement and thereby deriving "successful" measures for adaptive solution evolution.

■ Segregate responsibilities by way of ownership, entitlement, and administration based on the loopback-based customer-user experience insight.

■ Take the inherent BI to a higher level by using information intelligence to transform the context-based and content-based solution into a concept-based solution—one that enables business users to "create-their-own-BI" solution: dynamic ETL to dynamic DW to dashboarding to dynamic customization to dynamic customer experience, all tied in a lateral fashion by the single pillar of intelligent information in action.

8.6.2   Data to Information Transformation and Presentation

This subsection explains information access in terms of anytime, anywhere, by anyone availability and delivering the right information in the right way at the right time to the right user. The combination both of these comes under the umbrella of prime-time data-to-information management.

Information Access in Terms of Near Real–Time availability of OLTP Data

This refers to collecting and computing data from an operational data source or OLTP system as it is being created and enabling it for consumption by BI systems. At least two key imperatives are necessary criteria to implement this in the real world, as outlined in this section.

There must be continuous operational integration of data as it is created in the source system with the BI system(s). The synchronicity and speed at which this data moves from source to target is integral to this imperative.

Data can be moved from source to target or it can be virtually federated without actually moving from the source; a hybrid approach uses the former for the data loading and the latter for the data consumption. Near real–time availability may or may not involve an EDW. In the former case, real time is generally interpreted to mean the access and availability of data anytime, anywhere, and by anyone—that is, on demand. When there is no EDW involved, this imperative is more emphasized by continuous availability, activity, and access of data-to-information in a near real–time fashion—that is, zero or minimal latency between the time it is created and the time it is consumed. This is where the continuous data integration mechanism comes into the picture.

The mechanism of data movement, followed by virtual data federation, is useful when the variability in changes is high *and* data needs to be persistent, as in EDW/data marts, for further consumption for front-end facing applications other than BI systems such as disconnected reporting, historical analysis, and time-series trending, for example. The data virtualization–powered technique is optimal of just-in-time (right-now) as opposed to point-in-time (right-time) processing and presentation of information as it is being created, directly serviceable to the dashboard.

This can be implemented in at least three ways:

1. By:

    a.   Using an enterprise service bus to achieve continuous operational data sourcing, processing, and delivery. This can use the traditional ETL-ELT methodology by following the 'Load Completely First, Then Load Deltas Only" iterative, and then SOA-enabling this process as part of the automated DI workflow. Here DI as a service can be used as an enabler of this methodology.

    b.   Using ETL-ELT for the initial load and then DI as a service to bring in the deltas only. Use data virtualization to do the heterogeneous data sourcing of the deltas.

3. Applying a data virtualization API to enable mash-up, massaging, and messaging of the initial (the first time) and the deltas (on a recurring basis) to conform them to the consuming format and delivery of the same. The above two steps give the dual advantage of moving the data from contextual source systems into the target environment and then use it in the manner desired.

4. Using near real–time asynchronous *(no oxymoron here!)* dynamic data services to pull data as it is created in the operational source in a service-oriented fashion and directly federate it to the BI dashboard.

Using Data as a Service or Information as a Service

Data as a service is the starting stage of the data-to-information lifecycle and plays a pivotal role in the sourcing/ETL and transformation stages. *Information as a service* primarily drives the presentation stages and beyond. Both types of services are necessary for process modeling and building the source-to-target information-in-action model, implementing it, and customizing it. Figures 8.2 and 8.3 illustrate this concept.

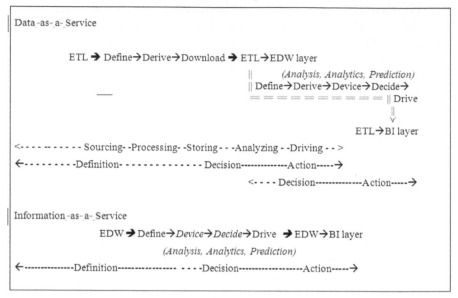

Figure 8.2   Visual view illustrating information as a service and data as a service from a people–process–technology perspective.

Both can be used interchangeably and involve DI as a service in regards to the following:

- *Building the bricks*: Synthesis and composition of source data and the interrelationships involved by using best practices—a set of processes, techniques, tools, and the like aligned to get the right result via best-fit selection, segmentation, and exception-mechanisms in place.
- *Piecing these bricks to construct the final brick*: Customization of the previous "bricks" into an integrated *data component* that encloses the contextual scope. This, in a way, defines a *reference architecture in context* that consists of at least a 3-tuple *(a reference methodology, target context, an integration methodology)*.

The difference lies in the scope and usability domains within which the integration services are applied in the real world. Data as a service can be considered more generic in scope of function and less broad in usage—it constitutes the lifecycle of building each individual data-brick. Though, as stated earlier, it primarily involves the data sourcing to storage phases, it can extend to the EDW and decision-enabling phases by facilitating on-demand and incremental data sourcing, computation, and exception-handling. A real-world use case of this is the consolidation of heterogeneous data marts into the EDW.

Information as a service can be viewed as having a larger scope of function and amplitude of usage, spanning across multiple data-as-a-service components. This comes into play during the information presentation phase, a critical piece of the EDW/BI pie. This can be used for servicing the EDW→BI layer as well as for operational BI (ETL→BI layer) and advanced interactivity functionality, such as on-the-fly external content integration (or data mash-ups), implementing dynamic dashboards by using a mash-up of multiple context-specific dashboards and solution-to-solution information access and availability without having to relocate the underlying data involved.

When to use what or both is a decision that depends on the business-case perspective—or in other words, *deciding between absolute and relative*—this means *the ability to apply either or both of them* to a solution-centric, business context–driven and process-oriented real-world customer implementation in a best-fit manner. A recommended rule of thumb is to use both in accordance with the practices outlined previously.

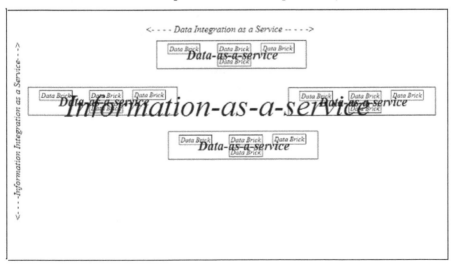

Figure 8.3   Isolating information as a service from data as a service for best degree-of-fit usability.

Dynamic Structured Data Access and In-Database Analytics: Practices for Best Degree of Fit

In-database analytics is a best fit for designing and implementing database-centric data structures, such as relational views, and logic-powered generation of context-specific models of the same, in close proximity to where the data resides. This is especially useful in distributed computing environments, where scalability and high availability are of primary concern. In database analytics can accelerate the implementation of a simulated high availability architecture that coperforms within the database where it is resident. This is not in memory, as the processing is preparsed, precompiled, and computed just-in-time; the results prefetched in the database. The delivery of the same can be in-memory based.

In-database analytics can be a best practice to store, compile ahead, and execute best-fit pragmatics of context-centric functionality-optimized development and deployment lifecycles. As a relevant example, consider designing and developing a best-fit architectural framework for discovering, analyzing, semantic enabling, and visualizing change dynamics in fast-paced solution implementations. The entire set of metrics involved can be generated, precompiled, and stored in-database as a change management analytics Web service that can be invoked as an API call or otherwise pushed to the application layer to be executed as an in-memory analytics cache.

In-database analytics is also a recommended practice for physical data consolidation and computation, with the corresponding analytics being stored as an executable procedure that mostly operates on the data residing in database.

This is due to the fact that dataflows for in-database analytics spaces follow the pattern: from data-file store to the in-database shared area to the database buffer cache to the solution tier. An additional intermediate file-system cache (AKA an in-memory database cache) such as RAM disk cache, NAND disk cache, MVs, and the like can also be used to optimize query access. This is a best fit to process data-intensive SQL-enabled computation, as stated previously.

Also, high-performance physical replication of data across distributed boundaries can benefit from this approach. A genuine use case of this approach is in-memory distributed caching to facilitate subsecond response to high-volume queries in near real–time, thereby preserving (location-based) access consistency.

A classic use case of in-database analytics is to precompile and store an industry compliance–enabled Information security engine that encapsulates not just data protection rules but also the associated logic, interrelationships, and metadata-driven intelligence, including componentized security-gateways. This leverages the in-database functionality that is optimal to the processing and realization of the same, as the data and/or content on which it operates also behave in an aligned fashion. This can then be used for scaling and add-ons across disparate access points.   This enables pervasive security implementation via detection and prevention of breaches right at the database entrypoint; and it can be generalized to act as a custom solution-to-solution data security analytic at any solution-tier level.

The primary drivers are:

- Security analytics adapt to changing solution environs by using in-memory distributed database activity monitoring.
- Distributed information architectures can leverage security as desired by way of a multi-tenant, multi-vector approach based on location, time, and cross-referencing boundaries.
- Accelerated compliance when implementing the same at the database or the VM in-memory level for ensuring and assuring virtual-to-virtual and virtual-to-cloud visibility, as well as monitoring data in motion and data at rest. This can be accomplished in a dynamic fashion by database-aware analytics that contain the above security model to leverage it in an elastic fashion as databases are scaled in and out vis-à-vis VMs and hybrid bases. By way of push-through, pop-up mechanisms, the security analytics can be localized on demand. This works in line with the functionality of the elastic topology of the distributed architecture.   Open source–based security analytic solutions are based on an SOA-based security gateway as well as, intra- and interdatabase security components that consist of a database-centric "native" KPI component and a database-agnostic "nonnative interface" KPI, with the two abstracted by way of a virtualized messaging framework.

Dynamic Structured Data Access and In-Memory Analytics: Practices for Best Degree of Fit

In-memory analytics is a best fit when there is no file I/O at all (to minimize). This is in contrast to other in-memory solutions, like in-memory database cache that minimizes file I/O but does not enable file I/O less data access; or RAM disks and SSDs that emulate a DB block disk in RAM and in NAND respectively. The key driver for using in-memory processing is to minimize memory and maximize speed of data access.

The fast response comes from building in-memory index structures that store only metadata values instead of business key values—in the case of regular in-database indexes, the 4-tuple {pointer, meta-data, key-values, row-id} values are stored.

In-memory DB caches are useful for read-only optimization, whereas in-memory databases or analytics-bases are useful for read-write optimization. In the case of the former, the cache is primarily shared across solution boundaries, whereas in case of the latter, the entire database or analytics-base is preloaded into memory, akin to an in-memory processing engine (not just limited to querying).

In-memory analytics can be used to generate analytics based on criteria and are a best-fit in use cases like deriving custom sales KPI from Sales 2.0 and socially relevant computing KPI for high-performance customer-centric analytics.

In-memory analytics can also be used for big data computation—for data-intensive or memory-intensive processing of large volumes of structured data (or unstructured data to be more generic) in heterogeneous formats and functionalities—by way of complex logic tied to the relevant data via caching algorithms – all in one place in-memory – eliminates the frequency of database-to-memory caching, serializes complexity pairing data to the processing context, and significantly reducing time to analysis.

As an alternative to EDWs or enterprise data marts, and for business scenarios that demand operational BI capabilities or real-time data access, can also function as in-memory analytics provides in-memory multidimensional stores of context-relevant master data and associated fact data and dynamic analysis of the same in RAM to reduce CPU cycles and I/O. These can then be materialized or federated as desired.

In-memory analytics is a best fit for implementing computation-centric data structures such as objects-based content that store both the data and its associated behavior as a class-based object. Typical functionality includes validation of input that is complex in structure, such as unstructured or very large objects like for data quality, metadata extraction from video-based content confined across varying dimensions, and the like. It is to be noted that the processing and management of the same is easier, simpler, and faster in memory—in close proximity to where such input comes from (i.e., the application-solution tier).

This is due to the fact that dataflows for in-memory analytics spaces follow a different pattern than that for in-database analytics. Since the entire analytics-base is cached in memory, data moves in singular copies from the database (i.e., the in-memory analytics-base) to the solution-tier via data management techniques like streaming replication by way of (virtual) data federation.

In-memory analytics is also a best fit when it is used as a cache repository of the associated computed result-sets. This can be then be utilized for distribution and delivery of the cached data for high-performance querying and high-availability of data for instant access. Even query performance–based baselines can be derived in dynamic manner and pre-stored in the database, as well as persistently cached for query optimization. Also, it enables autosyncing of the distributed and cached data. *The key here is to ensure that only deltas in data are synced incrementally.*

In either of the above cases, using a data virtualization engine as an in-memory compute-enabled analytics platform optimizes the management and pervasive use of the same. As a use case, database virtualization can be used to implement business-to-business integration and access by enabling a virtual pipeline of required information without moving the actual data across boundaries. Each individual database can be an analytics-base that acts as both a computation and access platform in a continuous fashion. Industry examples of in-memory analytics are McObject and other embeddable analytics engines such as Inter Systems Caché, eXtremeDB, Birst's SaaS-enabled In-memory BI Appliance, and the like.

Content-Based and Other Unstructured Data Access: In-Database vs. In-Memory Analytics

In-memory analytics is a best-fit methodology for content-based and other unstructured data access, as it enables resident caching of all required data in a DRAM-based embedded database that has the potential to store and service analytics on-demand. The hybrid compression of the data ranging into the terabyte scale can be cached in-memory by a factor of at least 1:5 and can service a user request in significantly lower number of seconds while delivering output data in the 5TB range for user access.

A *real-time data visualization grid* can be created and managed as desired using this methodology, so that business analysis can happen at the speed of instant access, anytime, anywhere, by anyone.

The top-tier best practices for adopting this strategy can help you navigate the maze of unstructured data, such as videos, graphs, recursive hierarchical drill-through data models, and similar other models:

- Use a combination of analytics to implement a custom application specially tailored for deep-dive processing of unstructured and/or semistructured content. This design can involve the following steps:

  1. Converting the analytic measures into a "pure code" state via native API interfacing that can execute on multistructured content without changing the underlying source code and that is computation-agnostic in terms of the DBMS/DMS engines, technology platforms, and orchestration dynamics. This means constructing a dynamic model that emulates or simulates the flow-pattern, as illustrated in Figure 8.4.

     This ensures commonality in containment and coordination for conformance across the disparate data/content at either end of processing. This also allows for merging 2D and 3D unstructured content which is essential for this type of processing.

  2. "Native" enablement can be done using standards-based constructs such as bitmaps, hex-maps, or Pix-maps that combine different bits and BI-wise operations to flatten/unflatten the

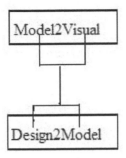

Figure 8.4   Flow-pattern for a dynamic model–based "pure code" state conversion of multistructured content.

complex data structures involved. The core logic of the API methods contains the analytic-specific code.

3. The native APIs so constructed can be delivered as embeddable plug-ins. This way cross-compatibility with minimal overhead can be achieved across databases, XML-bases, and unstructured content–bases.

- Use role-based workflows and process automation to enable cross-content interoperation.
- Use cascading style sheets and context-based subclassing to override the visual defaults so that a common graphics vector can be constructed that unifies the look and feel. This can be used for the model-to-visual and vice versa transformations.
- Use code-design patterns with ECMA-compliant scripts and XML/A-compliant access for exposing the bi-directional content at the application level. This can then be contained into an in-database procedure or an in-memory embedded KPI, depending on whether the consuming request is static or dynamic in terms of the 3-tuple {Input, Output, Context} and access-intensive with high-volume results for faster response. This helps convert logical design views into models and vice versa.
- Use event-driven initiation, initialization, instantiation, and state capture via complex event processing mechanisms such as agentless monitoring, transformation-aware code, and dynamic context switching.
- Use a data abstraction layer to decompose composite unstructured content such as video, social and graph-based data,

machine-generated content, dynamic information flows, and the like that enables rapid vector and scalar factoring of the same into a common representation tied by common semantics; supplement this with virtual data federation to provide a consolidated common view of the same.

- A variety of open source standards-based algorithms can be followed, such as unicode-enabling, in-database generation of the target analytics, Ajax, SAX (Simple API for XML), DOM (Document Object Model), DOM, and streams I/O reusable components.
- Embedded analytic frameworks for real-time, right-time access across disparate content by way of on-the-fly integration of the same from structure to semantics, using:

    1. Source-database resident processing via SQL-based extensions for optimizing analytic joins across boundaries, involving RDB content. Using analytics to optimize the SQL engine for iterative and recursion-depth intensive processing is a best-fit methodology to implement the same.

    2. Processing unstructured data by leveraging next-gen methodologies such as NoSQL (Not Only SQL), Hadoop/MapReduce frameworks and using optimized analytics on the same to accelerate synthesis and computation of unstructured content via "divide-and-conquer" parallelized vectors. SQL-enable the same using Hadoop/HBase design frameworks that store key-value pairs for super-fast querying involving processing speeds in the range of million records per second.

    3. Collapsing structured and unstructured content using associative in-memory analytics—processing relational OLAP, n-dimensional OLAP—to derive a hybrid in-memory table that caches data based on the principle of optimal usage (AKA Least Common Multile and Highest Common Factor) and refreshes it on demand. This is highly efficient in that it enables a personalized analytics engine to work locally in terms of multiple instantiations, each suited for a specific purpose, all executing in parallel or otherwise. Even XML document stores such as CouchDB, other in-memory engines like QlikView (a product of QlikTech), and even customized EDWs can be leveraged in this way.

        As an example, the open source–based Alfresco Content Management Solution (CMS) uses a Share Framework for unified interfacing by way of optimized design, architecture and presentation. The open-source vendor Rivet Logic has leveraged this framework as a complementary add-on to implement a unified CMS in its products Crafter Studio and Crafter Rivet.

Another open source framework for realizing unstructured content processing is the Splunk framework. The resulting computation logic can be executed in-database or in-memory depending on the solution footprint, dictionary-based search and retrieval (in-database), high-speed distributed data access (in-memory), and advanced business analytics for operational BI (in-memory), and the like.

Model-Based Data Access (Using LINQ to SQL, XML, and other Entity Framework Model-Based PLs): Practices for Best Degree of Fit

Here three innovative best-fit methodologies for model-based data access are outlined that use heterogeneous language and data models for effective business analytics:

1. Model-driven data access is a best-fit strategy in situations where the same data model needs to be used for mutually inclusive contexts. A good example is multitenant services based on multiple temporal and spatial dimensions. Here the time and geolocation dimensions are refactored based on the degree and latitude of the variance involved to yield one or more different result models. A best-fit use case for the same can be to convert logical design(s) involving time and location data into a persistent data model by tying them together based on common business attribute (i.e., join dimension).

    This can then be further extended into an adaptive asynchronous model for model-based data quality that factors in the analytics for inducing qualification and certification metrics to assess the relative deviation from the expected accuracy.

The above pragmatics can also be used to evolve a model for common query services of multicomponent data/content based on a design-to-model, model-to-visual interoperable language generation.

2. Another recommended best practice for model-based access is to ensure adaptability of the analytics model as the business model changes. This is possible by implementing an in-memory ROLAP architecture that houses both the n-dimensional design and the relational analytic design to eliminate preprocessing of data by dynamic syncing of fact-based measures with changes in dimensions. Data virtualization powered dynamic ETL and dynamic warehousing design patterns can be applied to segregate, summarize, and qualify data based on role-based imperatives so that the right information is available for the right analysis in a distributed and decentralized fashion—all in-memory to facilitate a near real–time analytics model that is responsive to the business dynamics. This is akin to an in-memory n-dimensional analytics engine in trending contrast to the traditional EDW where the necessary dimensions, facts, and other data are collapsed into a predesigned model that serves as an entry point for all multidimensional analysis.

3. Model-based metrics can be used to enable business transforms (i.e., function-based measures) to evolve into business transformational models (i.e., intelligent KPI models) by using a combination of one or more of the above best practices. This aids in model-based mining and analysis for VLDB systems.

A Best Practices–Driven Methodology as a Strategy for a Successful Business Case for Data-to-Information Transformation and Presentation by Way of Integrated Access to Availability and Dynamic Computing to Integrated Analytics

1. Synthesis and analysis of information and its application to a contextual problem/review/research/Proof-of-Concept (or POC)/prototype

   1.1 Managing data by using inclusivity, exclusivity, and exceptionality metrics. Setting tolerance limits at each intersection point, inflection point, decision point, interaction touchpoint, access point, performance (criticality) point; and recursively within each level of point.

      1.1.1 Automating the same by notifications, alerts, passed dataflows as business rules that exhibit adoptive, adaptive, reactive, proactive, and pre-emptive capabilities.

      1.1.2 Managing data by using exceptionality increases data to information assurance across the solution lifecycle timeline and hence, user confidence backed by this support across the customer user experience lifecycle timeline.

1.1.3   Clarity in requirements and roles definition—this enables, qualifies, and accelerates change management, thereby extending the changes to be reflected pervasively by implementing dedicated and/or multitenant change controls. This process-flow can be applied at all levels of solution componentization.

1.1.4   Data quality is critical to any data management portfolio and must meet the following necessary inclusions: Accuracy of scope in terms of right information for the right purpose to the right people at the right time; accuracy of design in terms of interrelated process composition and their workflow—this includes source format and related aspects like data containment or native versus nonnative aspects, linkage, lineage, and the like; data transformations in terms of technofunctional process flows and execution flows; data presentation in terms of a collaborative customer view, dynamic data mash-ups, and the like; data quality criteria in terms of definition, derivation, and boundaries; quality assurance in terms of quality control process models; and the testing, verification, and validation of the same using the quality controls, predefined acceptability criteria, and context-specific application of the same to the real-world business case. This confirms the quality of criteria, quality of services, and quality of conformance to industry standards, GRC specifics, and customer-user experience—or quality of standards enforcement for information I/O, information security, information technologies/information architectures, information audit, information assurance, and the like.

1.2   Applying the above POC end to end to simulate a real-world project of similar type.

1.2.1   Managing the solution lifecycle with a process-driven and business-case oriented methodology.

1.2.1.1   Managing the solution lifecycle by structuring it into segments, each of which can be managed independently and therefore can be integrated and correlated in an interoperable fashion. It is vital that each sub-component must be capable of executing on its own as a standalone solution (e.g., isolating the EDW/BI solution into data management, application management, identity management, etc.).

1.2.1.1.1   Within the data management segment, it can further be broken down into modular components such as data sourcing and ETL; EDW; BI; beyond BI continuum—advanced analytic appliances, predictive analytics–based reasoning—useful for elastic management of solution evolvement and devolvement (if needed); Web user experience management; Enterprise Performance Management (EPM); Enterprise Feedback Management (EFM); cross-solution data management; cross-business-to-business data management; data management for cross-platform development and delivery (e.g., physical-virtual-hybrid deployments); cloud-to-cloud, solution-to-social; customer-user experience lifecycle across variable dimensions

1.2.1.1.2   Automation of the same for execution and management

1.2.1.2   Designing and implementing business rules for data quality, starting from the dimensions of data scoping, profiling, cleansing, clustering, transforming, masking, protecting, loss-prevention, data federation, and data access and availability; to time-and-location variance cum standard deviation and enabling access and availability independent of these variants; data virtualization to avoid physical data replication using virtual data federation, which eases and accelerates dynamic MDM and EDW anytime, anywhere, by anyone; data as a service, information as a service, DI as a service, and information integration as a service; database virtualization; data auditing; data discovery for comprehensive data analysis; and unifying structured and unstructured data by way of in-database analytics, in-memory analytics, and model-centric analytics—integrated query, analysis, analytics, and BI-driven informatics

1.2.1.3 These have to be prescriptive (best-fit practices) as well as predictive (for information assurance vis-à-vis risk assurance) in addition to being subjective, descriptive, and objective. Business Solutions and Support (or BSS) and Operations Solutions and Support (or OSS) are one side of the coin when it comes to solution efficiency—they raise the bar on customer satisfaction/SLA fulfillment. The other side is solution assurance using prescriptive and predictive-based quality controls that not only add to the business value by ensuring reliability, availability, and security, but also increase the visibility of the solution overtime ahead of those times—thereby increasing confidence and adding assurance (this is a big deal) to the overall business.

1.2.1.4 Data/information quality is composed of quality planning—defined quality roles and quality controls and a segregation of duties–enabled mapping of the two; the depth of details involved for implementation; and quality control—actual implementation of the quality of service rules, using quality-in-depth strategies such as the enforcement of quality tolerances solutionwide and quality assurance policies derived using quality control/predictive analytics–based models.

1.2.1.5 It is critical to note that "best practice" and "best degree of fit" do not necessarily go together; in most cases, the latter overrides the former. This is because solution effectiveness and credibility ratings are driven by the overall solution acceptability levels (not just addressing severity levels) in terms of managing any and all data, from preplanning to postdeployment. The 3-tuple {people, process, technology} values define, determine, verify, and validate the solution as a set—not individually. This 3-tuple, factored across dynamic and static dimensions and qualifiers that are not easily quantifiable, poses a challenge in providing and putting into practice an acceptable level of efficiency benchmark for any EDW/BI solution. No two business cases are the same and hence the need for analytics and BI-enabled decision rules in addition to analysis that can be used to validate the solution against the business case on a prime time basis.

1.2.1.6 Baselining the change controls and quality controls to enable roles-based, rules-driven data management processes into a sort of gold standard for EDW/BI data management by determining the depth of implementation details (what-to-do and how-to-do) across the dimensions of business context, quality of service, and business-case scenarios.

8.7 Best Practices for Auditing Data Access, as It Makes Its Way via the EDW and Directly (Bypassing the EDW) to the BI Dashboard

Real-time data audit monitoring by common grid console(s) that enable visibility into runtime production environments can be implemented by:

- Asynchronous monitoring and capture of the audit trails and so forth to identify blockers and outliers of end-to-end audit activity that deviate from the compliance-enabled audit policies induced in the solution workflow.
- Premodeled graphs based on the captured audit-flows can be put to work using analytics KPI that execute in a dynamic publish–subscribe and hot-pluggable fashion to output just-in-time visualization of the audit process as it progresses in continuous execution from EDW to BI.
- Pervasive auditing by way of real-time and offline auditing of data across disparate boundaries, using localized audit trails and merging them using physical or virtual clustering based on common audit criteria. This decentralized localization of auditing enables auditing for compliance with segregation of duties.
- Creating audit intelligence by way of audit, automate, auto-wire, accelerate, and adapt:
    - A unified auditing standard for qualitative, regulatory, and customer-centric value.

- Customizable framing and unframing of auditing by context—for dynamic EDW/BI environments—as in the case of scenarios demanding location-awareness or in environments involving physical-to-virtual hybrid infrastructures. In the latter case, the auditing framework must be implemented across every cross-tier boundary, be it intraphysical, intravirtual, interphysical, or intervirtual layers.
- Using XML-powered intelligent metrics to audit fine-grained security controls that block Command Line Interface (CLI) and/or API access and vice versa, based on network, database, solution, and user-centric statistics.

Data access can be audited in a number of ways, including

- Native database auditing.
- Extending native auditing to *adaptive auditing* by enabling multi-factored auditing at the individual solution tier such as database, EDW, in-memory layer, presentation layer, and across perimeters.
- Using open source profiling benchmarks to dynamically discover data changes over time, context fit-in, and degree of persistence, and audit the same by classifying them into the categories of slowly changing data, rapidly changing data, or constant data, relative to context best fit. This can help in correlating computational complexity of data in context versus contexts in context.
- Using pervasive audit capabilities by auditing of proactive and reactive security, compliance, and business process-to-user interaction measures; the level and depth to which these processes are visible; and bidirectional flow-based auditing.
- Auditing of data at a more fine-grained level to capture row-level and column-level change management, including auditing of queries, auditing of column stripping and the associated context (especially during data federation) and multilevel time-stamping; auditing of data quality processes; query-rewrite and optimization metrics; and the like. Factoring in session-based policies tied to a unified secure key framework is necessary and sufficient for intrusion prevention and proactive controls.

8.8 Best Practices for Using XML in the Open Source EDW/BI Space

The evolution of XML from an eXtended Markup Language to a document store to a document management model to a trans-messaging mechanism to an in-memory computation and/or transit platform to its ability to leverage intelligence signifies the next-generation trends of using XML for architecture, technologies, methodologies, and cross-language convergence. This section focuses on the best-fit use of these practices in an open source EDW/BI space. The following bullet points outline some of these to derive measurable BI analytics for measurable business value:

- Take XML to the next level by leveraging the next-generation unification trends in XML processing, from unification of data structures to unification of data access to unification of languages—thereby enabling unification of analytics, resulting in a Unified XML Model. Some of these trends are as stated in the beginning of this section.
- The next generation of touchscreen—from human touch interfaces to remote touch (AKA sensing) interfaces to human–computer interfaces—can be realized by leveraging XML in combination with HTML, UML, XACML, XML/A, Web Ontology Markup Language (also termed OWL), ebXML, or SQL-enabled XML for convergence-centricity, thereby enabling:
  - Agile-to-Mobile-to-Visible-to-Value by seamless integration of embedded analytics and mobile (data-in-motion) analytics using SQL-enabled XML-based access and assembly of content in multiple formats, breaking the complexities across cross-technology, cross-nativity, cross-compliance, and cross-structure barriers.
  - XML can help accelerate this process by leveling language-based semantics across disparate technology-oriented languages, such as Java, .NET, C++/C, and NoSQL, and proprietary languages, such as streams-based declaratives and the like, to abstract a *common data management language model* that can be implemented declaratively or via API.
- XML can be used for CLI-to-API and vice versa dynamic interfacing based on conditional runtime binding. This type of implementation in any EDW/BI solution goes a long way in opening dual

entry points in a user-controlled fashion—thereby easing the administration via automated flip-flop mechanisms during system crashes, critical disaster events, and the like.

- XML can be used to bridge the online to offline gap in terms of data delivery to disconnected access points by using it as an in-memory coherent cache that syncs online content with offline interactive content and vice versa as the changes are being made.
- XML can help in easing model-to-model integration by way of merging using preset and machine-generated metrics pertaining to:
  - Semantics
  - Taxonomy
  - Metadata
  - Business rules

  This spans the business drivers of coherency, consistency, durability, and high-availability, and best fits into the dynamics of data-driven facts-based analytic integration.

- XML can power associative processing of hierarchical and poly-morphic data Associations discovered using scale-in in-memory data domain–based metadata replication and scale-out data staging. A cross-compare and -contrast KPI matrix can be autogenerated using XML as the data staging in-memory processing store to correlate cell variants with polymorphic variants grouped by hierarchy levels and super-sub linkages.
- Using XML content authoring and interoperability frameworks such as XMetal Solutions for Content Lifecycle Management (a product of JustSystems) can help in accelerating discovery and collapsing of unstructured content.

8.9   Best Practices for a Unified Information Integrity and Security Framework

The best-fit strategy for achieving unified information integrity and security is to architect the design components by pairing {data–content value, data–business value} at every level of the solution architecture in place, including at end points {data source, data target} and {data in motion, data at rest} in a bidirectional manner. Augmented by a security gateway such as an SOA-enabled gateway for perimeter security that can be deployed at the Web access layer or other perimeter boundaries, this enables a robust and data-driven security methodology powered by open source technologies. Some of the best practices recommended for this approach are as follows:

- Delegated information authorization by application solution based on a permutation of:
  - Principle of optimal privileges: multifactor authentication by combining role-based access control with identity-trusted access control
  - Fine-grained access control to content (securing by protecting from unauthorized access)
  - Fine-grained dependency control—access control lists and access control dependency lists—to both content and context (e.g., users, user roles, etc.)
- Applying dynamic domain-level contexts via autogenerated/static application contexts: This allows out-of-box and outside-of-use-scope application-level ID-enablement. Apply log-based auditing to this and the result is application-aware/context-aware capture for integrity and security. This includes external contexts too.
- Multifactoring security: This is achieved by using the following steps:
  - *Reasoning-based identification* that uses predetermined behavior patterns and trends based on end-point login information correlated with the associated usage logging. The initiator can be *a signature-based recognition*, like biometrics hash-mapped with login ID and fine-grained dependency controls applied to the login ID. This is then factored by the *reasoning-based ID* to arrive at a final status of authentication equaling one of {SUCCESS, FAILED}. This can be standardized as the first-level

    ```
    OpenSourcePerfect_Security_Context(. . .)
    ```

    that can be transformed into a reusable multitenant security firewall deployed in line with the intersecting boundary of the enterprise intranet and external network.
  - Apply the principles of delegated information authorization and dynamic contextualization as a second-level security factor to determine the amplitude and visibility of the information that can be accessed or changed. SQL-compliant fuzzy logic matching can be used to implement this for real-time monitoring and detection of false positives. This also aids in preventing zero-day attacks.

- Apply semantic tagging to union of the above two steps to de-identify the security context from the solution context – The resulting tag stores the complete multi-factored security context relative to the solution context as an independent entity. This can be made persistent in a pre-configured repository or in line as a secure file store that gets auto-synced with the changes in real time via role-authorized management console. The entire process is completely transparent to the users, from corporate to end point. This implements proactive security controls not only for authentication and authorization but also for modern-day threats like abnormal SQL injection, insider threats like privileges escalation and elevation, intrusion detection in real-time, perimeter-based threats, and the like.
- Architecting a service-oriented, process-driven model by combining the above sub-steps results in a *solution-aware security framework*. Using an open source methodology has the unparalleled benefit of asynchronous execution and streamlining of the same across heterogeneous end-point solution boundaries involving varying databases, development and deployment platforms, architectures and methodologies, and data-to-application ecosystems, by way of:
  - A unified security standard for qualitative, regulatory, and customer-centric value. Factoring in session-based policies tied to a unified secure key framework is necessary and sufficient for intrusion prevention and proactive controls.
  - Customizable framing and unframing of security by context—for dynamic EDW/BI environments—as in the case of scenarios demanding location-awareness or involving physical-to-virtual hybrid data centers.
  - XML-powered intelligent metrics to block CLI and/or API access and vice versa based on network, database, solution, and user-centric statistics. This adds to the risk-aware capabilities of such a framework.
- Achieving multifactored integrity by using the following steps:
  - A clear and concise definition of "out-of-normal" rules, along with the boundary, inclusivity, exclusivity, and cohort-based (set-based combinations of inclusion, exclusion, or negation) conditions that can be classified as violations. This is a quintessential

piece of the integrity pie and begins with the requirements analysis phase. It must involve business analysts, solution architects, and everyone in between who is responsible for overlooking the solution from concepts to customization.

The recommended best practice is to consider the imperative of "native" versus "all other" data, not only in terms of data structure and function, but also by way of data computation.

The scoping of *native* functionality in terms of the driving database/EDW involved can take several meanings, such as the ability of *all other* data to dynamically interface with data that is native to the driving DB/EDW; or the ability of the driving database itself to automatically activate/deactivate implicit DB/EDW functionality based on compile-time and run-time optimization levels. In the former case, *native* refers to the internal DB storage and structure format, as well as the accessibility cost, which means the native data conforms to these guidelines and does not need extra computation/transformation to enable DB-compatibility for storage, structure, access and operation. The imperative of *native* in the context of integrity is that native functionality is more robust in relevance and qualification of information input-through-output.

As regards the latter, this imperative emphasizes self-management for self-service enablement by the driver DB, which in turn bookmarks or blueprints information integrity implicitly to inherent capability level, especially by way of declarative enablement.

- *Rules-engine based verification and validation*: Using predefined and machine-generated business rules that take into account the input, output, interaction, traction, transition, transformation, reflection, and state-enablement parameters for a particular business function(i.e., process) and use them to verify against context profiles and validate against baseline tests. This involves advanced test analytics for fast, asynchronous searches of multiplexed data content sets; automated metrics for rules generation based on semantics, performance (by way of cost of processing and resource utilization), and compliance; and automated event-based notification by way of active alerts (state-preserving) tagged with business-friendly outcomes. Some of the recommended best practices to implement this are:

- Validating the data quality framework in place for least probability of success to determine "true" negatives to the greatest level of certainty. This can be done using two different context sets as input to the data quality framework. Here, the context set must include the {content/data, integrity-rules-set} combination and must be tested for associative and mutual exclusion of context sets involved.
- Auditing of this process end-to-end to aid in enlisting best-case/worst-case pragmatics by way of tested-results certification.
- The scope of these is only as limited or unlimited as the scope of the integrity in demand.

- *Re-engineering* the above practices to retrofit into a "live" solution context to identify best-case/worst-case domain contexts that can be reused for both quality and integrity control designs, as well as in production environments for real-time agile/iterative testing. Semantics can be used to rationalize the integrity context framework and make it context-centric as opposed to context-specific. This can be made persistent in a preconfigured repository or in line as a secure file store that is auto-synced with the changes in real time via role-authorized management console.
- Architecting a service-oriented, process-driven model by combining the above substeps results in a *solution-aware integrity framework*. Using an open source methodology has the unparalleled benefit of asynchronous execution and streamlining of the same across heterogeneous endpoint solution boundaries involving varying databases, development and deployment platforms, architectures and methodologies, and data-to-application ecosystems by way of:
  - A unified integrity standard for qualitative, regulatory, and customer-centric context-specific value.
  - Customizable framing and unframing of security by context for dynamic EDW/BI environments, as in case of scenarios demanding location-awareness or involving

physical-to-virtual hybrid data centers that demands precedential integrity to preferential integrity. The key point is that the former does force-include all the necessary factors in addition to the sufficient ones.

8.10   Object to Relational Mapping: A Necessity or Just a Convenience?

From the open source perspective, it is prudent to state that object to relational mapping, or O→R, is both a necessity and a convenience when it comes to using it. This means O→R can be used in either or both of these ways to achieve the desired output.

The best practices that can be followed in terms of O→R implementations are described in this section.

8.10.1   Synchrony Maintenance

To maintain synchrony between disconnected or in-memory resident DB caches and the foundational DB/EDW that is relational data model oriented—particularly when such data is non-native relative to the driving DB or is non-compliant by form, structure, content, and computation for relational storage, access, and change, or for SQL-enablement.

A typical scenario can include bidirectional data access and presentation of unstructured or less qualified content, or composite data structures that store interlinked data at highly recursive depths. Here O→R serves an abstraction layer to encapsulate, decapsulate, and thereby insulate the presentation of such data from the processing of such data for efficiency and scalability, as well as representational accuracy. *This O→R mapping can be implemented as an API that can dynamically interface with the calling solution or solution component on as as-needed basis by way of dynamic services or runtime-resolved API calls using invoker rights privileges; thus, it can be active but not live always in terms of execution. Or it can be even be compiled and stored in the database as a packaged procedure or in memory as an embedded routine.*

This scenario reflects O→R usage as both a necessity and convenience—in that order of precedence.

A second scenario can be to streamline or optimize intra- or intercomponent process implementation and execution. A good example of this is when using multiple data services that are disparate in functionality but are being shared across solution tiers or across applications. Though the solution-implicit orchestration capabilities can be leveraged, the O→R can be used to augment/extend the synchronization of inter- with intradata services end to end, thereby enabling cohesive interoperability among them. This translates into DI as a service–to–DI as a service interoperability, and results in an efficient architecture that eliminates end-to-end siloization.

A more pervasive use of this scenario can be the integration of cloud and non-cloud deployed solutions. The steps to be synced in a pipelined, parallelized workflow can be (but are not limited to) the following:

1. Migrating/replicating (physically or virtually) non-cloud solutions to a compatible SaaS-enabled environment—This includes data to database to EDW to dashboard syncing without affecting the reliability, security, and integrity of the same.

2. Defining related workflows as object-classes and then using O➔R to serialize and enumerate the same for in-RDBMS leverage.

3. Using the solution security framework (as described earlier in the section on "Best Practices for a Unified Information Integrity and Security Framework") to context-frame the necessary security on the above object-based topology.

4. Delivering the cloud-to-non-cloud integration as a service or model for best-fit use—This implicitly automates the implementation-to-customization process.

This best practice fits into solutions demanding a greater degree of resiliency as opposed to efficiency, such as those implementing cross-protocol information exchanges that involve frequent data-in-transit processes but can afford some additional downtime by way of WAN-optimized bandwidth and the like.

8.10.2 Dynamic Language Interoperability

The implementation of dynamic language interoperability is a next-generation imperative for realizing language-independent information access and analysis (with only SQL at the fixed query language throughout). Combining information as a service with O➔R to realize the *consolidated customer view,* data, both raw and processed, can be partitioned into multiple compute-centric segments by way of big data, data spread, and distributed storage of content, data-model orientation, and the like; a unified query interface from coding to compliance can be constructed in the following manner:

1. Designing an in-memory analytics-based query engine to access unstructured data (such as binary large object (BLOB)–based or Hadoop Distributed File System-based or graph-based) that breaks the computational complexity to the order of near-SQL efficiency. Here, each such unstructured data component can be instantiated as an object of corresponding class by using cross-technology, cross-messaging methodologies such as XML-models, embedded object bases, document containers, graph-centric visualizations, and so on.

2. Applying SQL processing to leverage in-database processing efficiency and SQL-compliant declarative query access.

The primary business and solution benefits of this approach (a combination of information as a service with O→R) are:

- Data and computation abstraction for simpler and flexible data exchange
- Reduction in complexity, enabling faster access and analysis
- Improved performance, fine-grained insight, and ensured compliance from data to dashboard and beyond
- Greater degree of customer satisfaction by ensuring multilateral information assurance, thus boosting both the adoption and adaptation factors to a higher level, which in turn results in "less IT, more business" by value and by consumption.

8.11   Summary

This chapter dealt with the best practice pragmatics for data management dynamics involved in development, deployment, and integration of EDW/ BI solutions. Beginning with a convincing justification as to where, when, and how open source data management plays its role in EDW/BI implementation as a *unified set of adoptable standards and their subsequent implementation as business rules for horizontal and vertical business solution growth/optimization—from concepts to components to compliance and beyond*, it delved into the essential best practices for data/information access and delivery by way of factoring into the data lifecycle as it progresses from the data sourcing phase through the EDW into the BI stage to evolve into an intelligent information lifecycle that enables a best-fit information architecture across the DI, EDW, BI (with and without EDW) tiers. Special sections covered the best practices for auditing the data lifecycle, using XML and model-based data access and unified information integrity and security frameworks for EDW/BI. The chapter also highlighted the use of data as a service as compared to information as a service in the context of data management for EDW/BI. It concluded with some leverage on object to relational mapping in terms of necessity and ease of use. The next chapter discusses the best practices for application management in granular detail across the multitier-enabled implementation and the cross-dynamism and analytics involved across each interaction point of the end-to-end solution spectrum.

Chapter 9

Best Practices for Application Management

9.1 In This Chapter

- Using Open Source as an End-to-End Solution Option: How Best a Practice Is It?
- Accelerating Application Development: Choice, Design, and Suitability Aspects
    - Visualization of Content: For Better or Best Fit
    - Best Practices for Autogenerating Code: A Codeless Alternative to Information Presentation
    - Automating Querying: Why and When
    - How Fine Is Fine-Grained? Drawing the Line between Representation of Data at the Lowest Level and a Best-Fit Metadata Design and Presentation
- Best Practices for Application Integrity
    - Sharing Data between EDW and the BI Tiers: Isolation or a Tightrope Methodology
    - Breakthrough BI: Self-Serviceable BI via a Self-Adaptable Solution
    - Data-In, Data-Out Considerations: Data-to-Information I/O
    - Security Inside and Outside of Enterprise Perimeters: Best Practices for Security beyond User Authentication
- Best Practices for Intra- and Interapplication Integration and Interaction
    - Application Consistency: Information Coherence, Persistent versus Intermittent Caching in Multiple Tiers
    - Application Web Interaction and Communication: Cross-Data Source Information Access, Analytics, and Availability; External Data/Content Integration on the Fly

- ▪ Continuous Activity Monitoring and Event Processing
- ▪ Best Practices to Use SOA-based Methodologies: Data Services versus Data Integration Services; SOA over Information Presentation; Information as a Service on the Go
- ▪ Best Practices to Leverage Cloud-Based Methodologies
- ▪ Best Practices for Creative BI Reporting
- ▪ Summary

9.2   Introduction

This chapter treats application development from two aspects, namely, solution orientation and product orientation. From business intelligence (BI) to the fore to BI encore, enterprise data warehouse (EDW)/BI solution–application management begins with the consumer/customer/competitor trio, from concept to customization and beyond. The power of advanced analytics lies in its ability to autotag value-added metadata to the actual data, thereby enriching it—*without using any database (DB)/EDW/data-store/data-source infrastructure in place*. It details on dimensional data views (i.e., derived dimensions) and cell values in content-grid views. The subsequent sections talk in more specific details about Web-massaging and its relevance, if any, to Web mashing, Web interfacing, and forward-facing API; best practices for certain special topics in application integrity; and intra- and inter-application integration and interaction. The final sections discuss best practices for cloud enablement and creative BI reporting from an application management perspective.

9.3   Using Open Source as an End-to-End Solution Option: How Best a Practice Is It?

Drawing upon the paradigm of the *Open Source Perfect* (as explained in Chapters 1–3), the imperatives of architecture as a precedence factor over other criteria, and the three-in-one convergence of information-centricity, business-centricity, and customer/consumer/competitor-centricity, the business value of such a solution option is measurable as close as possible to a time to deliver from the primary users' (e.g., user, end user, customer, intelligent customer) perspectives. Hence, it is prudent to conclude the following as an executive summary as far as mainstream BI is concerned:

- ▪ Use open source methodologies as an add-on to augment, automate, and accelerate certain business processes.

- Adoption of open source can be be fitting during "rip-and-replace" scenarios. Even open source–based techniques can come in as value-added services.
- Use open source to implement functionality that makes it otherwise difficult to conform with IT or GRC policies. This way you can unplug your embedded component without disrupting the underlying service. Typical use cases for this are business to business, customer to business, customer/consumer/competitor to business–social, and the like.

With small to medium-sized businesses to medium to large enterprises adopting open source BI as mainstreams or collaterals, and more of them as mainstream itself, the road to open source BI as a mainstream channel for global information services and BI-on-the-go is not far off, especially when cosupportive technologies such as data virtualization and DW, shared and cloud computing, scalability on demand, dynamic visualization, and dynamic SOA have already beaten the heat in proving the customers' trust.

Figure 9.1 gives a bird's-eye view of an EDW/BI solution manager from the open source methodologies perspective.

9.4   Accelerating Application Development: Choice, Design, and Suitability Aspects

Open source architecture enables you to build your own EDW/BI solution with choice, design and suitability in terms of flexibility to extend/unplug components on demand; codeless design using interactive and visual controls; and above all business and operations productivity by delivering *optimal more with optimal less*. A series of clicks, mouse moves, drag-and-drops, and even voice-activated controls, and your dashboard is ready. Yes, truly it is, and this can even include real-time data analysis.

The good news is that this is for both better and/or best-fit.

The key performance indicators (KPIs) are:

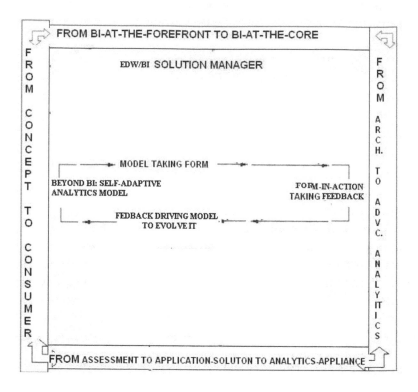

Figure 9.1　Bird's-eye view of an EDW/BI solution manager from the open source methodologies perspective.

- Cross-referenceable lists of choice by usability domain, line of business, pervasive scoping, and pervasive coupling
- Information amplitude and granularity of detail needed
- Data-driven design, grouped partially by technology and partially by user interactivity
- A best-of-breed solution, technology platform, and tools, and a hybrid approach of bridging them using best-fit common factors/refactors of the *Open Source Perfect* strategy (outlined in various sections referring to the same phrase in Parts I and II of this book). As an example, for a best-fit cloud-management solution, one that is hypervisor-agnostic can be the selective choice by functionality (like Abiquo's Next-Generation Cloud Management). And the independence of this manager keeps it from being tied to a specific hardware or vendor, which keeps it adaptive in the future, too.

For example, UShareSoft's Uforge Image Builder can be used to build the beta-release of a best-of-breed solution component factory that can be emulated for best-fit scenarios. The requirements herewith are additional criteria for rapid application development:

- Follow the design closely with the design component meant for it. Do this each time the design or the design component changes itself or its parameters via autoalert notifications, voice-enabled signaling, or social media real-time feeds. These are a KPI of customer feedback to the solution/product fed via RSS, social media feeds, and the like. Input this into a customer relationship management (CRM) solution via CRM2.0 (e.g., Social CRM, Salesforce Chatter, etc.)
- Enable customer engagement throughout the enterprise via collaboration and communication. This accelerates the customer-user experience lifecycle and attunes the solution component as it is being developed. Also, at every point of module completion, the completed module should be injected into a subsuming mesh net and regression-tested against real-world business process workflow (don't exclude testing for edges or pin-drops in the data). In certain cases, it makes sense to offline the solution component and test it in a private/public cloud (for reengineering or reverse-engineering purposes).

The following classification schemes are worth considering when using open source for EDW/BI solution development and deployment:

- Rapid application development and deployment
- Rapid application usage, customization
- Rapid application personalization: portability, mobility, visibility
- Rapid application personalization: adaptation, device-agnostic, customer/consumer/competitor-agnostic
- Rapid analysis, intelligence, and advanced analytics (includes predictive analytics)
- Rapid analytics, informatics, informatics CoE

The first set of classifications elicits the following best practices when it comes to development, deployment, usage, and customization:

- Online, on premise (non-Web platform), on device, on air, onto the cloud: high-definition (HD) rendering of content by context:
  - Platform-agnostic scalar and vector graphics processing, with digital signage and display rendered in the form of HD text; visual (object)–based software development kits that are codeless, per se.
  - Support for industry standards compliance in regards to target content presented: character sets, collocation sequences, encoding, including Unicode, natural language (NL) semantics, and the like.
  - Endpoint device-compliant rendering, with instant or near-zero latency in autorefresh/autosync of backend data (processed) to the visualization interface.
  - Support aspect-oriented visualization, especially to address rapid analysis (time to assess), rapid intelligence (time to insight), advanced analytics (includes predictive analytics too; time to implementation and user-driven feedback) and rapid information (time to informatics in action, or return on customer).

The second set of classifications elicits the following best practices:

- Support for funnel-ins/fan-outs of heterogeneous content in an interactive fashion
- Seamless support for Adobe Flex-enabled Flash; and Open Web standards like XML/CSS; and HTML5 higher dimensional visualization
- Support for user-friendly and business-compliant terminology in a consistent and coherent fashion
- Support for industry GUI standards such as JSF, WPF, and Silver-Light; Adobe Air/Flex; HTML5; Ajax/HTML; Python/PHP/Perl; and the more enriched open source frameworks like ICE Server Faces (Infobright Community Edition).
- Rapid analysis, intelligence, and advanced analytics (includes predictive analytics)
- Rapid analytics, informatics, informatics Center of Excellence (or CoE)

Industry vendors include:

- Birst: the world's first solution as a service (SaaS)–enabled BI appliance
- BIRT: Business Intelligence Reporting Tools
- Tableau software's BI solutions (for competitive BI)
- Integration of the open source EDW/BI with develop-build-deploy 360°, mobility 360°, visibility 360° components such as Aquia's Commons, an open source social business software; Alfresco's ECM Solutions; RivetLogic's ECM Solution, an open source content, collaboration, and community management solution; SPRINGCM (cloud enterprise content management); Open-Text's ECM Suite 2010; M-FILES' M-Files Professional (document management in the cloud); or Google Enterprise's Google Search Appliance and Google Apps.
- Connotate has developed Agent Community, a cluster of intelligent software agents for idea generation, personalized monitoring, precision harvesting, and data mash-ups.

This applies to all users, naïve to non-naïve. Use of database (DB)/repository–configurable table(s) grouped by domain, solution-usage, and customer/consumer/competitor contexts is recommended on the server side; it can subsequently travel on the go in the form of exported XML files/file templates.

9.4.1   Visualization of Content: For Better or Best Fit

Content and big data management do involve large-scale management, and both demand agility of scale, which means the appropriate business process (i.e., information as a service) and technology (protocols, prototypes, plots; i.e., information integration as a service) always sync one on one.

These architectures map results of such large-scale analytics onto big data models that allow disparate content-to-content integration by way of virtualization, visualization, or view-based location. Hence, it's always better to include this in the interest of a best-fit design. Visual content enables richer presentation of facts and thus helps identify cutting corners; also, when mining for patterns in sets, it can identify whether co-related visuals are based on "live" datasets.

Some special use cases of visualization in large-scale analytics can be to coalesce two reference business models, where each one belongs to a line of business but has a large set of dimensional, factual, reference, metadata, and additional attributes. The resulting coalescence will merge from the bottom up—from the physical design to the logical design to the conceptual common view of customer-360°.

A second one can be for interactive analysis on real-time data by allowing the end user to perform 3D ops on 2D graphs by using a mouse and an optional keypad to simulate 3D models from 2D ones for content interaction based on layered strata of siloed datasets.

9.4.2   Best Practices for Autogenerating Code: A Codeless Alternative to Information Presentation

Autogeneration of code comes as an accelerator when it is necessary to obfuscate metadata and then tag it to the master/reference. Even anonymous-identifying personally identifying information (PII) data can help blockages, especially when the data flows bidirectionally.

XML in-memory stored and in-memory database cache(s), as well as in-database, can be used as open source–based enablers and accelerators of the same.

Multiple architectures are in the works in at least three big data categories (courtesy of EMC2):

1. *Machine-generated data used for aggregation.* This can be leveraged in situations where both data volume and velocity, as well data complexity, are huge. The result is machine-generated data that is aggregated and then analyzed using Hadoop HDFS. Subsequently, the results can be fed into ROLAP (or Relational Online Analytical Processing) systems for advanced analysis and CoE.

2. *High-definition data captured for aggregation.* This can be leveraged for fine-grained use in database (like HBase, a low-latency, high-rate records-processing DB engine).

3. *Social networking data.* The data that "speaks exponential volumes," some of it manually person-fed, some autofed and some autogenerated (different from autofed in that it is autogenerated based on internal event processing or scheduling). Examples include a social graph that is autogenerated based on "status" ele-

vation of a fan on Facebook who is also a customer of the EDW/
BI solution.

Business case examples include deriving custom sales KPI from Sales
2.0 for integrated analysis with socially relevant computing.

9.4.3   Automating Querying: Why and When

Automatic querying is used to test intra- and intercomponent functionality.
It can be defined as:

1.   Autoquerying additional business attributes when the primary
     business facts are retrieved

2.   Dynamically constructing a fully static query in memory, based
     on external (e.g., user input) criteria

3.   Dynamically constructing a fully dynamic query in memory
     based on external (e.g., user input) criteria

4.   Auditing of queries based on business operations context(s)

5.   Reverse-engineering of visual queries into SQL-enabled or Com-
     mon Query Language–based queries

6.   Autogenerating output from interactive visuals that work behind
     the scenes to autoanalyze and generate an intelligent query on the
     fly and subsequently respond in subsecond timeframes

7.   Automating BI as a service, or automating any of its components
     for information as a Service on the go.

8.   Automating and accelerating any of the seven tasks listed above.

The first three tasks in the list can involve the dynamic processes of virtual data federation. The task listed at number 5 can involve a visualization
query scenario. In reference to the task at number 1, this is quintessential
when autotagging granular metadata from a dynamic federated view to the
actual data values, observations fetched by the query. Simply stating, this is
pulling the context as per the content prefetched for retrieval. Examples
include a graph and its associated data source lineage; a customer intelligence Flash view and its associated customer/consumer/competitor–trending information; as well as the individual strategic indicators.

A second use case can be audit queries due to strict governance, reliability, and compliance or technofunctional requirements. Again, the queries pertaining to prediction-based business value proposition are a best fit for this category. The implementation details of auditing or automating querying cannot be narrowed to one set of lists, but the underlying approach seems to be the same, using dynamic SQL or a dynamic query string consisting of a multipart declarative composite.

When a business process connected with context-aware or risk-aware input source is set to activation, the underlying context or risk awareness is not completely stateable until runtime. Almost all such queries that address this scenario must be automated.

A testing framework consisting of steps 1 through 8 can be autogenerated whose dynamic variables can be code-listed, as in Listing 9.1, along with the EDW/BI solution–application users' and resources' allocation credentials being master-listed in persistent tables or model-definitions.

```
(
  (master_data_context, master_data,
   input_enabled, output_enabled,
   relay_enabled, state_of_master_data),
   shareable_across_lob,
   searchable_across_lob
)

(
  (meta_data_context, meta_data,
   input_enabled, output_enabled,
   relay_enabled, state_of_meta_data),
   shareable_across_lob,
   searchable_across_lob
)

(
  (input_context, input_data_context,
   input_data, input_state),
  (output_context, output_data_context,
   output_data, output_state),
   shareable,  searchable
)
```

Listing 9.1 Dynamic variables of a testing framework, consisting of list steps 1 through 8.

9.4.4 How Fine Is Fine-Grained? Drawing the Line between Representation of Data at the Lowest Level and a Best-Fit Metadata Design and Presentation

The word *fine* is only fine-grained to the lowest depth or recursive depth that its business dependency tree dictates, or to the highest recursive depth in case of recursive hierarchies. In general, the foundational data warehouse (DW) can consist of data at its lowest level of granularity. Higher level dimensional tables and/or ROLAP designs can be the basis of metadata designs, provided the following conditions are met:

1. Metadata can be stored in the EDW in native format and is SQL access compliant.

2. It is accessible by one or more of its dependents.

3. It is measurable by itself. This means facts-based reasoning can be done using this metadata item.

4. It has a scope of its own that allows for inter-metadata shareability.

5. It can be shared using a name or a taxonomy-friendly name across other applications within its scope.

6. It can be imported/exported as part of the overall solution view in a ROLAP or XML model.

7. It conforms to open standards but is specification-explicit.

9.5 Best Practices for Application Integrity

Application integrity is not just consistency, coherency, currency, and commonality, but also about preserving these Cs over time—in fact, over the customer-user experience lifecycle of the same. Such a design demands reusability as a design driver. A *reusable application design* that complies with structured and modular patterns of each inherent component enables both isolation by way of independent execution, multitenant reusability, and in-memory distribution-enabled replication, while at the same time managing these four aspects across all layers of the end-to-end solution. The best-fit practices for the same can be enumerated as follows:

1. Use global and domain-specific contexts (it does pay off if these are defined using common and open standards) to isolate/insulate the EDW/BI solution across lines of business.

2. Design filter translators that can take common standards–compliant parameters with respect to data type. This will help aid in object-based/Web services–based in-line execution. Allow for reporting time-based parameters to DEMUX JOIN with the column closest in granularity to the fact-based time dimension. For multiple granularities, join from the lowest through the highest.

3. Avoid n-dimensional cubes in-memory. Instead mash them into dimensionally spread ROLAP slices that are autorefreshed on the fly or on demand and then autojoined based on the user/domain application context; and stream-federate the results in an orderly fashion. Using open source gives the best-of-breed solution.

4. Socially enable your business solution through dynamic interfacing with Facebook, LinkedIn, and the like. This in turn enables create business–social intranets that can be delivered as software social-nets or hardware social-bots. Remember to deploy this social software so that it faces the end users' side. Classic examples of BI-enabled social-nets are MicroStrategy's cloud-based service named MicroStrategy Gateway, which constructs an enriched relational model of the Facebook social graph; and MicroStrategy Wisdom, which unlocks the wealth of personal information contained in Facebook using advanced analytics.

Open source analytics can help build a hot-pluggable bridge–application programming interface (API) that maps the R-model from the social graph to a customized analytic model, obtained by MicroStrategy Wisdom, to result in an independent business–social BI component that is platform agnostic, DB/DBMS agnostic, and dynamic SOA compliant. The enriched output model can be reused again for example, against a .NET Entity Framework Model (object model). In this manner, integrated analysis can be performed using cascading inputs and outputs, which are multitenancy enabled. The entire process can be made persistent as an advanced analytic metrics function, or BI information as a service; the underlying workflow (i.e., the process-flow) bridges the social graph to the custom analytics and streamlines it with the rest of the process flow as BI information integration as a service. Subsequent visualization via instant charting and analytic dashboards can aid in accelerating the analysis process by way of on-the-spot analysis and the like.

5. Address searches on unstructured text using secure-rights-aware filters for non-ROLAP layers; for example, in the Web server and/or application server (just a reminder that both can be different), in-DB cache, object cache, in-memory distributed cache, and the like. When using ECM, it is recommended to use the inherent content management features first, supplemented by declarative enhancements that merge into the driving feature as a transparent abstraction. Industry examples in the open source arena include Alfresco ECM; Coveo's CIAS (Content Information Access Solutions); AvePoint's DocsAve, ProofPoint, and MarkLogic; and the like.

6. For searches inbound to the database, use the DB-native SQL-enabled search engine. Augment with NoSQL/XML/LINQ/CQL (Common Query Language) wrappers to combine SQL- and Non-SQL search results.

7. Use semaphores, assertions, annotations and index-organized data-structures to help speed up the access and retrieval of content-centric queries, especially when all of the inherent relationships for a data item need to be retrieved inline as part of the data itself or tagged via URL or similar. Visualized tagging of the retrieved data/content for quick views for relevancy makes a lot of sense.

8. The underlying business process flow/work flow can be fed to a dynamic data grid that can smart-store and reuse them on demand. The same holds true for data (-flows) as well. Here the individual cached (data, workflow) can be prioritized based on a workflow database table.

When sharing data between EDW and the BI tiers, always ensure that the "true" object identifiers (business OID, machine-generated OID) are preserved natively in a persistent manner. These can go in the form of custom context info as part of a row in a ROLAP table or an XML-/SQL-compliant column in a streams database. Additionally, tying them with the solution–application context and client identifiers makes the integrity more robust and yet flexible. The key indicator for a reusable and adaptive design is one that enables isolation with insulation by way of components—these are more than the COM/DCOM objects of the Microsoft methodology.

Some of the primary vendors in the open source search space are:

- Concept Searching's conceptClassifier: Automatic identification and extraction of concepts; automatic classification and taxonomies management
- Smartlogic's Semaphore: An open source semantic search platform
- Lucid Imagination's Lucene/Solr–powered enterprise search platform
- Brainware's Globalbrain: A multiple format intelligent search solution

9.5.1   Sharing Data between EDW and the BI Tiers: Isolation or a Tightrope Methodology

The following callout is reiterated from the previous section to highlight the importance of a loose-coupled SOA methodology used in solution-to-solution integration.

When sharing data between EDW and the BI tiers, always ensure that the "true" object identifiers (business OID, machine-generated OID) are preserved natively in a persistent manner. These can go in the form of custom context info as part of a row in a ROLAP table or an XML-/SQL-compliant column in a streams database. Additionally, tying them with the solution–application context and client identifiers makes the integrity more robust and yet flexible. The key indicator for a reusable and adaptive design is one that enables isolation with insulation by way of components—these are more than the COM/DCOM objects of the Microsoft methodology.

The primary ways to share data between EDW and BI tiers are as follows:

- Using data as a service and DI as a service
- Using service-oriented architecture (SOA):
    - SOA-centric information components

- SOA-centric workflows
- SOA-centric visual flows
- SOA-centric intuition, innovation, invention flows
- SOA-centric intuition, innovation, invention
- Using Web services (exposed via API)
- Using XML as a service
- Using an ESB, akin to the likes of Apache ESB
- A static/dynamic combination of the above
- *A case for information on the go*

The road ahead for implementing an open source BI-driven global information service and BI on the go seems to be not far off, especially with cosupportive technologies like dynamic data virtualization, dynamic EDW, shared and cloud computing in the competitive lanes. Secondly, scalability on demand, dynamic visualization, and dynamic SOA have already beaten the heat in proving customers' trust.

9.5.2   Breakthrough BI: Self-Serviceable BI via a Self-Adaptable Solution

Let open source EDW/BI self-evolve to become next-generation BI in a series of steps, the primary ones being:

1. Assimilate, anchor, accelerate, automate, adopt, and adapt big data into the EDW/BI solution. Design and implement analytics that are receptive to frequent change dynamics. This ensures the adaptability of the same down the road.

2. Use the same (high-definition or high-level) conceptual architecture, on a plane of common view of concept comprehensible by business, social, technology and corporate teams.

3. Use EDW-ROLAP design tuning while the solution is up and running. Analyze (some large) tables for row-level and column-level statistics. (The same holds good for user-level statistics.)

4. Prepackage commonly called procedures/functions in shared memory areas or virtual machine (VM)–enable the same into shared memory realms.

9.5.3   Data-In, Data-Out Considerations: Data-to-Information I/O

Data-in, data-out as a primary EDW/BI process plays a pivotal role in enterprise business operations and insightful decision making. In this context, the following best-fit options are recommended for its implementation:

- *A multichannel approach* consisting of siphoning source data and qualifying it for further steps (data virtualization is key here, as well as for data mining from the context of data-cues extraction and data lineage and linkage). Optimal data processing levels are performed via virtual data federation, data as a service, data integration as a service, and information as a service for BI on the go; SOA-centric data as a service is used to feed/sync the BI dashboard. As an example, the Talend 4.2 Open Source Solutions XML Mapping allows transformations between structured (relational) and XML (unstructured) data.
- *A multidimensional approach* that breaks the complexity of both the data and the processes involved. Dynamic ETL, dynamic EDW, dynamic SOA, and self-serviceable BI are key game-changers that accelerate the solution processes execution. Talend 4.2 XML Mapper in combination with an inline Web-based business process modeler can be leveraged to synthesize existing models, compare and contrast them, and derive additional functionality on the fly or on demand.
- *A multicomponent approach* in which each individual can exist on its own as well as in coordination with its related components.
- *A multiservices approach* with pub-sub models for predefined/scheduled functionality, ESB for 24×7and data-in-transit requests; dynamic SOA for operational BI and visualization, and the like.
- *A multiendpoint approach*, with anytime/anywhere/anyone, right information/right purpose/right people/right time, and reliability/availability/security build-your-own BI functionality from the comfort of a laptop or mobile device.

9.5.4   Security Inside and Outside Enterprise Parameters: Best Practices for Security beyond User Authentication

Enlisted are some of the best-fit practices beyond authentication that, when put into place, can turn reactive security automatically into proactive security by way of "live" flagging and enabling of the same in *real time*:

- Enforce WPA (Wireless Preferred Access) and WPA2 at each and every intra- and interaction point. This includes physical, virtual, perimeter, endpoint, and wide-area network (WAN) layers of the end-to-end solution.
- Rely on modular and secure shell scripting.
- Design and build self-manageable and data-driven security solution components, such as:
  - Autoconfiguration of default policies based on Role Based Access Controls (RBAC), Attributes Based Access Controls (ABAC), or Fine-Grained Access Controls (FGAC).
  - Autoextension (using FGAC) of add-on policies/policy rules based on actual usage stats, persistent threats, surveillance, and intelligence-based composite maps that illustrate the most vulnerable to least vulnerable zones of the end-to-end solution usage.
- Realizing deduplication in a risk-assessed manner helps a lot for high- and real-time traffic flows over the WAN, such as voice, video, VoIP, Web, and the like. Decentralization, virtual federation with centralized EDW, and unified grid console-based administration are the recommended bests for such a realization.
- Leveraging the cloud for backup, archiving, and administration of the same.
- Leverage perimeter security across all endpoints including intranets and extranets.

9.6   Best Practices for Intra- and Interapplication Integration and Interaction

In addition to the best-fit practices pertaining to application component–to–appplication component and solution-to-solution highlighted in Chapters 2 through 8, this section completes the so-called interprocess communication and interoperability of the EDW/BI solution lifecycle sliced into the following subareas:

1. API and solution development (SD)–API
2. Caching and caching API
3. Web interfacing and forward-facing API (can include cloud too)
4. Optimization of resources

The first two subareas define the consistency in terms of information coherence and persistent vs. intermittent caching in multiple tiers. The second two of the four sub-sections discuss the same in reference to Web-interfacing and Forwarding-facing API and correspond to "Application Web Interaction and Communication"

1. API and Solution Development (SD)–API

1. Track, trace, and monitor the end-to-end code for both methods and behaviors.

2. Focus on modular and structured code with cross-platform portability in mind.

2. Caching and Caching API

Caching enables the use of multiple frontends to handle n requests per second. When implemented, it yields higher throughput. In-database cache is enabled by default and set to a marginal size that depends on the Web server and/or the application server installed. Some of the best practices that can help in superior performance are as follows:

1. When the custom code is not an issue for latency or resource contention, placing data/content in RAM rather than on disk is usually faster for high-performance query access, immaterial of the content and distribution of the same. Then this data will and should be the most frequently accessed/processed and is normally out-of-sync with the underlying EDW/DB in terms of access paths, storage patterns, and distribution—yet is mutually exclusive in the result-sets output.

    For SQL-to-SQL access bidirectionally, if the data-to-data involves object(s)-to-relational, caching the same, sometimes with the appropriate result-set(s), does render it faster, especially in operational environments.

    Object caching comes in multiple flavors such as:

    a. Object caching for navigational data

    b. Object caching for queries across distributed data sources. Binary large object (BLOB) caching is one such type of object caching. PDFs, documents, images, and the like are cached in-memory and served to per http(s) requests.

    c.   Object caching for publishing page layouts, not the content/data in them, along with the URL entire key.

InterSystems's Caché and Objectivity's Solution provide two powerful solutions for information transformation from unstructured-to-structured object/object-related data or content.

---

2.   Relocating data closest to its point-of-usage is a recommended best practice when the data is dynamically shuffled around a dynamic grid as it is simultaneously accessed, changed etc. without losing its state-of-integrity.

A dynamic collaboration content grid is a good business case for the same. In such a scenario, a Content Delivery Network does the load balancing in an intelligent fashion.

---

3.   Keeping track of query timeouts for non-SQL based data/content access. This can be set at the application and/or domain levels, set at the user-controllable domain level, or merged/matched with the analogous SQL-based

```
QueryTimeOut( )
```

    values converted to seconds.

4.   Deciding the enablement/disablement of server-side publishing mechanisms to override the web.conf values. The setting

```
<ObjectCache maxSize="100">
```

    overrides the default for the same as set in the web.conf file.

The parameters publishing cache hit ratio and total number of cache compactions (related to performance monitoring) are key technical indicators (KTIs) for monitoring when object code caching is enabled. Others parameters to watch out are cache duration, cache type, and cached object type.

---

5. Varying the caching by http header, validate the same—create anonymous cache profiles that are different/separate from the page output cache profiles. The next step is to create test cases that simulate multiple concurrent users' testing environment.

3. Web Interfacing and Forward-Facing API

A forward-facing API can include a Web graphic user interface (GUI), Web rich Internet application (RIA) portal, or a (private) cloud. Here are some best-fit practices:

1. Using XACML policy server for cloud compliance

   a. Implementing attribute-based access control (ABAC) using XACML (2.0)

   b. Using XAACML 3.0 for delegation by way of federated identity

2. Using solution-aware or risk-intelligence identity

   a. Implement security at every I/O level

   b. Implement the same in the transport-carrier mechanism (ESB etc.)

3. Implement 1 and 2 as stated above at every I/O point of the product/solution

```
=================================================
|                        |  Presentation        |
|    Web Perimeter       |                      |
=================================================
|   SOA Tier                                     |
=================================================
|   ESB Tier                                     |
=================================================
|   EDW/EDM/ROLAP       |        ODS            |
=================================================
         ^                        ^
        | |                      | |
====================            | |
|  Legacy Systems   |===========| |
====================
```

4. Derive policy rules to comply to corporate/new/amended governance, risk, and compliance standards. Pipeline/federate and

stream them as needed based on endpoint usage–functionality mappings.

4. Optimization of Resources

It is often recommended as also a followed practice to initialize frequently used programs to be cached in memory the first time the solution application is loaded into memory. However, there can be situations when a different but needed program must be executed, thereby commanding instantiation and/or initialization of the same in live production environs. This must be done during off-peak hours, and its state must be made independent of the other programs. *When dealing with cross-tier transporting involving bidirectional bits flow, this factor of stateless transfer of data but statefull transfer of context by way of what it represents in terms of output must be taken into account.*

By tweaking the memory parameters and using dynamic cross-lists for custom resource allocation, the optimization of memory, CPU, throughput, and response time can be realized. Parallel execution and pipelined streaming of data/content can prove faster if a stack-based data-structure more often needs more memory than allocated. This type of polling mechanism can be dynamically implemented.

Chapters 4 through 8 have emphasized isolating the various tiers of the EDW/BI solution into seamless components of EDW/EDM/ROLAP/ODS layer(s), as well as a BI layer with the two loosely coupled by ESB tier/SOA tier/presentation tier.

The isolation by way of technofunctional independence aids in getting point-in-time memory usage (calculated as a percentage) by way of fine-grained alerting on server performance metrics. The arguments that parameter the same are sufficient enough to enumerate, analyze, and optimize these metrics.

Also, finer granularity in alerting can include deciding who is alerted (determined by RBAC+ABAC), SMTP alerting only, alerting of logs-based event outcomes, and automation of responses to alerts via feedback mechanisms.

9.6.1   Continuous Activity Monitoring and Event Processing

Throughout the earlier sections of this chapter, as well as in the earlier chapters, it was emphasized that business continuity of an EDW/BI solution relied heavily on continuous data integration, continuous operational BI, and continuous feedback management. It is the third component that this section addresses, in a way—more so in terms of the foundations for the same.

Three key indicators drive business value from this aspect, namely,

(i) Self-serviceability—Uses user-interaction, runs the required EDW/BI processes and displays the output(s) or continues the channeling of the same.

(ii) Knowledge mining and using it to self-manage—Discovers user-driven patterns, transforms them into data/tuples/rule-sets, autofeeds them with new user data, and evolves the design by rewiring them into workflow.

(iii) Customer feedback—This can refer to any kind of input from the customer based on any platform or combination of platforms of use, including face-to-face interaction. This is kind of an interprocess for the one stated above.

The various processes involved are divided into two primary categories:

1. Solution health information
2. Solution health assurance (minus security view), in terms of unbreakability by function, too load-stressed to handle, too many users to handle, disaster-recovery failures, and the like.

These are discussed in detail below.

1. Solution Health Information

- *Solution snapshot capture (of live environments)*: This involves end-to-end capture of (content, context, end-user attributes) cross-tiers. This also records the state of the end-to-end solution minus the logon credentials that are stored separately or key-hashed differently.
- *Solution operations statistics—metrics and measures*: These involve the various defaults, thresholds, inputs, outputs, break-evens,

break-points, outliers, and non-quantifiable ones like "raising the bar on" or "lowering the bar on" derived from the qualifiers.

The capture process can be further subcategorized into:

- Tier-level capture of live application stats, EDW/EDB activity monitoring, process/workflow monitoring, user-activity monitoring, cross-correlation between tiers of similar nature, auto-incident discovery, and autoresolution of the same.
- Auto-alerts notification based on severity of incident and built-in autorespond mandates, followed by autosynced notifications.

Complex event processing triggered by break-points across tier-boundaries, dangling cache pointers (unsafe memory management) or implicit standard suspend/resume process signaling, process dependency states list–based analysis, and the like; add preemptive user downtime to shutdown. This is a key business value driver.

- *Solution analyzers*: These do the code analysis and logic (techno-functional) analysis, the latter to a certain measurable degree based on the solution snapshot and operations statistics collected as well as can do the same on an as-of basis. OPNET Technologies, Inc., is a vendor who offers products such as Advancd App-Transaction Xpert (ACE Analyst) for application capture and import strategies, AppInternals Xpert (Panorama), and AppResponse Xpert (ACE Live).

2. Solution Health Assurance (Minus Security)

This refers to unbreakable ability by function, too load-stressed to handle, too many users to handle, or disaster-recovery failures for the duration of the solution lifecycle. In a way, this category overlaps with information assurance, mostly at the critical juncture when the solution is going to snap due to one or more of the above reasons. Prudent solutions to subvert this type of incidents include:

- Live solution testing by capturing a "live" snapshot of the current system, accelerating the load and scalability by way of simulation or emulation
- Creating pseudo-users who emulate real-world users and repeating the testing, as well as storing their settings
- Adopting WAN optimization techniques like deduplication and optimization of voice, video, Web, VDI, VoIP, and PCoIP that handle most of real-time traffic.
- Securely offshore backup-enabled data and secure on demand and fast access to the same, 24×7 (EVault Solution's EVault offers an Open Source solution for the same that also allows intelligence search for backed up data offsite (and in the cloud).

Bridge the offsite EVault cloud with the onsite live production cloud using cloud-connects. This is taking secure backup, recovery, and retention to the next level.

Best Practices to Use SOA-based Methodologies: Data Services versus Data Integration Services; SOA over Information Presentation; Information as a Service on the Go

It has been established through customer success stories and research reports that SOA-centric business processes, vis-à-vis their implementations, have been proven successes after adopting SOA-methodologies into their business operations workflows. Talend open integration solutions was named in one such report, namely Gartner's "Cool Vendors in Application and Integration Platforms, 2011." Talend uses SOA to leverage real-time DI. Enlisted are potential pivot points of what an SOA-centric solution can deliver:

- From data services to data integration services, data virtualization by way of virtual data federation; transport of the same data (-in-transit) for near real–time DI necessary for operational BI; SOA is leveraged statically and dynamically for information integration and application-to-application integration.
- Dynamic SOA is pivotal to high-volume real-time data federation, formulation, and streaming.

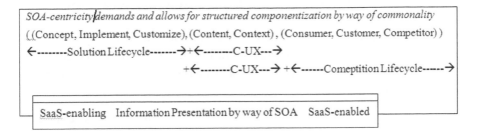

SOA-centricity demands and allows for structured componentization by way of commonality

((Concept, Implement, Customize), (Content, Context) , (Consumer, Customer, Competitor))

←--------Solution Lifecycle-------→ +←--------C-UX---→

+←--------C-UX---→ +←------Comeptition Lifecycle------→

SaaS-enabling   Information Presentation by way of SOA   SaaS-enabled

- SOA-based solution also allows for SaaS-enabled as well as SaaS-enabling of the component module for modular reusability or hot-pluggable usage of the same. Information solution on the go is possible by SaaS-enabling and SaaS-enabled BI on demand engines that can be embedded (true in-memory or RAM-disk based in-database cache) and accessed in near real–time/on demand. Controls for the same needs to be implemented in dynamic SOA environments.

A Business Case for SOA Methodologies via Commonality

Using SOA methodologies not only enables but also accelerates the injection of optimized or supplementary information architectures that address the paradigm of commonality among domains. This subsection outlines two such trending industry domains, namely, big data and solution-to-solution collaboration by isolation.

- By being SaaS-enabled, an advanced big data analytics engine can be leveraged in an existing EDW/BI environment with near zero hassles.
- By being SaaS-enabling, this SOA module can have another compliant big data analytics engine embedded in it by API or otherwise. This is managing big data the easy way.
- Coupled with heterogeneous sourcing, from data to data models, SOA can help ease the big data complexity and variance in change by integration and disintegration of any data (in-store to in-transit) and thereby help churn unified views of customers in as accurate and accessible a manner as possible.
- An SOA methodology can be designed to isolate applications in such a fashion that all of the inherent APIs have the control to "know" where the info flows by the use of the same (API).
- Virtualization is not a viable option when delivering a universal OS for mobile, as it is very volatile and loses control at the physical level.

9.6.2 Best Practices to Leverage Cloud-Based Methodologies

Focusing on the key business drivers for cloud computing as pay-as-you-go pricing, automation, shared-platforms, and it ability to run on commodity hardware, here are some highlights that can be marked as recommended principles to put into practice:

1. Design and implement a compute OS or compute cloud that is self-service enabled and can be instantiated in a few clicks into a VM, SOA-enabled as well as SaaS-enabling for use as an on-premise ISO image.

    An example of doing one such prepackage is using UShareSoft's Uforge Image Builder. It provides a self-service appliance factory for Cloud Computing.

Again shown in Figure 9.2, open source scores here by easing the design pragmatics leaving many more choices on the table as shown in Figure 9.2. The key capability here is the centralized provisioning of the inherent load balancing from a custom-built portal, custom API, or via a different segregation of duties–compliant and SaaS-enabled deploy "Compute-OS" solution.

Building A self-service appliance factory for Cloud Computing

0. Proprietory Solution Stack	2. Open Solution Stack
1. Open Solution Stack	0. Proprietory Solution Stack 1. Legacy Application(s)

0. Proprietory Solution Stack ||		|| 0. Proprietory Solution Stack
1. Lecagy Solution Stack	|| Open Solution Stack <--> Open Solution Stack ||	1. Lecagy Solution Stack
2. 3rd Party Solution Stack ||		|| 2. 3rd Party Solution Stack

Figure 9.2 A example of building a self-serviceable appliance factory for cloud computing.

2. Leverage the elastic flexibility vs. reliability, availability, and security over time for data (including) e-mail backup, archival, and restoration, especially historical. As personally identifiable information and mission-critical data move to the virtual private cloud or hybrid cloud, all other not-so-critical data can migrate to the cloud using a "push into/pull out" on-demand strategy and pay-per-use billing. Cloud-enabling archival and e-mail also con-

tribute to the pervasive anytime, anywhere, anyone functionality and value of the EDW/BI solution.

3. Cloud as a sandbox for test-driven development as well as a sandbox for results-trusted value. This gives the true "cloud nine" confidence backed by support from the trusted metric results, such as:

   a. The most versatile agility with the finest of granular testing from dimension to detail: fine-grained business rules for iterative development-to-unit testing and similar rules for verification-validation-to-results-valued

   b. Open source opens up the gates to any analogous standards-compliant IT ecosystem (hardware server, OS, middleware, integration and integration services tier(s), presentation layer, beyond presenting-mash-boarding, end-point delivery

   c. From "I get your point" to "BI's the point" to "going beyond the BI point," cloud is a safe haven to do all things ethical, from penetration testing to validation-to-value that are commensurately measurable. Test for a preview PoC here at a fraction of the cost and at least on par with the payload—from unit testing to business technofunctional testing (if your SLA allows it) to regression and stress testing.

4. Leverage cloud for deployment of large-scale solutions with flexibility at hand: The right orchestration is the key in terms of services in the cloud, and a matrix-driven deployment cheat sheet is the initial document to be created.

   This outlines the statement of plan as a first step, followed by gap-fit analysis (yes, there is a gap-fit analysis for deployment, too). And subsequently, the actual deployment steps are to be executed in the order determined, as in the preview plan.

   a. Decide upon physical, virtual, hybrid cloud, or just a hosted service. The recommended practice in this scenario is to deploy it to a hybrid cloud.

   b. Large-scale deployments need to be cloud-compliant in terms of deployment *and* operations—with the emphasis on *and*.

   c. When it comes to users' enablement, "inclusiveness precedes all other," meaning anyone in the company from corporate to customer support can access the cloud-enabled EDW/BI solution. Engage business users in this overall process and the hits for quality of solution will be very high. As a result, time to value is less and the "value" is at least on par or more.

RightScale Technologies is a trending vendor who does automation and orchestration in the cloud. Other top-tier vendors are OpSource (OpCloud), Amazon Web Services EC2 and S3, GoGrid, and the like.

5.   Leverage the cloud for e-vaulting backup and alternative (physical) replication strategies. Deduplication in the cloud is a huge game-changer when it comes to intelligent offline data storage. Faster, secure, and scalable access to it, SLA-compliant and built-to-last trust (this is still in the evolutionary stage)—all at a fraction of the cost of conventional equivalents.

9.7   Best Practices for Creative BI Reporting

This is at least twofold in its creativity. First, it addresses the optimization of reports execution and output; second, it addresses the optimization of reports robustness.

Some of the best-fit practices are:

1.   Using disconnected analytics or connection bases for BI enablement: The power of disconnected analytics lies in its ability to auto-tag value-added metadata to the actual data, thereby enriching it *without* any DB/EDW/data-store/data-source infrastructure in place.

   a.   Customer Lifecycle Experience Dashboard vs. Measurable Results (functional goals, KPI, score-carding)

   b.   Business Lifecycle Experience Dashboard vs. Measurable Goals (acquisition, on-boarding, attrition, retention)

   c.   Solution (Technoprocess) Experience Dashboard vs. Measurable Goals (business value proposition–strategic roadmap)

   d.   Solution (Dynamic Information Fabric) Mashboard vs. Measurable Objectives (collaboration without boundaries; secure file-sharing in the Web)

2. Thinking out-of-the-box reporting: canned reporting; operational BI reporting; *n*-dimensional reporting; proprietary; otherwise, and so on.

    Open source reporting services can streamline the process of loose-coupling two or more combinations of reports/report-centric (data_context, metadata_context), or a dynamic set of reports based on a (RBAC, FGAC, ABAC) combination of access control. This in turn can execute virtually federated queries to generate the necessary data/content in prime time and on-demand using the FAST method described in my book *Oracle Embedded Programming and Application Development*; high-volume query responses are in the order of 5x–10x seconds.

3. Build reusability as a design pattern:

    a. Leverage operational robustness of EDW/EDB: In additional to OLAP resiliency, BI systems demanding real-time data must have the operational robustness of subsecond online transaction processing (OLTP) data analytics. This mandates an operational BI system that facilitates continuous sourcing, processing, and delivery of data as it is created. Ingres Vectorwise, JasperSoft, and Pentaho are some of the major players of this type of BI. PostgreSQL Plus, and MySQL Enterprise are also geared to provide this kind of richness in information insight.

    b. Leverage inherent on-chip computation: For scaling operational BI analytics at the speed and efficiency of a ROLAP engine in terms of adaptive native in-database processing (reduced CPU cycles)—context-aware, application-aware. This can involve a custom compute OS by coalescing and coagulating OS, apps server, and the existing database management system (DBMS).

    c. Perform integrated analysis (JasperReports v3.6): Proactive workflow provides active-state and instant visualization (e.g., instant charting, widgets, and Flash-based maps).

    d. Perform intelligent execution by rationalization of data (algorithm-driven computation) and query processing: In a typical scenario, the query process caches the compressed data in memory and hands it to the query engine, which in turn has to deconstruct the compression algorithm inherent in the same and then determine the appropriate decompression algorithm to apply and subsequently execute it. This is an overhead in terms of recompression of data.

A second intuitive approach to service the query requests is to use the compute-OS methodology, which puts the compressed data in memory and inputs it to the compute-OS (query) engine, which is intelligent enough to identify and determine the optimal decompression routine and subsequently execute the query request. Ingres Vectorwise does this by using its intelligent query processing technique, which dynamically understands and applies the appropriate decompression algorithm on the compressed data in memory and directly passes it to the CPU cache for execution.

The key difference here is that the decompressed data is not stored in-memory but is processed in the CPU via the CPU cache, and the results are passed on to the transaction context. As a result, there is an isolation of the query engine functionality from the related in-memory/on-CPU cache processing in terms of decompression and execution. Open source enabling this isolation by way of separating the transactional context-based decompression and execution from the query processing (i.e., query parsing, access path optimization, and in-memory caching) helps deliver split-second query response times as well as efficiency by way of query throughput.

Open source techniques can accelerate this "divide-and-conquer" strategy of optimally load balancing the in-memory and query-engine processing to leverage the best order of fit computation involved.

The notion of a compute-OS as a prototype for an open source analytic computation platform is illustrated in Figure 9.3.

4. Optimization directors: Performance indicators normalized into actionable business rules that can be streamed as reusable vectors (these can be time-bound, space-bound, location-bound, outlier-bound, or cross-border bound) refactored by content-only, context-only, or content-in-context.

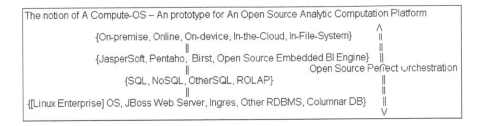

Figure 9.3   The notion of a compute-OS as a prototype for an open source analytic computation platform.

5.   Vector-specific execution of Ingres Vectorwise:

a.   Vectorized processing of the CPU by harnessing all of the relevant hardware in use.

b.   Cache-aware algorithms that autodecide the best fit in a way the data flows and is computed in the CPUs.

c.   Compressed columnar storage on disk, immaterial of the data variance involved (data variance is measured as the factor of data variety multiplied by data velocity). This is the greatest challenge of big data query processing—and some times of processing it ahead of schedule, by which time the same data might have changed.

The current trending big data analytics appliances for BI reporting and beyond are:

- Birst: The world's first SaaS-enabled in-memory BI appliance
- BIRT: Business Intelligence Reporting Tools
- Tableau software's BI solutions (for competitive BI)

6.   Contextual integration by way of ubiquitous platform and data structure support—Java, SOA, BPM-BPE, and the like—to deliver analysis against any data and/or datasets:

a.   Robust data mining (as both subjective and objective integration enabler)

b.   Advanced analytics and predictive analytics as accelerators for business analysis

c.   Rich visualization and interactivity with REST-enabled (Representational State Transfer enabled) "active" and "live" reporting, which can consist of data grid views and cell content grid views for non-matrix and matrix-enabled custom views

d. Completely modularized and feature-rich support for the fast-changing enterprise, that is, the mobile-enabling and mobile-enabled enterprise

e. SaaS enabled and cloud enabled to provide vertical and horizontal flexibility

f. Rich metadata abstraction and interfacing, including Web interfacing and Web messaging

7. BI-to-BI advanced reporting and collaboration capabilities, including platform-to-platform and peer-to-peer (can include person-to-person too) cross-operational functionality.

8. Cross-domain reporting by way of integrated analytics merged with report bursting.

9. Integrated analysis with multitenancy and contention-aware concurrency. This can be done by combining steps 5 and 6. Of special mention are those that enable n-temporal dimensioning where $n >= 2$. Visuals re-engineering and reverse engineering to autogenerate reference models, as per the collateral context domains. A query domain, an analytical reasoning domain, and a cross-collateral analysis domain are worth mentioning.

This is a value metric in terms of increasing the customer lifecycle. And this is a lot of value, because the more customers you have, and the more times you have the same customer, then the more dollars you get and the more competitive your business intelligence. Hence the data proposition (by way of data structure and structured analysis) leads to value proposition (by way of CI).

10. By allowing dynamic construction of report contexts that contain one or more of {identities, reporting domain specifics, access semantics, sort and search semantics} that can be standardized, template enabled, or personalized for further customization. A primary use case of this is in discovering unknown/new metadata contexts that can be defined by {meta-state, meta-object, meta-functions, meta-api, meta-context}. This approach has two key benefits:

a. It enables one-click generation and implementation of personalized reports by the business user, and not the IT or development teams.

b. It preserves the report meta(data)-state in addition to the involved data state—a huge plus for cross-platform portability and interfacing.

9.8 Summary

This chapter dealt with application development from two aspects, namely, solution orientation and product orientation. From BI to the core to BI to the forefront, it emphasized that EDW/BI solution application management too begins with the customer/consumer/competitor trio, from concept to customization and beyond. It reiterated the fact that the power of advanced analytics is in its ability to autotag value-added metadata to the actual data, thereby enriching it without any EDB/EDW/data-store/data-source infrastructure in place. It detailed dimensional data views (i.e., derived dimensions) and cell values in content-grid views. The subsequent sections gave details on Web massaging and its relevance, if any, to Web mashing, Web interfacing, and forward-facing API, and best practices for certain special topics in application integrity and intra- and interapplication integration and interaction. The final sections discussed best practices for cloud enabling and creative BI reporting, from an application management perspective.

The next chapter gives details about going beyond BI reporting to drive business value by way of business analyses, BI, and business analytics—powered by advanced analytics.

Chapter 10

Best Practices Beyond Reporting: Driving Business Value

10.1   In This Chapter

- Advanced Analytics: The Foundation for a Beyond-Reporting Approach (Dynamic KPI, Scorecards, Dynamic Dashboarding and Adaptive Analytics)
- Large Scale Analytics: Business-centric and Technology-centric Requirements and Solution Options
- Accelerating Business Analytics: What to Look for, Look at, and Look Beyond
- Delivering Information on Demand and Thereby Performance on Demand
- Summary

10.2   Introduction

This chapter focuses on the best practices beyond reporting—those that add to the business value of an open source–based enterprise data warehouse (EDW)/business intelligence (BI) implementation. It explains the use of dynamic key performance indicators (KPI)– and scorecard-based rankings in scenarios where multivariate analysis is the key imperative. The topics on dynamic extract, transform, and load (ETL) and dynamic dashboarding are touched upon with respect to the appropriate context. It emphasizes the use of adaptive analytics as a key component of advanced analytics and as a foundation for BI beyond reporting. The subsequent sections touch upon some essential indicators when dealing with large scale analytics and accelerating business analytics in terms of what to look for, look at, and look beyond while including them as part of an EDW/BI solution. And the last (but not the least) section outlines how, by delivering information-on-demand and thereby performance-on-demand, it is possible to deliver business value on demand too.

Obtaining granular level of detail from data sources to data delivery and achieving the cross-dynamism and analytics involved across each interaction point of the end-to-end EDW/BI solution spectrum are indispensable. When it comes to delivering business value, there are some essential indicators in terms of categorizing the landscape, keeping in mind that the customers/consumers/competitors (AKA, the users producing, consuming, and subsuming the data) are the driving factor. And the corresponding design architecture is a matrix-based on-demand scenario in the real world. Add to this the *big data* element, and the complexity is accelerated, akin to managing a maze of *n* dimensions. The good news, though, is that as data evolved in structure, function, and volume, so did the technologies, architectures, and methodologies in place for creating, accessing, assessing, delivering, distributing, and dimensionally conforming that data in a correlated fashion. Using open source methodologies for implementing the *Open Source Perfect* data management platform for EDW/BI, is perhaps the best-fit practice option in today's data-centric wireless information-seeking world. Using advanced analytics involving accelerated business analytics and large-scale analytics as well as predictive analytics, these challenges can be overcome and even overturned in the road ahead of BI beyond reporting.

10.3   Advanced Analytics: The Foundation for a Beyond-Reporting Approach (Dynamic KPI, Scorecards, Dynamic Dashboarding, and Adaptive Analytics)

In today's trending business–social world, the term *big* is too commonly used to truly indicate bigness. From the legacy mainframes to the midrange supercomputers and SPARC stations to currently trending and evolving commodity hardware and hardware appliances, and hardwired software appliances to the palmtops that compute faster than a mainframe of yesterday. And as service-level agreements (SLAs) become dynamic in their revisions and reviews—one-on-one with the changing business needs, the new dynamic of customer-centricity is redefined and augmented with new rules, roles, and workflows to be injected into the revised SLA but also into the existing solution landscape. This mandates a new way of redefining the existing solution infrastructure—one that allows for this elasticity-on-demand. This is where advanced analytics, dynamic dashboarding, and adaptive analytics play a pivotal role. This takes BI to a higher level that is above the reporting capabilities of the same. The architectural framework for the same is a mix/match/merge of multiple architectures that enable high-definition dashboards, keeping the usage-identity semantics more or less the same. Listed here are some of the best practices that, when followed, raise the bar on data proposition (by way of data structure and structured analysis) leading through to value proposition (by way of competitive intelligence) using advanced analytics, scorecards-based ranking, and dynamic metrics–based measurement, as well as real-time transactional data availability "as-is."

1. *Leverage operational robustness*—From the database to the dashboard ace, operational robustness is a quintessential business process. The selectivity choice must be driven by keeping the business user in mind. As an example, MySQL doesn't have all the operational robustness of ExtremeDB or Ingres. Ingres Vectorwise or JasperSoft BI server are more tailored toward BI (especially operational BI) as opposed to Oracle11g OBIEE Suite or the recently released (in October 2011 at OOW 2011) Oracle Exalytics In-Memory Analytics Appliance.

2. *Leverage inherent on-chip compute capabilities*—For scaling operational business analysis at the speed and efficiency of a ROLAP engine in terms of adaptive and native in-database processing (reduced CPU cycles). This makes the computation context-aware or application-aware. This can involve a custom compute-OS (operating system) by coalescing and coagulating the OS, the apps server, and existing DBMS. Figure 10.1 depicts the notion of a compute-OS for BI.

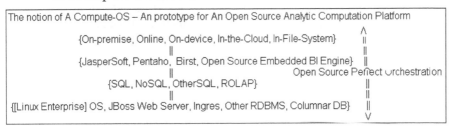

Figure 10.1   Notion of a compute-OS for BI

3. *Leverage integrated analysis*—This is implemented by way of proactive workflows that provide active-state persistency and instant visualization (e.g., instant charting, widgets, and Flash-based maps).

4.   *Leverage intelligent execution by rationalization of data (algorithm-driven computation) and query processing*—In a typical scenario, the query process caches the compressed data in memory and hands it to the query engine, which in turn has to deconstruct the compression algorithm inherent in it to determine the appropriate decompression algorithm to apply, and subsequently parse and execute it. There is an overhead in this process when it comes to recompression of data.

Another approach to servicing the query requests is by using the compute-OS methodology that puts the compressed data in memory and inputs it directly to the compute-OS (query) engine which is intelligent enough to identify and determine the optimal decompression routine, subsequently apply it, and finally execute the query request. Ingres Vectorwise does this by using its intelligent query processing technique that dynamically understands and applies the appropriate decompression algorithm on the compressed data in memory, and directly passes it to the CPU cache for execution.

The key difference here is that the decompressed data is not stored in-memory but is processed in the CPU via the CPU cache, and the results are passed on to the transaction context. Thereby the query engine functionality is isolated from the related in-memory/on-CPU cache processing in terms of decompression and execution. Open source–enabling this isolation by way of separating the transactional context-based decompression and execution from the query processing (i.e., query parsing, access path optimization, in-memory caching, etc.). This delivers split-second query response times as well as efficiency by way of query throughput.

Open source techniques can accelerate this "divide-and-conquer" strategy of optimally load-balancing the in-memory and query-engine processing to leverage the best order-of-fit computation involved.

Optimization directors are performance indicators normalized into actionable business rules that can be streamed as reusable vectors (these can be time-bound, space-bound, location-bound, outlier-bound, or cross-border bound; refactored by content-only, context-only, or content-in-context).

The key here is to extract and optimize relevant, meaningful KPI from existing KPI by using analytics (AKA measurable metrics) or derive entirely new KPI that are functionally relevant and efficient at the same time.

The accuracy of this is at least KPI^2.

Vector-specific execution of Ingres Vectorwise can be described as follows:

a. Vectorized processing of the CPU by harnessing all of the relevant hardware in use, thereby reducing CPU cycles. Vectorization balances concurrency versus parallelism in terms of fair-shared execution.

b. Employs cache-aware algorithms that auto-decide how best fit in a way the data flows and gets computed in the CPUs.

c. Compressed columnar storage on disk immaterial of the data variance involved (data variance is measured as data variety factored by data velocity). This is the greatest challenge of big data query processing—and sometimes processing it ahead of schedule, by which time the same data might have changed.

d. Ingres Vectorwise can also perform the following:

- Optimize disk storage by implementing columnar storage, lightweight compression, cooperative scanning and Flash drives.
- Optimize memory hierarchies (AKA recursive depth-levels)
- Optimize CPU usage by adaptive vectorization

5. *Leverage contextual integration by way of ubiquitous platform and data structure support*—Java, SOA, business process management (BPM)–business process execution (BPE), and the like, to deliver analysis against any data and/or datasets:

a. Robust data mining (as both subjective and objective integration enabler)

b. Advanced analytics and predictive analytics as augmenters and accelerators for business analysis

c. Rich visualization and interactivity with representational state transfer (REST)–enabled "active" and "live" reporting; this can consist of data grid views and cell content grid views for non-matrix and matrix-enabled custom views

d. Completely modularized and feature-rich support for the fast-changing enterprise (i.e., the mobile-enabling and mobile-enabled enterprise)

e. Solution as a service (SaaS)–enabled and cloud–enabled to provide vertical and horizontal flexibility

f. Rich metadata abstraction and interfacing, including Web interfacing and Web messaging

6. *Leverage BI-to-BI advanced reporting and collaboration capabilities*—Including platform-to-platform and peer-to-peer (can include person-to-person, too) cross-operational functionality.

7. *Implement cross-domain reporting by way of integrated analytics merged with report bursting.*

8. *Leverage integrated analytics that support multitenancy and contention-aware concurrency*—This can be done by combining steps 5 and 6 above. Of special mention are those that enable n-temporal dimensioning where $n >= 2$; visuals reengineering and reverse engineering to autogenerate reference models as per the collateral context domains. A query domain, an analytical-reasoning domain, and a cross-collateral analysis domain are worth mentioning.

This is a "value" metric in terms of increasing the customer lifecycle. And this is a lot of value, because the more customers a business has, and the more times those same customers return to the business, the more the dollars and the more competitive the business intelligence. Hence the data proposition (by way of data structure and structured analysis) leads to value proposition (by way of CI).

Allow for dynamic construction of report contexts that contain one or more 4-tuples of the form {identities, reporting-domain specifics, access semantics, sort-and-search semantics} and subsequently standardize, template-enable, or personalize them for further customization. A primary use case of this is in discovering unknown/new metadata contexts that can be defined by {meta-state, meta-object, meta-model, meta-API, meta-context}. This approach has three key benefits:

a.   It enables one-click generation and implementation of personalized reports by the business user, and not the IT/development teams.

b.   It preserves the report metadata state in addition to the involved data state—a huge plus for cross-platform portability.

c.   HTTP session state is managed by random generation of code followed by execution of the same during the deinitialization process of such a session.

9.   *Use custom property mappings for serialization to induce persistence and GRC-standards compliance*—Defining one-to-one mappings between key objects and value objects is essential in computing the qualitative, by way of object-relational models that can be derived based on commonly agreed upon input/output criteria. As an example, high-level conceptual models for real-time dashboarding can be automatically generated using real-time data feeds as source data, KPI-based [key object, value object] pairs, and the algorithmic mapping function that takes these inputs to output a relational SQL-compliant output pair as [output context, output value]. This works agnostic of the input variables irrespective of form, format, or function and is also platform-agnostic by outputting in industry standards–based unified formats, such as XML models, XML docs, HTML/XML, and HTML5/Flash/AJAX (for rich visualization). A business use case of this design strategy can be adopted to deliver generic digital displays—from digital dashboards to grid-based consoles. Using open source graphics and image libraries such as OpenGL, BGL (the Boost Graph Library), Geometric and Geospatial libraries; OpenFlow-like protocols to illustrate the intercomponent image/graph analysis flow(s), open source workflow application programming interfaces (APIs) like Apache Lucene Solr and Chef bring an in-depth user experience.

The key concept here is that the entire process is highly transparent when it comes to the end-point usage, even if some of it involves end-user interactivity.

A good use case for this is while performing aggregations and summarizations on non-SQL compliant data where an object→object mapping is transformed into a near equivalent object→relation mapping. This can then be passed as a parameter to a chain of pipelined functions that are capable of handling multiple grouped-elements computations on the same set of input data and yielding zero, one, or more rows.

10. *Inter-analytics and intra-analytics KPI*—This involves cross-programming language, cross-frameworks, and cross-semantics application programming interfaces (APIs). Using these types of API along a common workflow to streamline coordination and cooperation across them helps in constructing a customer success imperative (CSI). This framework can consist of the following:

   a. Open source interfacing API that consists of front-facing (towards consumer-end) API as well as backstaging API (from the front-facing interface to the backend systems like apps server, other performance-boosting middle-tier API and hybrid-DBMS server/s)

   b. Open source cloud–enabling API, which can be used to automate SaaS on demand or in near-real time. The reliability of SaaS factors in to raise the bar on critical issues like Web perimeter security, SOA-centricity, and EDW/BI firewalls at the EDW, middle, and BI tiers, as well as Web perimeter firewalls and bridge-firewalls that serve as elastic switches to become enabled or disabled on-demand.

   c. Open source semantic expression API

   d. Open source regular expression API

   e. Open source custom property mapping API

   f. Open source integration services API—This is function-to-function integration including the underlying context of the same (e.g., structured data–to–unstructured data integration by making use of the integration services).

g.   Open source workflow API, which can a part of the open source orchestration API. Other open source solutions in this arena include the open source OpenFlow, Solr, and Chef.

h.   Open source interchangeability and compatibility API – This is to programmatically interface with source ←→target language synchronous execution – without the use any specific third-party or other migration tools.

i.   Open source container API to ensure interlanguage, intermetrics, and interplatform deployment functionality as well as the SOA and Web services–based RESTful, agentless messaging, massaging, management, and monitoring of the same.

j.   Open source streaming API, which is useful for asynchronous execution of complex functions that are callable from SQL, such as pipelined chains that "emit" rows one by one as they are generated, as opposed to the traditional SQL set-based row operations. The greatest advantage of doing this is twofold. Firstly, it is asynchronous, thereby releasing the control to the calling environment. Secondly, they improve efficiency of execution by outputting row by row as they are created and/or updated there by reducing the overall response time as well as reducing the number of executions (including recursive and iterative executions).

k.   Open source embeddable API, which can include open source SaaS-enabled API and open source SaaS-enabling API.

l.   Open source services integration API is not the same as open source DI services API, in that it is larger in scope and function, as in service-to-service, cloud-to-cloud, internal-to-external, business-to-business, and business-to-social, and the like. Depending upon *the variety and variability of the serviceable functions involved*, this API can be collapsed or expanded on demand, as the business need dictates.

11.   *Build a prototype for the cloud-enabled enterprise for business operations as well as business-to-business integration*—It is worth the trustworthiness for such a solution deployment with respect to a better/faster/easier, governance, risk, and compliance (GRC)-compliant, and pervasiveness (in terms of solution scope). This can be implemented as a private cloud with all of the organization's personally identifying information (PII), critical, or sensitive data residing in the private cloud and the administrative , not so frequently used functionality, like archiving, auditing, audit trailing, logging; and time period–based push-through data, like end-of-month reports and the like, as well as a standby copy of the enterprise ecosystem in the public cloud.

12.   *Use XMLA and XML-as-a-service as a transport mechanism for data-in-transit*—Even XML can be used as an in-memory staging container for intermediate processing.

13.   *Beyond-the-buck business value*—A EDW/BI solution architecture that is capable of delivering Asynchronous execution coupled with synchronous results, thereby preserving the concurrency and parallelism with respect to execution; consistency and bi-directional state-of-transit is recommended for high throughput demanding applications like Web portals etc. where the customer value is measured in ranges of sub-second response times,. Here, a distributed in-memory data grid is dynamically constructed that deviates from the relational database management system (RDBMS) and ACID compliance (Atomicity-Consistency-Integrity-Durability) of processed data by being abstracted by a BASE architecture. The SQL and ACID properties are still enforced per se, but are delayed till the reconciliation stage, when all of the "active" transactions (AKA query-based pub-sub or online transactions) are synced to be flagged as "completed successfully."

All of the above best practices can be developed and deployed as software adapters, software accelerators, advanced analytics, or software analytic appliances that are hot-pluggable without any intervention to the live user environments.

Figure 10.2 depicts the value proposition of an EDW/BI solution implemented in the *Open Source Perfect* way, and the elbow-shaped dotted arrow leads to the illustrated decomposition of the same, as depicted in the central rectangle with the text "SOLUTION 360° BUSINESS VALUE").

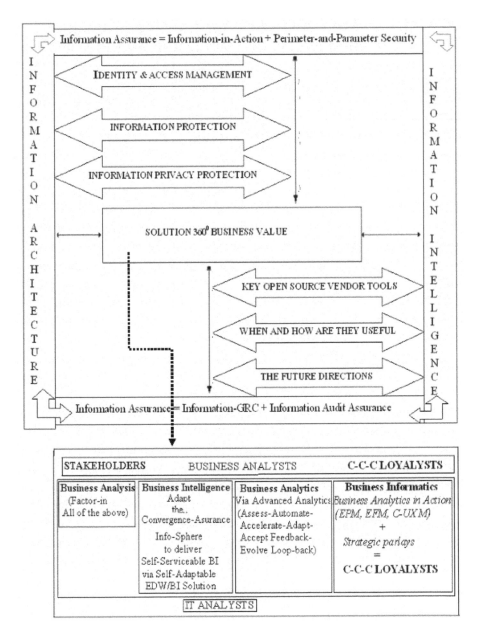

Figure 10.2   Value proposition of an EDW/BI solution implemented the Open
Source Perfect way, with the elbow-shaped dotted arrow
leading to the illustrated decomposition of the same.

10.4   Large Scale Analytics: Business-centric and Technology-centric Requirements and Solution Options

Accelerating analytics for scalability in the range of tens of thousands of users and converging into Petabytes and n-dimensions, especially when at times one or more of the n dimensions is large in the range of 1 to 100 is a mission-critical project by itself.

Viewing master data management as a business process and taking the steps necessary for its efficient execution by way of symmetric and/or semantic metadata, implemented as a service-oriented technological component, automatically builds new or enhanced analytics into the information lifecycle. Engaging business users in this process provides the dual benefits of leveraging the right people at the right time while also transforming the underlying business process into a decision process—a potentially high value for tactical and strategic business decision optimization. The implementation of the same can be done by way of business rules in action as part of the solution orchestration and interaction.

Optimizing the solution MDM strategy also results in domain knowledge–enhanced reporting, thereby adding an extra layer to the overall business benefit. As stated in the earlier section, a data element has the highest potential value at the time it is created, rather than down the road. Hence analyzing such data generates greater value in terms of better metadata extraction, running it through the information MDM cycle and outputting information that is rich in context per se, as well as time saving. Hence, better data brings better (dimensional) analysis and therefore decisions, which in turn bring better decision rules and connected/disconnected knowledge sets. This in turn raises the bar on information assurance.

Based on the above details, the following list is a set of business-centric requirements followed by the appropriate technology-centric requirements.

10.4.1   Business-centric Requirements

1. *Trust in open source gone mainstream*—Backed by a vibrant open source community in almost every tier of EDW and BI, from newbie to newsmaker and programmer to project lead, the availability of "SOS" help is pretty much everywhere. There are even live on-premise sessions supplementing the online forums. The information generated by these communities is hands-on proven, customer-implementation tested and trusted. And of course most

of them come free—all those participating from the pundits to the naïve are the navigators of the evolutionary open source ecosystem.

2. *Data identification for large-scale analytics*—Identify the data itself and the corresponding source lineage and linkage with respect to other similar data.

3. *Data usage: Identify the users of this big data and the related primary uses*—In other words—what will they be using it for? As an example, discover how large-scale analytics can help in corporate planning and forecasting, internal auditing and compliance, or ad hoc reporting.

4. *Data analytics*—Improvisation of the identified data by enabling it to best-fit into the solution ecosystem.

5. *Dealing with data in prime time*—This includes data-at-rest, data-in-motion, and data-(NOT LOST)-in-transit, as well as real-time or near-zero latency data.

6. *Scalability for performance*—Given that horizontal scale-out and vertical scale-up of data are transfinite across complexity-in-format and non-uniformity-in-API, the primary driver to address is how to balance uniformity in structure and storage with uniformity in information input/output (I/O) semantics. And not all access languages and storage formats conform to a one common presentation-only syntax and semantics. The key solution indicator here is to converge/coalesce/coagulate business scope–related entities into a single unit that can interoperate with similar such units, both inter-unit and intra-unit-wise.

7. *Plan, evaluate, and prototype handling of large-scale analytics*— Starting with a high-level conceptual view, a requirements analysis chart and a logical model, plan for the prototype development by identifying potential must-haves, pain-points, and all possible interaction touch points across the solution boundary—from stakeholders to end-users. *Planning must include the data quality and future-proofing prerequisites as well.*

8. *Use fast search to locate such data and how it can correlate with existing master/facts-based data.* The key criteria in this respect are: large objects packed index-organized data stored in the data base or flat-file that is SQL/NoSQL/LINQ compliant for access and storage.

9. *Querying and reporting (Ad hoc querying, "as-is," and "as-of" reporting).*

10. *Rich visualizations that are completely transportable.*

11. *Data mining for what-if analysis (forecasting and planning).*

12. *Predictive analytics for information and risk assurance.*

Predictive analytics can be used as an add-on advanced analytics tier on top of or juxtaposed with the forecasting (AKA the data mining tier) for delivering greater degree of probability in case of mission-critical business scenarios, as seen in:

- Out-of-tolerance conditions that are classified as rare.
- Emergency incident response when the decision to subvert to an auto-failover or hot-standby lies in the subsecond range.

13. *Interoperability with external analysis tools like spreadsheets.*

14. *Data sourcing to data storage to data signage to data display signage to dynamic dashboard signage*—Securing the data (encryption, ACID compliance for data integrity, systems monitoring and surveillance).

15. *Context-specific information presentation via dashboard, online portal, RIA, and corresponding analytics for targeted business analysis.*

16. *Interfacing with external/co-existing solutions*—Reliability by way of fault-tolerance of SaaS integration with third-party applications.

Fault-tolerance has a tolerance limit too. To prevent a solution/system from unanticipated snapping, preventive tracking, tracing, trapping, and audit trailing by implementing active and passive surveillance, in addition to in-lined security, can accelerate this process. The key takeaway is to include this as an iterative process as part of the identity, access, and authority processes.

---

17. *Data retention and archiving policies across disparate datasets*—By way of complexity (of data), computation (of data), connectivity

(of data by way of data virtualization), and competitiveness (of actionable metrics by way of measurable results).

18.   *Vendor viability* via customer success stories, business use cases, users' references, and the like.

10.4.2   Technology-centric Requirements

1.   *Focus on what's needed, not what's there or what's more.* The contextual relevance of adopting large-scale analytics for current and future business operations is a key business driver.

2.   *Calculate risk-aware metrics* like total cost of ownership (TCO)/ return on investment (ROI)→return on customer (ROC), the ability to collect data from heterogeneous sources and the data load performance per run, data load throughput (#loaded/#total) across all runs with or without custom groupings, complete data load audit trail, data compression ratio, query performance, and overall system stability including data/information volatility and automatic backup, recovery, and load balancing. Here data volatility refers to the ability of the data to stay persistent as well as "enabled" as required by the SLA, so that it can be managed on-demand if needed by flagging it as "active" and vice versa. This technology requirement is very critical when dealing with very large database (VLDB) scenarios in which query performance in subsecond ranges is given precedence over all other impacts and most of the data is unstructured.

3.   *Include scalability*: dynamic allocation of resources; user controls triggered lockout across any tier of the solution; poor performance in terms of bad throughput; latency in near real-time environments, etc.

4.   *Virtual vs. physical*: It is important to note that a virtualized EDW/BI infrastructure is more flexible than an equivalent physical one per se. And flexible is not always the same as reliable. Selecting a virtualized platform-as-a-service or software-as-a-service, leaving the infrastructure-as-a-service to the physical host, is a decent choice when it comes to development and quality assurance (QA) cycles (including the trending DevOps from the {urban}code team); and might as well be a good choice for small to medium-sized businesses (SMBs) where the primary focus is on getting things done in an elastic, efficient, and economical

manner and at the same time benefiting from pay-as-you-go or pay-by-the-drink models; there are very little upfront costs and no or near zero downtime in maintenance. Today with the cloud revolution, so to say, which enables your business to go with you, even larger enterprises are in deep thought about the cloud and its features in terms of security, reliability, and high-availability; and most importantly about the cloud being a business delivery model and platform.

5. *Frequency of data analysis*: This can be measured as a range of "most frequently" (meaning more often than hourly) to "least frequently" (meaning hourly) analysis—This is important due to at least two reasons: namely, first rapidly changing data and second, the data being collected is servicing downstream solutions that are mission-critical.

6. *Security issues*: Address using code inlined with security policies that are vendor-neutral (as far as possible). The code can be written in XACML (eXtended Access Control Markup Language), as it works at any/all levels of the solution stack.

7. *Implementation time*: This includes time-to-delivery, time-to-insight (the new imperative created by the industry for solutions based on data virtualization methodologies).

The author would like to add the (probably new) metric time-to-results (from the customer experience perspective) that in turn can be used to measure the return-on-customer as opposed to return-on-investment.

---

8. *Types of data being used include*: Data differing in structure; currency (current, historical, or mined); data classified as outdated or out-of-normal-range; data currently unused but likely to be used in the near future; data inclusion, exclusivity, or a combination of both; data that is machine-generated (randomly or auto-generated as part of the workflow or process flow); dataset as baseline from the front-end; data phased-out after execution or automarked as "inactive"; and metrics-based (programmatically derived from another predefined metric in which case both the derived and the deriving metric are predefined by way of logic used. Other types of unstructured data formats can include log-based data, high-volume data (e.g., CDR), networking monitor-

ing and surveillance data, event-based data such as clickstreams and SEO trickle-downs, metered data, converged multimedia data, text data from documents or other n-net sites, and last but not least, operational (AKA transactional) data in near-real time.

9. *Number of disparate data sources being used in the analysis process*: Grouped by types of data being used.

10. *Types of analyses being done*:

    a.   Deconstruction and/or indexing of unstructured data such as social media text, conversations or other multimedia content

    b.   Consolidation/clustering of proliferated data sources for business analysis

    c.   Proprietary and open source application integration

    d.   Advanced analyses such as data mining, stochastic-cum-scholastic tests, etc.

    e.   Data profiling, preparation, and processing for data mining, grouped by target usage context. As an example, preparing data as a training set for data mining relies more on statistical datasets where as preparing data for predictive analyses relies heavily on statistical, summarized, as well as graph/unstructured content that is typically more column-oriented than row-oriented.

    f.   Multidimensional visualizations involving game-changing patterns

    g.   Ad hoc query and reporting for on-demand click-to-report needs.

11. *Segmentation of use of data for analysis by lines of business*:

    a.   Informatics centers of excellence; corporate centers of governance

    b.   Self-serviceable help desks, interactive tables, and touchboards

    c.   Online information center, contact center, call center

    d.   Enterprise data warehousing and business intelligence (social interoperability solutions, support, and operations)

e.   Business to business integration, offline to online to cloud migrations and the bring your own data center (or desktop) telecom

f.   Governance, risk, and compliance (GRC)

g.   HRMS, HCM, talent management systems, learning management systems

h.   Business and IT (solutions, support, and operations)

i.   Sales 2.0

j.   Educational/training/learning media

12.   *Technology as an enabler and enhancing factor to ease the expertise in implementing the following for analysis*:

a.   Dynamic consolidation of source data onto physical storage

b.   Federated streaming of the same using inline virtual views to eliminate staging tables (as far as possible)

c.   Virtual replication by way of dataset streaming based upon query requests

13.   *Historical or not, data is data*: And this applies to all data in-store, in-transit, and in-cloud. Hence, if the solution demands that the history of data be maintained, it must be done. The key differentiating factors here are manifold. First, to determine a baseline as to what time range can we go back in history to sustain the impedance match between "current" data (i.e., data as of now) and the time period in the past? Second, is archival of the same and access on-demand a viable solution? Third, can historical data be treated as "live" data when it comes to delivering right data for the right user at the right time for the right job? And if so, how much of window sliding can be allowed in this case?

14.   *Fine-grained data analysis*: This does not mean summarizing data at any dimensional *n*-key level or vice versa. There is a subtle difference between separately aggregating data physically based on temporal, spatial, and business variable dimensions and doing the same by implementing each one of them as virtual entities to be accessed on-demand. A good use case for the latter is dynamic data federation, in which an intelligent data grid picks up the right query tables to construct a virtual view on demand that can

parameter the user-query-context and respond back in a significantly shorter amount of time. The reason this is fast is because this level of aggregation is done as a post-process just in time before the rows are released to the user, assuming all other so-called "large data" has been preserved earlier.

15. *Analysis of unstructured data (text, audio, images, or video)*: This depends on the primary criteria detailed as follows:

    a. *Rate of creation of new data required for storage and analysis*—This is critical when such data is in raw format – both structured and unstructured. This is nothing but a cross-correlation of frequency of creation measured in units of time interval vs. granularity of the same for storage and analysis. As an example, consider n GB of raw data per day involving f cycles overall. Here the granularity is "daily" and the rate of raw data creation is n GB/day.

    b. *Amount of raw data stored and analyzed in addition to static datasets*—This can include SCD data and/or facts-based system-of-records/CDR or unstructured data like IVR data, multimedia data, network data, XML binary documents, and the like, measured in multiples of 1G or higher.

    c. *Rate of aggregation/summarization of raw data* segmented by context-specific business attributes, and incremental materialization/virtualization of the same with existing data.

    d. *The rate of decommissioning of data*—This includes purging policies as well as data retention policies.

    e. *The implementation platform/methodologies used to manage large-scale analytics*, such as a relational database management system (RDBMS) like IBM DB2, MySQL, Oracle, Sybase Adaptive Server, and the like on standard hardware; an EDW appliance like Netezza, Exadata, Exalytics, EMC Greenplum, Teradata, and the like; a specialized DBMS like Aster Data, Infobright, Paraccel, SybaseIQ, Vertica and the like; flat files; distributed file systems and databases based on them like Hadoop/ HBase/Hive, Oracle SecureFiles and the like; in-memory databases; in-database engines like JasperSoft BI engine, LogiXML's Logi 9 BI Platform, and the like.

- Use of RDBMS or hybrid DBMS as the primary EDW/BI data source. For example, RDBMS in conjunction with Aster Data n-Cluster for large-scale analytics either by way of an embedded engine or by API-based plug-and-play adapters to the same.

- Use distributed file-system based DBMS like Hadoop/Hive/HBase for high-performance access to data rows/columns from external sources of unstructured content. This performs the dynamic computations in-memory in a distributed-DB fashion and then coalesces the results.

- Use a target native ETL/ELT/ETL-T data integration methodology for intelligent information integration across lines of business, business-to-business, and business-to-social interoperability. According to the type of optimal computational order, the appropriate data/content storage mechanisms need to be in place. As an example, processing large binary objects in memory by first doing the O→R mappings and then computing the same might not yield the same flexibility as opposed to directly accessing it from a large-object analogous DBMS storage entity when the processing involved is SQL-intensive. In this case, external table-like structures can be used to provide SQL-enabled access and/or updates to the content of the same. In certain other cases, managing the O→R mappings and other complex linkages in large-scale data can benefit from using an algorithmic share-every-thing computation platform like Hadoop/MapReduce and then SQL-enabling the same using HB/Hive.

1. The transformations on the source DB end enable efficient "source-DB" nativity

2. The transformations on the target DB end enable efficient "target-DB" nativity

3. The third one, that of ETL-T, refers to postprocessing after the ELT phase is completed and before the

actual transformed data reaches the interfaces upstream (e.g., EDW + BI; operational BI; ESB for data-in-transit; dynamic SOA-enabled Web services; HTTPS/UTPS/FTPS/ requests from online and portal URL/URI sites; etc.). In occasional cases, the postprocessing could be the data discovery/data mining process for gaining insight into the fine-grained data lineage and linkage that is critical for data quality/data virtualization processes ahead of the game.

16. *Virtualization and visualization marshalling of search algorithms*: In addition to querying, reporting, forecasting, and trending analytics, a BI dashboard can be used to leverage powerful contextual searches based on a combo of fully set, heuristic/AI algorithms that enable deep-dive insight into often ignored but sometimes (even though rarely) required data. This brings the Ruby-on-Rails part of the search process to halt if the search involves what is referred in EDW terms as "finding a needle in a haystack" or "finding a haystack of needles in haystacks" Just imagine combining each of these two individual searches. I definitely think it is quite a challenge when it comes to variety, complexity, volume, and standard variance of such data. Therefore the corresponding analytics must find "the one needle from the haystack of haystacks," work on it and deliver the required results.

17. *VLDB and large-scale data analytics rationally depend on the following key business drivers for both selection and implementation*:

   a. *Atomicity*: key from the visibility and transparency point-of-view

   b. *Usability*: solution pragmatics must be at least inclusive of the current or trending technologies from the information convergence and assurance viewpoints

   c. *Manageability*: administration and security via segregation of duties (SoD)–based hierarchical points of grid consoles

   d. *Reliability*: architectural fit, performance, and scalability from the load-balancing and customer-centric dynamics standpoints

e.   *Agility*: capabilities of solution one-on-one with changing business needs; solution durability also factors in here

f.   *Adaptability*: customization, personalization, and integration

g.   *TCO/ROI*: whether software meets cost and benefit requirements

h.   *ROC/VOC*: Return on customer based on voice of customer

10.5   Accelerating Business Analytics: What to Look for, Look at, and Look Beyond

Every business relies on its consumers and hence, when it comes to driving business value, the customer/consumer/competitor imperative (AKA the users producing, consuming, and subsuming the data) is indispensable. Given that the corresponding design architecture is a matrix-based and on-demand one and complexities get value-added in the form of *big data* elements, *n*-way temporal dimensioning, and the need to access historical/static datasets for trending analyses—it's like navigating an entangled web. The good news though is, as data evolved in structure, function, and volume, so did the technologies, architectures, and methodologies in place for creating, accessing, assessing, delivering, distributing, and dimensional-conforming of that data in a cross-correlated fashion. Using open source methodologies for implementing the *Open Source Perfect* data management platform for EDW/BI, is perhaps the best-fit practice option in today's data-centric wireless information-seeking world. The process of using business analytics in the form of advanced analytics, large-scale analytics, and predictive analytics by way of exploration, experimentation, and evolution can be accelerated quickly, easily, and efficiently to adapt the business KPIs to the solution operations cycles as the changes occur in real time. Using dynamic capture of entire data flows along with the associated master data and metadata; optimizing them for on-demand quality, and rewiring the BI processes beyond reporting, takes the use of pervasive BI to a new/next level and today is poised for custom-BI platforms like BI-on-the-go; disconnected-BI platforms, mobile-BI, and BI-in-the-cloud, to name the trending ones. The following outlines some key insightful consideration and best-fit practice pragmatics in the road ahead of BI by way of what to look at, what to look for, and what to look beyond for BI beyond reporting.

1. (*What to look for*) Identify the functional area and its dependents. Identify the functional roles corresponding to each level of functional area along with their dependent roles. Factor role hierarchies into this and the results are far more intriguing. This lattices an *n*-dimensional matrix of functional areas, roles, and each of their dependent hierarchies. Now apply the dimensional and facts-based reasoning, taking into account the about factors, and the goal of accelerating business analytics boils down to:

    ```
    BI + Business Analysis = Business Analytics
    Operations + Continuous Operational Integration
    = Continuous Operations
    Business Analytics + Continuous Operations =
    Business Operations


    Competitive BI + Business Analysis = Competitive
    Business Analytics
    Operations + Continuous Operational BI =
    Continuous Operations
    Competitive Business Analytics + Continuous
    Operations = Competitive Business Operations
    ```

(What to look for; what to look beyond) This brings to light an often-overlooked proposition: that personalization and multitenancy go hand-in-hand and that global contexts are realizable using localized user controls. A business case by a class on its own is using SaaS as a services delivery model, in addition to being a deployment model in the cloud—a single competitive business analytics application that can be downloaded and/or accessed pervasively across multiple heterogeneous access points.

2. (*What to look at; what to look for*) Use in-database embedded analytics that follow a preplanned, SLA-compliant development and deployment strategy and aligned with the corporate and industry standards to speed up the computation of the underneath logic as the data that the embedded analytics use is closest to where such data resides. Even using a transparent cache is still close to getting to in-database processing. Secondly, embedded analytics are highly portable by way of SaaS-enabling them (i.e., they can subsume external embedded metrics/engines). Examples of open source vendor implementations are JasperSoft BI Suite; Talend

DI Suite; Microstrategy BI Suite; LogiXML Reporting and BI Toolkits, BIRT-Actuate BI Reporting Tools, and the like. The third essential driver for using embedded analytics is their ability to adapt to trending changes in a way that the deltas can be hot-plugged as add-ons and work just fine. *Interestingly, these add-ons can be hot-unplugged on-demand.*

3. (*What to look beyond, what to look for*) Cloud as a business-to-social model vs. cloud as a next generation IT-as-a-service model that conforms to the anytime, anyone, anywhere paradigm. Do the pros outweigh the cons? Why and how?

4. (*What to look at; what to look for; what to look beyond*) Viewing the cloud as an evolution from next-generation train of thought to next-generation business (model) in line with this train of thought?

5. (*What to look at; what to look for*) Add-on without losing off cloud-based storage modules can be designed to support SaaS enabling as well as SaaS enabled, so that all existing internal/proprietary/external storage modules can be combined within the cloud-based storage module. This way the existing IT ecosystem need not be seamlessly streamlined with the add-on just embedded into it.

This concept of adding on without losing off can be generalized to implement lossless migration, upgrades, transitioning, streamlining, and the necessary spread across business domains, users, spin-offs, and the like without any compromise on operational efficiency or user experience.

In terms of open source tools for large-scale analytics, the 2011 Ventana Research Survey, entitled "Process and Technology in Managing Large-Scale Data," highlighted the vendor Cloudera as a top *n*-tier highly powerful solution. According to the report, Cloudera offers enterprises a powerful new data platform built on the popular Apache Hadoop open source software package. Cloudera claims that it can "unlock the storage and processing technologies of the world's biggest Web companies, allowing our growing list of global customers to use Hadoop to solve problems and achieve their particular business needs."

6.   (*What to look at; what to look for; what to look beyond*) Using cloud computing for business-to-business integration—a trustworthy fast lane or just another EZ pass?

   a.   Cloud enablement involving SaaS, PaaS, and IaaS. S-a-a-S enablement can include *both* SaaS-enabling and SaaS-enabled functionalities.

   b.   Bringing feedback to the cloud, by way of EPM, customer experience management, and enterprise performance management. Let the customer's voice (courtesy of Vovici Software's Voice-of-Customer Feedback Management Platform, www.vovici.net) signal as the voice-in-the-cloud, in both strategic and operational directions.

   c.   Cloud-based compliance—Is there a specification for this from the Open Source Initiatives as well as from the Open Source Standards Committee(s)?

   d.   Cloud-to-cloud and cloud-to-NOT-cloud integration—This can include the real-time, right-time, on-demand streaming of virtualized instances of fully functional cloud-enabled solutions, either federated (accessed from a single point-of-virtual-cloud) or replicated (multiple virtual copies are distributed in a desired fashion).

   e.   Virtual private cloud—This is also termed virtual private SaaS (VPS) and in turn consists of an interoperable combination of a hybrid cloud (on-premise and cloud, mostly public) that in turn is hosted in a "true" hosted SaaS platform or another SaaS-based cloud, and is used on demand. The latter is very useful in protecting a company's mission-critical data and records. The highest scoring benefit of such an implementation is its ability to protect and preserve such data for the duration of the company, business solution lifecycle or otherwise.

   f.   Solution-application portability—This is by any means the most favored advantage any solution can ask for. Implementing a cloud-enabled SaaS as a complete, fully functional, dynamic SOA-centric Web service and exposing it by a callable API that is scoped out (in a serialized fashion) or becomes persistent either in the EDW layer or the interfacing-services layer. The author has stressed this strategy multiple times in earlier chapters and believes it is by far an easy alternative to other choices. A cross-platform, cross-runtime service can execute this API.

g.   Automation must be treated as a necessary condition for cloud computing. This can be a design fabric for cloud-enabled testing of dev-ops from the unit testing to the functional system testing to the stress/regression testing and finally to the quality assurance (QA)/user acceptance testing (UAT) levels. The pragmatics of such a design is the same as those for using cloud as a delivery-cum-deployment platform. The difference between the two is the manner in which the test cycles are built/developed and run.

h.   Scalable computing in terms of big data analytics and elastic computing capabilities, by way of data virtualization and dynamic data and knowledge grids. InfoBright, Vertica, and ParAccel columnar databases (all of which are open source) use the dynamic knowledge grid to leverage ultrafast query performance and distributed query processing. Even EnterpriseDB evolving on top of PostgreSQL has similar capabilities. Other spawned open source versions include Fedora, MongoDB, and the like.

7.   *Do-IT-yourself metrics*, by way of custom analytics and predictive analytics. As customer requirements change, custom analytics ensure greater visibility into their contextual domains, thereby aligning interaction requests, multiplexed query results in response to these requests, and autofederation/syndication across physical and virtual boundaries. The "open-ness" of open source methodologies makes it receiver-agnostic and user/IT-controllable in addition to exposing the source API. The latter enables custom functionality to be embedded into the code programmatically independent of the original source. Open source makes it easier to implement customized functionality even when the solution is running live. Also, it eases the way administration is centralized and streamlined across the solution landscape. Enlisted below are some guidelines for implementing a do-IT-yourself analytic framework.

a. Leverage shared resources, user-driven customization for fast and synced adaptability.

b. Architect advanced analytics to ensemble a pub-sub design where intelligence is inducted into it so that it can autoallocate and autodelegate each subscriber's requests and subsequently service them in a platform-agnostic manner; this is quintessential for big data analytic domain or for that matter any data analysis.

c. The "intelligence" is gathered based upon behavioral patterns of the form {User, Context, Content} where each such 3-tuple defines the self-serviceability of the particular user during the course of multiple interactions within his contextual domain, and the content [seek | re-seek | un-seek] categorically classified as (SEEK, NO-SEEK).

d. The focal point here is to capture the hard corners or the so-termed *blind spots* that are necessary though seemingly naïve.

10.6 Delivering Information on Demand and Thereby Performance on Demand

Delivering information on demand can be conceptualized as users' primary information resource under the umbrella of prime time information management, from the standpoints of accessibility and availability. Taking an open source–based cloud-enabled approach to business information management, from real time to right time, speeds up competitive intelligence, thereby enhancing solution efficiency and business performance on demand. Here "on demand" can refer to both near-real time (transactional or clickstream or social content) and/or historical data (in terms of relevancy of the information in context).

The information requirements of today's businesses have gone beyond mission critical to evolve with changing trends in customer-centric dynamics:

■ The business user of yesterday is today's intelligent customer, covering the consumer, customer, and competitor umbrellas

■ The enterprise information management of yesterday is today's business information management (BIM) spanning the functional IT-intelligent customer–social landscape. This is as great a challenge in the software development lifecycle to customer–user experience lifecycle as it is in high potential. On-demand business processes get scope-creep where SLAs are relatively flexible, and this directly impacts both the tactical and operational roadmap of the ongoing live environment. The strategic roadmap can face some challenges too, with respect to increased sparseness in individual disconnects.

These changes shift the imperatives and dynamics of managing information end-to-end to include:

- Assess, access, adopt, automate, adapt, and assess mechanisms
- Real time to right time information analysis to delivery
- The ability to isolate the design paradigms of both

This section highlights an intelligent BIM framework taking an open source–based and cloud-enabled approach for implementing the underlying pragmatics in prime time.

Business intelligence and predictive analytics are made for the competitor. Business analysis relies on both of them for fine-grained visibility of the KPI in context; this boosts the on-demand access and availability of information anytime, anywhere, by anyone – still ensuring and assuring authorized access and change management, protection, loss, anonymous ID, and encryption of the same.

The framework is termed "information access and availability on-demand by way of innovative business information nets," or BINets for short. The design pragmatics of its implementation are outlined in this section.

10.6.1   Design Pragmatics

The primary focus is on using social, virtual, and cloud technologies to create an on-demand, anytime-anywhere accessible information platform that is termed a BINet. BINets can be created in a click-and-configure fashion by the end-users' use of proper authentication/authorization credentials to enable a "my information net, my way" platform. The technologies, architectures, and methodologies underneath that enable the development and deployment of the same are:

1. The trending customer-centric dynamics that aid in personalization. Dynamic ETL, dynamic EDW and BI, all three serviced and serviceable by dynamic SOA.

2. Using social, virtual and cloud computing technologies to evolve the on-premise experience into a competitive and connected interactive center-of-business information experience that is anywhere/anytime accessible and available. Simply put, it is a *cloud-enabled virtual information management solution* in which the end-user personalizes his/her analysis experience according to his/her changing business demands.

3. Taking the information platform off-premise and onto the cloud brings it closer in terms of location-independence, fine-grained visibility, and services orientation. The problem is role-based security. Dynamic SOA-enabled services do not handle role-based access control in as scrutinized and efficient a manner as GRC measures require, hence a fine-grained access policy needs to be formulated. The primary choice can be to use group-based policies that are predefined at the base authentication level (that can be *n*-factored at the same time) and subsequently hashed by random (AKA dynamically) generated SoD-based rules, signature stamped or otherwise. A recommended fine-grained access control can be a composite policy of {local_authentication, SoD-driven_Authorization} enforced at every level of solution implementation. *Even this can be further extended with the endpoint of interaction by using one single login in one simple click by typing in endpoint security as a third factor. This could even make it cloud-proof when used in such ecosystems.*

4. Gaining insight without losing sight: enabling preemptive, reactive, and proactive diligence using proactive intelligence and advanced analytics.

5. The more convergent the inherent technologies, the more divergent (for optimal outreach) the BINet's capabilities.

6. Socially relevant, competition-enabled, disconnected analytics power the BINets.

The key business driver here is the reliability of SaaS (such as for archival in addition to usability) and to a certain degree the resiliency of the same to aid, augment, or accelerate the recovery of cloud infrastructures in times of disaster or grid failures.

10.6.2 Demo Pragmatics

The above design can be implemented and demonstrated via a POC as follows:

1. Use live snapshots of the social intranets and extranets, and deploy using a private cloud and/or a virtual private cloud. This creates an on-demand, anytime/anywhere accessible platform that is in a way personalized to a specific {domain-context, user-context}.

2. Enable click-and-configure functionality using SOA-centric Web services.

3. Build authentication and authorization credentials based on the "my BINet, my way" paradigm. This can be inlined into the BINet's information entrust policies via one single intelligent sign-on. The key here is to follow a digital signature that is hardened for the most severe attacks.

4. Implement such a multifactored metric using Map/Reduce logic in which multiple authentication and authorization rules converge at a common ground such that the probability of error is $+$ or $- c$, where c can be a cessation co-efficient determined by the business.

5. Enable enterprise-level agility by using mobile analytics, virtualization, and visualization meet the socially relevant, competition-enabled, and disconnected analytics to power the BINet by using historical KPI merged with live KPI and subsequently hashed using factorized API.

   The key here is that each of the factored/factorable routines must have an entry and exit scope clearly defined and be components-based, services-oriented, and tied by lightweight integration services. Secondly, exposing the same by means of reusable platform-agnostic API is huge plus. Dynamic parameterization of the same by appropriate scoping gains another plus. As an example, an API call can be scoped at the call level or global level (across calls). Ensuring that cross-call persistence is critical when Web-enabling DB routines or processing them in-database as prewrapped guest-language routines inline with the DB (AKA native-to-native computation).

6. Other necessary and sufficient criteria include performance optimization for online deployment and execution, dynamically state-changeable API, and the most demanding one, these API being endpoint device–agnostic. Integrated analytics based on common mobile endpoint protocols, standards, and transformative business rules as well as convergence parameters need to be incorporated. This can be done quite robustly using data to dashboard virtualization API.

7. The cloud serves as an architectural enabler, integrator, orchestrator, accelerator and adaptive-connector of the same. Examples of open source vendors for cloud-enablement, orchestration, and administration are Right Scale (cross-vendor cloud management services), OpCloud, Chef (for Automation in the Cloud), Amazon Web Services' Cloud Formation, OpenStack, StandingCloud (a packaged, preconfigured, one-button appliance), and the like.

8. Use live snapshots of social intranets and extranets for deploying personalized cloud-centers (AKA private clouds).

10.7 Summary

This chapter focused on the best practices in EDW/BI beyond reporting—those that add to the business value of an open source–based EDW/BI implementation from the core. It explained the use of dynamic KPI, EDW, and scorecard-based rankings—from leveraging operational robustness to on-chip compute capabilities to integrated analysis and execution and business-to-business, platform-to-platform and peer-to-peer BI. The topics on dynamic ETL and dynamic dashboarding were touched upon with respect to the appropriate context. It also focused on using adaptive analytics as a key component of advanced analytics and as a foundation for BI beyond reporting. The subsequent sections dealt with large scale analytics by way of the business-centric and technology-centric imperatives; and accelerating business analytics in terms of what to look for, look at, and look beyond while including them as part of an EDW/BI solution. And the last but not the least section outlined how by delivering information-on-demand and thereby performance-on-demand, it is possible to deliver business value on demand too. The next chapter discusses how to apply open source EDW/BI in the real world by way of EDW/BI development frameworks.

Chapter 11

EDW/BI Development Frameworks

11.1   In This Chapter

- From the Big Bang to the Big Data Bang: The Past, Present, and Future
- A Pragmatic Framework for a Customer-Centric EDW/BI Solution
    - Solution Customization: Key Considerations
    - Driving the Solution To Be Business-Centric, Data-Driven, and Model-Based
    - Prioritization of Business Functionality across the Enterprise: Pervasive Yet Unconstrained
    - Eliminating Complexity with a Better, Easier, Faster Solution
    - User Adoption of the Solution: Hard and Soft
    - Context versus Content
    - Precedence and Design Pragmatics for Best-Fit Contextual Standardization
- A Framework for BI beyond Intelligence
    - Embeddable BI: SaaS-Enabling versus SaaS-Enabled Solution
    - E-mailable BI
    - Adaptive BI
    - Self-Service BI
    - BI on the Go
- A Next-Generation BI Framework
    - Key Design Pragmatics
    - Use of the BI beyond Intelligence Framework Components
    - Preventive and Proactive Monitoring, Diagnosis, Root Cause Analysis, and Resolution for a Zero-Tolerance Limit
    - Measurement for Extreme Visibility: Behind the Scenes across All Interaction Touchpoints

- Localized Monitoring of Individual Touchpoints and Globalized Correlation of the Measures
- A BI Framework for a Reusable Predictive Analytics Model
  - Using Data Visualization as an Accelerator of (Predictive) Analytics
- A BI Framework for Competitive Intelligence: Time, Technology, and the Evolution of the Intelligent Customer

11.2   Introduction

This chapter focuses on the best-of-the-breed enterprise data warehouse (EDW)/business intelligence (BI) frameworks and their implementation details. We begin by highlighting the relevance of big data, from the Big Bang to the *Big Data Bang*, and outline the trending and future directions in customer-centric dynamics from a BI perspective via an in-depth look at a pragmatic framework for a customer-centric EDW/BI solution that is accessible anywhere, anytime, by anyone, and maintains the integrity of our goal of providing the right information for the right purpose to the right people at the right time. Following that, we examine the framework for BI beyond intelligence, which focuses on advanced analytics and big data analytics. The next section addresses a next-generation BI framework, highlighting a self-adaptable BI solution for self-serviceability. It uses business analysis, BI, and business analytics to deliver business informatics and, as a result, business value as a key design imperative. The next section focuses on a BI framework for a reusable predictive analytics model. The final framework is the one for competitive intelligence, which discusses time, technology, and the evolution of the intelligent customer.

11.3   From the Big Bang to the Big Data Bang: The Past, Present, and Future

These days, it's all about the big data bank, or in other words, the core of the big data bank—from online transaction processing (OLTP) and operational data store (ODS) to business analysis, BI, and beyond, the foray of business analytics—needs the appropriate business rules, processes, and sometimes even advanced methodologies to harness the "big data" for *speed*, *scale*, *score*, and *storage*.

As it was pointed out in Part II (specifically in Chapters 5 through 8 and Chapter 10), it is evident that:

- The *big* is more about the rate at which the structure and form of data is changing and the manner in which the data is being accessed and stored. This includes the data spread and spend (cost) involved in such processes.
- The *big* includes archived data, to-be-backed-up data, and in-the-cloud data.
- Big data is managed just like any other data—as needed and as the right information for the right purpose to the right people at the right time. This is "managing all data" in the same (business) process-oriented manner.

This being the past (in terms of "as of"), current (in terms of "as is"), and trending (in terms of "trending"), the future of big data as a next-gen (in terms of "future") processing and analytics accelerator is no misnomer, as enlisted by its functionality as below.

- Analytics on any/all big data give small to medium-sized businesses (SMBs) to enterprise(s) scalability, no matter what. Virtualized databases are the way to go in designing and implementation of the same. Big data involves loading and analyzing data from "live" Web transactions, online content sites, social networking sites, as well as wikis/information-nets and the like. This in turn, turns the business into a real-time business. Combining this with right-time data (i.e., data already stored as "as of" data or historical data), we arrive at a new imperative "prime time" that is now. SMB, enterprise, or corporate, all business is prime time—that includes real time and right time.
- Big data, too, can be virtualized, Web 2.0 content-enabled, mobilized, and synthesized/serialized/serviceable by way of business rules/SaaS, etc.
- Applying searches on big data to gain new insights in existing data to improve relevancy via fast-actionable-synchronized-tested (FAST) search for quicker response, using open source search solutions such as Lucene/Solr search (Web-enabling, SOA-enabling, and SaaS enabling the same), accelerates knowledge discovery for BI and business analytics. Database (DB)-enabling the same solution-component aids in native-enabling the same for seamless integration with SQL-enabled software components.
- Big data enables the use of advanced analytics for relevance-enhanced query output, thus ensuring consistency of information,

both extracted and analyzed. Metadata information on the big data is also an indispensible asset when it comes to selecting the right data for the right job.

■ Virtualization of complex binary data by way of dimensional ID-ing enables efficient storage and access. In this way, it can also take part in transformational queries such as star queries. Virtualization also enables big data to be part of a unified view of data that is shareable by multiple consumers.

■ Virtual data federation involving physically distributed data and content (i.e., data and big data), delivers the best of the best when it comes to query output and query performance across live geolocated sites, thereby providing a certain amount of location independence.

■ Automation of these processes provides accelerated business performance.

The trending and next-gen BI metrics, such as fine-grained visibility into existing data, data/text mining, content discovery, integrated analysis, competitive intelligence, and the like, are integral to the trending and future of BI and BI beyond intelligence.

Software analytic appliances for big data also hold the future of big data.

11.4   A Framework for BI Beyond Intelligence

A framework for BI beyond intelligence involves advanced analytics. Big data analytics and/or predictive analytics are different from forecasting/time-series trending. We describe the topic of advanced analytics here via methodologies for raising the bar on BI that are implementable as a framework. Table 11.1 lists the aspects covered in this regard.

Table 11.1   BI beyond intelligence aspects.

BI Beyond Intelligence Aspects
Raising the bar on BI using embeddable BI and BI in the cloud
Raising the bar on BI: Good to great to intelligent
Raising the bar on the social intelligence quotient (SIQ)
Raising the bar on BI by mobilizing BI: BI on the go

The value proposition for a BI beyond intelligence framework is the BI assurance that it is capable of delivering to benefit enterprises and SMBs.

11.4.1 Raising the Bar on BI Using Embeddable BI and BI in the Cloud

Cloud computing is going mainstream as the next-generation enterprise IT, available anywhere, anytime, to anyone. Especially in today's demanding, though seemingly constricted, IT and services market, enterprises and SMBs have both realized the need for a more agile, visible, and elastic business model and for this to be practical, cloud computing will be used as one of the key implementation drivers for a new innovation landscape of IT. Data and application virtualization will be the other major game-changers.

Given that software as a service (SaaS) facilitates the agility and elasticity demanded by a virtualized or cloud-enabled solution, implementing BI as a service for both enabling and enabled functionalities not only raises the bar on BI but also provides a design pattern for a framework for BI beyond intelligence.

The key implementation indicators here are service-oriented architecture (SOA) and software as a service (SaaS).

11.4.2 Raising the Bar on BI: Good to Great to Intelligent

This subsection aims to introduce the concept of the business intelligence quotient (BIQ) and how it can be used as a metric for accelerating time-to-insight and keeping the customer/end user in perspective. It enlists the five best practices companies can follow right now to graduate from being a good company to a great company and finally to an intelligent company.

Strategies

With a multitude of intelligence quotients being used to measure peoples' all-around success (e.g., IQ, emotional IQ, social IQ, and the most mystical of all, the spiritual IQ), it seems to make sense to do the same for business or companies to gain a 360° quantification for their performance—not just from a return on investment (ROI) perspective, but from a customer/end user experience perspective. As trivial as it may seem, this is by no means an easy task. Viewing a company as a conglomerate of people performing in various roles and driven by a set of business processes, the accuracy of such an IQ extends beyond numbers. The phrase "win-win" creates business value only when the business benefits of easier, faster, simpler, sharper decision-making capabilities by all users—from the corporate to the front desk—are realized when they are needed most. To this effect, here are a list of High-Fives that enable companies of any size and industry vertical to raise the bar on BIQ:

1. Restate the fact that BI is everybody's business. This is a key driver in BI adoption and empowerment by all users of a BI solution, from the corporate staff to the customer/end user. Educating that better BI means better decision making, which leads to efficient actionable analyses across the company spectrum (i.e., the why and what of a BI solution) is a key performance indicator (KPI) in getting all of them eye-cued. A unified view of the contextual customer is the KPI for a higher BIQ.

2. Data, data everywhere—but I can't see it, no matter how I do my search! Follow this as both the means and ends of adopting BI: Companies must be able to trace and track the silos of data that are present in various forms, from paper to prediction, across the length and breadth of the companies' resources. Then a robust BI solution can "refine" all of this data to derive the right information that is useful to the right user at the right time. So, the sooner your company gets going on the "gold data rush," the faster the time to insight, which is the time taken to analyze and arrive at decision points that, when implemented, can improve business/operational efficiency.

3. Enumerate the potentials of BI as the innovative invention of a superior customer experience: BI helps provide autonomy to the customer/end user by combining self-service functionality with interactive and responsive controls that place the power to drive the business solution in those users' hands. And companies should focus on differentiating between customers and end users in terms of power users and contextual business roles. This is the new dynamics of being *customer-centric*. Proper enlisting of users versus roles versus business needs and maintenance of the independence and isolation of data/metadata access and presentation is vital to a higher BIQ. And this is where managed metadata comes into play by allowing some of the business context to be custom-defined by the end users! By correlating customer/end

user–centric aspects with their existing BI solutions, companies can efficiently manage their metadata and streamline their business processes.

4. Right time information is the *new* BI imperative, and it prevents the data burst: From real time to right time, time and data truly don't wait for any user today! This can be both real time and point in time, or just-in-time relevance and authenticity of information enables efficient use of the same and is essential to a better BIQ. And the ability to integrate/interoperate with multiple existing solutions and data sources provides a value beyond revenue. Nothing is more critical to a business than the consistency, currency, and protection of all of its data-cum-information in a way that is secure, reliable, and available anytime, from anywhere, and by anyone authorized. To this effect, companies must lay out security and governance, risk, and compliance policies, as per requirements, from the early stages in their operational lifecycle (a typical plan starting from concepts all through to customization). This approach ensures that the data/information lifecycle is in sync with the business process lifecycle. Enforcing multifactor authentication, distributed data replication, and/or data federation/syndication; rich search analytics; and industry standards–based architecture go a long way in getting the right data at the right time in the hands of the right user.

5. Consider BI as a strategic solution for your business: BI is more than just a decision-making tool. For any company, it is an evolving solution that reinvents itself based on customer/end user experience to adapt to the customer/users' changing needs. It extends beyond intelligence to become a strategic decision-making enabler. Companies must keep this focus when deciding on a BI solution—one that can adapt to current and future business requirements. By doing this, the return on customer will be higher, which is an intelligent metric for quantifying success—in terms of both business value and customer/end user experience. This requires a self-adaptable BI solution that enables a greater degree of self-service BI. A best-fit IT solution based on gap-fit analysis, in terms of access optimization, embedded analytics, SaaS enablement, and operational BI capabilities, accelerates the operational efficiency. This again raises the BIQ—*better insights yield better results.*

Conclusion

The next generation of BI is driven by a new dynamics of customer-centric imperatives that include faster time to insight, right-time information availability and accessibility, enhanced self-service by way of self-adaptability, business process–driven and business services–oriented, multitenancy enabled, and one that relies on active and passive security and compliance. Not just having the ability to analyze big data, but the ability to enable big decisions that add strategic value, derived from any and every data source, however big or small, and across the enterprise BIQ is the new business–IT KPI for a BI solution. A fine-grained analysis of business-centric requirements, followed by a robust plan for putting the above outlined principles into practice, can help companies in raising the BIQ—and in establishing an intelligent company, one that is tailored towards and geared by the customer/end user.

11.4.3   Raising the Bar on the Social Intelligence Quotient (SIQ)

This subsection aims to introduce the notion of social intelligence quotient (SIQ) and how it can be used as analytics for accelerating business efficiency in terms of growth, customer satisfaction, and value. It also introduces the notion of business–social as the new business as usual. To get to the facts of the matter, it highlights five best-fit practices companies can follow right now to elevate themselves from being great business enterprises to being great business–social enterprises—ones that score an SIQ on a higher level.

Strategies

In today's world, the word media is no longer proprietary to the conglomerate of the news and press. With the multiflexed, multifaceted growth of social media sites richer in content and live usability, the phrase "keep in touch" seems to have advanced too quickly to "get connected" on LinkedIn, to "like us" on Facebook, and to "follow me" on Twitter. And YouTube seems to be nothing short of a 360° revolving channel across the globe—in any desired direction and manner. As curious as it might seem, social media is gaining an edge as the unique and universal platform for near real–time communication, collaboration, and coordination—right from the palm of your hand. Helped by revolutionary technologies of 3D visualization, digitization, and beyond, social networking has resulted in what I call the age of "Socially Enabled Digital Intelligence." Refactoring this paradigm into the Business–IT innovation landscape, it seems to make perfect sense to leverage the social content sphere for business innovation to quantify performance using a new imperative: the SIQ, or more precisely, the business–social intelligence quotient. To this effect, here is a list of the high-five concepts that enable companies of any size and industry vertical to raise the bar on SIQ:

1. *Business–social is the new (intelligent) business model.* The new "business as usual" is the "business–social" relationship. This is the new baseline of business modeling that's gaining speed—and an open source approach speeds this up to go mainstream! This approach greatly simplifies, standardizes, and seamlessly imbeds the end-to-end pragmatics from concepts to customization. Use of open source software as a business analytic (i.e., as a business model analytic to derive the business analytics behind the growth of the business) drives the awareness, adoption, and adaptation of an open source–enabled EDW/BI solution, by way of the customer/user experience feedback loop. Using open standards and open source methodologies, as far as possible, for the end-to-end social analytics implementation enables consistency, control, and flexibility of the solution infrastructure handling the complexly unstructured content, and also adds to the robustness of the built-in security framework.

2. *Use social analytics for business process mining.* Apply research as an agile process to social content by way of iteration cycles of search, research, and research again on social media sites. Sometimes this can be done in a pipelined fashion, too. Not only can data and information about trending and behavior patterns be uncovered, but new details in regard to process/model patterns can be discovered, eventually leading to business process/model mining. Social media content is a best fit for this purpose, as it is open source–oriented and aligns closely with the facts in context. This can help in getting to the core of social analytics for business process mining via implementation using a plethora of programming languages, technologies, techniques, and tools—from scratch programming to fast-actionable-synchronized-tested (FAST) search algorithms to context-aware vectorized appliances. These can seamlessly search, store, sync, simulate, and socialize the mined data-to-information-to-knowledge-to-intelligence around a business context to evolve into a business process that can be standardized as a model for business process execution

and, further, as social analytics for business process mining. Remember that SEO is still an imperative that, when optimized, can accelerate this end-to-end process.

The newly introduced Facebook Timeline (a live Facebook profile) can help accelerate as well as enhance the relevance of social analytics.

---

3. *Recognize the social landscape as the evolving and emerging additional dimension when architecting a best-fit EDW/BI solution.* Today, as business moves to business on the go (or business on the fly, to be precise), this seemingly slight shift in business model has enormous potential to transform the business–IT–customer landscape into a business–IT–customer–social landscape, with the following benefits:

    a. The business accelerates from improvement to involvement

    b. The business–IT forecast looks all *cloud*-y (regardless of climate change!), from cloud bursting to crowd sourcing

    c. The business–social grows wiser than business-as-usual as data grows from intelligent to information-in-action

    d. The business network communicates and collaborates to become business competition, from inside the net in the real world, through the Internet, to the social net, resulting in competitive business processes

    e. The business services (including BSS and OSS) evolve into business–social services thereby granting them tenure—and business assurance through the customer lifecycle of the business

4. *Improvise social to become self-serviceable.* This a boon to the so-called social customer in that it delivers currency of information in near real-time. Businesses can leverage the "gold" mines of intelligent information as more and more data mining becomes practical—in unimaginably fast, actionable, synchronized, transparent and social ways—wherein users across all touchpoints interact in a 360° variance to feed and feedback their (business) input. This self-serviceable input can then be automatically

rewired as "intelligent business rules" via the tenor of self-adaptability of the open source BI solution in near-real time.

5. *Take social intelligence to the next level by making it pervasive social intelligence.* Let the social prevail, so that businesses become the social enterprise. Getting to know how social analytics can aid the decision making that drives business success is not just new knowledge—it can be a key business driver, as shown in best-fit use cases and customer success stories like using social media for recruiting, eLearning, and talent management; or using CRM software to drive CRM adoption via the customer experience feedback loop.

Conclusion

The new level of next-gen BI is driven by a new dynamics of customer-centric imperatives that include the new faster time to social insight, in addition to faster time to insight, right-time information availability and accessibility, interactive and adaptive self-service, business process driven and business services oriented, multitenancy enabled, and relying on active and passive security and compliance. The social customer is the evolved business customer and relies on social media feedback as a primary factor for ranking business performance. Hence the need for a context-aware EDW/BI solution that is also social enabled. Building a social context around the BI analytics in place is a necessary business requirement for any BI integration—and a social analytics framework of excellence is the right starting point for making the business socially intelligent.

11.4.4   Raising the Bar on BI by Mobilizing BI: BI on the Go

Mobilizing BI has the following aspects:

1. Enabling BI on the go via on-demand access to BI solution from a mobile device

2. Accessing the BI solution from within a cloud

3. Inter- and intraconnectivity and operations

A framework for the same can be designed as a 360° mobile analytics appliance that can be SaaS enabling as well as SaaS enabled for delivery. The framework pragmatics can be implemented as follows:

1. A cross-mobile-device BI solution model being enabled via role-based access control. The end-point device security and governance, risk, and compliance controls, as well as attribute-level controls, must all be enforced.

2. On-demand decision support using an information model for BI that can be reused based on contextual relevance. This model can be subsumed by the cross-mobile-device BI solution model. This way, the core BI model is isolated from its mobilizing aspect. The implementation of the same can be via an SaaS BI engine that can be linked or embedded in the consuming application. The result is an SaaS-enabling and an SaaS-enabled BI engine.

3. Building an enterprise application-solution for BI on the go can modernize BI while streamlining it strategically, in addition to making it flexible for pervasive use. This gives BI on the go the same treatment, as on-premise BI when it comes to implementation, meaning that the BI-on-the-go solution can adhere to a standards-based compliance rules set that consists of:

    a. Contextual information model (semantics, taxonomy, rules, metrics)

    b. Contextual metadata model (taxonomy, master data, metadata)

    c. Declarative application programming interface (API)

    d. ACID-compliant integrity – ACID stands for Atomicity, Consistency, Integrity and Durability

    e. SNMP (Simple Network Monitoring Protocol) monitoring

    f. Rules-based administration

The enterprise BI on the go can be implemented by virtual application(s) streaming in real time.

1. Using the cloud as a deployment and/or automation abstraction of the above.

2. In the case of accessing BI solution from within a cloud, the cloud-enabled BI engine can be linked to the mobile-device BI model or the remotely accessing user context. The mobility man-

agement can also be done from within the cloud, with the enterprise only having to specify the dynamics of the same.

11.5   A Pragmatic Framework for a Customer-Centric EDW/BI Solution

This section describes of a pragmatic framework for a customer-centric EDW/BI solution using open source architecture(s). It details the design and implementation of the framework by considering following techno-functional imperatives:

- Solution customization: key considerations
- Driving the solution to get business-centric, data-driven, and model-based
- Prioritization of business functionality across the enterprise: pervasive yet unconstrained
- Eliminating complexity with a better, easier, faster solution
- User adoption of the solution: hard and soft
- Context versus content
- Precedence and design pragmatics for best-fit contextual standardization

Along these perspectives, we explore the understated design imperatives that will be part of the framework methodology:

1. The need for a customer-centric solution. The famous quote "no two snowflakes are alike" applies to the phrase "customer-centric" too, in that

    a. No two customers are the same

    b. No two end-users are the same

    c. No two business solutions are the same

2. Changing trends in customer-centric dynamics. The KPI involved here are as follows:

    a. Context-specificity drives content-specificity

    b. Customer is different from the (end) user

    c. Customer experience is different from (end) user experience

d.   Consistency of information that is exposed to the customer/end user takes precedence over consistency of functionality—a key indicator of choice for the specific solution infrastructure (DB, DW, BI tools, etc.) and solution architecture (customer-centric design of the IT solution)

e.   Business value of a solution is better decided based on return on customer (ROC) than return on investment (ROI) and/or TCO (Total Cost of Ownership)—a better business benefit value

f.   This means that the business impact of the solution measures the ROI, and not the IT impact—going beyond custom implementation; the leveraging of customer experience and the user experience enables the solution to evolve beyond intelligence

3.   Key business indicators of DW/BI solution architecture, as elaborated in the following points:

a.   Anytime, anywhere, anyone accessibility—enabling any user, with any query, at any time, to get the right answer (that is, an answer that can lead to actionable decisions)

b.   Business continuity—with enterprise-wide reliability, availability, and security

c.   Enabling business users to have "behind-the-wheel" control of the BI solution:

  ▪ Understand the customer/user stance: The choice and design of the solution should be "organic," in that their key criteria must grow from the users' perception of data—how the users and analysts peruse, reason, and use the data by turning it into information via fact-based analysis.

  ▪ One size doesn't fit all anymore, as today there is more than one ALL: Solution usability extends beyond current industry demands, and requires *intelligent solution adaptability* (i.e., as current, comprehensive, and consistent as possible) - way down the road – irrespective of changes in the Business Goals, Industry Trends, Technology, Customer-base

- to not only cope with change, but also to leverage it to your advantage.

d.   Self-service BI—self-service interactivity and responsiveness with minimal IT intervention

e.   Unprecedented flexibility in terms of unbounded and instantaneous "analyze-and-derive" action-response capability—prebuilt KPIs do not always facilitate this, as all-KPI based reasoning doesn't promote new areas of discovery (e.g., for improvement, trends, and the like)

f.   Shareability of information and business results across the distributed enterprise

g.   Information assurance in addition to information security (both data and users)—anywhere, at any time, by anyone—in terms of risk assessment and mitigation and quality assurance.

4.   Key IT indicators of DW/BI solution architecture, as explained in the following points:

a.   Anytime, anywhere, anyone accessibility requires both real-time and right-time accessibility (instantaneous and continuous, yet intermittent and persistent)—A unified data centralization framework combined with a unified data integration framework at the source data level as well as at the data/content delivery stage, resulting in unified information presentation from the standpoint of anyone/anytime/anywhere accessibility without compromising on efficiency and productivity, and having the ability for SOA enablement as well as having SOA-enabling capability via data services that can be embeddable in any existing SOA-based services and/or on-premise platforms.

b.   The foundation for such a solution calls for a seamless workflow that is event-based and is in line with the infrastructure management, capable of real-time and on-demand data services, application services, and portability.

   ▪   How the data flow is coordinated and synchronized also depends on how the code is written. This has a ripple effect, because the security of data also depends on security of code, and this in turn propagates to the security of sensitive and customer-specific data throughout the end-to-end solution, both internally and externally, providing protection from unauthorized user access (and insider threats) for both static data and data in transit as well as from data breaches and data loss prevention through robust database, user, and network activity monitoring and bidirectional audit-logging of the same. Oracle11g's preintegrated Advanced Encryption and Masking, Secure Backup, and Advanced Security; Oracle Database Vault and Label Security; and Oracle Configuration Management for Security, Audit Vault, and Total Recall provide a "defense-in-depth" methodology in achieving bulletproof security of data, from end to end.

■ The key indicators significant to the solution are knowing the specifics of the data: who, where, why, when, how. Based on this are the optimal performance indicators in terms of ability to handle high-volume data flows—instant response to query requests based on temporal effects in data, flattening unstructured content and merging it with external content, real-time availability, high throughput in the case of transactional data updates, and the like. This in turn ensures that information is available at the right time at the right place for the right user. The Oracle11g database includes high-performance and high-availability features of group policy invocation, column-based fine-grained access control, fine-grained dependency control, transactional data consistency cross-databases, the implicit design and self-tuning capabilities can accelerate and automate data management and optimization. The best practice is to design the data flow in sync with the business process flow, which not only aligns IT processes but also provides business agility, eliminating the need for IT intervention in the long run—and leaving some scope for extensibility and innovation. This adds to an ideal data infrastructure flow, up to the end-user presentation layer for data availability and access. Oracle11g provides some of the greatest and largest technologies, such as like enterprise data integration, dynamic data provisioning, dynamic data services based on SOA Web services that provide both agility and mobility of information within the enterprise and beyond, and in-memory data replication and processing for ultra-high performance.

■ Interactive search capabilities on all kinds of data/content, using declarative, direct SQL-based full text– or regular expression–based searches that yield meaningful results, and having the least response time.

c. Separate the DW and BI layers, which minimizes/eliminates silos in the solution architecture, like middle tiers and metadata layers. Let the DB do most of this work as far as possible; use in-memory database (IMDB) cache to eliminate a middle tier for distributed data federation (on premise and on demand), and use in-memory data replication (of both operational data and historical data). This distributed grid can be stitched in-memory to the application/solution layer.

■ Flatten cube-based data into ROLAP cubes, but preserve the "intelligent refresh" of the same—allowing the real-time and batch data changes to trickle-down to the ROLAP cubes on the fly.

d. Combine accessibility (the right data at the right time to the right user) and availability (reliability, availability, and security) via a unified connectivity and integration framework comprising comprehensive management and control over connectivity of all solution touchpoints, including end-user devices), security within and beyond the enterprise (Web-based SOA appliance secure gateways, local policy enforcement, and access control)

e. In perspective of the separation of DW and BI layers— data access and data integration are two symmetrically different processes. Data integration promotes data access.

■ The key to efficient data access is using the right data access connectors/adapters.

■ The challenges posed by complex data for both data access and data integration are eased; unstructured data requires data quality, too.

■ Incorporate operational BI to enable direct access to (source-system) data to the BI solution, bypassing the data warehouse.

■ Operational DI doesn't necessarily provide real-time data, but it provides the right data any time, keeping the EDW current for anytime/anywhere/anyone access.

f. Reliability, availability, and security:

■ Introduce virtual data federation by creating context-aware federated data views based on a virtual metadata dictionary that is created via an "abstraction layer" (i.e., a single view) and then federated downstream into other DB-based applications.

■ Create on-the-fly joins based on different data subsets to populate this federated data view.

■ Introduce shared services using SOA-based deployments (driving business agility and continuity using SOA connectivity and integration)—with the ability to share agnostically across multiple domains.

■ Augment role-based access control and fine-grained access control with context-based identity and access management; the roles allocation and roles separation is based on content-aware/solution-aware policies that are federated based on context-specific attributes/domains.

   ■ Role-based access control is more static in nature

   ■ Context-based access control is more dynamic in nature

- Implement using SOA-based security; Oracle ESB now supports XACML (eXtended Access Control Markup Language) enabled and XML threats
- Cross-site Scripting (XSS), Cross-site Request Forgery (XSRF), and XML eXtended Entity (XXE) security
- Delegated authentication coupled with local authorization

5. User perception of data, data access and data integration. This refers to the user-interaction across all needed touchpoints and can involve:

    a. Self-service-enabled interactivity via controls

    b. Business-savvy language semantics

    c. User-friendly presentation: high-definition data visualization that is easy to navigate

    d. Integrated single view: Context-specific, time-sensitive

    e. Actionable :Turn data into informative decisions that can be put into action and beyond—leveraging this actionable customer/user BI insight to evolve/create *new* BI analytics (that promotes the BI efficiency) beyond the IT solution lifecycle, encompassing the customer lifecycle.

6. Data access and data integration are two symmetrically different tasks.

7. Data integration lays the foundation for data access. Both contribute towards accelerating BI informatics.

    a. Data integration promotes interoperability of data between disparate databases, applications, hosted data services, and the like.

    b. Data access is all about data availability in a unified manner that is consistent, comprehensive, and coherent across all business domains—and context-specific too.

8. Data services and data integration services are two separate tasks:

    a. Data integration services

- Are about processes that trigger a data integration task based on events
- Streamline a (new) data integration process into a data integration workflow.

b. Data services

- Are primarily related to data access (either data already in place or transformed/derived/aggregated/merged data from new and/or existing data)

c. Both data services and data integration services can be exposed as Web services based on SOA (both provide and consume Web Services using SOAP (Simple Object Access Protocol), WSDL (Web Services Description Language), XML (eXtended Markup Language)).

Figure 11.1 depicts an architectural design that can be adopted for implementing this framework as a loosely coupled and modularized EDW/BI system—delivering it as a model, as a product, or as an application solution.

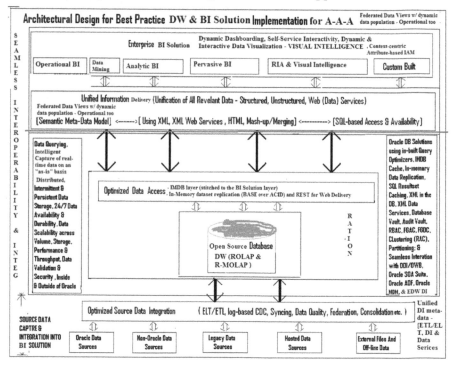

Figure 11.1   A pragmatic framework for a customer-centric EDW/BI solution.

1. Key implementation indicators:

    a. Standardization

    b. Synchronization (and streamlining)

    c. Virtualization (enables real-time streaming of the BI solution across all solution touchpoints → from on-premise users to beyond-the-enterprise access via remote access application delivery and endpoint devices)

    d. Automation

    e. Elimination of solution silos like metadata layers, middle tiers, and the like

    f. Monitoring of predefined KPIs in Out-of-Box (O-O-B) solutions—they don't permit discovery of new analytical metrics

2. Key prize-for-price indicators:

    a. A customer-centric BI solution based on commonality, comprehensiveness, and coherency, defined by industry-recognized standards

    b. Efficiency in terms of high performance and unbreakability

    c. Continuous BI in terms of:

    - Business continuity (reliability, availability, security)
    - Continuous event processing
    - Operational BI and connected workflow (dynamic or static)
    - Self-service driven
    - (Sort of self-)adaptable, by enabling the solution to evolve and innovate—leverage the harvested customer experience to dynamically create new business analytics that provide far-sighted decision making that can be put into action

11.6   A Next-Generation BI Framework

This section describes of the pragmatics of a next-generation EDW/BI design model that builds upon itself to evolve, enhance, and extend as a self-adaptable BI solution for self-serviceability. It details the design and implementation of the framework with regards to the key indicators, the use of BI beyond intelligence components, preventive and proactive monitoring, diagnosis, root-cause analysis, and resolution for a zero-tolerance limit, localized monitoring of individual touchpoints, and globalized correlation of the measures. The subsections that follow describe this design framework as a business driver for taking BI to the next level by way of leveraging open source architectures to efficiently, effectively, and adaptively integrate enterprise performance management (EPM) and EDW/BI.

11.6.1 Taking EDW/BI to the Next Level: An Open Source Model for EDW/BI–EPM

The framework describes an open source model for an EDW/BI–EPM through connectivity with and continuity of the EDW/BI model constructed using open source methodologies, with an ongoing live enterprise performance management (EPM) system. Herewith the key indicators for the same:

- The role of an open model for open source BI and EPM: Connectivity
- Next-gen trends in customer-centric dynamics, from user to intelligent customer
- Open source model for an open source BI/EPM solution architecture: Business-centric drivers. KPIs for this framework include:
  - Business processes as key information architecture drivers—solution architecture
  - The new and next-gen dynamics of customer centricity (consumer, customer, competitor)
  - The BI dashboard is more than just an intelligent graphic user interface (GUI)—it is the outlook for an evolving customer–user experience lifecycle
  - Starting small also means starting where the contextual business data is functional (right data–right user–right time–right process)
  - Let security be its own "role" model: Collaborative information sharing with all security and governance in place; localized authentication plus delegated role/policy based multifactor authorization–Segregation of Duties (SOD)
  - Self-service-enabled user interaction—from business users to power users to IT to corporate to end users

- Business analytics versus BI versus business analysis
- Open source model for an open source data warehouse–BI/EPM solution architecture: Implementation-centric drivers. The KPIs for this framework are as follows:
  - Dynamic views via virtual data federation encapsulated as XML-enabled open source BI viewlets
  - Data virtualization is different from data services virtualization: the latter involves business process/workflow; the former can include database virtualization as well
  - Open source BI-based dynamic dashboarding, dynamic EDW, dynamic ETL
  - Information design versus information architecture: SaaS-enabling, SaaS-enabled, and embedded capabilities

Figures 11.2 and 11.3 illustrate information design versus information architecture.

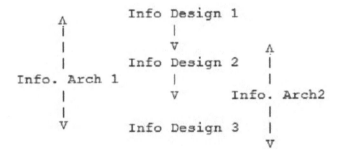

Figure 11.2   Illustration of information design versus information architecture.

- Users' perception of business analytics, BI, and EPM: From data to the dashboard
- Open source architectural framework for a best-fit open source BI/EPM connection solution

11.6.2   Open Source Model for an Open Source DW–BI/EPM Solution Delivering Business Value

The open source model for delivering business value aligns with the strategic and tactical imperatives of the intelligent analyst and intelligent customer across the spectrum of design, development, deployment, and

```
Information Architecture
        -> Business-processes as key drivers for Information architecture & solution
           architecture
                -> The new & next-gen dynamic of customer centricity
                   (Consumer-Customer-Competitor)
                -> The BI dashboard is more than just an intelligent GUI - it is the
                   outlook for an evolving C-UX lifecycle
                -> Starting small also means starting where the contextual business
                   data is functional (right data -right user -right time -right process)
                -> Collaborative information sharing with all security & governance in place;
                   Local multi-factor authentication with delegated (Roles/Policy based)
                   Authorization (SOD) - Oracle IRM
                -> Self-service enabled user interaction-from business users to power users to
                   IT to Corporate to end-users

        -> Info Design 1
                -> Design Patterns for context-aware algorithms, accelerators, etc.
                   [This can be reused across Info Designs]
        -> Info Design 2
                -> Risk-aware processes for the domain in context
        -> Info Design 3
                -> Business Rules that drive Advanced Business Analytics
                            -> For Information Virtualization
                            -> For Information Visualization
                            -> Business2Social Interoperability
        -> Info Design 4
                -> KPI for dynamic ETL, EDW, and Dash-boarding - a depth-driven dimensional
                   analysis that enables business dimensional data integration and insight
                   on-the-fly as in Mash-boarding
        -> Info Design 5
                -> Design & Code accelerators for sub-second request response times
        -> Info Design 6
                -> Designing for deployment
```

Figure 11.3   Illustration of information architecture.

integration. Figure 11.4 illustrates the open source model for such a solution delivering business value.

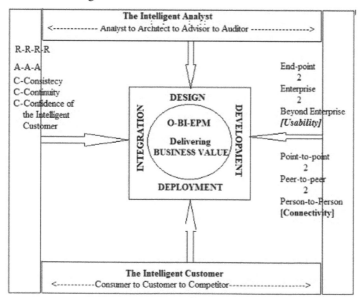

Figure 11.4   An open source model for an open source DW–BI/EPM solution delivering business value.

11.6.3 Open Source Architectural Framework for a Best-Fit Open Source BI/EPM Solution

The architectural framework for a best-fit solution can be listed as follows:

- Flexible and customer-centric consolidation of (existing) apps, middleware apps, and third-party BI and EPM systems, disparate or otherwise, into a unified open source (apps, middleware apps, etc.) BI/EPM that is capable of being dynamically instantiated and deployed
- Improvisation and/or modernization of this consolidated platform as an open source BI/EPM as a service module. This can be exposed as a Web service or as an API-based or URL-based SOA call:
  - Use open source–based (SOA-enabled) SaaS models in combination with cloud-computing powered enablers for automation, acceleration, adaptability, self-serviceability, and reusability
  - Federate and/or syndicate these SaaS modules on a context basis
- Promoting open source BI/EPM to be its own role model for security—Applying industry-standards compliant, customer/consumer/competitor-specific policies for governance, risk, and compliance; end-to-end security; and risk assurance on an ongoing or on-demand basis.
  - Construct security rules as business rules that can be wired, rewired, or unwired on the fly. This is a key design indicator, especially the "assurance" part, as customer confidence is also dynamic 1:1 with the changing business requirements.
  - Use open-source compliant SaaS-enabled and SaaS enabling techniques to accomodate the above security business rules so that they fit into the Web-application centric, portal-application centric, and/or SIEM (Security Information Event Management) domains. And all of this must be actionable in a hot-pluggable manner.
- Other probable business use cases of this model include:
  - A pervasive integration and implementation platform for EPM-centric performance tracking, profiling, measurement, analysis, reporting and optimization
  - A reusable information integration model: From real time to right time

Deployment Scenarios

Typical real-world deployment environments of this framework include:

- Augmenting existing OBIEE (Oracle Business Intelligence Enterprise Edition) and EPM implementations with extended business integration and functionality via co-location or on-demand business operational models
- A totally new implementation, either as a collateral to existing systems or as a replacement for retiring systems in place

Using the Open Source BI/EPM Framework for Linear Integration of Legacy Systems with Trending State-of-the-Art Data Integration Platform(s)

- Leverage the potential of preimplemented SaaS modules to create a virtual dynamic hub of EPM-related information across any number of legacy systems, both within and behind the corporate firewall.
- Pump this data to BI dashboard (or engine), routed through the open source data integration interface, for performance scorecards, talent management, or other analyses like deriving/extracting intelligent KPI for advanced performance analytics.
- The key business drivers here are:
  - High yield in terms of processing throughput
  - Greater flexibility and accuracy in the performance management process, from goals to accomplishments (time-to-performance) and from access to assessments (time-to-recognition).

These bring true value to the business—both tactically and strategically, continuous operational intelligence!

11.6.4   Value Proposition

This framework can be a highly scalable solution alternative from the Proof-of-Concept (P-o-C) stage to the cloud and beyond. In terms of its value proposition:

- It transparently and cost effectively balances the "build new" versus "buy and extend" equation.

■ No need to shift the current foundation of business solution systems and open source software; an open source methodology minimizes the cost and optimizes the "better, faster, easier, optimal outreach" value proposition.

■ A higher return on customer can be realized by enabling a longer customer–user experience lifecycle—user-confident flexibility and ease of use, business semantics–enabled interaction, self-serviceability in a plug-and-play fashion, and the like.

■ A win-win for both the business and the customer base: higher return on customer means a competition-proof TCO/ROI ratio and a happy customer!

11.6.5 The Road Ahead . . .

Evolving this into an open source BI/EPM connect model for the intelligent customer, and implementing it by way of the business-centric drivers described, is the real ROC and true customer success story.

11.7   A BI Framework for a Reusable Predictive Analytics Model

Coupling information with the most relevant insight is quintessential to a high confidence–boosting predictive model and more so for a reusable one when domain variables can change their values as well as their volume.

A BI framework for a reusable predictive analytics model can be designed using the details in the enlisted bulleted lists below. The actual theoretical and algorithmic details and pseudo code are not discussed. The workflows/processes involved are outlined.

■ The visibility of sensitive data to the accessing user is key implementation indicator to a reusable predictive analytics model. In this respect, in-depth data mining from data and content to discover both sensitive data and metadata plays a prominent role in accelerating the decision support process.

■ Native lean data discovery: Auditing data on a fine-grained basis and autoflagging columns as sensitive based on selectivity, contextual effectiveness, and efficiency enables sensitive metadata discovery. Autoenabling this feature for the primary BI data source(s) enables the nativity that is required. The *lean* here applies to the competitive nature of data discovered.

- Unified predictive analytics services view: Real-time data visualization via data virtualization enables as-is data to be analyzed as it is processed and autocorrelates it with confidence intervals to arrive at predictive measures that timeline the target context for 'lean' (cross-business-to-business) and cross-business-unit positivity.
- The power of advanced analytics and predictive analytics: Build robust analytic models combined with rich data mining models by leveraging the self-adaptability of the BI solution that facilitates customer targeting in a more sophisticated manner.
- Disconnected analytics can accelerate this process by providing the right information for the right purpose to the right people at the right time.
- The predictive analytic KPIs can be different from the EDW metrics themselves. Data mining models must be applied on these KPIs first to determine the appropriate confidence and support.
- Using uplift modeling after determining the degree of confidence, and applying it in real-time data, gives best-fit confidence based on inclusive and exclusive critical success limits.
- Integrated analysis using data from operational sources, and on the fly data-/content-mashing by means of hot-pluggable connectivity right out of the box, can extend the solution to the competitive edge.
- At every tier of the solution model implementation, a SOA process for a metadata module can be build that services commonly shared functionality (i.e., deterministic prediction-based models).

11.8 A BI Framework for Competitive Intelligence: Time, Technology, and the Evolution of the Intelligent Customer

The perspective of native lean data from a contextual relevance perspective is the result of the changing trends in customer-centric dynamics outlined in the section entitled "A Pragmatic Framework for a Customer-Centric EDW/BI Solution." This functional partitioning of the customer, driven by the market timelines, trending technologies (that helped in higher business value), and the constantly changing consumer demands raises the need for a customer-centric, customer/consumer/competitor solution.

Supplementing the competitive intelligence highway pragmatics as described in the subsection "Taking Business Intelligence to its Apex: Intelligent Content for Insightful Intent" of the section "Open Source DW and

BI: Much Ado about Anything-to-Everything DW and BI, When Not, and Why So Much Ado?" in Chapter 1, here we provide a competitive BI framework that serves as a prototype for a real-world implementation of the same:

- Build self-service BI analytics using self-adaptable BI. Here are the typical steps involved in implementing the same:
  - Data visualization and rich information retrieval, archival, reuse, and derivation of new context-specific customer-centric metrics from it
  - Use SQL/PLSQL, Hadoop/MapReduce, NoSQL, and O-O-B SQL-compliant analytic engines to flatten out processing involving big data and native SQL-enabling of the same
  - Leverage the role of data mining and predictive analytics in achieving self-adaptability and enabling self-service BI
  - Automating solution testing as well as the validation criteria generation process
  - Using an SaaS model to accelerate it for reliability, availability, and security
  - Autointegrate with any other solution accessing/running it using solution componentization by way of SOA and delivery by way of SaaS-enabled and SaaS-enabling capabilities
- Measure competitive insight as follows:
  - Integrate real-time analytics (operational BI) with predictive analytics to arrive at real-time confidence and support measures that reveal deeper insights into the competition, as is. This can bypass the EDW if necessary.
  - Incorporate value-adding metrics in addition to KPI for a superior customer–user experience and greater customer lifetime value. "Data mining" of data/content based on mission-critical business solution–centric attributes that support the value addition enables beating the best to be the best-fit in the competition.

The value here can refer to the value-added metric expressed in empirical values–based customer loyalty, overall competition, and the mission-critical business attribute of risk and complexity factor, measured in a percentage that is derived using predictive analytics. This makes the value addition lean more towards the competition. Include this as part of the core KPI for the EDW/BI solution.

■   Deliver the competitive insight using cloud and/or mobile-enabled BI. In cases where information-sharing is critical, a cloud service can be implemented by way of a private cloud.

The private cloud represents a unified access, services, and application solutions platform—with Enterprise 2.0, Web2.0, RIA, social networking apps, and business solution systems—both internal and external solutions converging in a single platform that is accessible and available anytime, anywhere, by anyone.

■   Build a unified customer experience analytics platform using the self-serviceable BI model, with integrated analysis of autogenerated business workflows and interactive input-based customer-centric feedback and performance. This gives the customer behavior factor to be considered for evaluating the customer lifetime value. Proactive monitoring based on real-time analytics captures the interaction at each and every touchpoint, and dynamic correlation and computation of the same with value-added metrics can factor into a customer experience metric for quantifying competition.

11.9   Summary

This chapter focused on the best-of-the breed EDW/BI frameworks and their implementation details. Starting with a rather nascent introduction of big data, it explained the past, present, and future of big data. The following section outlined the dynamics of a pragmatic framework for a customer-centric EDW/BI solution that is available and accessible anywhere, anytime, to anyone, while maintaining the integrity of providing the right information for the right purpose to the right people at the right time. This is followed by the section addressing a framework for BI beyond intelligence, which focused on a framework for advanced analytics and big data analytics. The next section presented a next-generation BI framework and highlighted the design of a self-adaptable BI solution for self-serviceability. The next section focused on a BI framework for a reusable predictive analytics model. The final framework is the one for competitive intelligence; it discusses the time, technology, and evolution of the intelligent customer.

The next chapter focuses on the best practices for optimization. Starting with the design criteria for accelerating application testing, it describes the best practices for performance tuning in online and on-demand scenarios and ends the chapter with a fine-tuning framework for optimality.

Chapter 12

Best Practices for Optimization

12.1   In This Chapter

- Accelerating Application Testing: Choice, Design, and Suitability
- Best Practices for Performance Testing: Online and On Demand Scenarios
- A Fine Tuning Framework for Optimality
- Looking Down the Customer Experience Trail, Leaving the Customer Alone: Customer Feedback Management (CFM)–Driven and APM-Oriented Tuning
- Codeful and Codeless Design Patterns for Business-Savvy and IT-Friendly QOS Measurements and In-Depth Impact Analysis

This chapter details some best practices for optimization with regard to testing, performance, customer–user experience, quality of service (QOS), and impact analysis. It also attempts to outline a fine tuning framework for optimality that is viable enough to be adopted for implementation. The primary business drivers for the optimization of the enterprise data warehouse (EDW)/business intelligence (BI) solution are:

- Enhancing critical BI business processes, such as those of data quality, metadata, and master data management
- Expand the depth and breadth of data usage in the EDW by using analytics that are data-driven, for example, ensuring that the right information for the right purpose is available to the right people at the right time
- Scalability to the desired level
- Adherence to compliance; for example, ensuring the right data is always available for auditing
- Breaking the complexity of business rules

- Improving performance of currently running processes; for example, self-adapting the solution for self-service BI

12.2   Accelerating Application Testing: Choice, Design, and Suitability

Accelerating application testing choice by design and suitability can be based on the following criteria:

- Concise, precise, and decisive goals for the business problem on hand vis-à-vis performance. As an example, consider segmentation of the solution testing into code profiling by functionality, component-level testing, regression testing, stress testing, configuration testing, and the like.
- An understanding the "what" and "how" of the problem being solved. As an example, separate the application test environment from the application build and release environment.
- The existing software infrastructure tier being used: programming languages, application stack, cloud stack if any, integrated testing suite, custom code, data-related components such as intra-ETL (extract, transform, load), data quality tools, data models for EDW and BI, database(s) etc.
- Data quality tools available and their reliability to certify the quality of data, from sourcing to subsuming, as the data is bookmarked for EDW/BI consumption
- A single unified interface to manage testing services (AWS (Amazon Web Services) toolkit) and Remote Method Invocations (RMIs). This must include automation of security practices such as principle of least privileges, multifactor authentication, separation of roles, securing private keys (for code signing), securing time stamping, and the like.
- Management of heterogeneous test-platforms for component testing. As a use case, cross-vendor cloud platforms accelerate testing done in the cloud, physical and virtual test beds, and the like.
- Tuning the parameters involved with regard to metrics that matter to both physical and virtual environments (e.g., metrics not related to O/S, storage configurations, CPU allocation, and the like)
- Tuning the database(s) involved to scale them to the required level
- Tuning by way of introducing custom code (using dynamic test builds)

- Whether point-to-point solution
- Whether optimized for Web delivery—for example, having the ability to decode compressed data sent over HTTP and the like.
- Whether exposable programmatically via an application programming interface (API)
- Whether extendable with custom metrics
- Whether accessible and/or available on any end device (e.g., mobile, virtual desktop implementation [VDI], remote device etc.)
- Whether service-oriented
- Whether real-time testing is enabled

Some best-fit optimization practices that can meet the above criteria are enlisted below.

- Use the Open STA (open system testing architecture) for all data testing, from sourcing to subsuming, and apply the DV (data virtualization) test to it.

If the data cannot be virtualized, then it hasn't passed the data quality test.

- Introduce custom code (using dynamic test builds) to accelerate solution testing. This can be done by incorporating reusable custom code components, such as those that monitor and alert solution performance on an incremental basis, data virtualization–enabled tests that function as a litmus test for data quality, slicers and dicers that output information as consumable by EDW/BI users, and the like. Actuate's BIRT platform offers a robust and unified platform for such custom code development.
- Test for data integration specifically using dynamically embeddable SaaS or hosted DI tools that can be hot-plugged into the EDW/BI solution. The required data/workflow for such testing can also be dynamically embedded in the process. Examples of such tools are Talend's DI Suite, Expressor DI tools, and FuseSource integration and messaging products and frameworks.
- Test for social media integration specifically using dynamically hot-pluggable components. The required data/workflow for such testing can also be dynamically embedded in the process. An example of a social content–based tool is Social Text. A test case

can be designed to integrate Social Text with the open source EDW/BI solution and implemented using the Cloud Foundry platform as a service (PaaS). Cloudy Foundry is an open platform as a service consisting of clouds, frameworks and application services. The sandbox testing platform can be custom-built by choosing any viable combination of these and cloud-enabling the solution provides the reliability needed to test the same in a somewhat OS-agnostic manner.

- Adopt packaged and preconfigured one-click cloud appliances such as Eucalyptus Cloud and StandingCloud to automate application testing. StandingCloud is IaaS (Infrastructure-as-a-service), single-click install and run.
- A cloud platform in the form of PaaS provides an agile platform for solution testing, especially for the reliability of SaaS.
- Deploy the EDW/BI solution in multiple cloud environments. Adopt a robust open source–based cloud management solution like the one from Rightscale for managing the EDW/BI solutions across the heterogeneous clouds deployed.

Tools such as
- p-unit (http://p-unit.sourceforge.net) can be used to unit-test and performance benchmark the EDW/BI solution. p-unit is OS-agnostic.
- Pylot (www.pylot.org) can be used for performance etesting and scalability of Web services.

12.3   Best Practices for Performance Testing: Online and On Demand Scenarios

This section describes a performance testing approach for an EDW/BI solution called LAAD or loading and analyzing all data. It is viable enough to be implemented in both online and on-demand scenarios.

Figure 12.1 depicts the LAAD model for performance testing in both online and on-demand scenarios.

Pregrow the test environment to accommodate current load and future data growth. The CLIF Load Injection Framework (http://clif.objectweb.org) can be used to implement this.

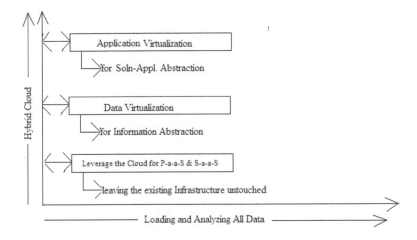

Figure 12.1   LAAD (loading and analyzing all data) model for EDW/BI performance testing

Additionally:

- OpenSTA can be used to measure scalability of simulated virtual user environments.
- OpenWebLoad can be used for load-testing the performance of the same for the corresponding Web-based deployment.
- The Cloud Foundry stated in the earlier section can also be leveraged to choose and provision online and on-demand sandboxes in the cloud. It is recommended that a separate sandbox be chosen to autogenerate test cases for the same.

Leveraging the cloud for PaaS and SaaS enables dynamic scaling in the virtual solution domain thereby bringing cloud agility.

Introduce and retrofit a design for synthesis of aggregated content into the EDW/BI solution architecture. Then test for structured BI output based on contextual searches or navigational links to the information.

- Use global and domain-specific contexts to isolate the cross-business solution and cross-line-of-business (LoB) borders.
- Scale performance in the following ways:
  - Scalability with and without big data (Hadoop-enabled or otherwise). Criteria such as storage of the big data and its migration to cloud/non-cloud environments must be taken into account.

- ▪ Out-of-Box (OOB) open source content management solutions such as Alfresco ECM and their interoperation with the EDW/BI solution. Extracting meaningful and actionable insights from the integrated content and at the same time securing the whole process are key performance indicators in this regard.
- ▪ Context-aware and secure rights–aware BI results for relational online analytical processing (ROLAP) and non-ROLAP tiers. A non-ROLAP tier can include in-database cache, in-memory distributed cache, etc. The BI results can be implemented as 100% embeddable reporting engines that are automated for testing purposes.
- ▪ Use dynamic in-memory knowledge grids to scale performance across servers.
- ▪ Dynamic knowledge grids can also be used for advanced analytics such as analytical or operational BI, advanced predictive analytics, and the like by:
  - ▪ Using data virtualization to pull rapidly changing data over from multiple sources across servers as it is created
  - ▪ Dynamically construct the knowledge grid based on contextual or runtime criteria in combination with business rules such as frequency of use for analysis
- ▪ Test for SaaS-enabling performance by embedding the EDW/BI solution in an existing enterprise resource planning (ERP) or enterprise performance management (EPM)/enterprise feedback management (EFM) solution in real-time or as a true-hosted solution, and see the results in an intuitive dashboard. It can also be embedded in an on-premise environment.
- ▪ Test for compression ratio in case of embedded analytic engines or databases. A compression ratio of 10:1 or better is recommended.
- ▪ Plan for testing using disparate workloads. This increases the reliability of testing process by increasing the likelihood of successful test runs and hence an assurance of successful runs in production.

This can be introduced as part of capacity planning to further accelerate the performance testing process. Increased collaboration between testing and planning teams leads to a truly resilient testing and deployment strategy.

As an example, accommodating a compressed workload to allow for proper decoding while exchange of data between client and server, as done during a Web deployment, is a recommended practice to consider while scaling such deployments. This can also be implemented using custom messages and Web polling.

12.4   A Fine Tuning Framework for Optimality

A fine tuning framework for optimality is needed to raise the bar on business value by way of an innovative business model through solution efficiency, an evolving information architecture, and context-aware intelligence. The efficiency of an EDW/BI solution demands a coherent and agile tuning framework that is resilient enough to guarantee assurance—from information to competition. The following set of rules can be adopted for the design of such a fine tuning framework:

- Re-examine the end-to-end information architecture from the perspective of the BI processes involved. This can be done by defining a set of goals, functions, resources, relevancy of data, priority of processes and iterating over the same till the EDW/BI optimization goals are met. As an example, The Open Group Architecture Framework (TOGAF) can be used for an optimized implementation of the information architecture of the EDW/BI solution.
- Enable caching for high throughput. This ensures that a large number of requests are handled per second. The key imperatives for caching are cache type, cached object type and verification and validation of caching-in-action.
  - Ensure that data resides in-memory, be it the application server or the in-memory (database) cache.
  - Ensure that data resides closer to the point of usage. Big data can be placed on content delivery networks.
  - Ensure that object caching is enabled for all data that involves (interactive) navigation and for distributed data access. The KPI for performance measurement in regard to object caching is the total number of cache compactions as a performance counter.
  - Ensure that binary large object caching is enabled. This gives the ability to cache binary documents and images and serve them on demand.

- Ensure that Web publishing takes advantage of caching for publishing page frames (this is different from the content in those pages). Of special mention is the publishing cache hit ratio parameter. Also ensure that page-output caching is enabled. This caches an entirely rendered page along with the key (for profile granularity).
- Ensure that the cache parameters are set appropriately. Some of the key parameters in regard to caching are cache maximum size, object cache maximum size, and cache duration.
- Verify and validate caching functionality by:
  - Setting up a *cache database table* that records the release of cached data and the associated workflow.
  - Setting up contextual cache profiles. As an example, set up an anonymous cache profile separate from Page Output cache profile.
  - Trace the cache performance by enabling concurrent execution
  - Varying the degree of caching by HTTP header
- Ensure that custom code is tweaked properly. It can call API that executes as natively as possible in heterogeneous platforms without source code change(s).
- Track "online" solution resource utilization (memory and CPU) by way of:
  - Memory usage (percentage): Point-in-time memory usage can be monitored by fine-grained alerting on server performance metrics.
  - Enabling alerting of SMTP, alerting of log-based events, and "automation of responses to alerts" via feedback mechanisms.
- Use tools for repeatable task execution, such as NTime (www.codeproject.com/dotnet/ntime.asp), to test the EDW/BI solution against its performance; this provides a veritable summary and detail of performance statistics at runtime. The use of tools enables the EDW/BI solution to be tested without having to incorporate code segments specially meant for debugging or performance-testing purposes.
- Use tools to unit test and performance benchmark the EDW/BI solution, such as p-unit (http://p-unit.sourceforge.net) or

HTTPUnitPerf. p-unit is OS-agnostic. Iterative profiling based on this can be keep track of changes in execution time.

- Accelerate BI using:
  - Operational analytics: Insight into data as it is and greater visibility into variety of data at greater speed.
  - Cloud platform: Aids and accelerates deployment of mobile BI and open source gives a best-fit boost to this; accelerates business continuity; private cloud ensures a best-of-both security strategy by way of protecting corporate sensitive data (keeping the EDW in the private enterprise) and deploying the BI layer in the public cloud.
  - Web services: Accelerates automation and integration of EDW/BI solution with existing/external applications.
  - Self-service BI scenarios: Reduce redundancy to the minimum by monitoring what's being created and what's not in the self-service environment. Self-service BI introduces BI collaboration and some components/objects (i.e., reports, dashboards, etc.) become common. Template-enabling these common information or duplicate EDW/BI objects can minimize redundancy by way of reusability.
  - BI governance: Evolve BI governance into a center of excellence (CoE).
  - Viable controls over self-service(d) BI: Identify self-service(d) BI objects in the un-governed zone and put some "viable controls" over them! Not all data needs to be audited or governed. Identify areas of such data, as well as the data by itself. Self-service BI can aid in this process when combined with collaborative BI people, processes, and analytics.
  - Custom analytics and custom metrics: Differentiate between analyses and analytics. Tune custom analytics based on the business analyses in context. This means that BI performance dictates the custom metrics optimization strategy, and this is the way typically it should be. Custom metrics gives greater flexibility in terms of hot-pluggability. The result is that this process shows how the analytic measures are performing (executing) based on the performance of the analysis. The inverse usually can refer to predefined KPI (or prepackaged KPI) and

tuning them to handle the solution performance can be hard if they have the same impact across solution tiers or boundaries.

- Models: Create a BI model that expands over time (on-demand model) as well as a capacity model based on CPU, memory, and the like to address the potential of supporting unlimited capacity.
- Impact analysis: Trace and track the changes taking place at the DB-level(s) and perform an impact analysis—both top-down and bottom-up—to determine the level of impedance linearity.
- Visualization: Ensure that visualization is both realistic and real time. The former means the visuals presented are understandable by *all* BI users, and the latter refers to anyone, anywhere, any time and right information for the right purpose to the right people at the right time access and High Availability (H/A).

12.5   Looking Down the Customer Experience Trail, Leaving the Customer Alone: Customer Feedback Management (CFM)–Driven and APM-Oriented Tuning

Some of the best practices in this regard are as follows:

- Build competency models based on customer behavior metrics as well as resource utilization measures cross-customer/consumer/competitor. The customer behavior metrics can include those that measure continuous improvement. This quantifies the value of competitive intelligence by correlating the trending market situation (i.e., the competitors' scores) with the customers' outreach.
- Enable autologging of interaction-based events and responses to these events across all interaction touchpoints as they happen.
- Enable auto-alerting of interaction-based events and automation of responses to alerts via feedback mechanisms. Examples of such events include user action–based navigations, one-click responses, and those that are cross-touchpoint.
- Use customer feedback–based improvements as enhancers of the inherent business processes. Automate the execution of the same to accelerate the application performance process. And automate the implementation of the combination of these two to accelerate the application performance management process itself. As an example, customer feedback profiles can be generated based on solution

functional categorization that can be subsequently transformed into action plans. Automation of plans by way of business optimization rules yields actionable results.

- Track and analyze the customer–user experience–related BI reports' usage with regard to their distribution, number of requests and queries made. This provides an outline of where, when, and how the customer experience trail is being used, thereby revealing the effectiveness of the customer–user experience management program in place.

The greater the utilization of the same, the more competitive the information will be to leverage it to a superior customer–user epxerience advantage. It is critical that data about the customer is obtained as it is identified and then made persistent so that it can be revisited if necessary. On a higher level of criticality is the ability to identify changes to pieces of the same data and update the persistent store appropriately. The latter process is not as easy as it might seem, as the business processes that directly or indirectly affect the changed data might also have changed over time. An open source EDW/BI solution can address this by way of an intelligent metadata or master data management model that takes care of these dynamic updates separately via Metadata/MDM model(s) and then cascades the changes to the right business process-based workflow(s) as needed. This takes care of both time-variant and location-variant processes in an effective manner.

12.6 Codeful and Codeless Design Patterns for Business-Savvy and IT-Friendly QOS Measurements and In-Depth Impact Analysis

- Enable codeless visual test editors for the primary EDW/BI solution language(s). Open source testing tools like LDRA Tool Suite can be used to implement the same. Additional information about the LDRA Tool Suite can be found at www.ldra.com.
- Build a resource management competency model for deep-dive impact analysis of system load vs. scalability. Design iterative test models that work on data-driven processes like data collection, data computation, and data virtualization.
- Execute the measurements as a set-based test operation as opposed to individual tests. This entails a pattern of correlating one set of results against another, thus increasing the chances of relevancy

across grouped business functions. As an example, the EDW/BI solution can contain flagged code that operates with and/or without debugging/performance-testing enabled; then a separate build can be executed.

- Use Opscode products that enable Web-based automation and adoption. The use of HTTPUnitPerf or Chef-like component patterns for quality of service (QOS) and in-depth impact analysis can significantly aid in accurate QOS measurements and analysis. The codeless design patterns based on Chef are by themselves an integration platform or SaaS product and are best suited to test SaaS-based solutions.

- Incorporate interaction-aided unit test case creation by way of automatic reverse engineering of the inherent EDW/BI model. The open source framework benerator can be used to implement this functionality. Additional information about benerator can be obtained from http://databene.org/databene-benerator.

- Use Python and Ruby on Rails Framework to code design patterns to augment the measurement process with custom metrics.

- Use cloud services APIs as virtual apps to obtain the desired results or as a starting point to dynamically call additional APIs to achieve the desired results. This method of implementation can be viewed as IT-friendly codeless "ready-to-execute" apps.

- Incorporate real-time analysis of (embedded) BI solutions by:
  - Testing automation and dynamic code analysis of (embedded) BI and operational BI solutions that consist of a set of automated testing rules that identify high-impact problem areas in "live" runtime scenarios. Directly testing in "live" environments yields better QOS results. The open source LDRA testbed can be leveraged to run these tests.
  - Automating testing at its primary levels (i.e., unit testing, integration testing, validation, and verification). Validation and verification can be implemented by automated source-code review analysis against predefined quality rules and standards, as well as autogenerated QOS rules based on contextual intelligence.
  - Executable code coverage analysis identifying executable code that has not passed the "live" testing phase of test automation. This ensures that such code does not get filtered to be executed in production environments the very first time. This metric is critical for both QOS and impact analysis.

- Memory usage profiling to proactively detect any memory leaks and trace runtime consumption statistics. Analyzing the latter statistics can help resolve solution performance issues by way of preemptive maintenance.
- Solution performance profiling to track and trace solution tier level (application tier and above) code that can be optimized for performance.
- Visual runtime tracing to enable point-in-time execution flashback. This enables reconstruction of solution execution behavior to get a dissected view of the same that can be employed for simulation in context-specific targeted scenarios. A good example of the same is using current and past data for measuring the competitive gradient of particular product. The visualization(s) can be in the form of workflow diagrams or UML sequence diagrams.

- Ensure that both representational state transfer (REST) and SOAP communication protocols are taken into account while deploying the solution to online environments. This can be done by testing using regular and binary XML messaging, Web services and RMI calls, and autoprocessing solution client identifiers. Additionally, SOAP enables the autogeneration of test cases for performance without measuring the traffic from client to server.

12.7   Summary

This chapter focused on some additional best practices for EDW/BI solution testing. Starting with some best practices for accelerating application testing, it touched on the details of performance testing using the LAAD (or loading and analyzing all data) framework. The subsequent section examined a fine tuning framework for EDW/BI solution optimality from the implementation and execution standpoints. The next chapter focuses on the best-of-the breed EDW/BI standards that can supplement the open source standards available.

Chapter 13

Open Standards for Open Source: An EDW/BI Outlook

13.1 Introduction

This chapter treats open source from an open standards perspective. Starting with easy definitions for open source and open standards, the remainder of the chapter dives into open standards *versus* open source—segmented by the primary tiers of a trending enterprise data warehouse (EDW)/business intelligence (BI) solution. These are different from governance, risk and compliance rules that are set forth as mandatory prerequisites with which any EDW/BI solution must comply.

The following is a repetition of a Focus.com Q & A answered by the author titled "Standards help create markets. Why is this important? Or is this not important?" (Available at http://www.focus.com/questions/standards-help-create-markets-why-important-it-not-important/).

Standards add the attributes of completeness, commonality, precision, and value to a software product or solution. First, standards help create quality products, and *quality* is the quintessential component of *all value*. Hence, the better the product quality, the more superior the customer experience. Second, quality is driven by and drives innovation. And innovation has *intelligence* built into it. Hence, from the crowd to the cloud, standards are the key business drivers as well as the key efficiency drivers that generate enhanced and accelerated metrics over time and thus become a strategic component of any business process. Although the concept of cloud computing has been floating around for a while, open cloud standards, just like any other standards, open the doors to key niche areas for improvisation and more.

As an example, cloud computing as it seems implementation fit today is primarily based on the notion of virtualization. Building cloud services versus cloud-based solutions is a recommended standard for enterprise IT. An example of a cloud service is a private cloud that services big data analytics for rapid deployment, prototyping, agility, and flexibility.

But a tagline like "Can you see beyond the clouds?" (slogan courtesy Voxel—see www.voxel.net) is not only a brilliant architectural design but also one that is open source, technology agnostic, and more importantly, one that explores beyond today's cloud computing domain —deriving yet another "Infrastructure That Always Fits" (slogan courtesy Voxel again). Eventually this approach may well be accepted by many businesses as the gold standard for intelligent cloud computing and implementation. Just imagine how many businesses can change gears by leveraging existing infrastructure and seamlessly integrating it with the Voxel Fabric, thereby raising the value of better business benefits, as they see it fit into any given infrastructure. Standards are always standards and will always remain as standards—the primary "standards" component that changes can be the breakthrough intelligence built into them that accelerates business efficiency and creates markets as dynamically as today's cloud bursting.

This chapter lists a set of practices that can be a used as recommended set of standards for an open source–based EDW/BI solution:

- Leverage speed vs. flexibility option while selecting an open source EDW/BI implementation option.
- Adopt consistency from planning to privatization, across quality and visibility into quality of processes. This can be implemented by a adopting a combination of open source standards, open governance standards, contextual customer standards, and SQL-enabled standards (including the most recently released ANSI SQL 2011). When the EDW/BI solution comes with a tiered solution, each tier can have its own set of standards specific to the core functionality of the tier, as long as they share the commonality across the vertical of the above open combination.
- Leverage native, generic as well as specialized SQL-compliant templates for data and information services. As an example, use SQL-only templates with generic XML-based templates and specialized content templates, like those based on Hadoop/Hive and MapReduce, to accelerate both data intelligence (DI) and data services execution.
- Create scope for self-serviceability as a model and reusability as a core design paradigm. Also, it's a good practice to enable self-service analysis. This can be done via semantic models, wizards, and templates. Semantics enable greater accuracy in regard to cataloging of every piece of content. As an example, the EDW/BI solution can be formed of the following interrelated components:

- EDW component
- BI component
- BA (business analytics) component
- Business–social component

Each of them can have subcomponents, such as user settings, admin settings, audit, dashboard, real time, service-oriented architecture (SOA) management, backup/recovery, and the like.

- Isolate and maintain custom code from standard API–based and SQL-enabled code. Maintain them in reusable codelets. *Let the code design reflect itself in the code debugging process!*
- Maintain separate code bases for data quality, master data management, BI, cloud bases, and business analytics with interbase modularization enabled depending on contextual business processes. This is very effective and efficient for elastic interprocess execution.
- Adopt service orientation and service-centricity at the same time. This means the design architecture must be SOA-based and the solution is delivered via software as a service (SaaS). Treat them as interdependent opposites. Use Web services as the delivery component of the SOA architecture and ESB or XML as the orchestration mechanism of the same. Examples include integrating EDW and BI layers, EDW/BI solution, and external systems, and the like. Web services can accelerate scalability of both integration and automation.
- In addition to architectural robustness, componentization, and tier isolation, inter- and intrapluggable ability is critical. This ensures the elasticity of the solution and can be implemented by the SOA enablement. Also, ensure that the integration processes can be administered centrally—centralized monitoring with decentralized (localized) user control.
- Effectively identify, prioritize, execute, monitor, and control—and thereby proactively optimize—the end-to-end solution lifecycle. Validation and verification of the same must be done based on solution behavior as the driver, and the toolsets for the same be selected following the same principle. This improves adaptive nature of the solution.
- Factor in query response time, data compression ratio, indexing/ data structure tuning overhead(s) and source data loading as primary criteria when determining the performance analysis of an

EDW/BI request/response task. These four need to be consistent across the analysis time period immaterial of location.

- Leverage the key rules for data compression for high performance:
  - The higher the compression ratio, the faster the row(s) movement.
  - The fewer the columns and the more redundant the data, the higher the compression ratio.
- Leverage star-query optimization wherever possible. This can result in very high-performing queries on large datasets by replacing unnecessary disk scans with lookups.
- Leverage data volume(s) versus average data compute time(s) and data transfer rate(s) to determine a *data transformation bookmark* that can be used for performance analysis, passive candidates' categorization, query-cost baselines, and the like.
- Implement contextual governance, risk, and compliance, taking into account interaction across all touchpoints. The implementation can be done using an SOA-enabled application programming interface (API) with the API call being either a serialized one that lasts only per invocation or a nonserialized one that lasts cross-invocations depending on the need. Build working prototypes and test them as applicable.
- Data virtualization can have the intrasolution standards as detailed in Figure 13.1. It is recommended to materialize the Relational Online Analytical Processing (ROLAP)-tier. For everything else, data virtualization can be the key driver.

| EDW-tier | {ETL Processes for Deltas: Pipelined, Partitioned, Parallelized}   EDW | C |
	{Dynamic Processes for Federation, Streaming: Data Virtualization}	O V
		M I
	Data Integration ←→ Information Integration ←→ Intelligent Informatics	M E
		O W
V	{EDW and BI: Continuous Processes for BI-Beyond-Insight}	N
BI-tier	{Dynamic BI: Continuous Processes for BI-Beyond-Intelligence} BI	

Figure 13.1   Data virtualization intrasolution standards.

- *It's how you view the data that matters the most.* And it's how you deliver the data that enables you to *make* the most of it. Treat data availability as a different business function from data visibility; this gives the customer/consumer/competitor-centric edge to the

EDW/BI solution. The data visibility can be implemented using a combination of data modeling and data mining correlated against data extrapolation to yield value KPI from data-based relationships. It is recommended that the data discovery rules are extracted based on commonality of {context, content, function} 3-tuplet. This can include custom indicators too.

I/O virtualization by using the logical view(s) layer as a disconnected database drastically improves the performance of both static and ad hoc queries, thereby enabling contextual customer data online 24×7.

- Provide the ability for data/information sharing by way of federation and syndication. Leverage the use of virtual data federation over distributed (physical) data replication. Factor in a weighting average in each of the following categories when determining overall value:
    - Data consolidation from multiple sources (homogeneous/heterogeneous)
    - Ultra-fast response to big datasets based queries (dynamic and unprecedented scalability)
    - Long-term retention of (historical) data
    - Pervasive range of deployment and faster time to deployment
    - End-to-end encryption
    - Dimensions of data for EDW and BI can be referenced by name as well as labels (especially useful for data synchronization)
    - Anytime/anywhere/anyone availability, and providing the right information for the right purpose to the right people at the right time, irrespective of the deployment platform, be it on-premise, online, cloud, mobile device, or other.
    - Support for analytics involving additional dimensions
- Provide the ability for content sharing (federation) and content streaming (syndication), using virtualization and/or replication. This must be done for regular (document) content as well as for social content.
- Provide content searching on structured and unstructured data as well as on all text. Allow for pattern matching based on event triggering, time intervals, and existing intelligence.

- Use social graphing for optimizing geolocation-based solution access and delivery. This can be implemented by integrating existing social networking systems with the EDW/BI solution. Using SocialText or OpenDesk solutions that are open source–based can accelerate or aid this process.
- Use of a dynamic control mechanism for autogeneration of the EDW/BI model in multiple formats is a good practice for externalization of the same. The output can be delivered in one or more of the following formats:
  - Declarative SQL-compliant language or integrated language script file
  - XML-DOC or XML/A-enabled file
  - View(s) based metadata or metadata file
  - High-performance Embedded database engine that is SQL enabled
  - Unified domain model (active)

The enabling/disabling of the same can be done based on interactive criteria, user-initiated or otherwise, based on specific workflow event initiated.

Enable seamless cross-component exchange at the following levels:

  - Data
  - Data model
  - Data mining/discovery model
  - Code
  - Process/process flow/workflow
  - XML/object/binary large object (BLOB)

One method to implement this is to use XML as

  - A transport mechanism (information carrier)
  - A transit store (information connector)
  - A compute-processing unit (information processor)
  - A heterogeneous data modeler (XML is an information modeler on its own)
  - And leverage the same on data, from messaging to massaging, as the data progresses from tier to tier.

- Specify execution/integration criteria for processes/programs based on:

- ▪ Entry point, exit point(s), exit behavior(s), startup/initialization code, serializable code, preprocessing and postprocessing code, specific execution criteria such as in-line with existing graphic user interface (GUI)/common container, external program, and the like.
  - ▪ Common grid console–based monitoring
- Enable the pervasive user control of dashboard(s) and the inherent master–detail linking of data involved.
- Integrate business analytics with operational processes, thereby easing the identification of the root-cause associated with the symptom(s). Open source can help accelerate this by embedding the root-cause symptom gadget into a reusable and adaptive API. It can be integrated into the dashboard using contextual show-only options. This way, business analytics can be used as both a connected and a disconnected BI process.
- An open source–based solution enables portability of source code across heterogeneous platforms on an "as is" basis. *This optimizes the time to deployment in addition to the execution of the deemed necessary-only BI processes defined and involved.*
- Use business analytics (BA) for identifying the high-impact activities in terms of return on customer, too. This is different from the item mentioned in the first bullet. This can be done using Out-of-Box (O-O-B)analytics KPI + measures to benchmark the results using value-added analytical baselines. A good example of a BI process that can be tailored towards this functionality is as follows:

```
MODEL (Data Mining) + FORECAST (Forecasting) +
DISCOVER (Data Discovery) + PREDICT (Predictive
Analytics) = Value-Added Business Analytics
Data Discovery ~ Visually Explore and Discover
Predictive Analytics ~ Real-Time Visualization and
Analysis
```

The result is identification of transformation business models that can be applied for business-to-business integration—the *Open Source Perfect* is the best fit for this!

- Using single source of data-views and timing the data for analysis by way of multipoint delivery mechanisms enables intuitive access to the data on an as-needed basis (getting the right information for the right purpose to the right people at the right time).

■ Enable autofederation of the source data to the appropriate target recipient based on the nativity of the latter.

■ Incorporate the functionality of centrally defining metadata as well as shareability of the same. Metadata includes administration and auditing-related metadata, too.

■ The *Open Source Perfect* BI enables source and target database independence. It is also capable of autodefinition of the metadata based on the intelligence captured from the connected data source(s), on the fly. It is prudent to provide a semiautomated version of this feature set. *As an optimization enabler, this enables only-necessary execution of the BI processes defined and involved.*

■ Isolate the EDW tier from the BI tier. Implement the deployment of both as an *integrated virtual machine.*

■ Isolate predictive analytics from BI dashboarding, yet keep it integration-enabled in a hot-pluggable fashion.

■ Ensure open source EDW/BI enables flexible deployment—start-anywhere, componentized deployment. Cloud "bursting" can be used to deliver this, with the EDW tier being in the private cloud and BI layer in the public cloud.

■ Ensure standards-based security. Allow information integration, enabling the sharing of metadata, security, dashboards, value-added metrics, and analytics in a tightly coupled fashion when it comes to computation/processing, but in a loosely coupled fashion when it comes to connectivity.

■ Provide normalized security rules across geolocation–based shared cloud environments. Do the same across cross-network DNS.

■ Baseline a consistent metric of security and use it to correlate relative performance.

13.2 Summary

This chapter focused on the best-of-the-breed EDW/BI standards that can supplement the open source standards available. Standards bring unified access to enterprise/proprietary data. From vision to innovation to action, implementing these standards can be a creator, manager, and evolver of best-in-class EDW/BI solution strategy: from the 0s and 1s of data to the streams of content and clouds.

13.3   References

The following reference has been used in gaining access to the information provided in this chapter:

Lakshman Bulusu, "Standards help create markets. Why is this important? Or is this not important?" (Available at http://www.focus.com/questions/standards-help-create-markets-why-important-it-not-important/).

Index

Milton Keynes UK
Ingram Content Group UK Ltd.
UKHW031125141024
449569UK00006B/431